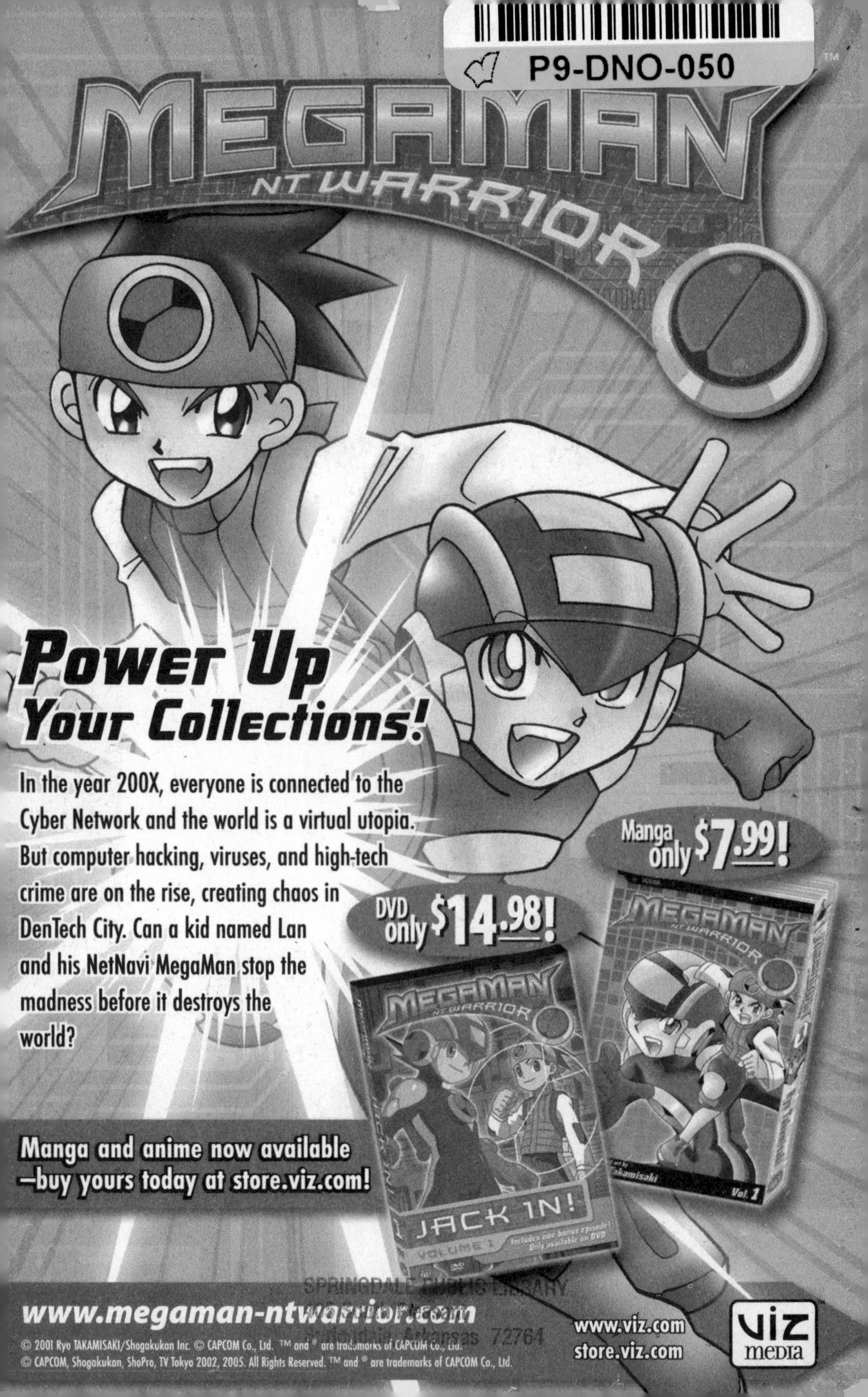
P9-DNO-050
MEGAMAN NT WARRIOR
Power Up Your Collections!
In the year 200X, everyone is connected to the Cyber Network and the world is a virtual utopia. But computer hacking, viruses, and high-tech crime are on the rise, creating chaos in DenTech City. Can a kid named Lan and his NetNavi MegaMan stop the madness before it destroys the world?
Manga only $7.99!
DVD only $14.98!
MEGAMAN NT WARRIOR
JACK IN!
VOLUME 1
MEGAMAN NT WARRIOR
Vol. 1
Manga and anime now available
—buy yours today at store.viz.com!
SPRINGDALE PUBLIC LIBRARY
Springdale, Arkansas 72764
www.megaman-ntwarrior.com
© 2001 Ryo TAKAMISAKI/Shogakukan Inc. © CAPCOM Co., Ltd. ™ and ® are trademarks of CAPCOM Co., Ltd.
© CAPCOM, Shogakukan, ShoPro, TV Tokyo 2002, 2005. All Rights Reserved. ™ and ® are trademarks of CAPCOM Co., Ltd.
www.viz.com
store.viz.com
viz media

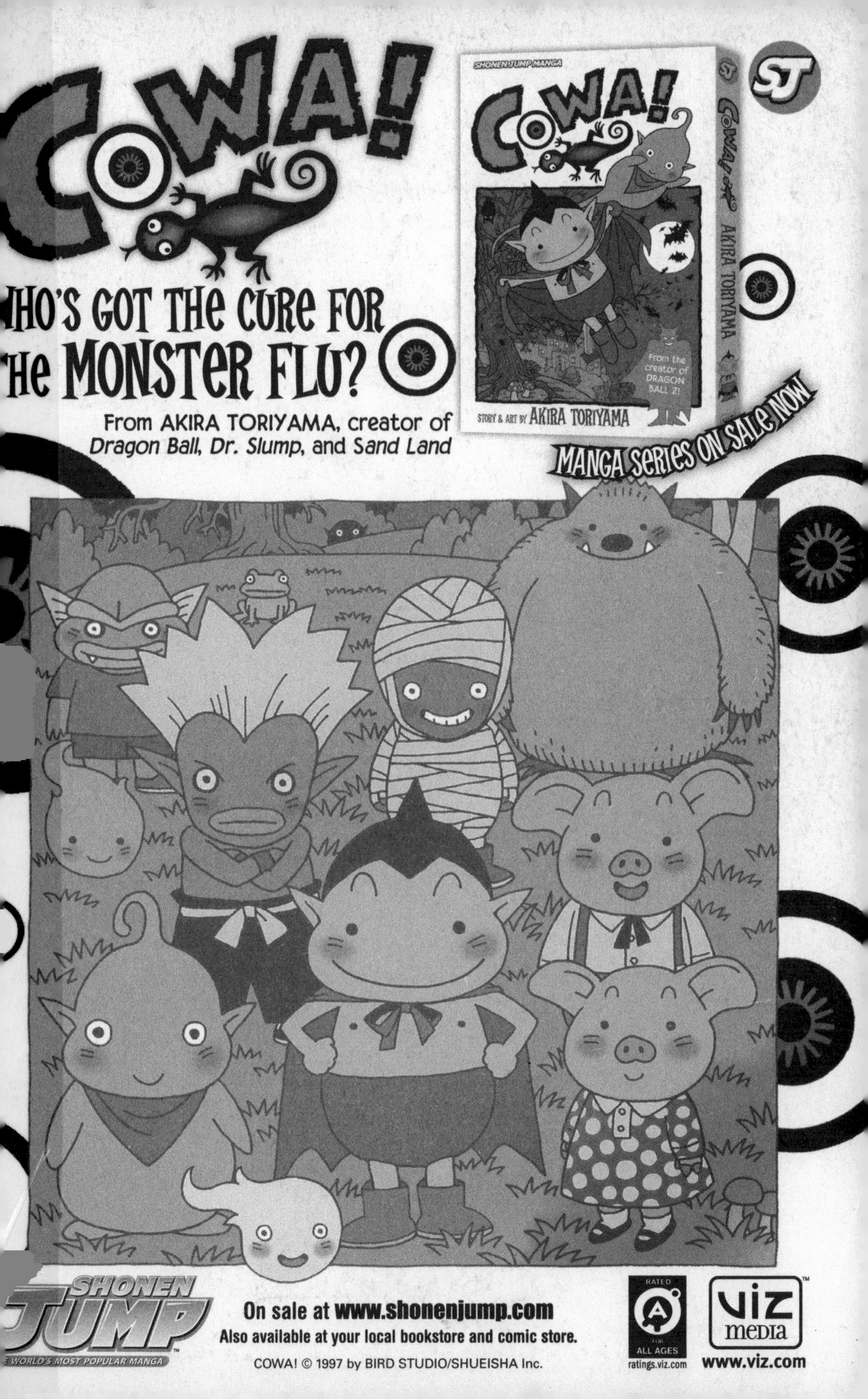
COWA!
HO'S GOT THE CURE FOR
HE MONSTER FLU?
From AKIRA TORIYAMA, creator of
Dragon Ball, Dr. Slump, and Sand Land
SHONEN JUMP MANGA
COWA!
From the creator of DRAGON BALL Z!
STORY & ART BY AKIRA TORIYAMA
SJ
MANGA SERIES ON SALE NOW
SHONEN JUMP
WORLD'S MOST POPULAR MANGA
On sale at www.shonenjump.com
Also available at your local bookstore and comic store.
COWA! © 1997 by BIRD STUDIO/SHUEISHA Inc.
RATED A FOR ALL AGES
ratings.viz.com
VIZ media
www.viz.com

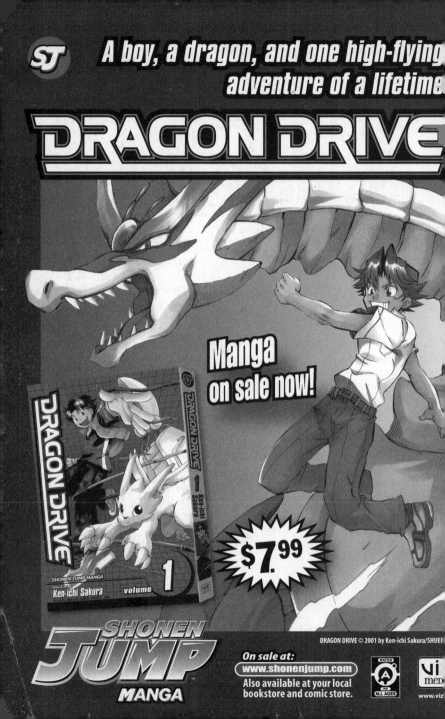

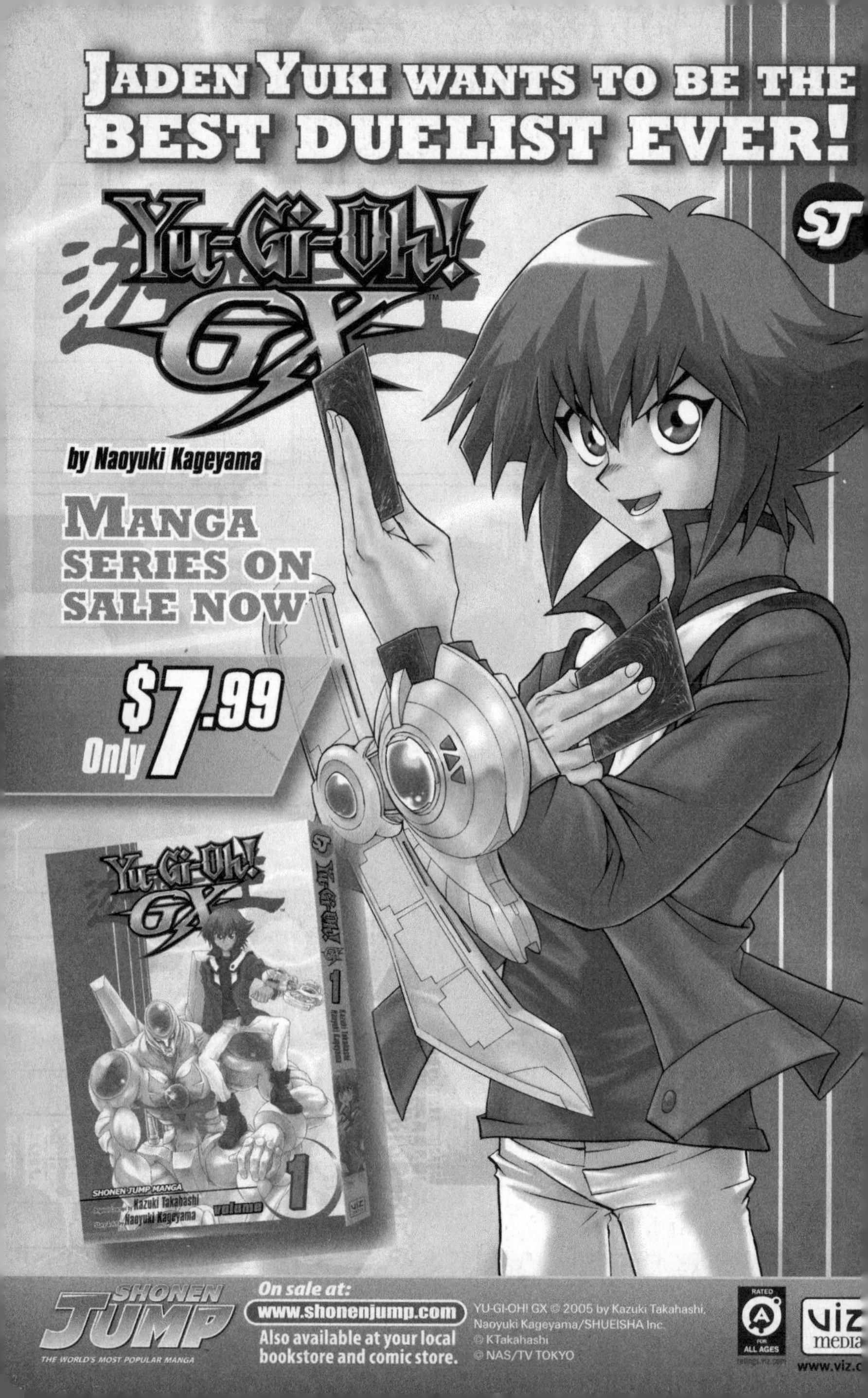
JADEN YUKI WANTS TO BE THE BEST DUELIST EVER!
SJ
YU-GI-OH! GX™
by Naoyuki Kageyama
MANGA SERIES ON SALE NOW
Only $7.99
Yu-Gi-Oh! GX
SHONEN JUMP MANGA
Kazuki Takahashi
Naoyuki Kageyama
volume 1
SHONEN JUMP
THE WORLD'S MOST POPULAR MANGA
On sale at:
www.shonenjump.com
Also available at your local bookstore and comic store.
YU-GI-OH! GX © 2005 by Kazuki Takahashi, Naoyuki Kageyama/SHUEISHA Inc.
© KTakahashi
© NAS/TV TOKYO
RATED A FOR ALL AGES
viz media
www.viz.c

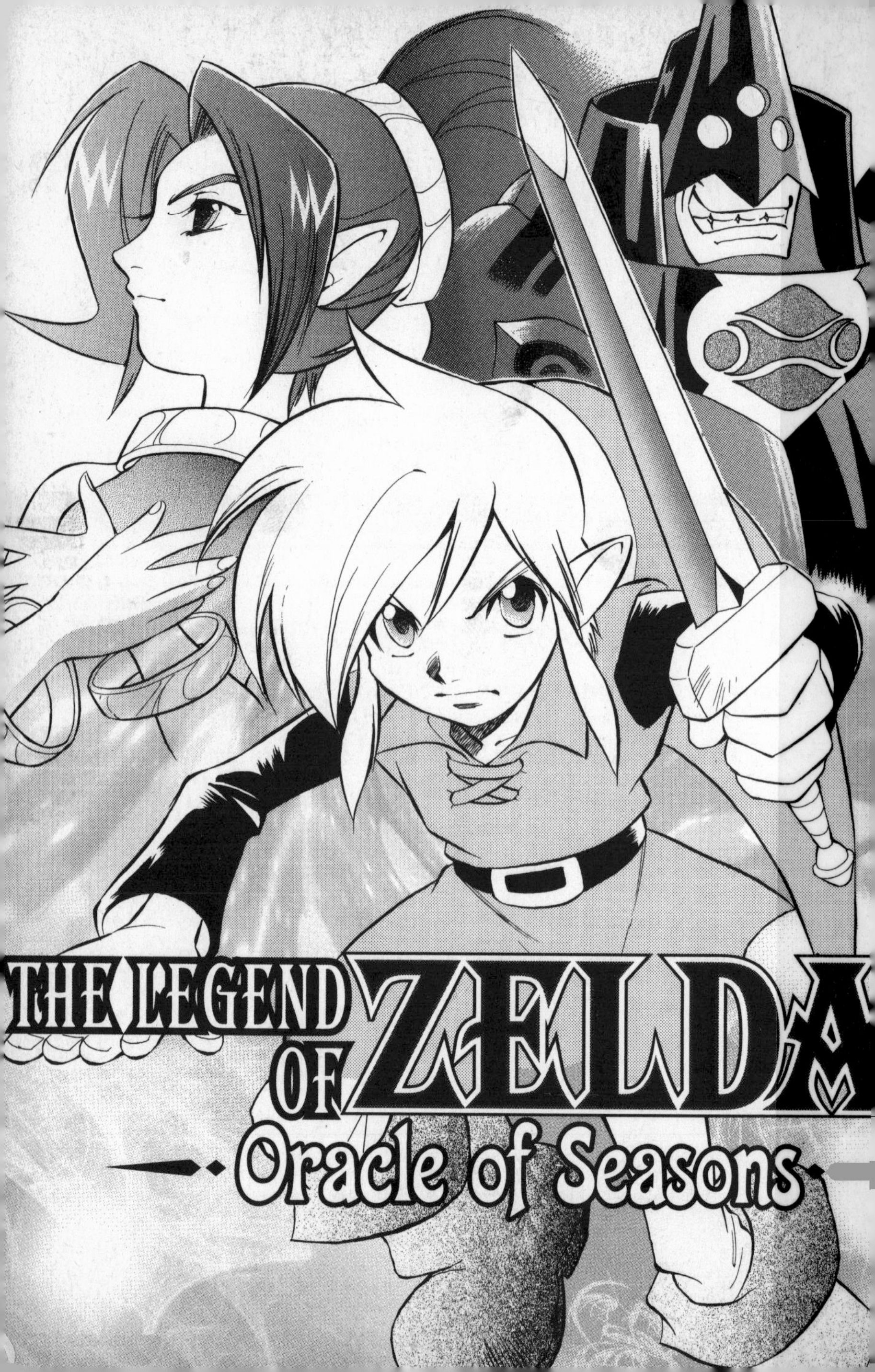
THE LEGEND OF ZELDA
Oracle of Seasons

THE LEGEND OF ZELDA™
ORACLE OF SEASONS

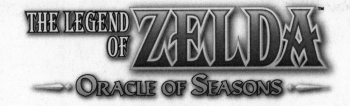

CONTENTS

ORACLE OF SEASONS

Chapter 1
Din the Dancer

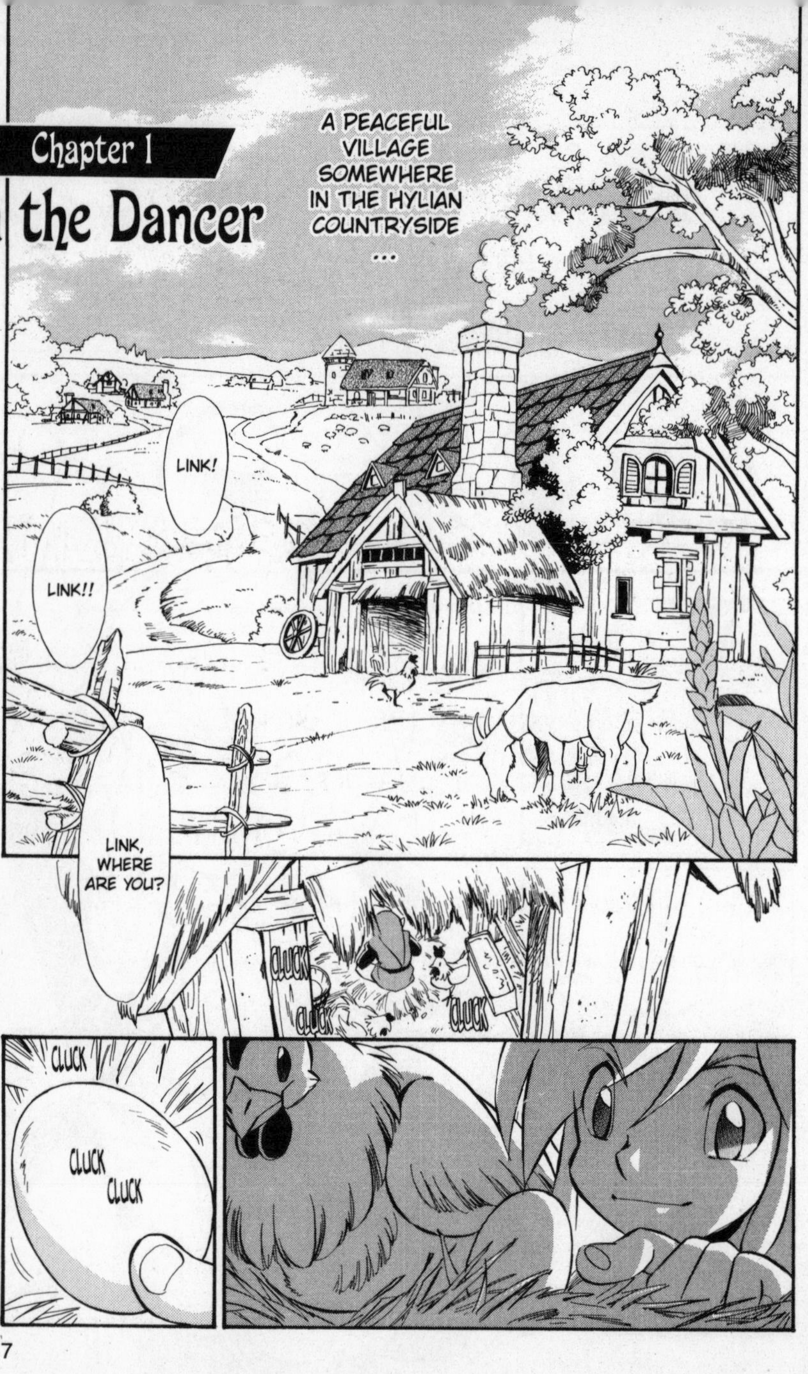

A PEACEFUL VILLAGE SOMEWHERE IN THE HYLIAN COUNTRYSIDE ...
LINK!
LINK!!
LINK, WHERE ARE YOU?
CLUCK
CLUCK
CLUCK
CLUCK
CLUCK CLUCK

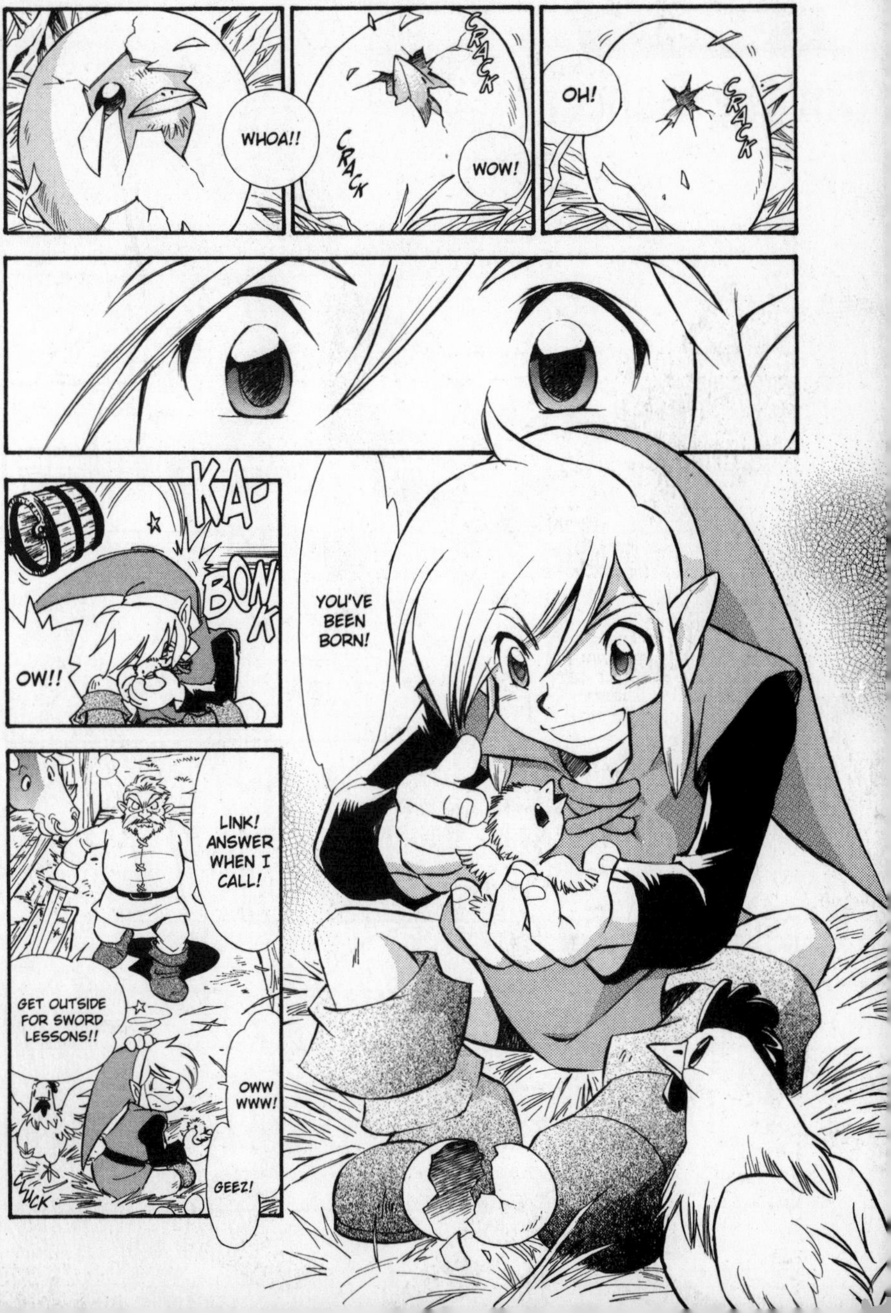
OH!
CRACK
CRACK
WOW!
CRACK
WHOA!!
YOU'VE BEEN BORN!
KA-BONK
OW!!
LINK! ANSWER WHEN I CALL!
GET OUTSIDE FOR SWORD LESSONS!!
OWW WWW!
GEEZ!
CLUCK

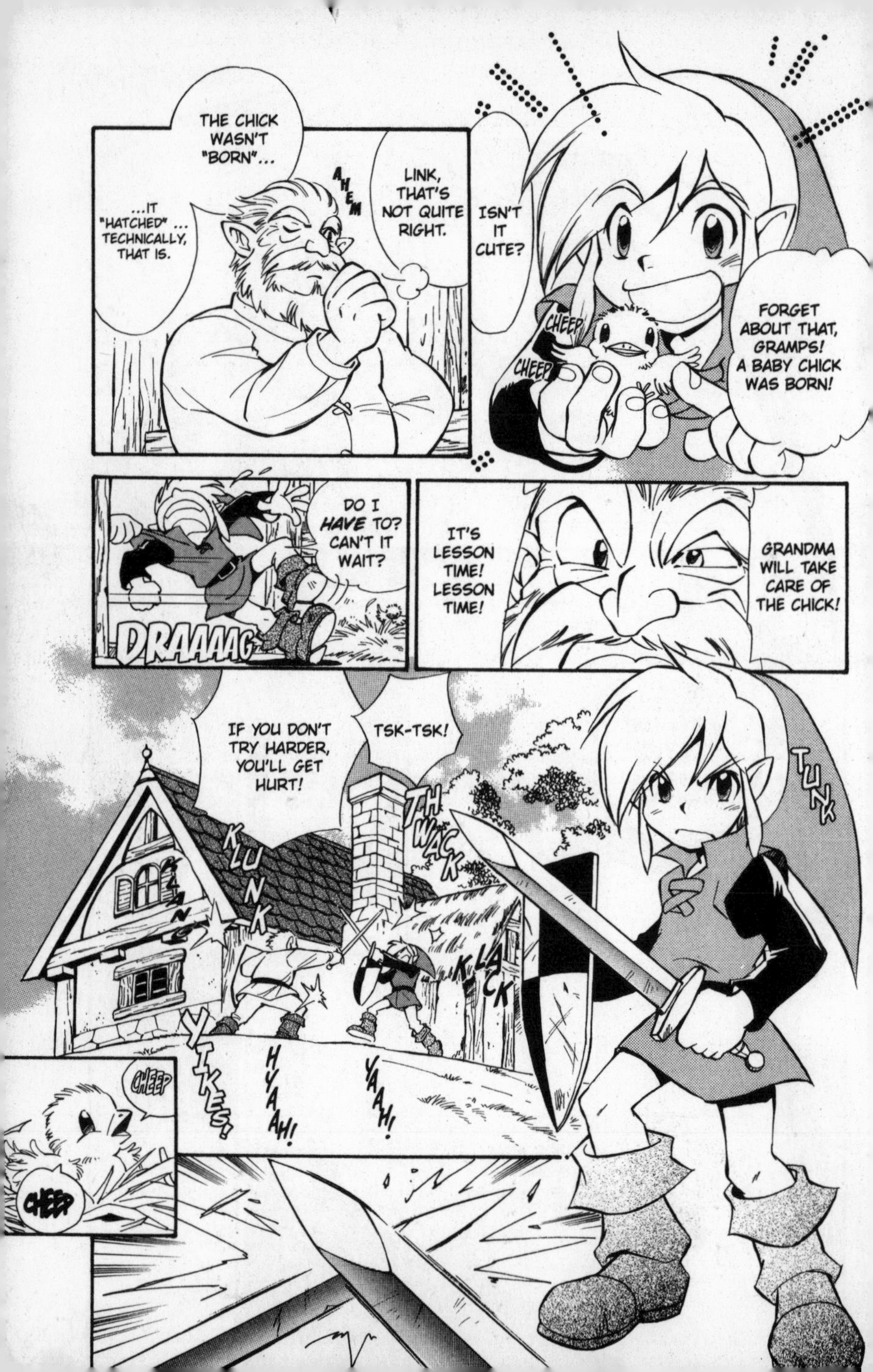
FORGET ABOUT THAT, GRAMPS! A BABY CHICK WAS BORN!
ISN'T IT CUTE?
CHEEP
CHEEP
LINK, THAT'S NOT QUITE RIGHT.
AHEM
THE CHICK WASN'T "BORN"...
...IT "HATCHED"... TECHNICALLY, THAT IS.
GRANDMA WILL TAKE CARE OF THE CHICK!
IT'S LESSON TIME! LESSON TIME!
DO I *HAVE* TO? CAN'T IT WAIT?
DRAAAAG
TSK-TSK!
IF YOU DON'T TRY HARDER, YOU'LL GET HURT!
TUNK
THWACK
KLUNK
KLANG
KLACK
YAAAH!
HYAAAH!
YIKES!
CHEEP
CHEEP

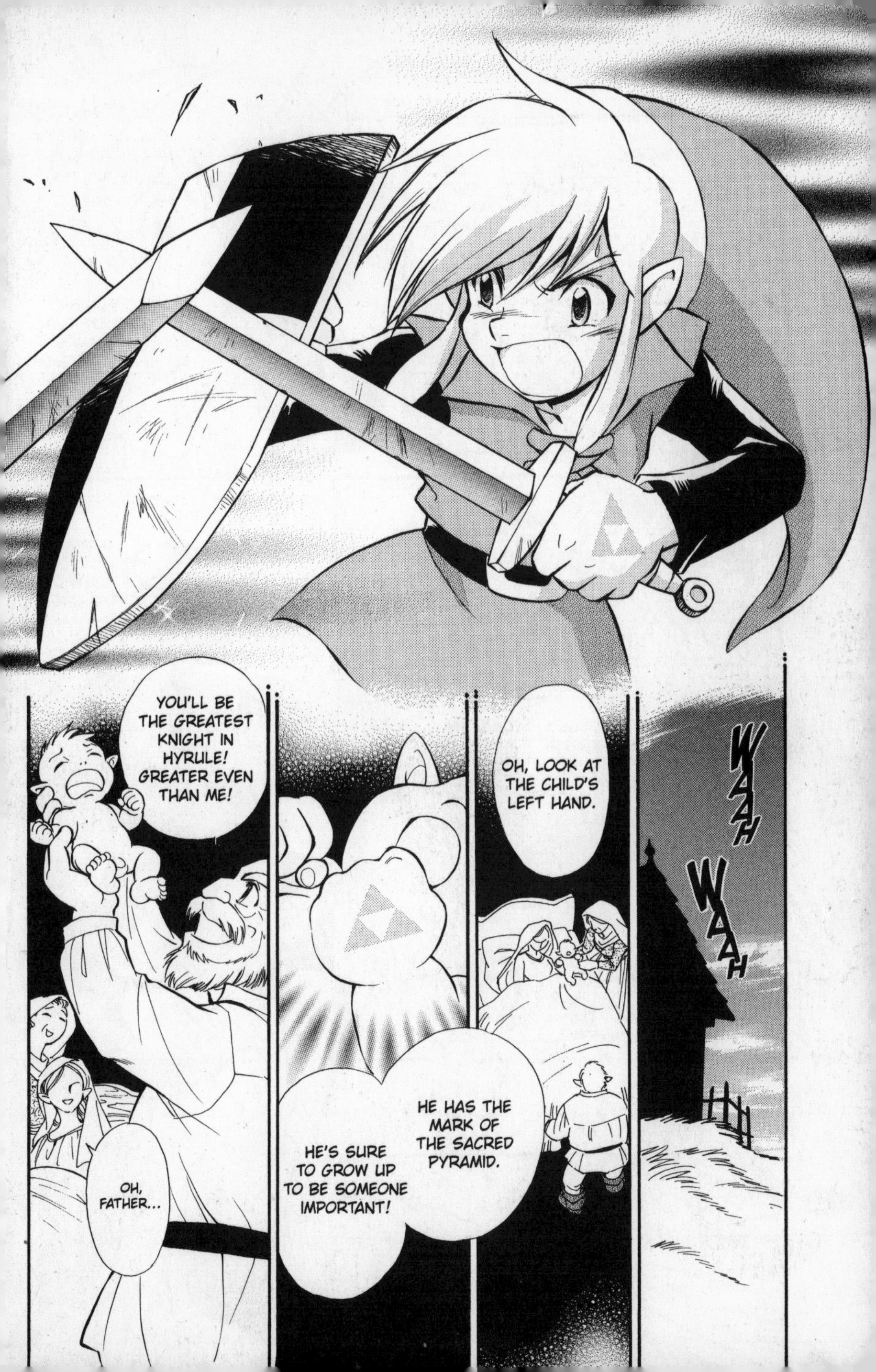
WAAH
WAAH
OH, LOOK AT THE CHILD'S LEFT HAND.
HE HAS THE MARK OF THE SACRED PYRAMID.
HE'S SURE TO GROW UP TO BE SOMEONE IMPORTANT!
YOU'LL BE THE GREATEST KNIGHT IN HYRULE! GREATER EVEN THAN ME!
OH, FATHER...

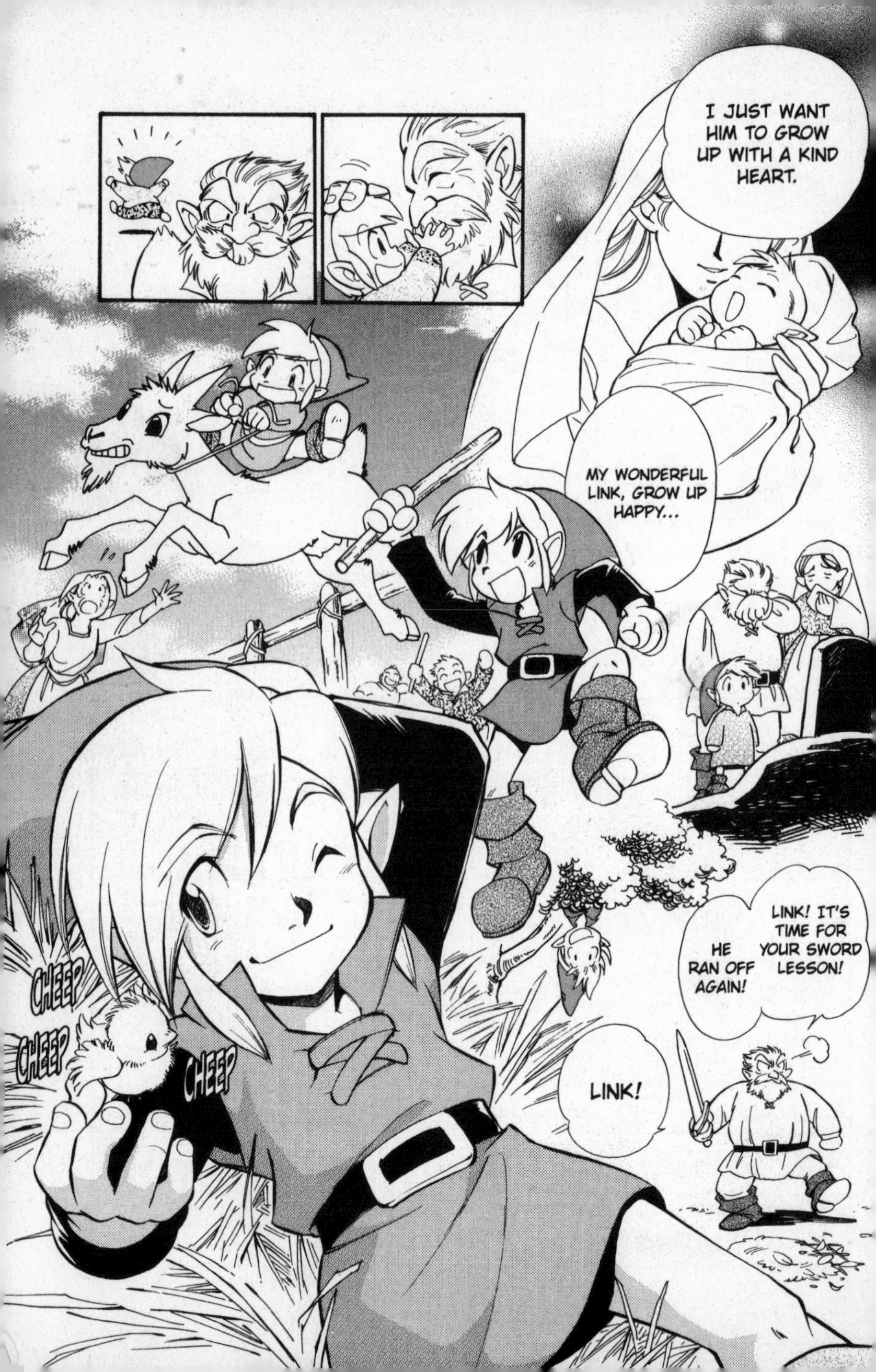
I JUST WANT HIM TO GROW UP WITH A KIND HEART.
MY WONDERFUL LINK, GROW UP HAPPY...
LINK! IT'S TIME FOR YOUR SWORD LESSON!
HE RAN OFF AGAIN!
LINK!
CHEEP
CHEEP
CHEEP

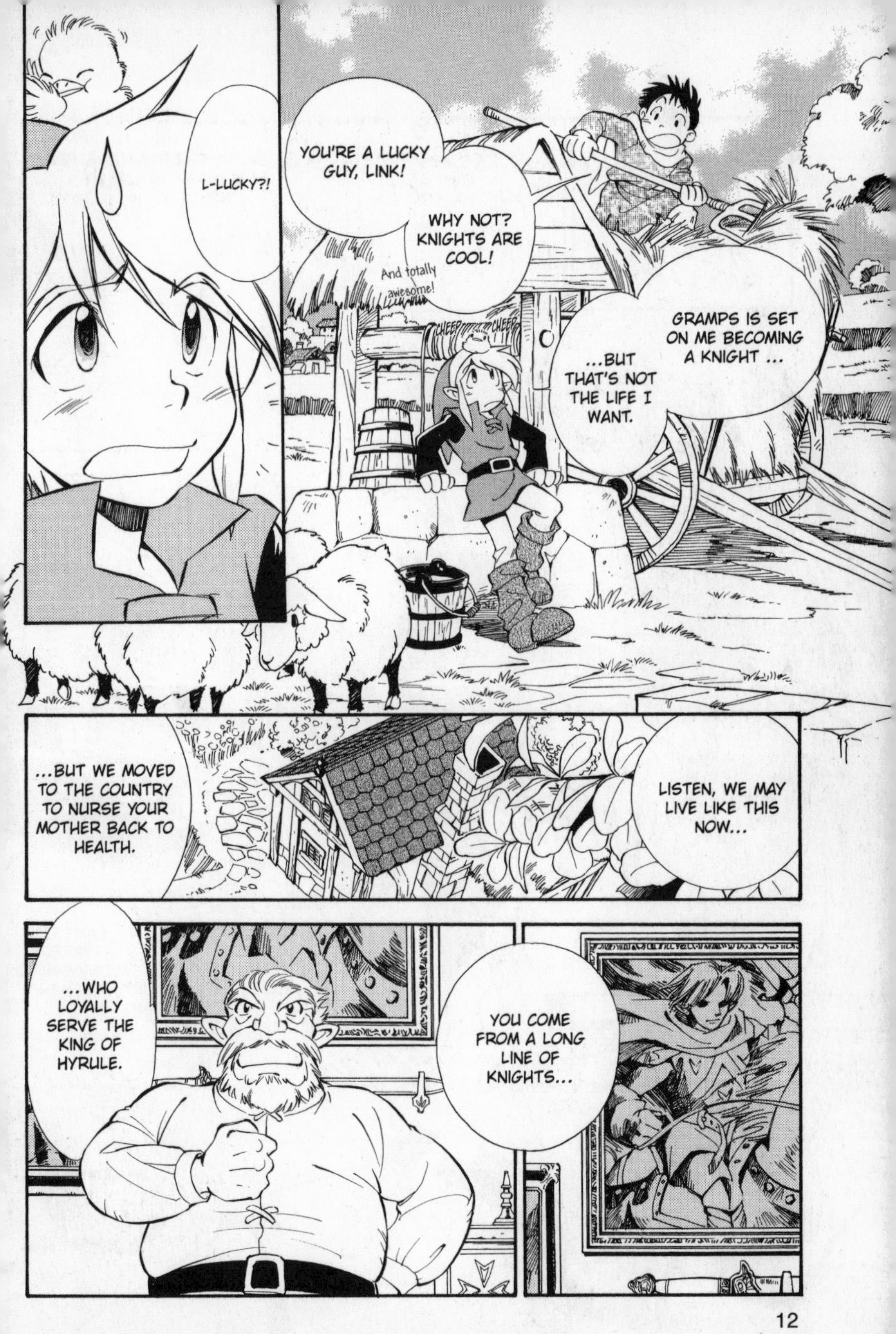
GRAMPS IS SET ON ME BECOMING A KNIGHT ...
...BUT THAT'S NOT THE LIFE I WANT.
YOU'RE A LUCKY GUY, LINK!
WHY NOT? KNIGHTS ARE COOL!
And totally awesome!
CHEEP CHEEP
L-LUCKY?!
LISTEN, WE MAY LIVE LIKE THIS NOW...
...BUT WE MOVED TO THE COUNTRY TO NURSE YOUR MOTHER BACK TO HEALTH.
YOU COME FROM A LONG LINE OF KNIGHTS...
...WHO LOYALLY SERVE THE KING OF HYRULE.

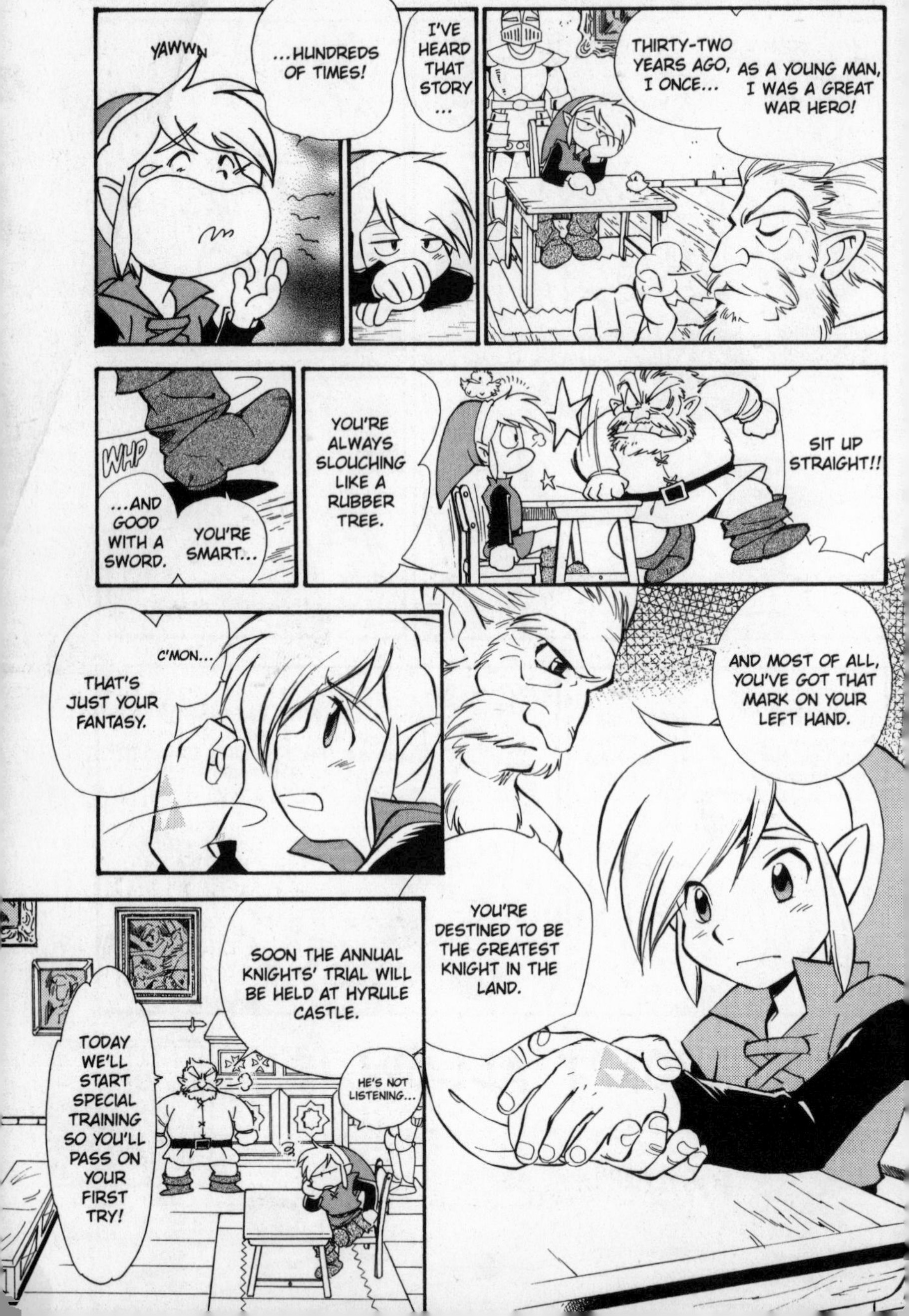
AS A YOUNG MAN, I WAS A GREAT WAR HERO!
THIRTY-TWO YEARS AGO, I ONCE...
I'VE HEARD THAT STORY ...
...HUNDREDS OF TIMES!
YAWWN
SIT UP STRAIGHT!!
YOU'RE ALWAYS SLOUCHING LIKE A RUBBER TREE.
WHP
YOU'RE SMART...
...AND GOOD WITH A SWORD.
AND MOST OF ALL, YOU'VE GOT THAT MARK ON YOUR LEFT HAND.
YOU'RE DESTINED TO BE THE GREATEST KNIGHT IN THE LAND.
C'MON...
THAT'S JUST YOUR FANTASY.
SOON THE ANNUAL KNIGHTS' TRIAL WILL BE HELD AT HYRULE CASTLE.
TODAY WE'LL START SPECIAL TRAINING SO YOU'LL PASS ON YOUR FIRST TRY!
HE'S NOT LISTENING...

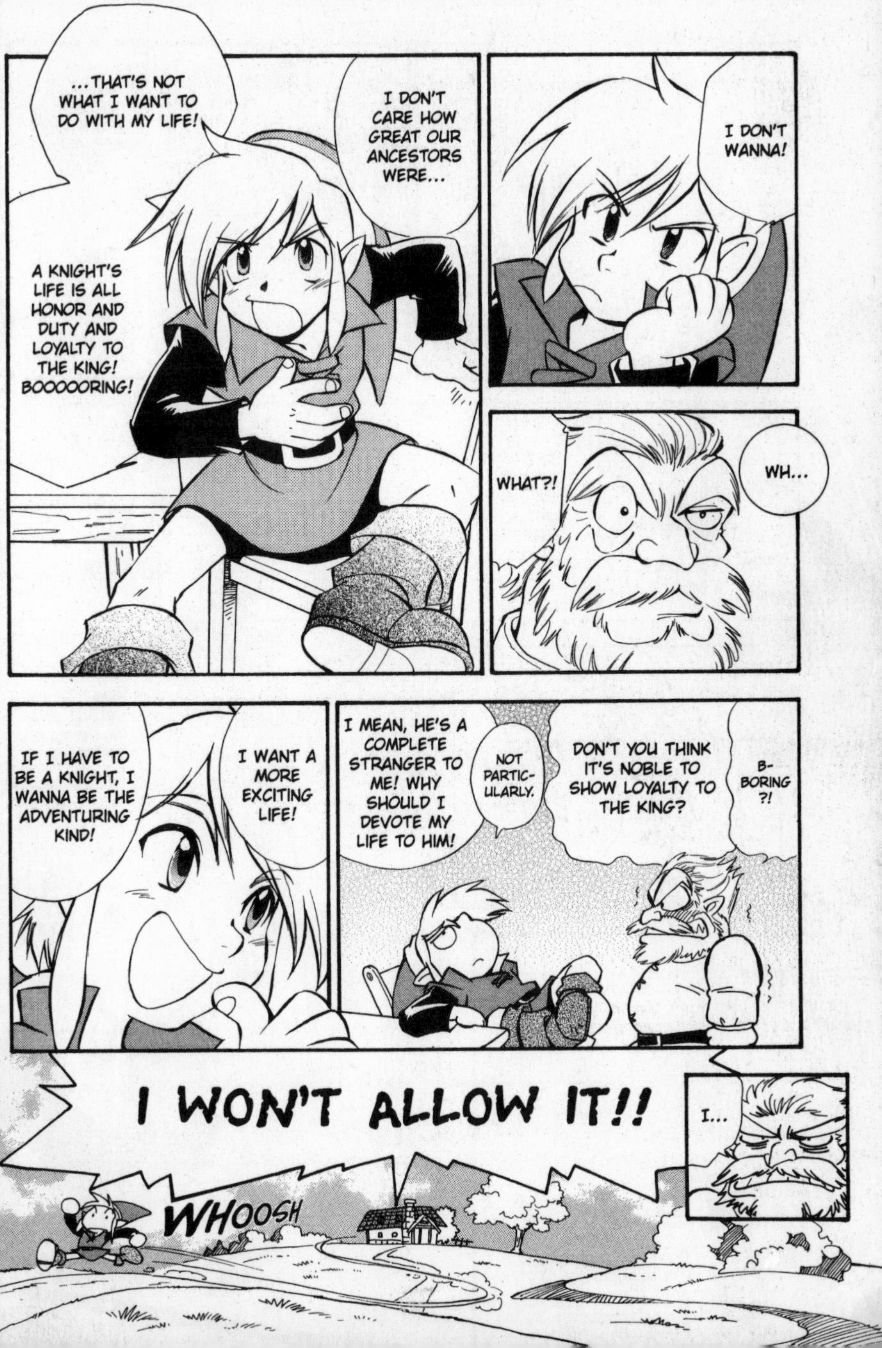
I DON'T WANNA!
WH...
WHAT?!
I DON'T CARE HOW GREAT OUR ANCESTORS WERE...
...THAT'S NOT WHAT I WANT TO DO WITH MY LIFE!
A KNIGHT'S LIFE IS ALL HONOR AND DUTY AND LOYALTY TO THE KING! BOOOOORING!
B-BORING?!
DON'T YOU THINK IT'S NOBLE TO SHOW LOYALTY TO THE KING?
NOT PARTICULARLY.
I MEAN, HE'S A COMPLETE STRANGER TO ME! WHY SHOULD I DEVOTE MY LIFE TO HIM!
I WANT A MORE EXCITING LIFE!
IF I HAVE TO BE A KNIGHT, I WANNA BE THE ADVENTURING KIND!
I...
I WON'T ALLOW IT!!
WHOOSH

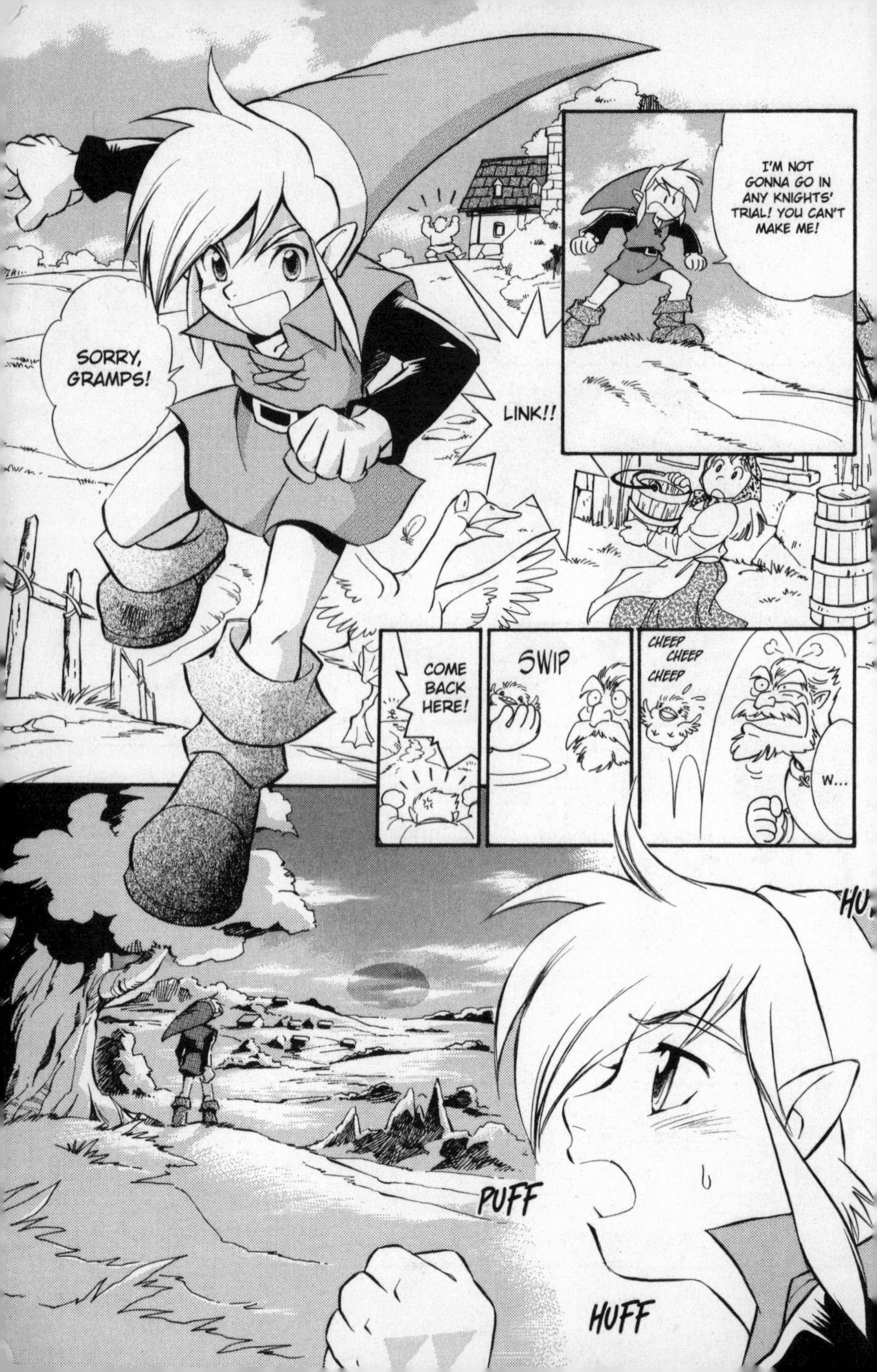
I'M NOT GONNA GO IN ANY KNIGHTS' TRIAL! YOU CAN'T MAKE ME!
LINK!!
SORRY, GRAMPS!
CHEEP
CHEEP
CHEEP
W...
SWIP
COME BACK HERE!
HU
PUFF
HUFF

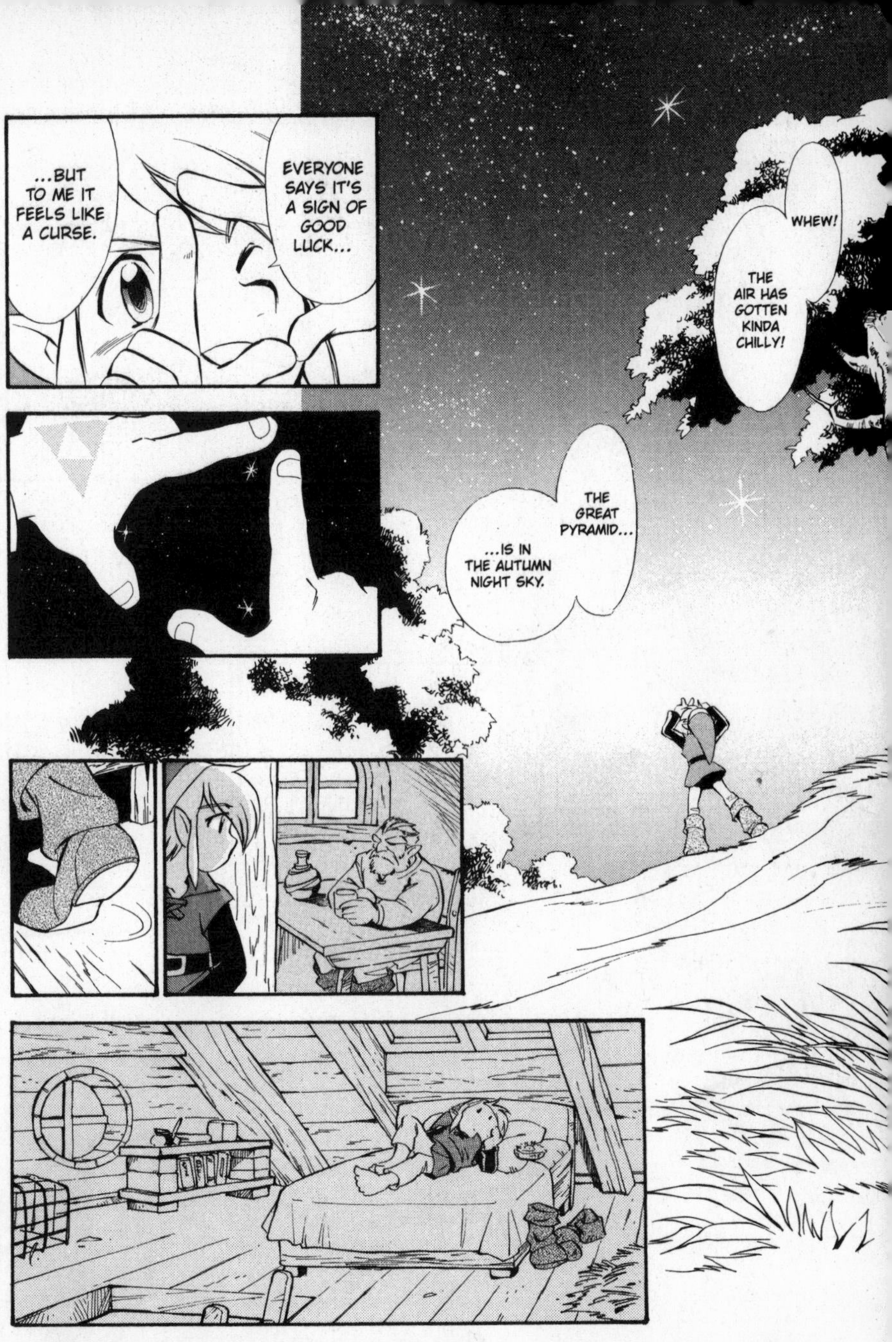
WHEW!
THE AIR HAS GOTTEN KINDA CHILLY!
THE GREAT PYRAMID...
...IS IN THE AUTUMN NIGHT SKY.
EVERYONE SAYS IT'S A SIGN OF GOOD LUCK...
...BUT TO ME IT FEELS LIKE A CURSE.

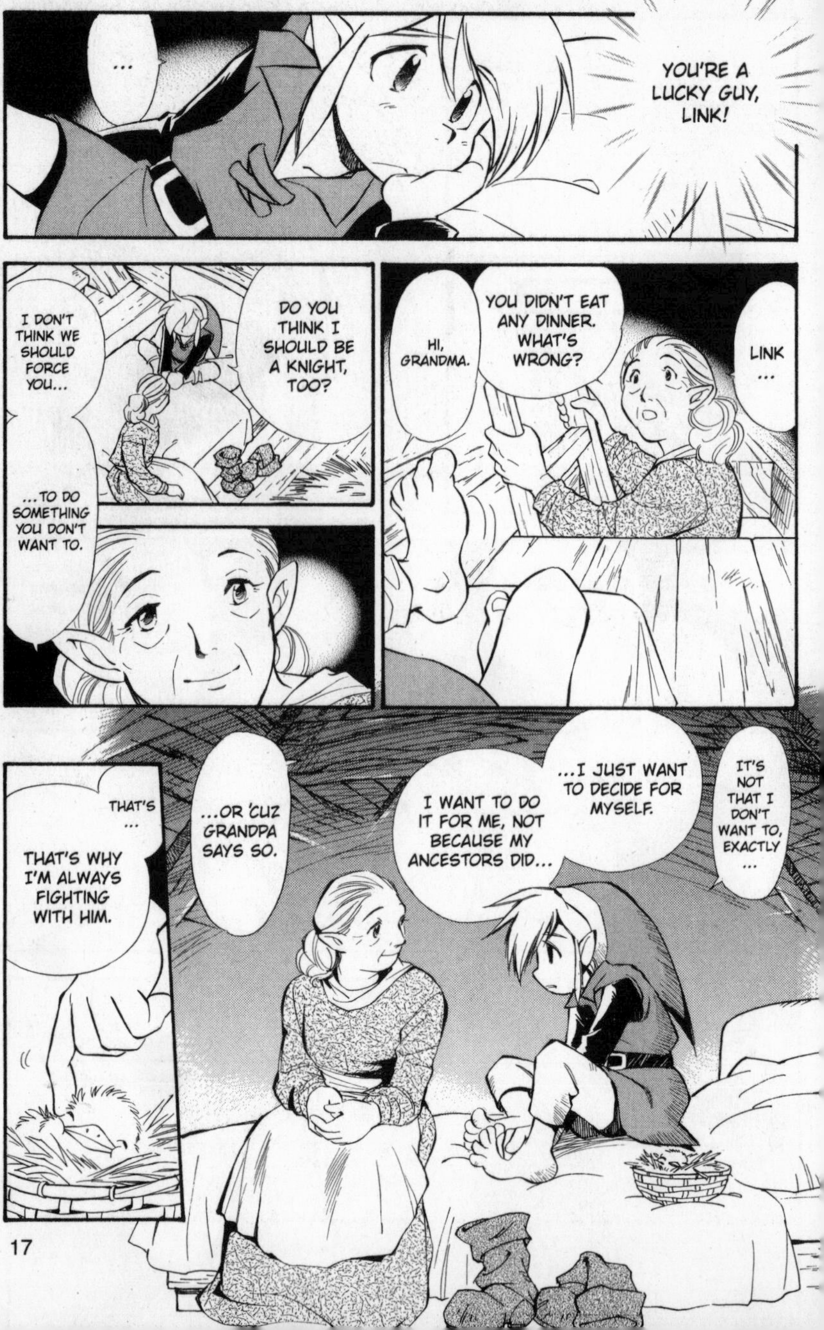
YOU'RE A LUCKY GUY, LINK!
...
LINK ...
YOU DIDN'T EAT ANY DINNER. WHAT'S WRONG?
HI, GRANDMA.
DO YOU THINK I SHOULD BE A KNIGHT, TOO?
I DON'T THINK WE SHOULD FORCE YOU...
...TO DO SOMETHING YOU DON'T WANT TO.
IT'S NOT THAT I DON'T WANT TO, EXACTLY ...
...I JUST WANT TO DECIDE FOR MYSELF.
I WANT TO DO IT FOR ME, NOT BECAUSE MY ANCESTORS DID...
...OR 'CUZ GRANDPA SAYS SO.
THAT'S ...
THAT'S WHY I'M ALWAYS FIGHTING WITH HIM.

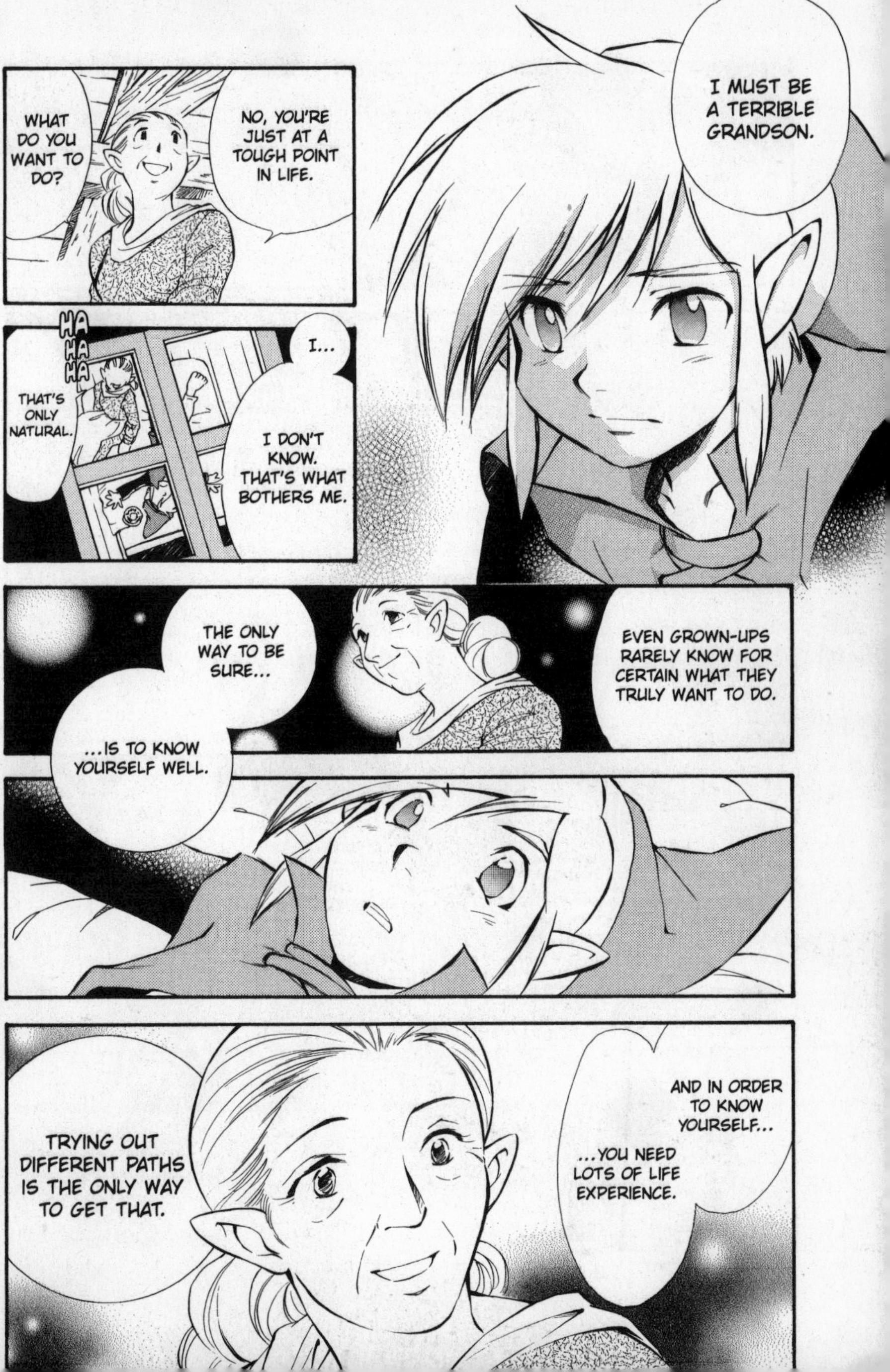
I MUST BE A TERRIBLE GRANDSON.
NO, YOU'RE JUST AT A TOUGH POINT IN LIFE.
WHAT DO YOU WANT TO DO?
I...
I DON'T KNOW. THAT'S WHAT BOTHERS ME.
HA HA HA
THAT'S ONLY NATURAL.
EVEN GROWN-UPS RARELY KNOW FOR CERTAIN WHAT THEY TRULY WANT TO DO.
THE ONLY WAY TO BE SURE...
...IS TO KNOW YOURSELF WELL.
AND IN ORDER TO KNOW YOURSELF...
...YOU NEED LOTS OF LIFE EXPERIENCE.
TRYING OUT DIFFERENT PATHS IS THE ONLY WAY TO GET THAT.

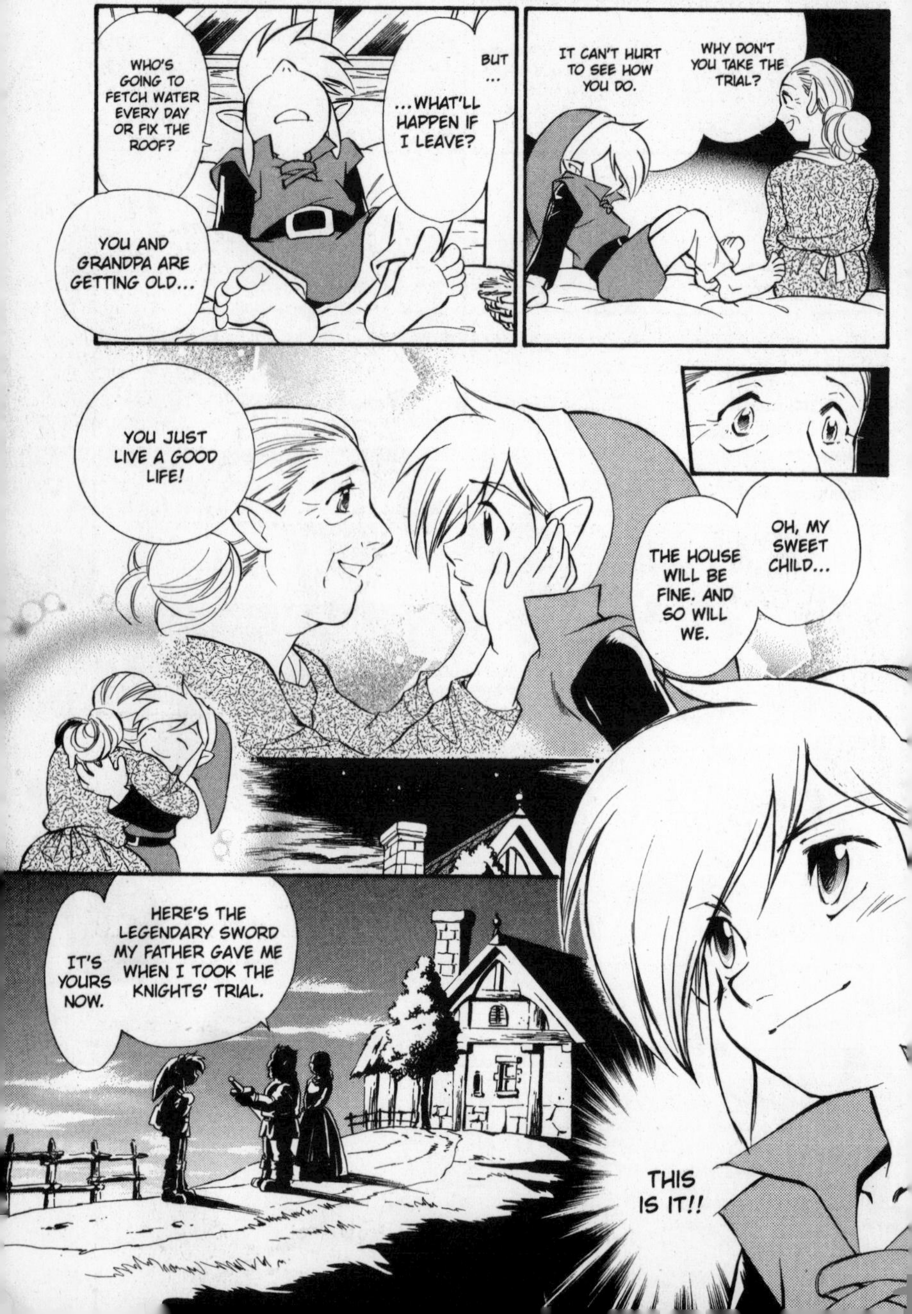
WHY DON'T YOU TAKE THE TRIAL?
IT CAN'T HURT TO SEE HOW YOU DO.
BUT ...
...WHAT'LL HAPPEN IF I LEAVE?
WHO'S GOING TO FETCH WATER EVERY DAY OR FIX THE ROOF?
YOU AND GRANDPA ARE GETTING OLD...
OH, MY SWEET CHILD...
THE HOUSE WILL BE FINE. AND SO WILL WE.
YOU JUST LIVE A GOOD LIFE!
THIS IS IT!!
HERE'S THE LEGENDARY SWORD MY FATHER GAVE ME WHEN I TOOK THE KNIGHTS' TRIAL.
IT'S YOURS NOW.

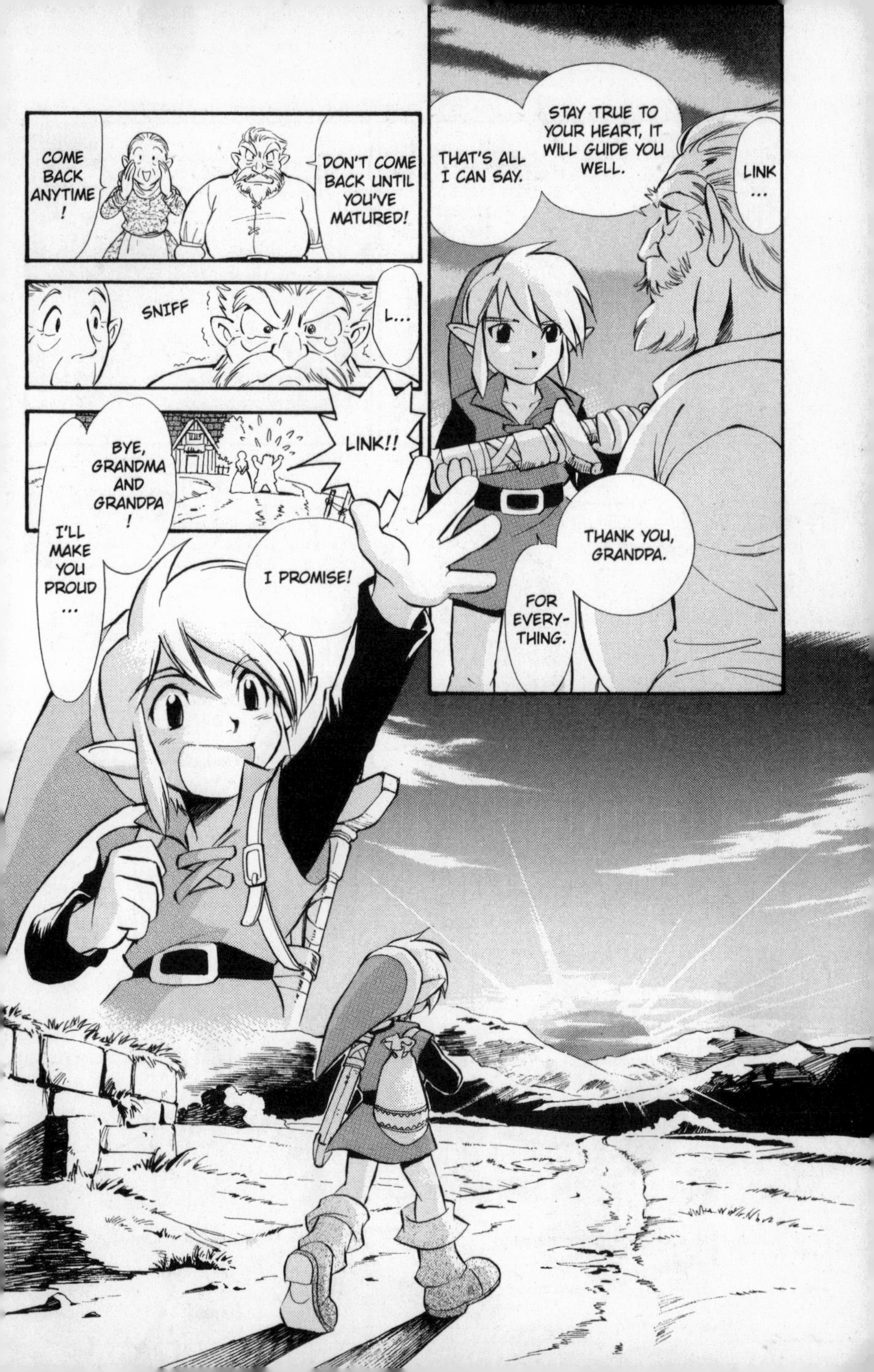
LINK ...
STAY TRUE TO YOUR HEART, IT WILL GUIDE YOU WELL.
THAT'S ALL I CAN SAY.
THANK YOU, GRANDPA.
FOR EVERYTHING.
DON'T COME BACK UNTIL YOU'VE MATURED!
COME BACK ANYTIME!
L...
SNIFF
LINK!!
BYE, GRANDMA AND GRANDPA!
I'LL MAKE YOU PROUD ...
I PROMISE!

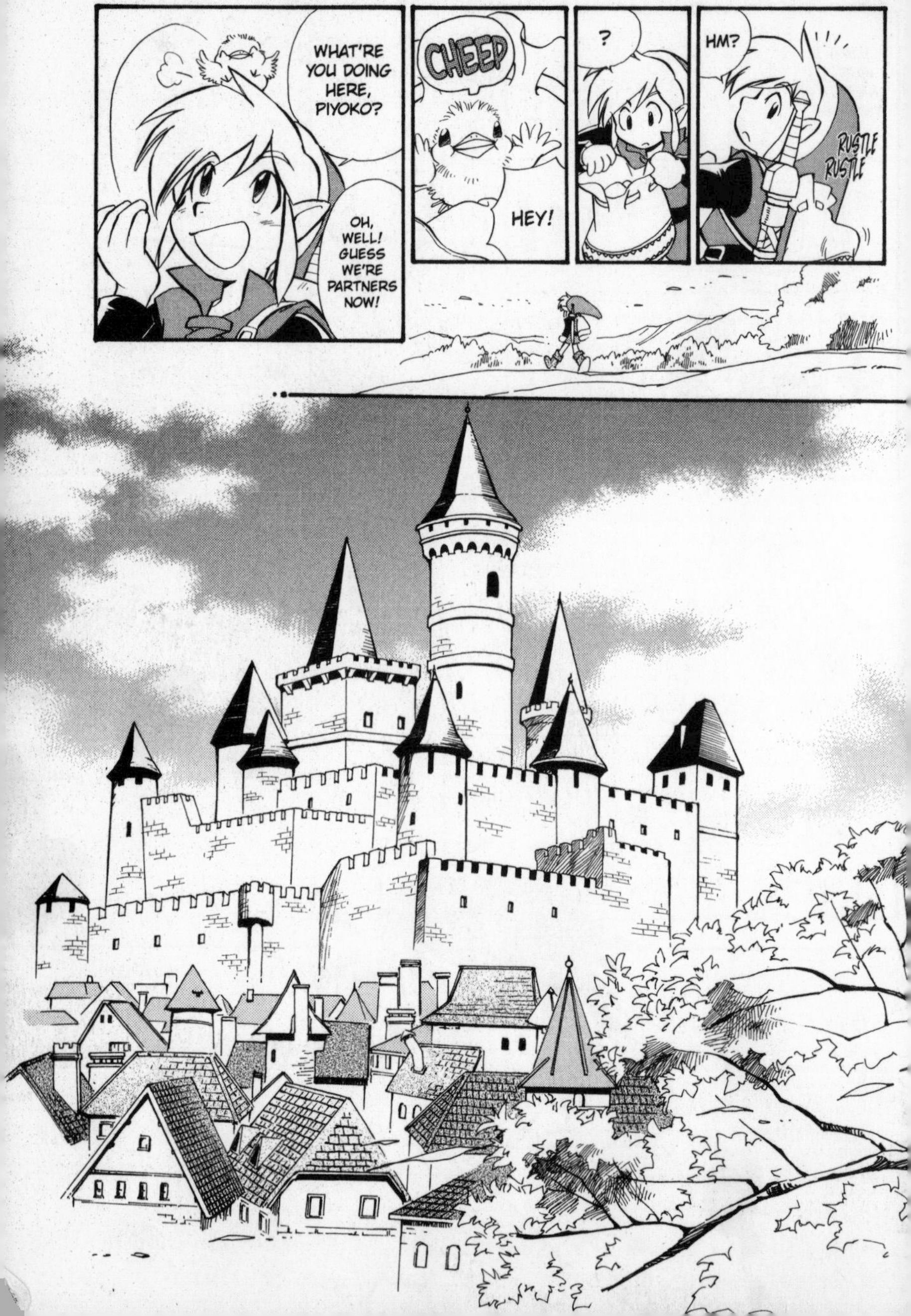
HM?
RUSTLE RUSTLE
?
CHEEP
HEY!
WHAT'RE YOU DOING HERE, PIYOKO?
OH, WELL! GUESS WE'RE PARTNERS NOW!

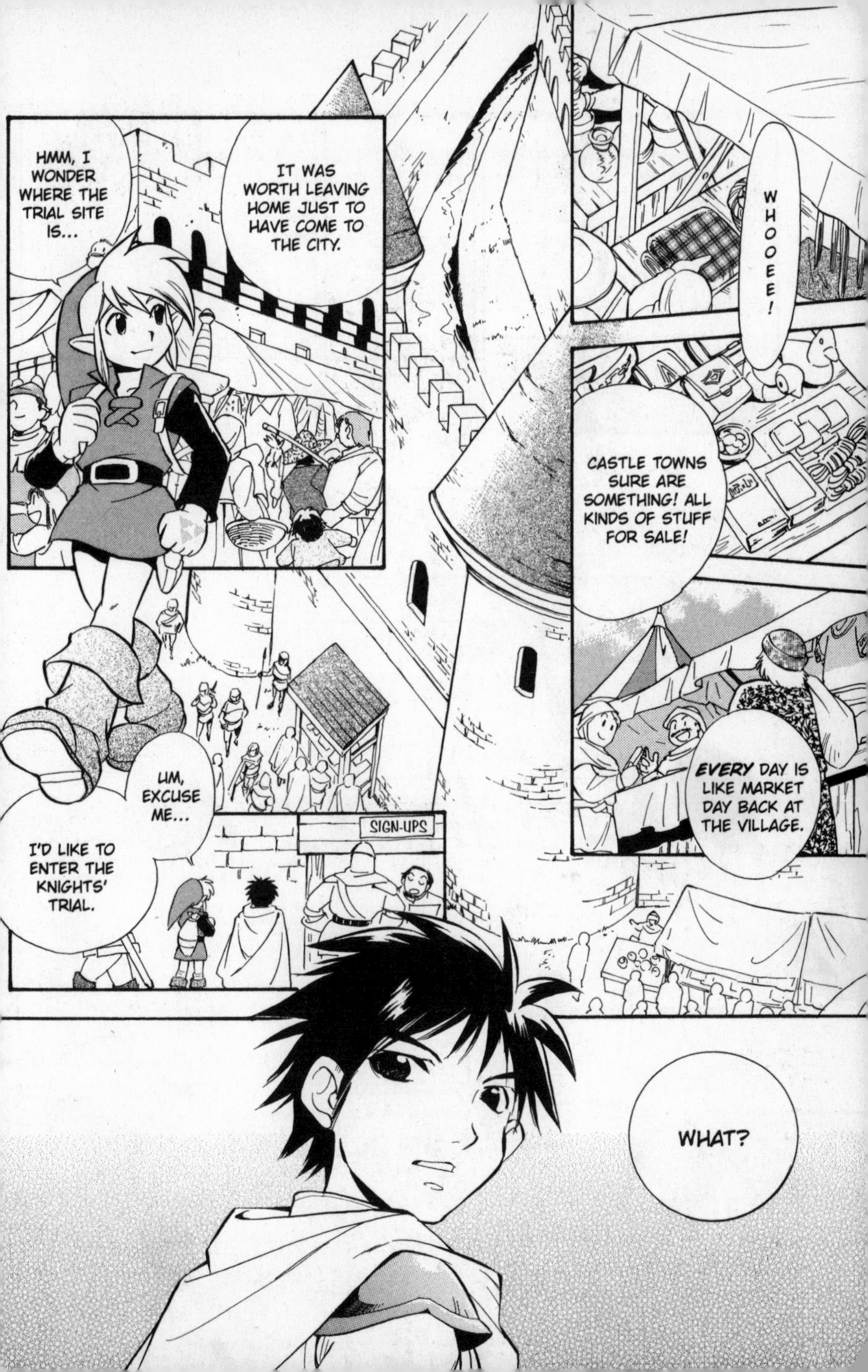
WHOOOEE!
CASTLE TOWNS SURE ARE SOMETHING! ALL KINDS OF STUFF FOR SALE!
EVERY DAY IS LIKE MARKET DAY BACK AT THE VILLAGE.
IT WAS WORTH LEAVING HOME JUST TO HAVE COME TO THE CITY.
HMM, I WONDER WHERE THE TRIAL SITE IS...
SIGN-UPS
UM, EXCUSE ME...
I'D LIKE TO ENTER THE KNIGHTS' TRIAL.
WHAT?

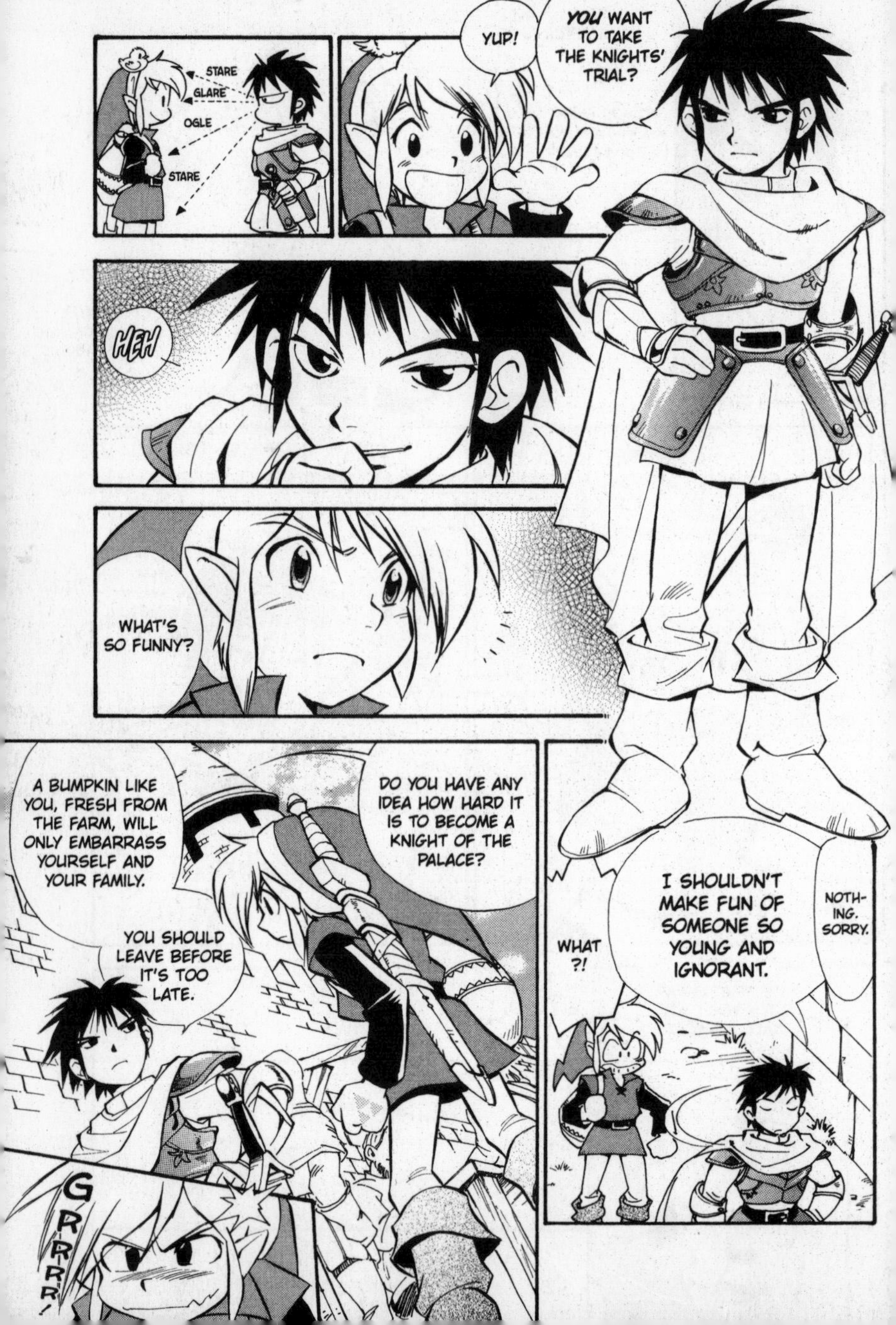

YOU WANT TO TAKE THE KNIGHTS' TRIAL?
YUP!
STARE
GLARE
OGLE
STARE
HEH
WHAT'S SO FUNNY?
NOTH-ING. SORRY.
I SHOULDN'T MAKE FUN OF SOMEONE SO YOUNG AND IGNORANT.
WHAT?!
DO YOU HAVE ANY IDEA HOW HARD IT IS TO BECOME A KNIGHT OF THE PALACE?
A BUMPKIN LIKE YOU, FRESH FROM THE FARM, WILL ONLY EMBARRASS YOURSELF AND YOUR FAMILY.
YOU SHOULD LEAVE BEFORE IT'S TOO LATE.
GRRRR!

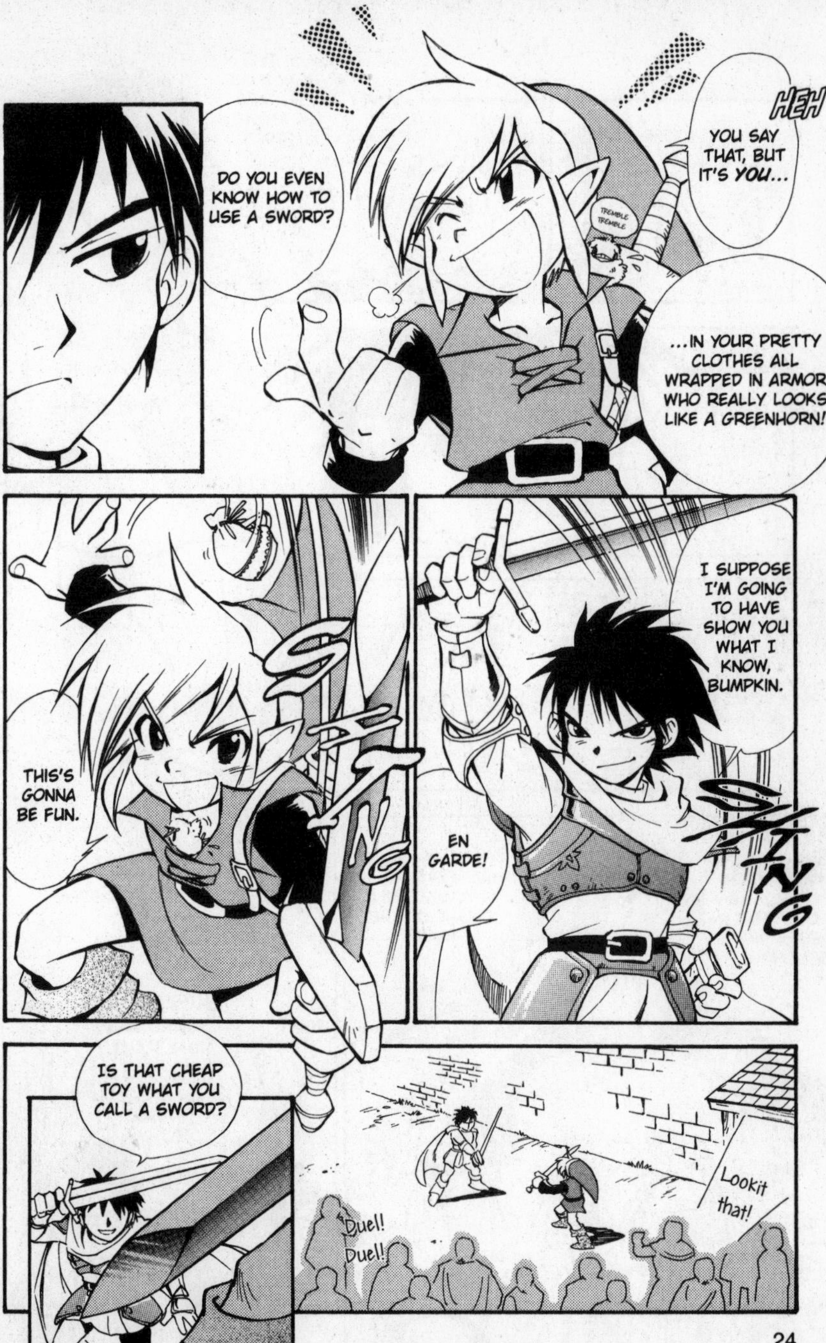
DO YOU EVEN KNOW HOW TO USE A SWORD?
HEH
YOU SAY THAT, BUT IT'S *YOU*...
TREMBLE TREMBLE
...IN YOUR PRETTY CLOTHES ALL WRAPPED IN ARMOR WHO REALLY LOOKS LIKE A GREENHORN!
I SUPPOSE I'M GOING TO HAVE SHOW YOU WHAT I KNOW, BUMPKIN.
SHING
EN GARDE!
SHING
THIS'S GONNA BE FUN.
Lookit that!
Duel! Duel!
IS THAT CHEAP TOY WHAT YOU CALL A SWORD?

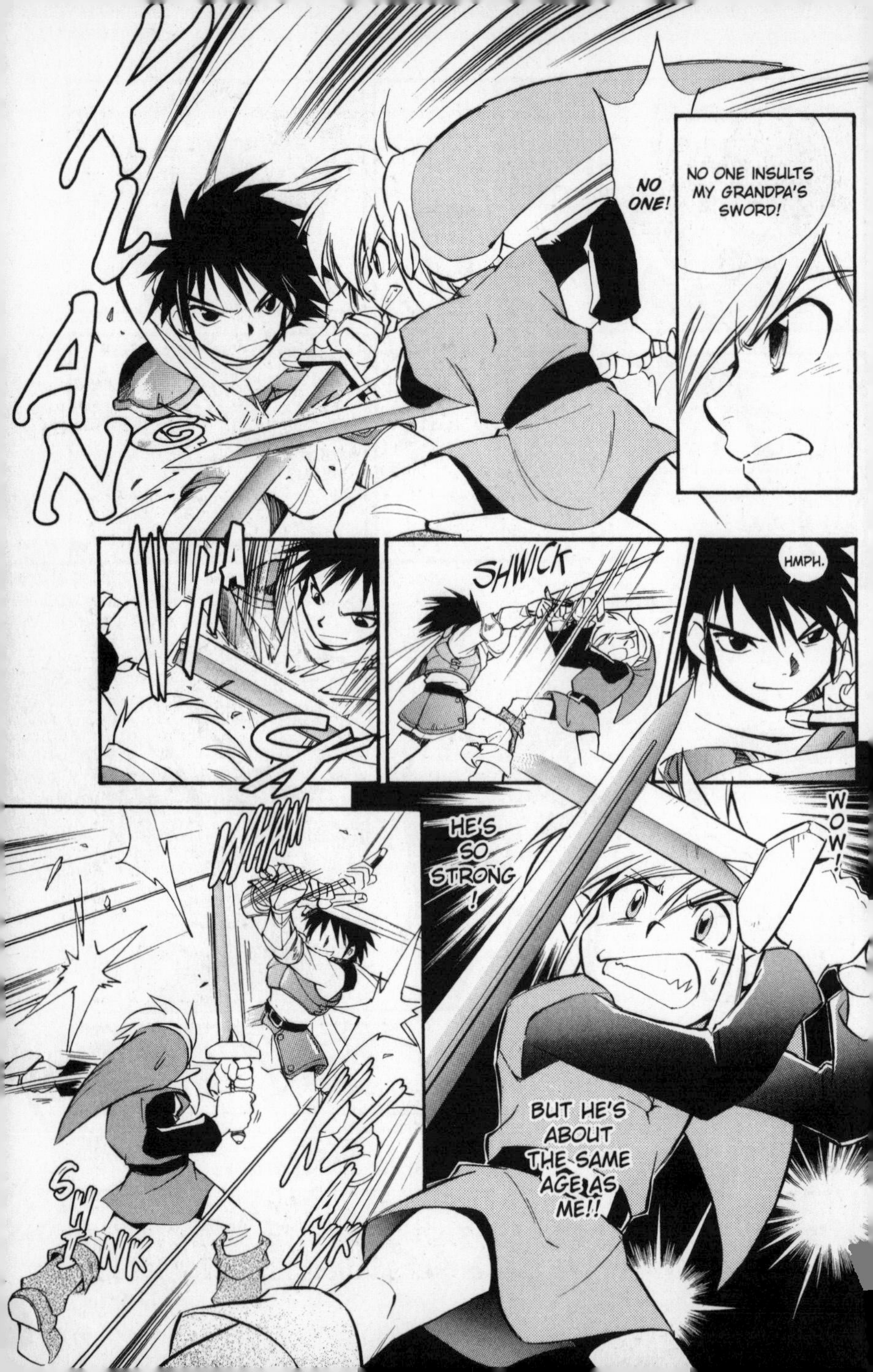
NO ONE INSULTS MY GRANDPA'S SWORD!
NO ONE!
KLANG
HMPH.
SHWICK
WHACK
WOW!
HE'S SO STRONG!
BUT HE'S ABOUT THE SAME AGE AS ME!!
WHAM
SHINK

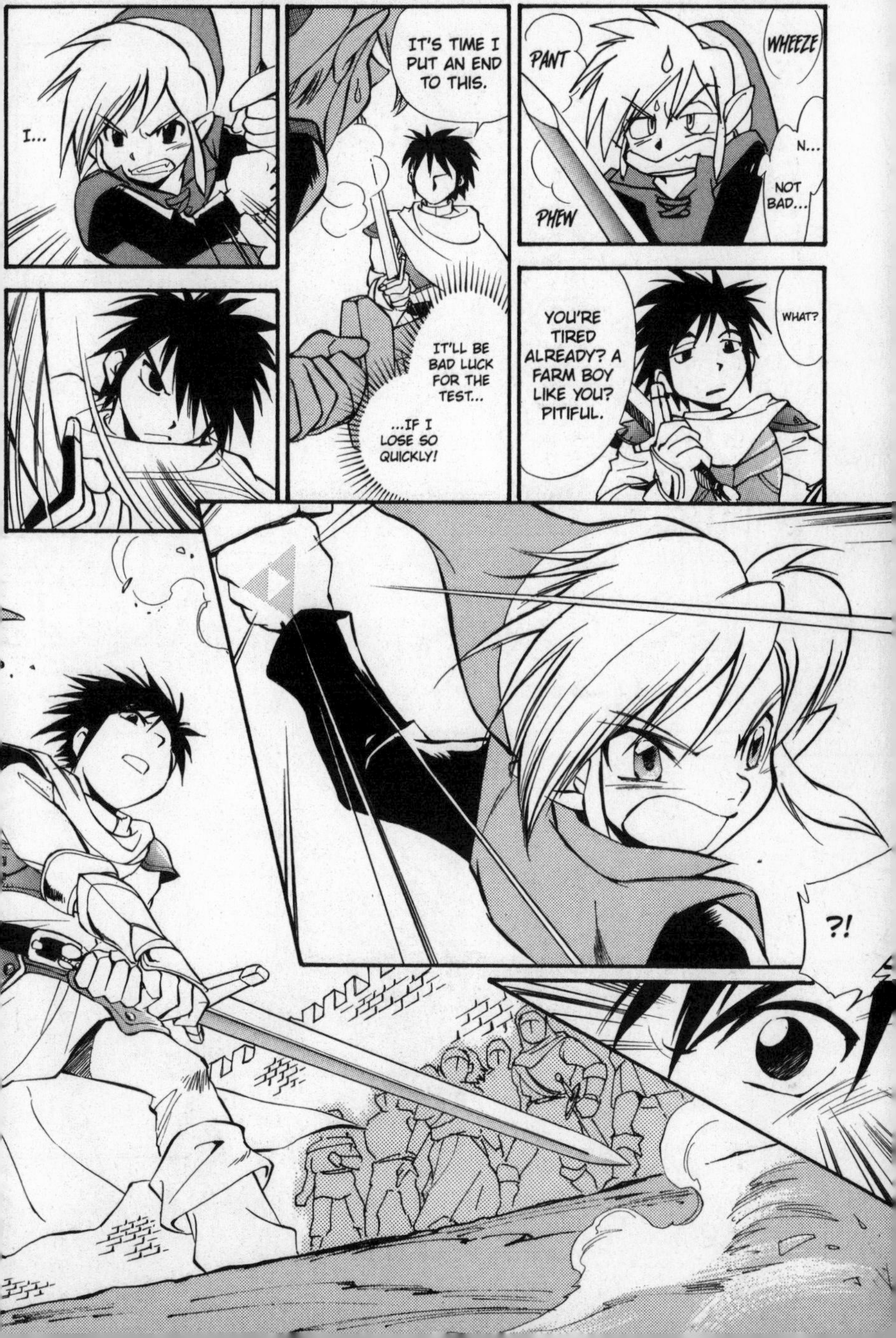
WHEEZE
PANT
N...
NOT BAD...
PHEW
WHAT?
YOU'RE TIRED ALREADY? A FARM BOY LIKE YOU? PITIFUL.
IT'S TIME I PUT AN END TO THIS.
IT'LL BE BAD LUCK FOR THE TEST...
...IF I LOSE SO QUICKLY!
I...
?!

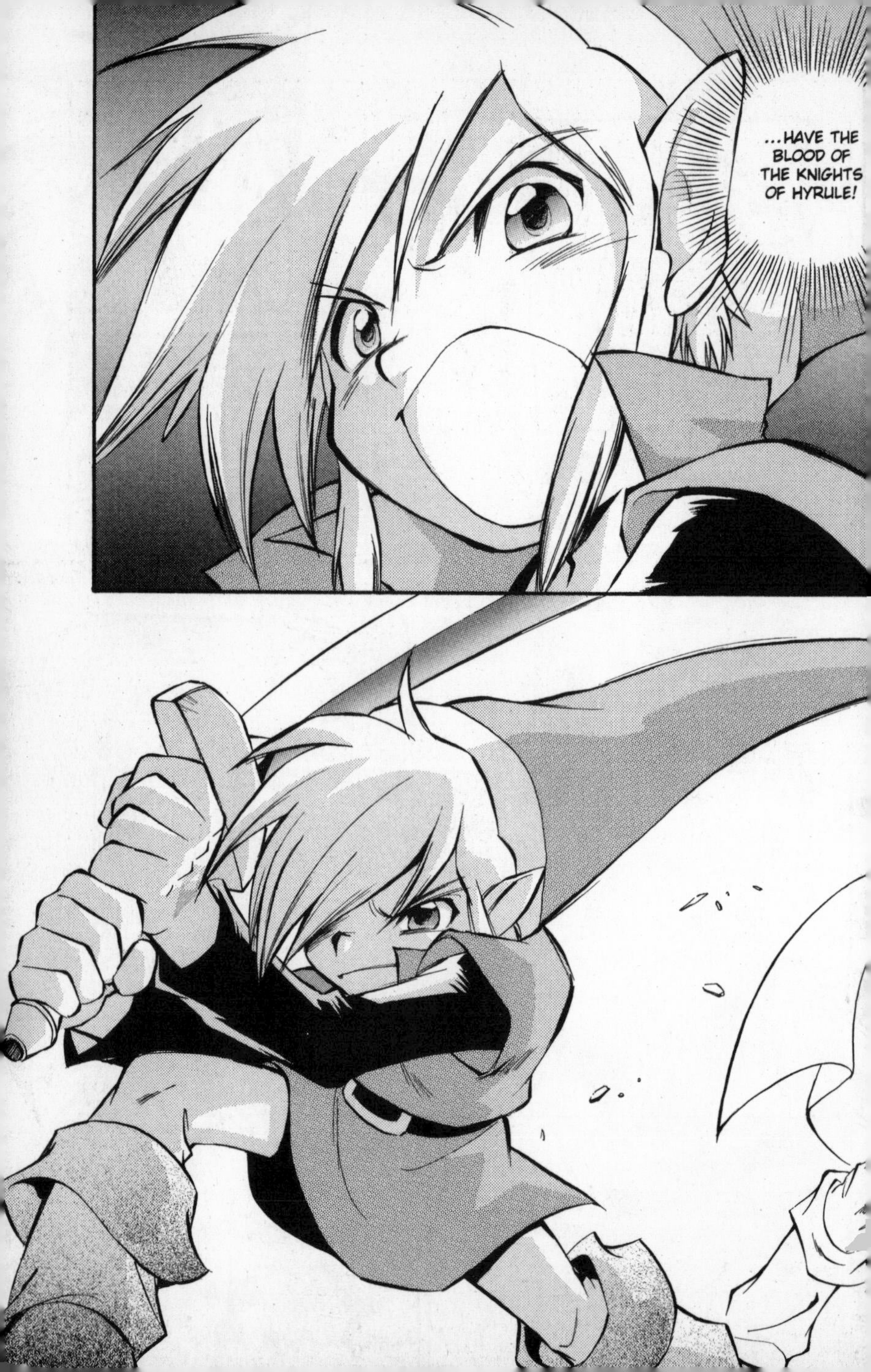
...HAVE THE BLOOD OF THE KNIGHTS OF HYRULE!

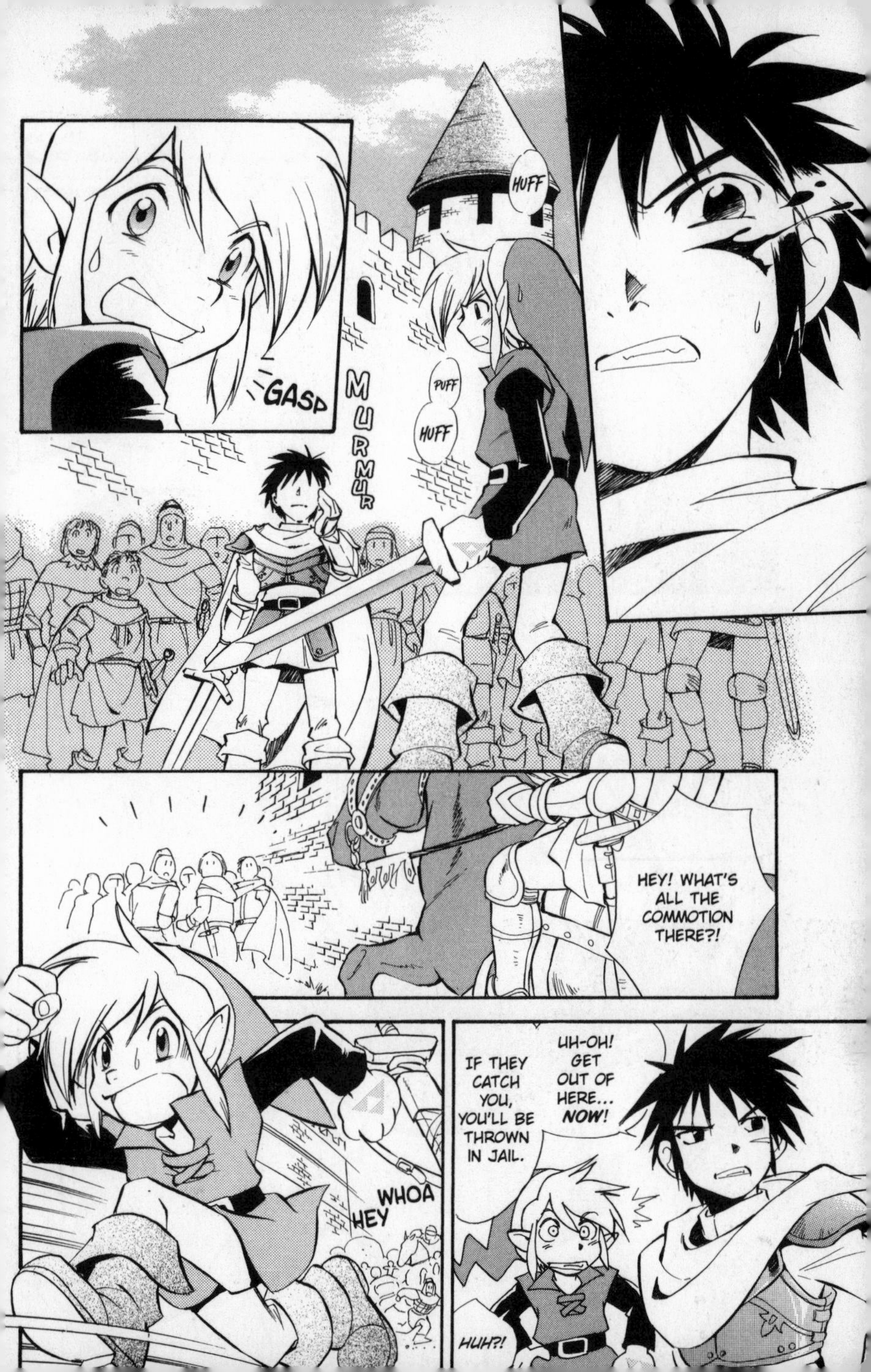
HUFF
PUFF
HUFF
MURMUR
GASP
HEY! WHAT'S ALL THE COMMOTION THERE?!
UH-OH! GET OUT OF HERE... *NOW!*
IF THEY CATCH YOU, YOU'LL BE THROWN IN JAIL.
HUH?!
WHOA
HEY

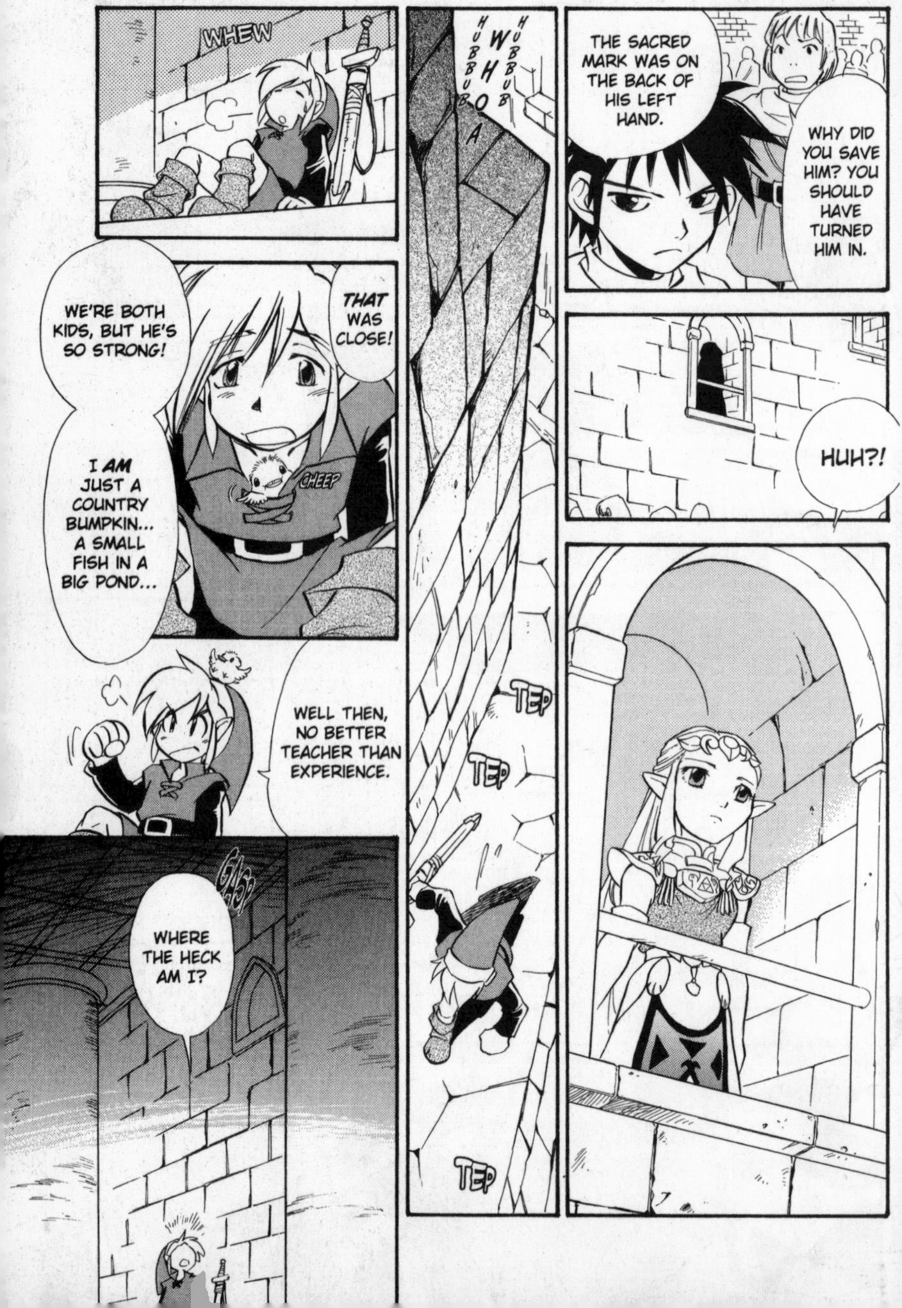
THE SACRED MARK WAS ON THE BACK OF HIS LEFT HAND.
WHY DID YOU SAVE HIM? YOU SHOULD HAVE TURNED HIM IN.
HUH?!
WHOA
HUBBUB
HUBBUB
TEP
TEP
TEP
WHEW
THAT WAS CLOSE!
WE'RE BOTH KIDS, BUT HE'S SO STRONG!
CHEEP
I AM JUST A COUNTRY BUMPKIN... A SMALL FISH IN A BIG POND...
WELL THEN, NO BETTER TEACHER THAN EXPERIENCE.
GASP
WHERE THE HECK AM I?

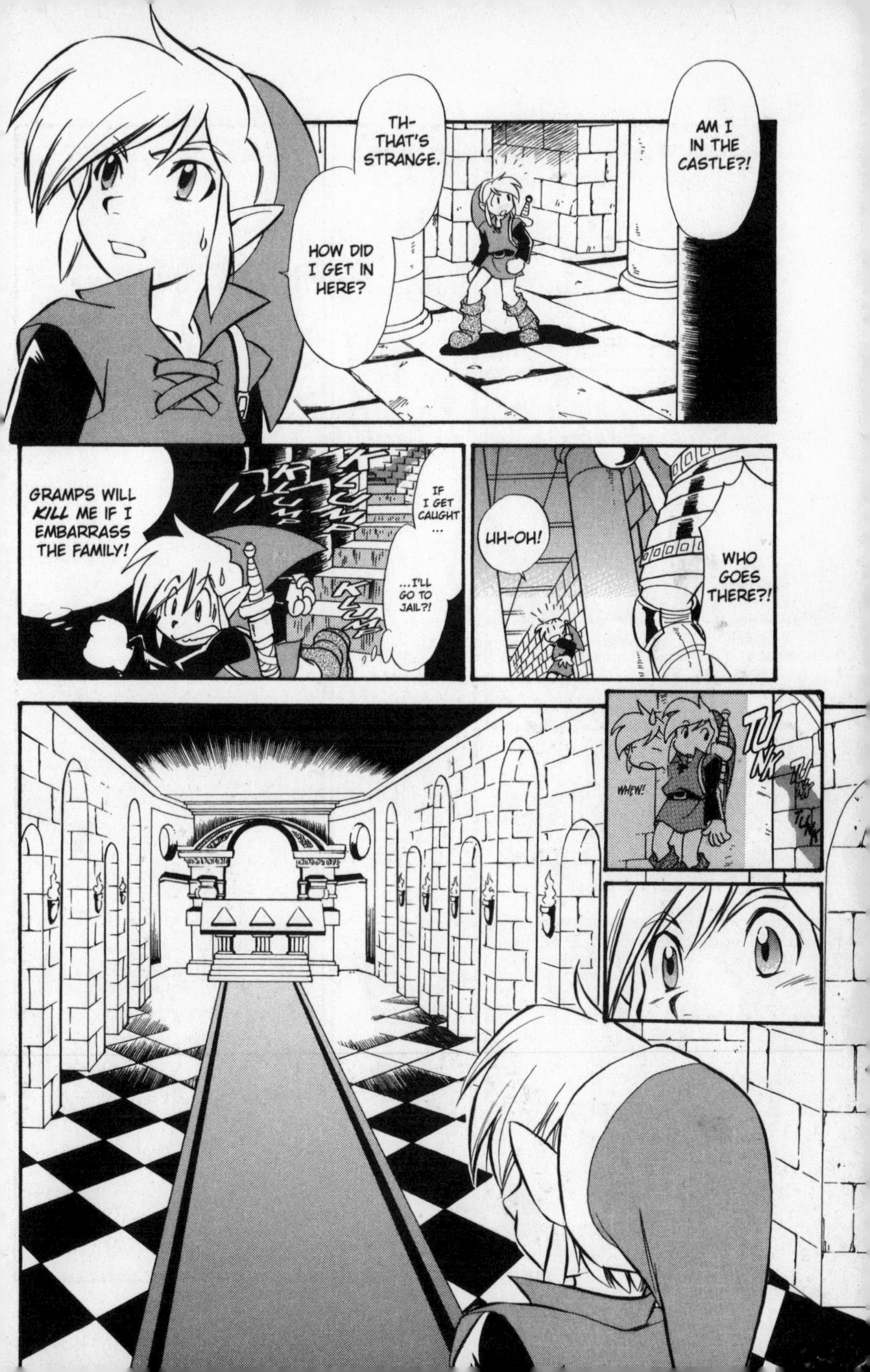
AM I IN THE CASTLE?!
TH- THAT'S STRANGE.
HOW DID I GET IN HERE?
WHO GOES THERE?!
UH-OH!
KLUMP
KLUMP
IF I GET CAUGHT ...
...I'LL GO TO JAIL?!
GRAMPS WILL *KILL* ME IF I EMBARRASS THE FAMILY!
TUNK
WHEW!

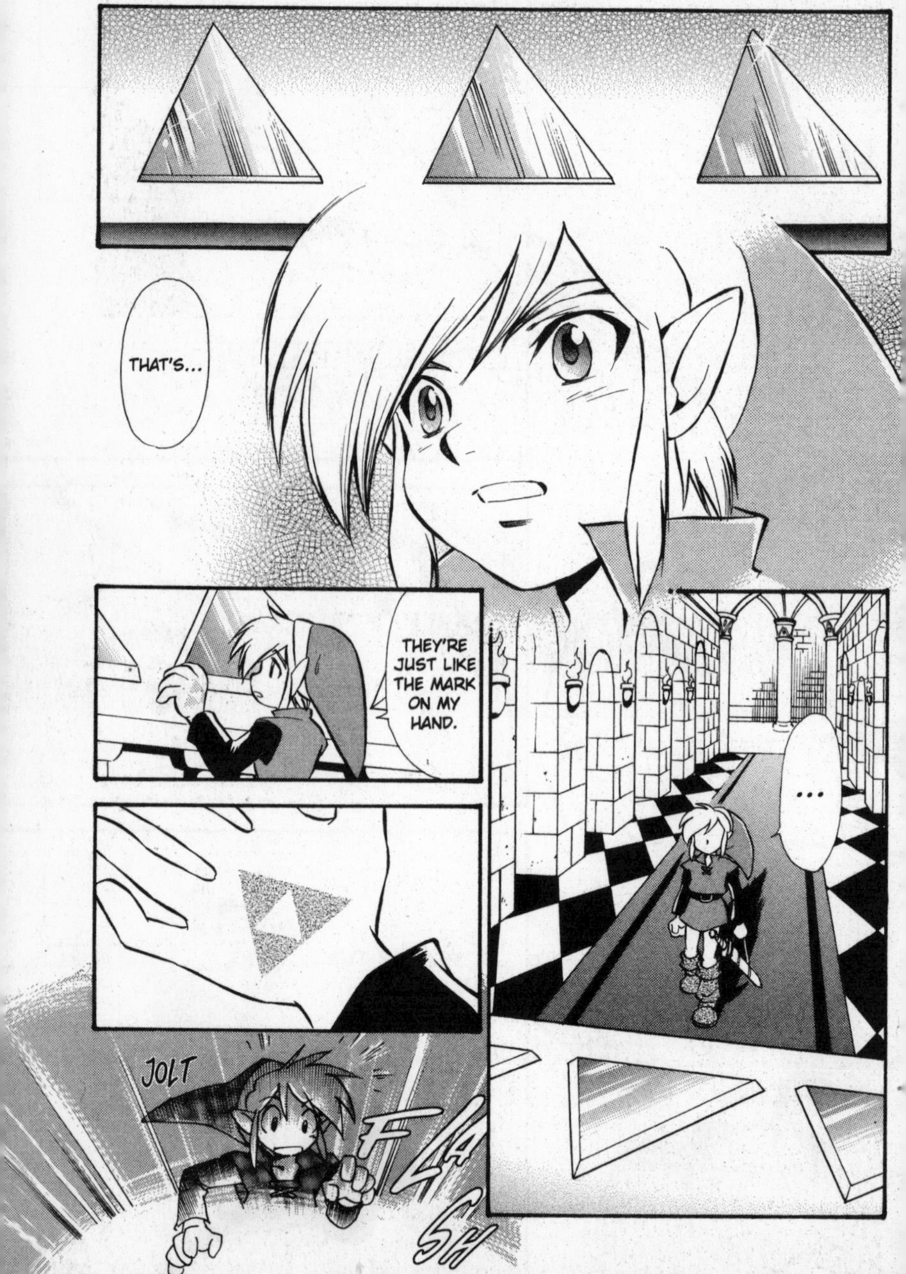
THAT'S...
...
THEY'RE JUST LIKE THE MARK ON MY HAND.
JOLT
FLASH

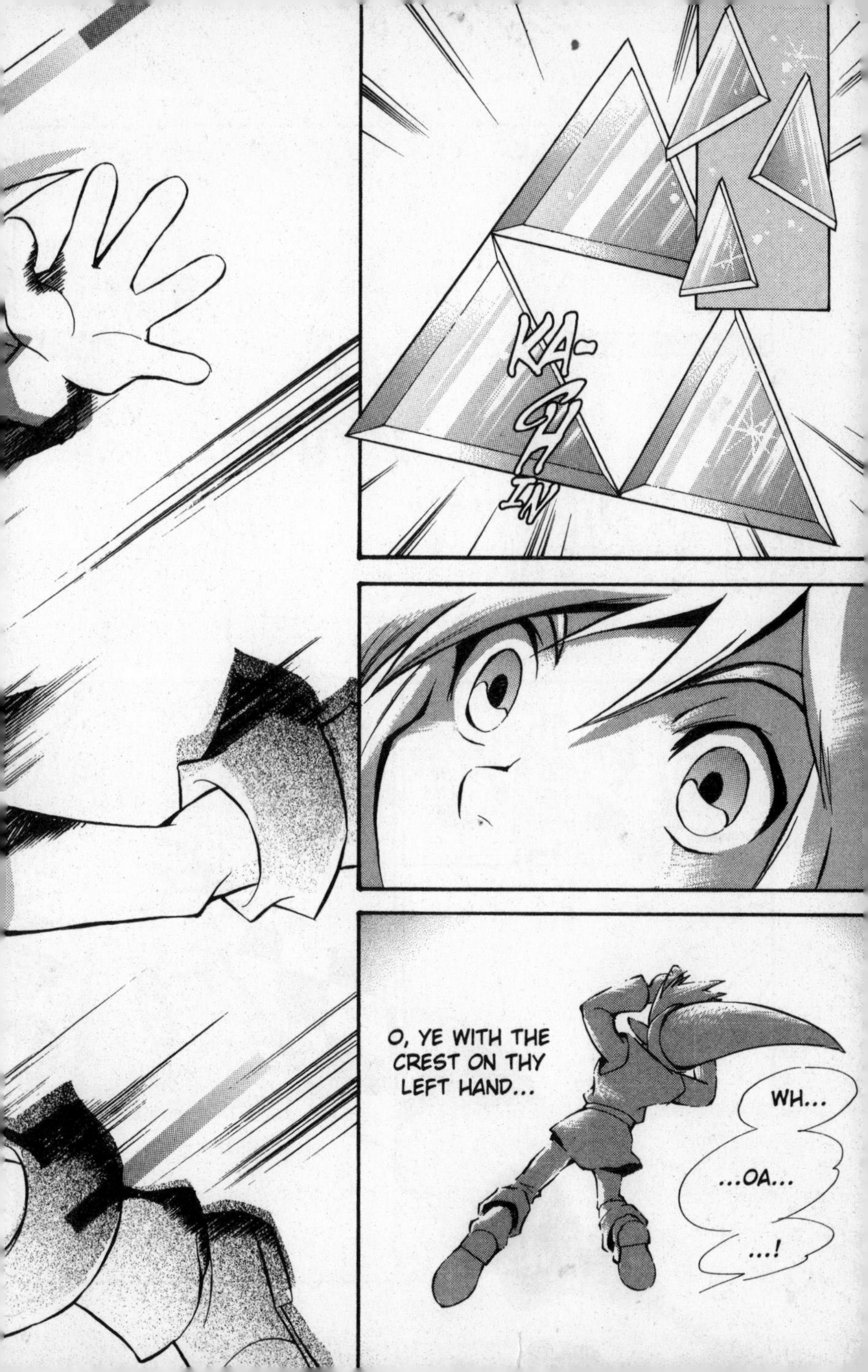
KA-CHIN
O, YE WITH THE CREST ON THY LEFT HAND...
WH...
...OA...
...!

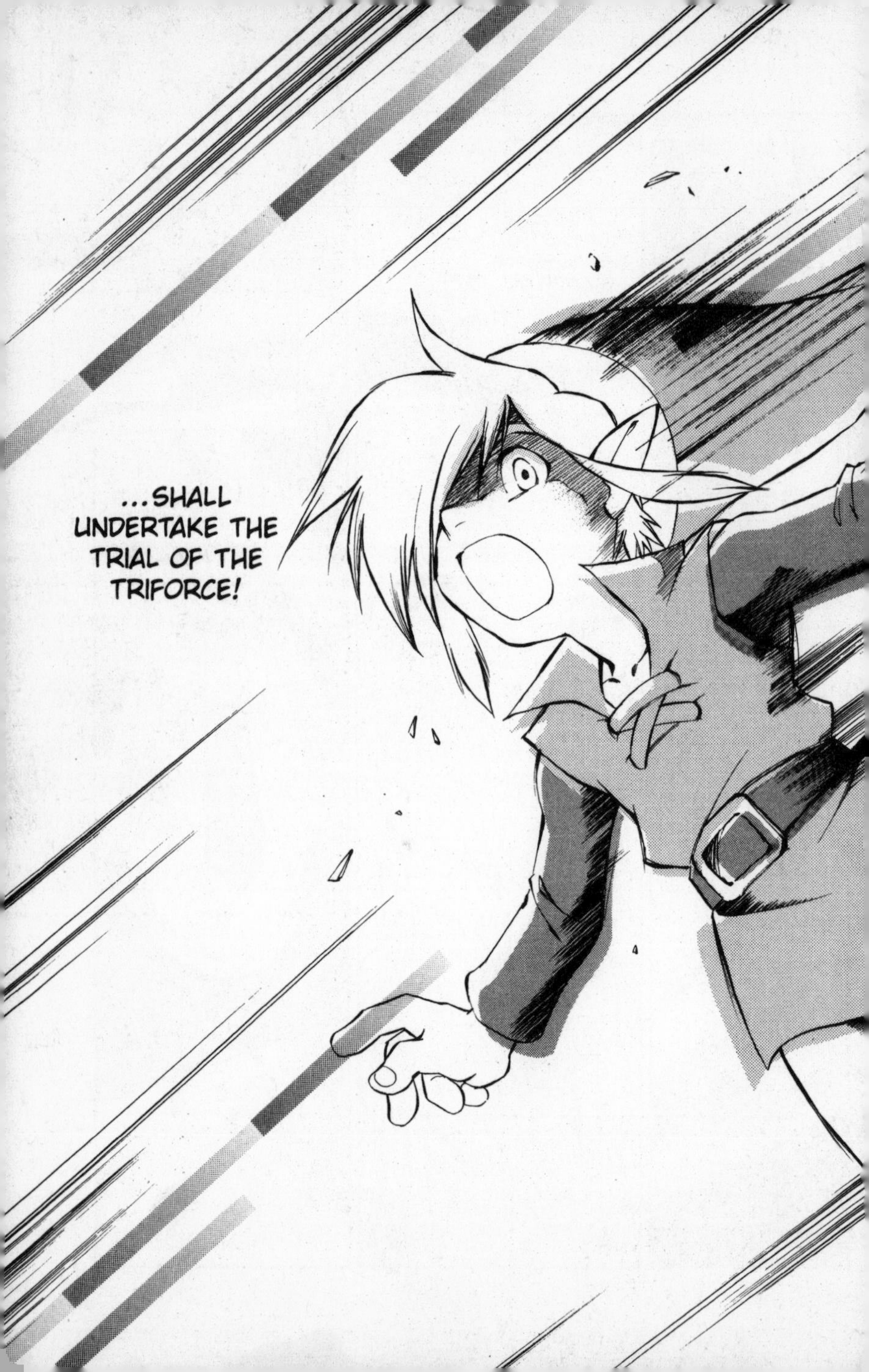
...SHALL UNDERTAKE THE TRIAL OF THE TRIFORCE!

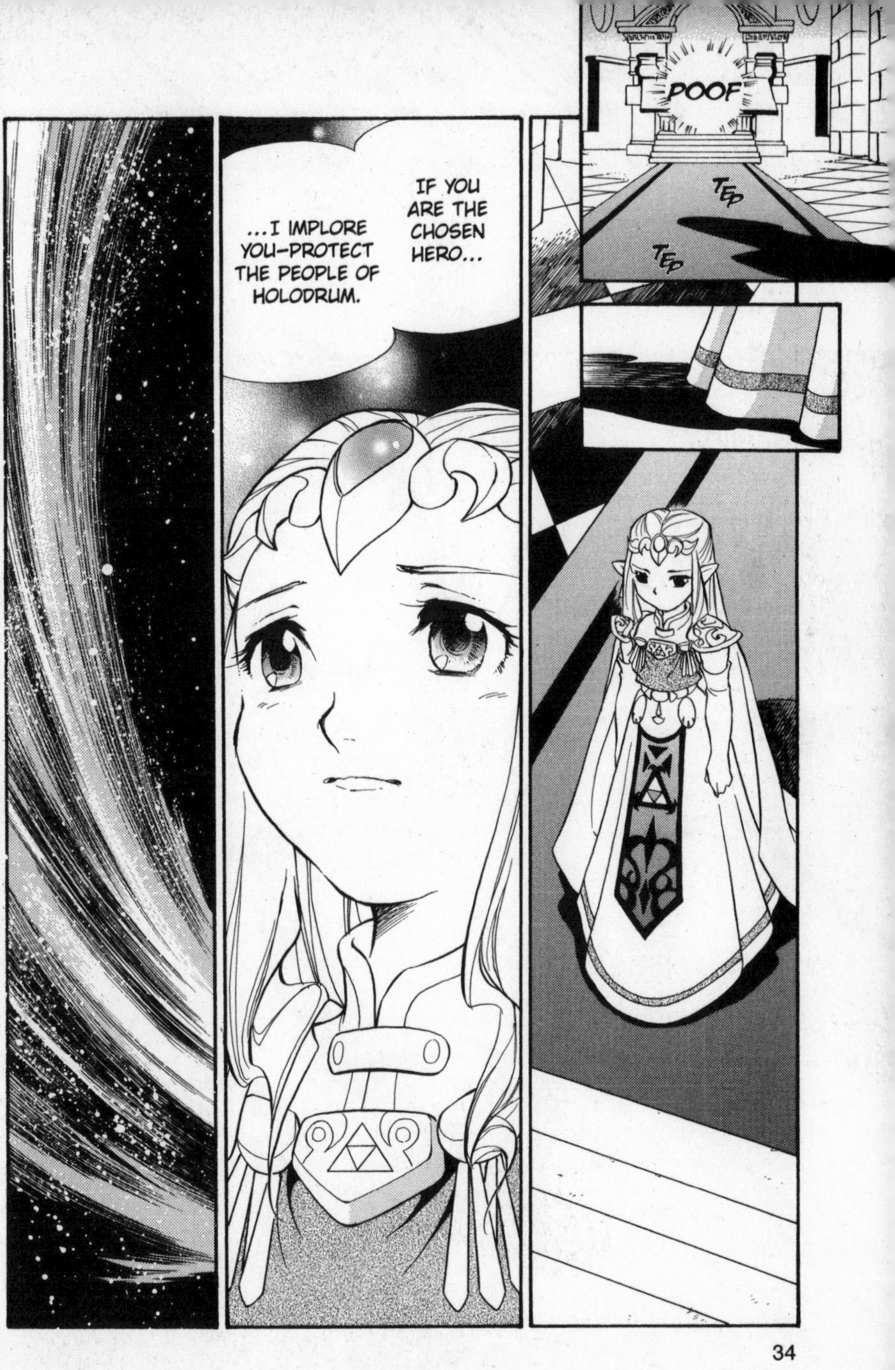
POOF
TEP
TEP
IF YOU ARE THE CHOSEN HERO...
...I IMPLORE YOU–PROTECT THE PEOPLE OF HOLODRUM.

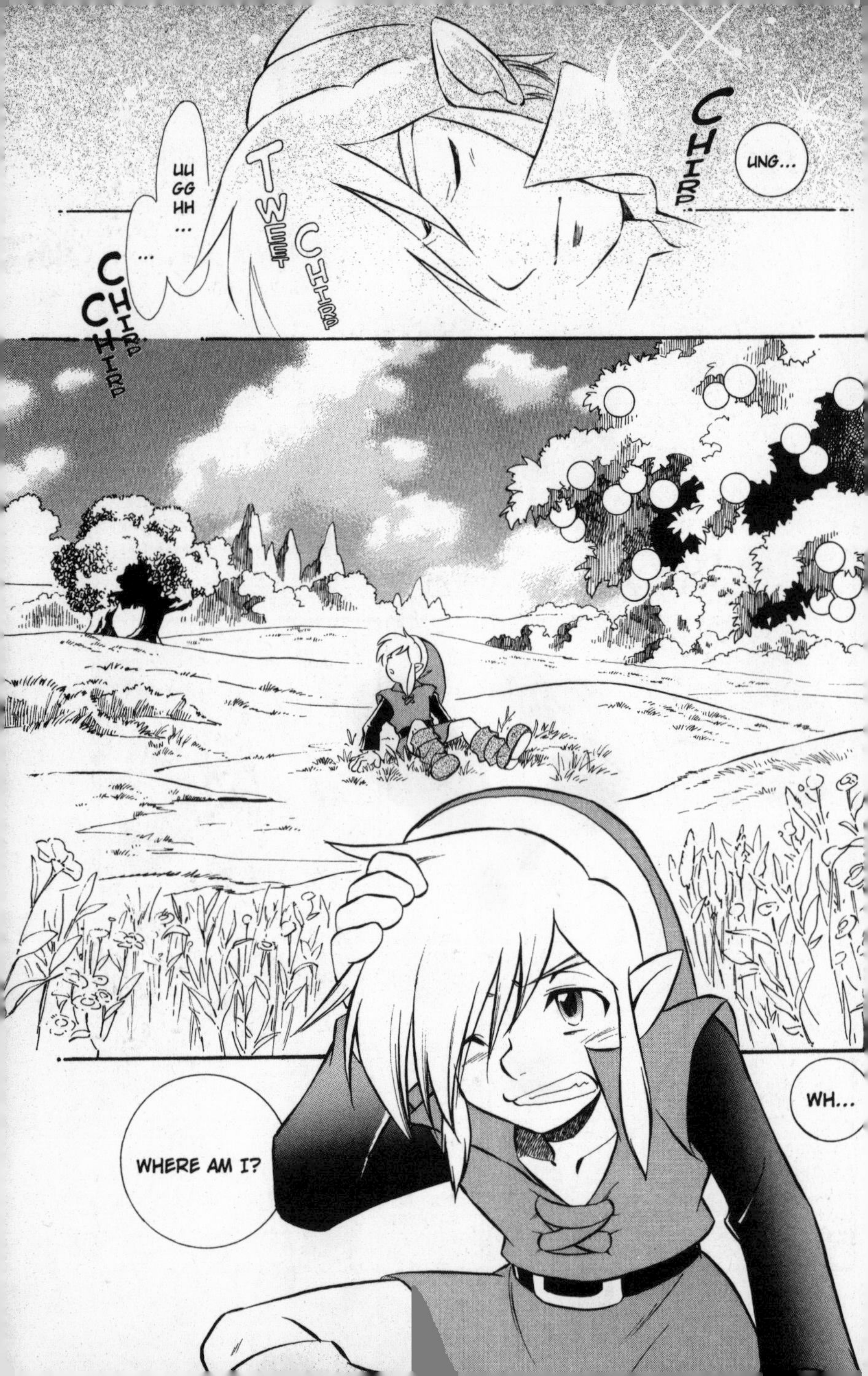
UNG...
CHIRP
UUGGHH... ...
TWEET
CHIRP
CHIRP
CHIRP
WH...
WHERE AM I?

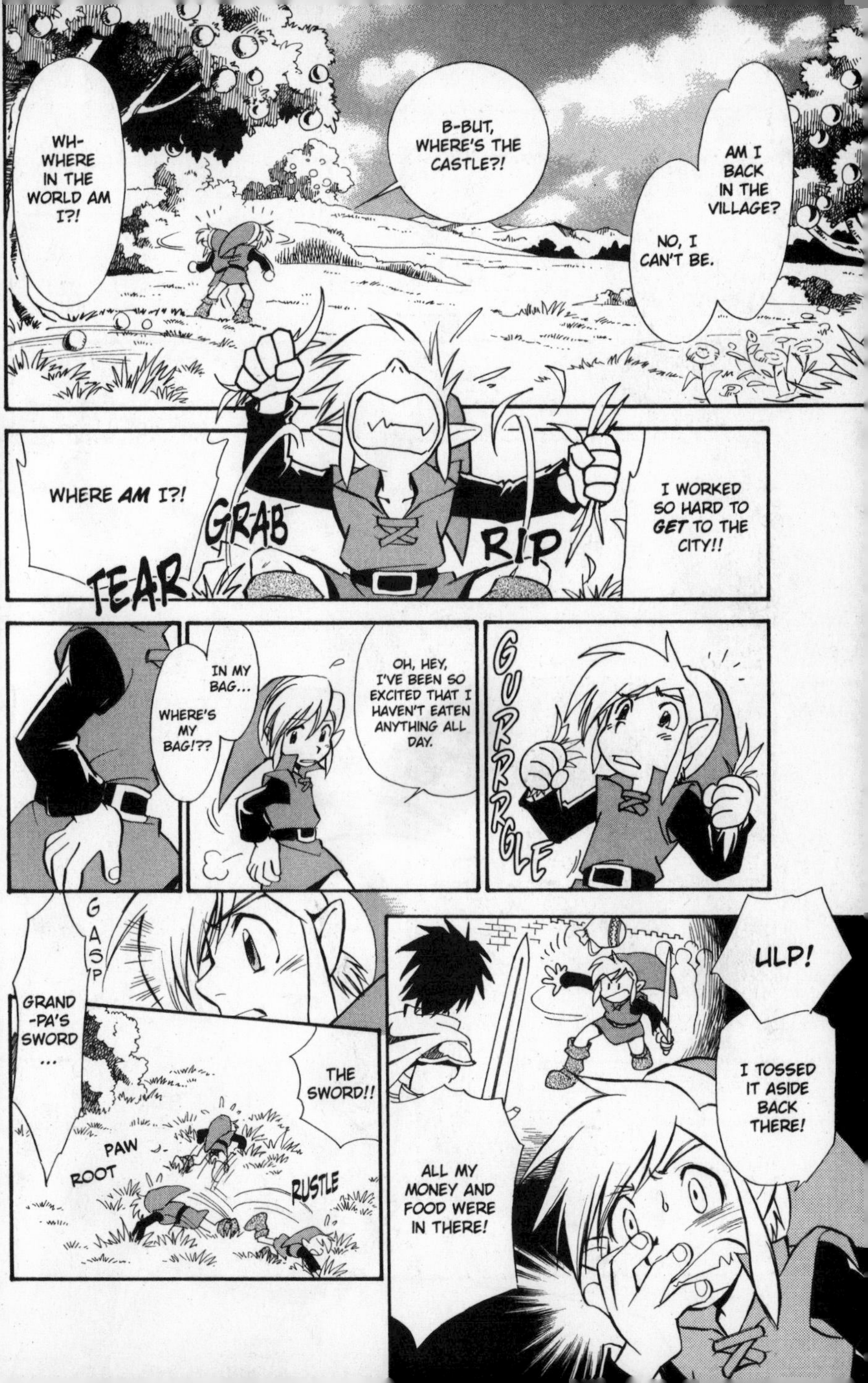
AM I BACK IN THE VILLAGE?
NO, I CAN'T BE.
B-BUT, WHERE'S THE CASTLE?!
WH-WHERE IN THE WORLD AM I?!
I WORKED SO HARD TO GET TO THE CITY!!
RIP
GRAB
TEAR
WHERE AM I?!
GURRRRGLE
OH, HEY, I'VE BEEN SO EXCITED THAT I HAVEN'T EATEN ANYTHING ALL DAY.
IN MY BAG...
WHERE'S MY BAG!??
ULP!
I TOSSED IT ASIDE BACK THERE!
ALL MY MONEY AND FOOD WERE IN THERE!
GASP
GRAND-PA'S SWORD ...
THE SWORD!!
PAW
ROOT
RUSTLE

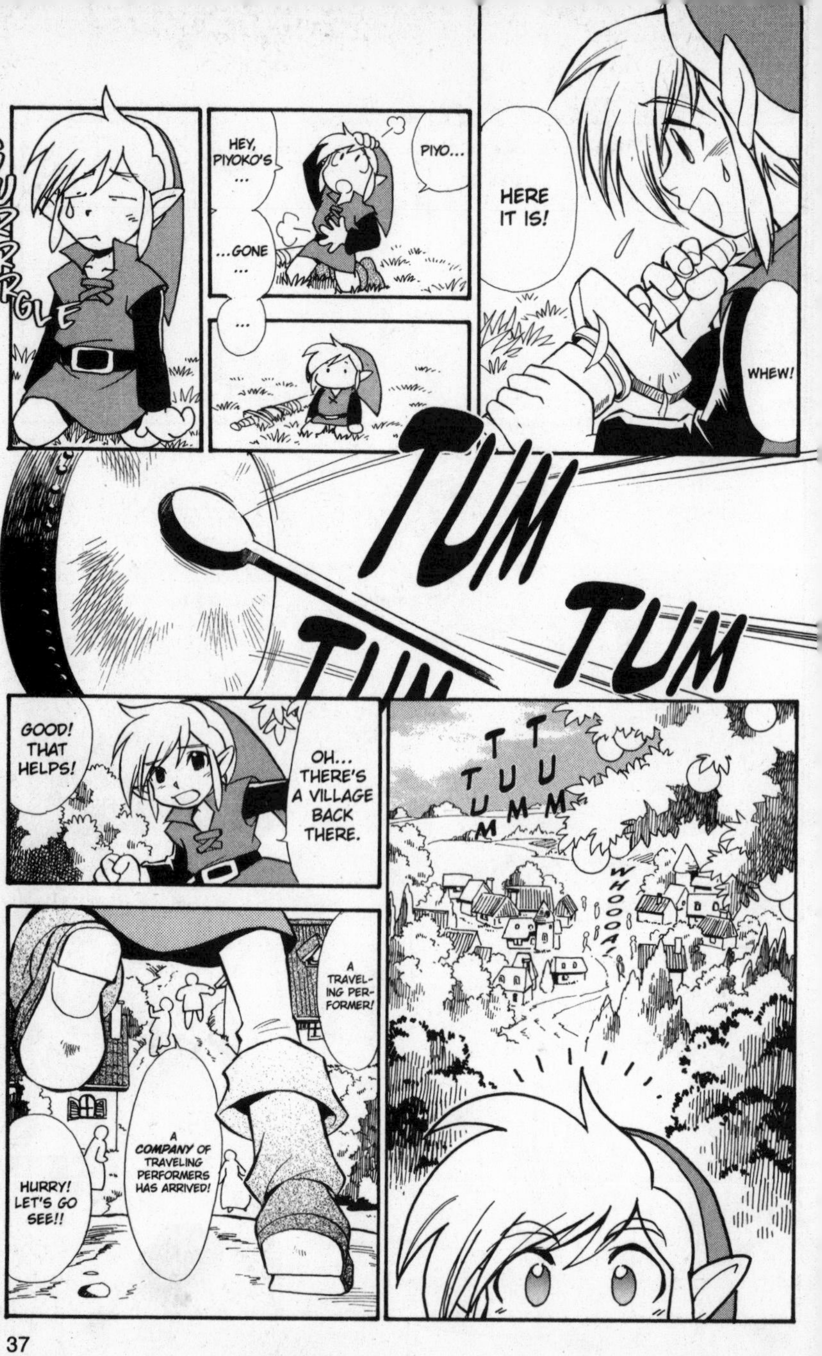
HERE IT IS!
WHEW!
PIYO...
HEY, PIYOKO'S ...
...GONE ...
...
GURRRGLE
TUM TUM TUM
TTUUMMM
WHOOOA!
OH... THERE'S A VILLAGE BACK THERE.
GOOD! THAT HELPS!
A TRAVELING PERFORMER!
A COMPANY OF TRAVELING PERFORMERS HAS ARRIVED!
HURRY! LET'S GO SEE!!

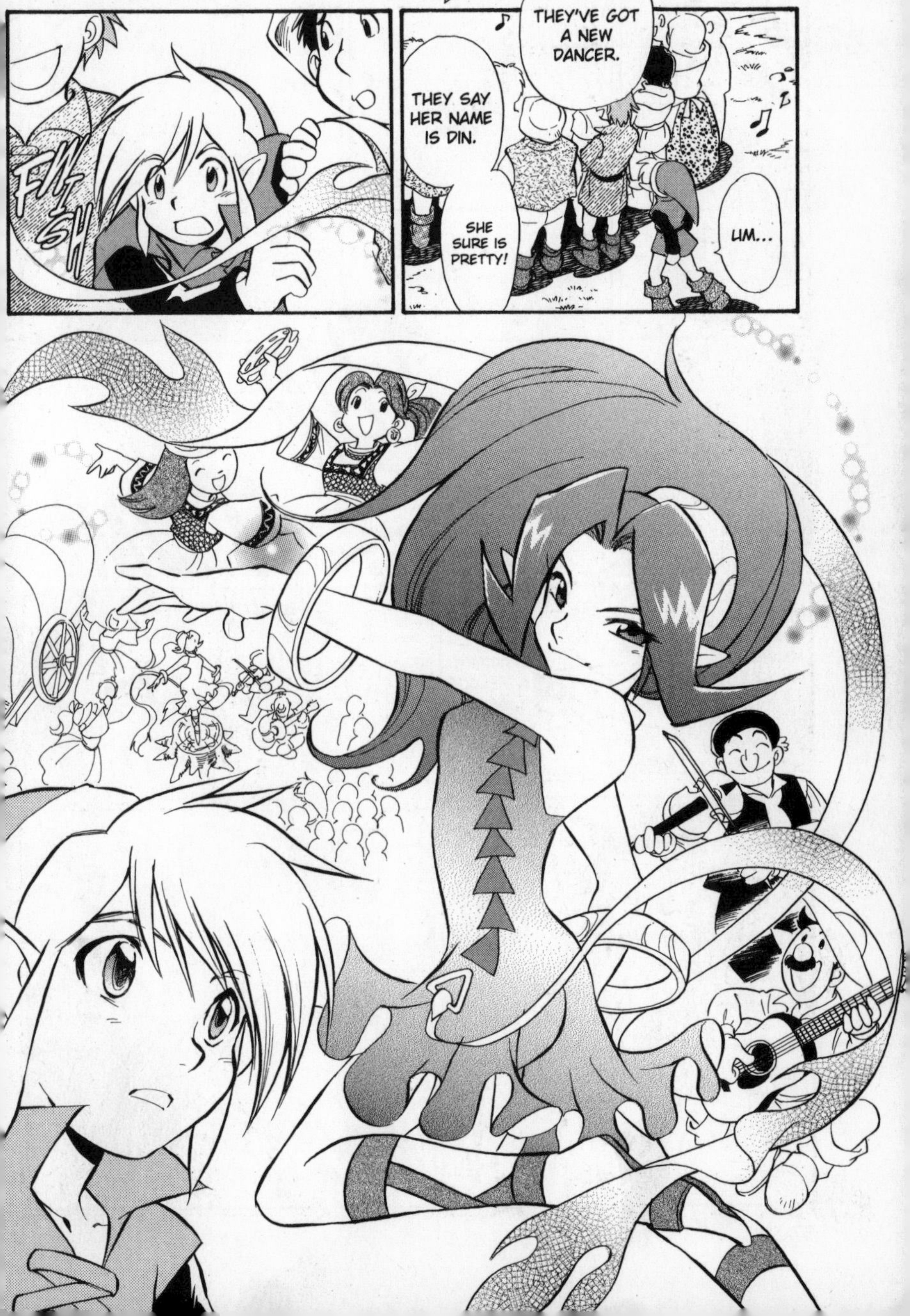
THEY'VE GOT A NEW DANCER.
THEY SAY HER NAME IS DIN.
SHE SURE IS PRETTY!
UM...
FWSH

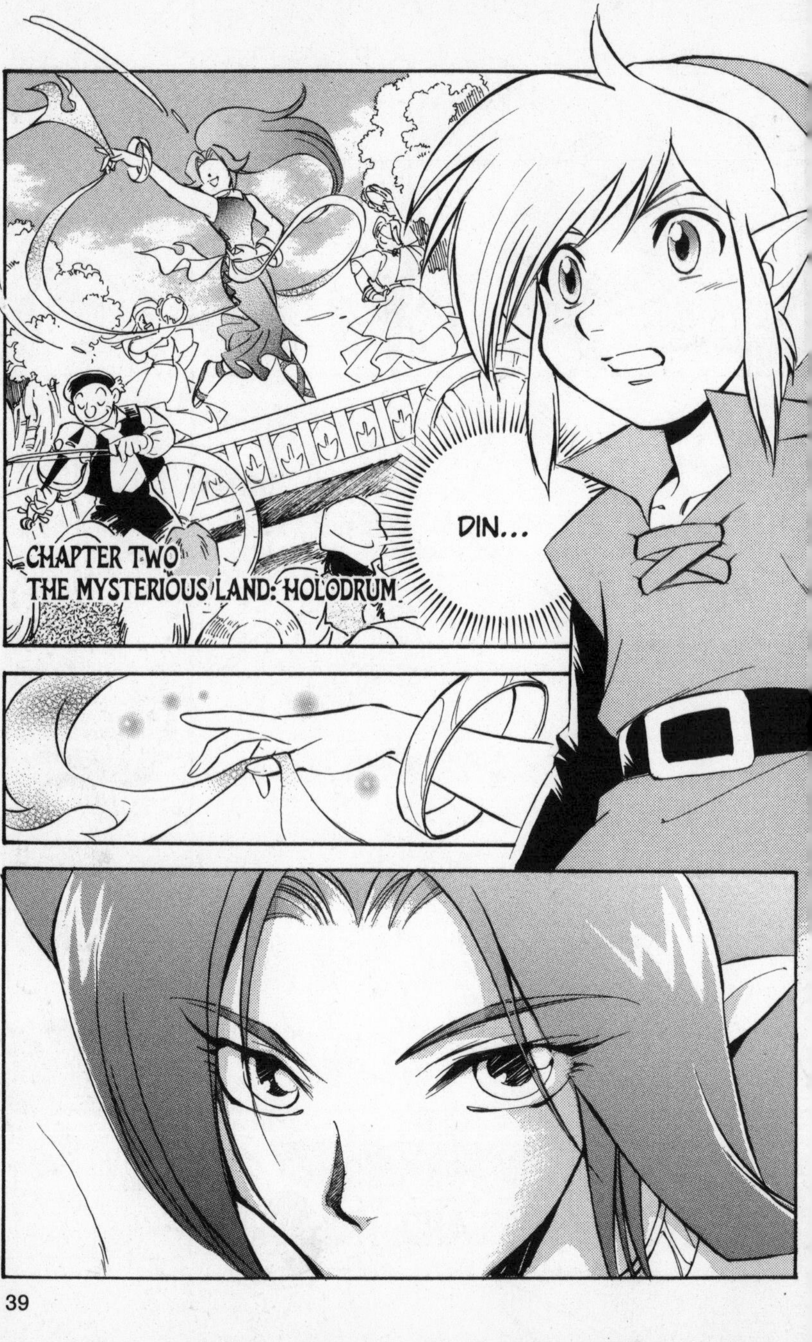
DIN...
CHAPTER TWO
THE MYSTERIOUS LAND: HOLODRUM

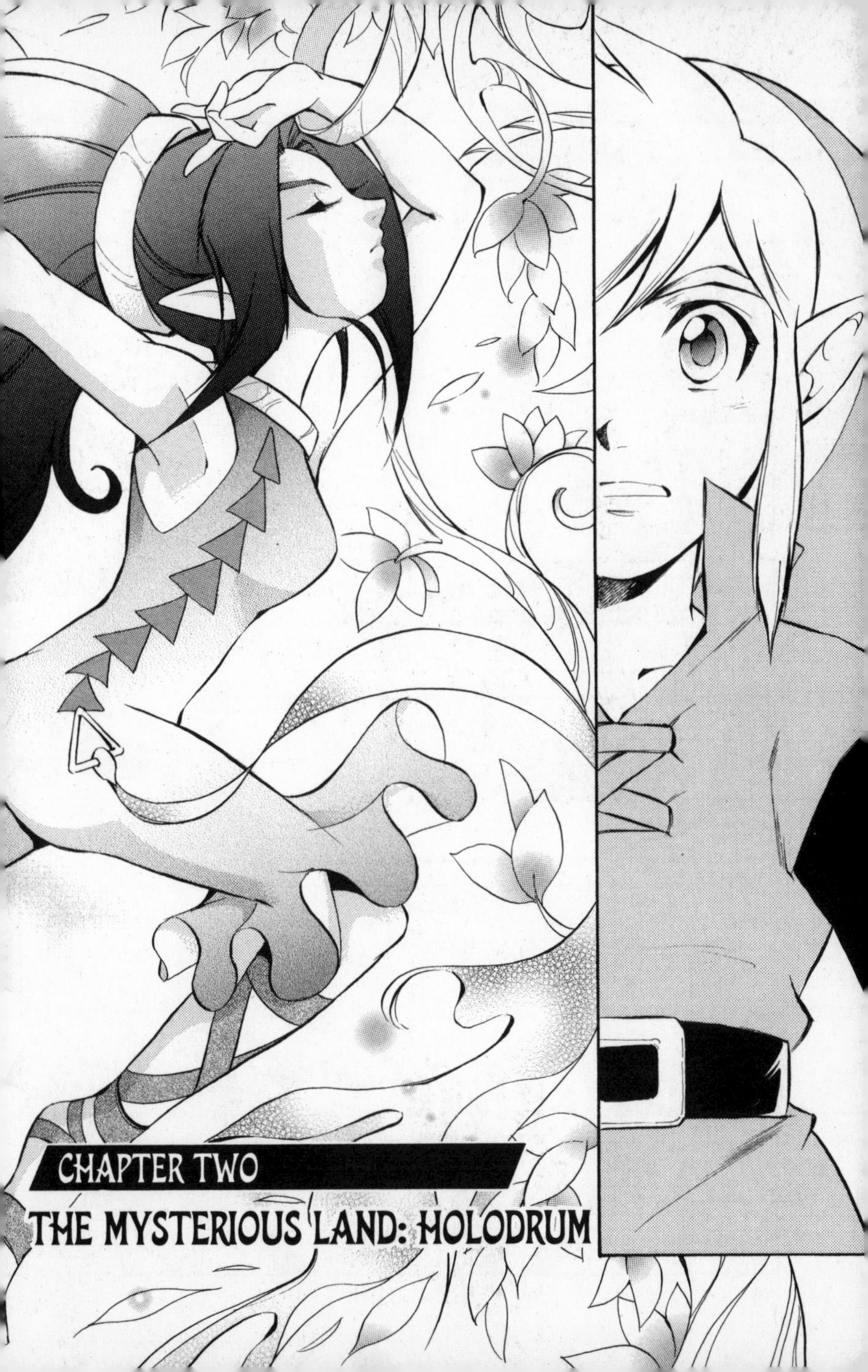
CHAPTER TWO
THE MYSTERIOUS LAND: HOLODRUM

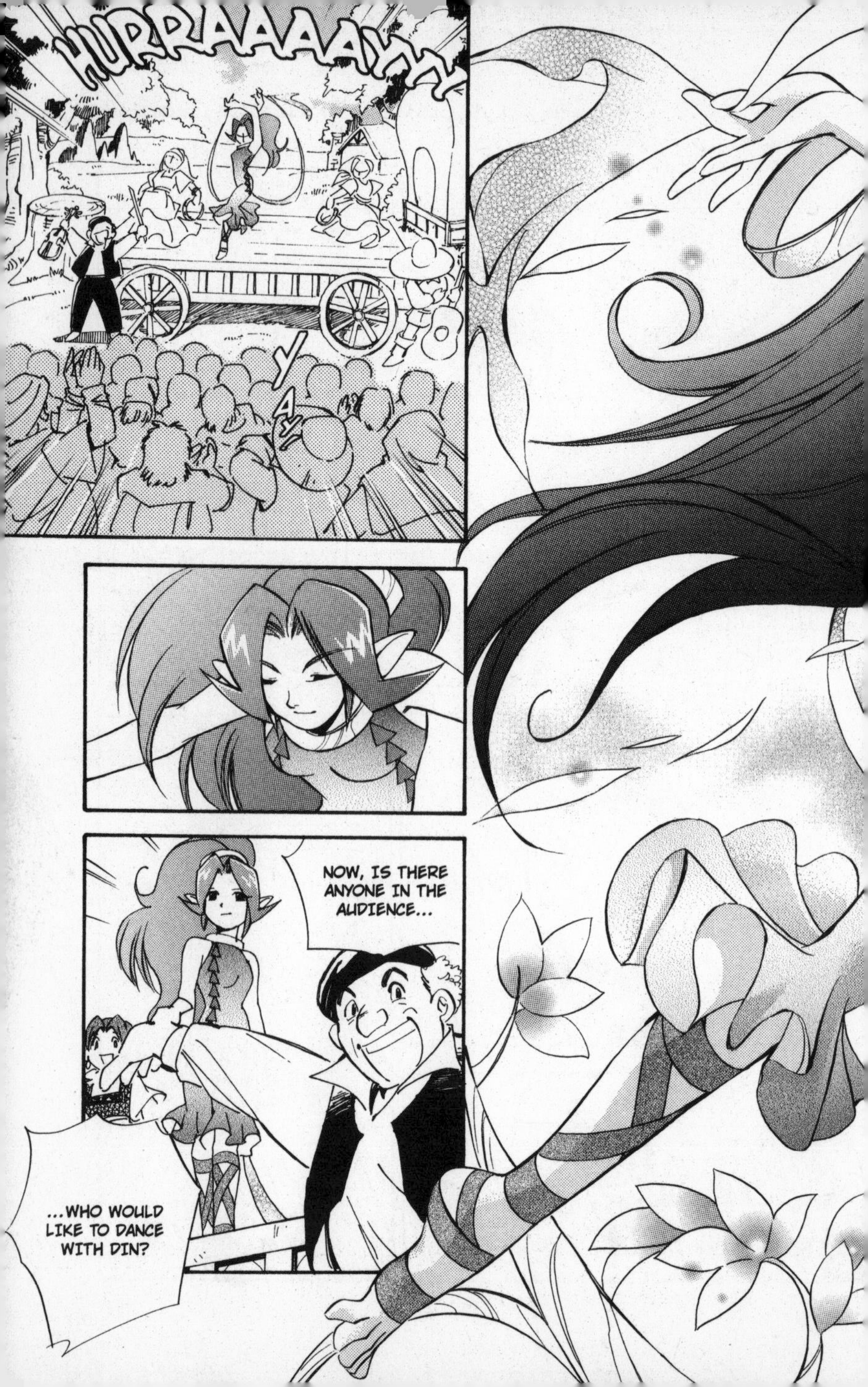
HURRAAAAAYYY
YAY
NOW, IS THERE ANYONE IN THE AUDIENCE...
...WHO WOULD LIKE TO DANCE WITH DIN?

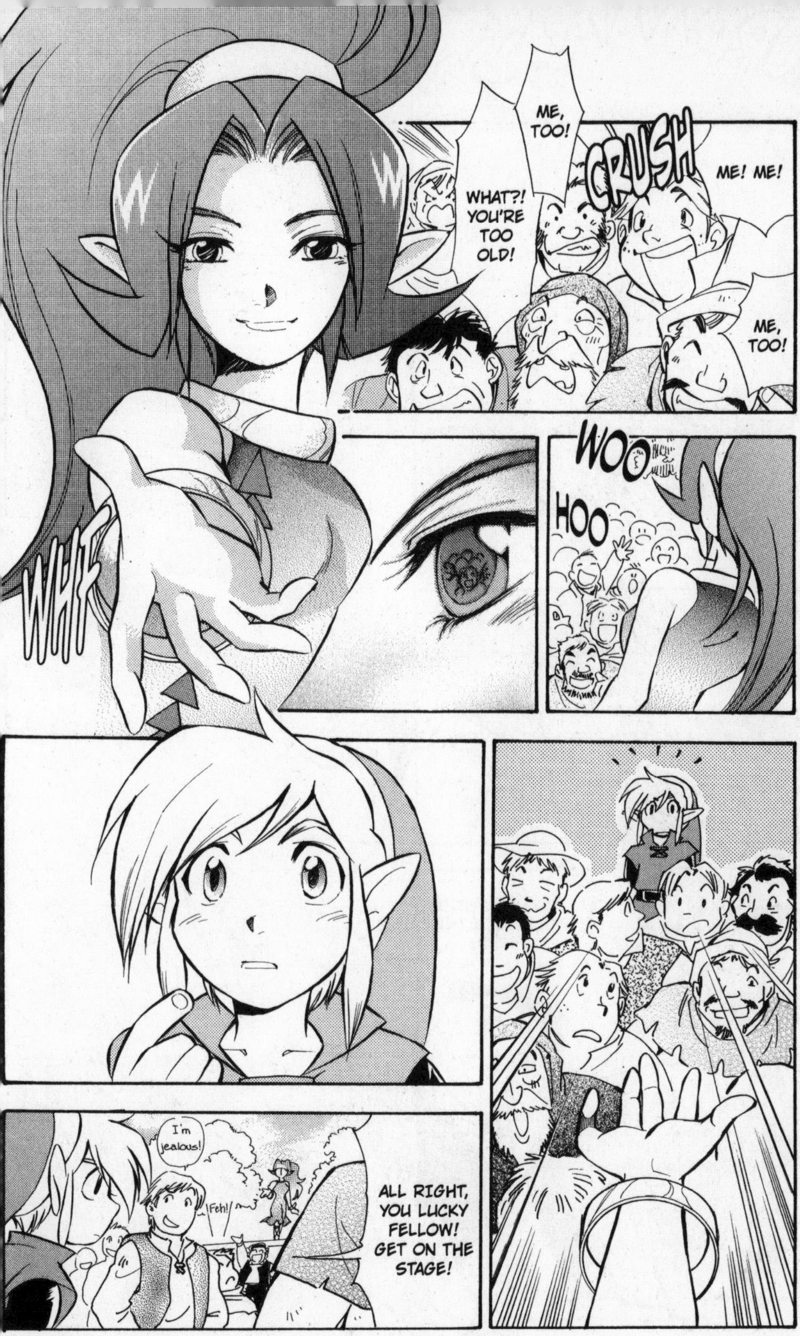
ME, TOO!
ME! ME!
CRUSH
WHAT?! YOU'RE TOO OLD!
ME, TOO!
WOO
HOO
WHIF
ALL RIGHT, YOU LUCKY FELLOW! GET ON THE STAGE!
I'm jealous!
Feh!

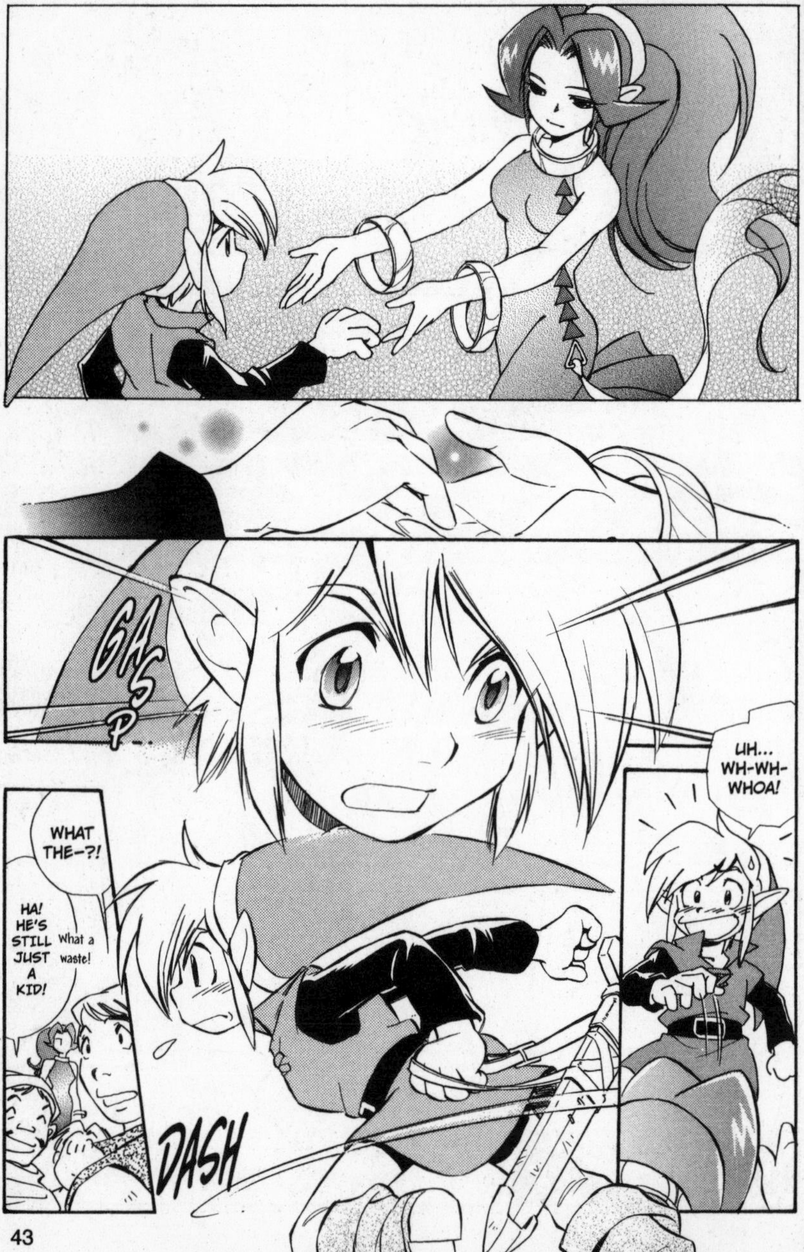
GASP...
UH... WH-WH-WHOA!
DASH
WHAT THE-?!
HA! HE'S STILL JUST A KID!
What a waste!

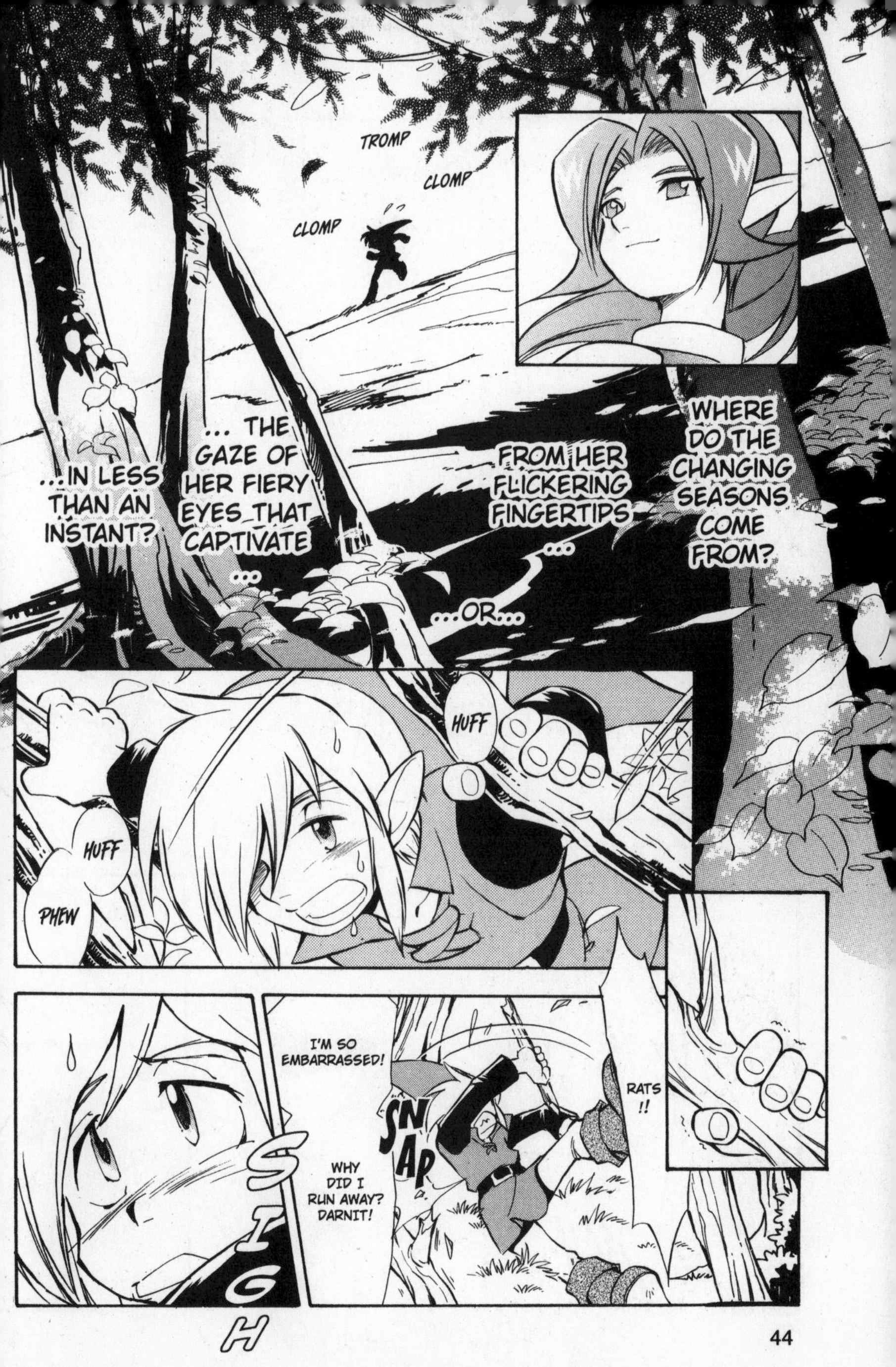
TROMP
CLOMP
CLOMP
WHERE DO THE CHANGING SEASONS COME FROM?
FROM HER FLICKERING FINGERTIPS ...
...OR...
... THE GAZE OF HER FIERY EYES THAT CAPTIVATE ...
...IN LESS THAN AN INSTANT?
HUFF
HUFF
PHEW
RATS !!
I'M SO EMBARRASSED!
SNAP
WHY DID I RUN AWAY? DARNIT!
SIGH

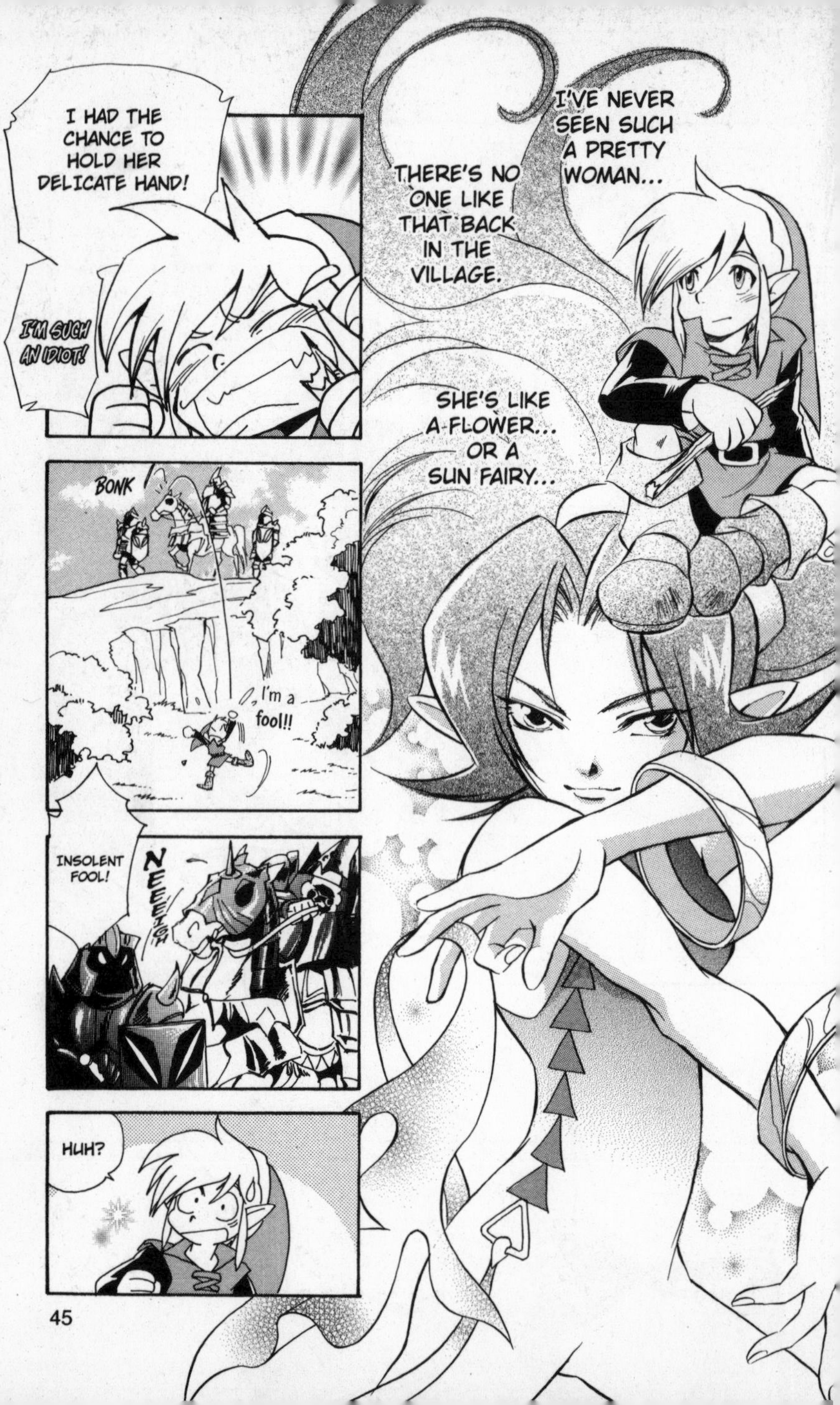
I'VE NEVER SEEN SUCH A PRETTY WOMAN...
THERE'S NO ONE LIKE THAT BACK IN THE VILLAGE.
SHE'S LIKE A FLOWER... OR A SUN FAIRY...
I HAD THE CHANCE TO HOLD HER DELICATE HAND!
I'M SUCH AN IDIOT!
BONK
I'm a fool!!
INSOLENT FOOL!
NEEEEIGH
HUH?

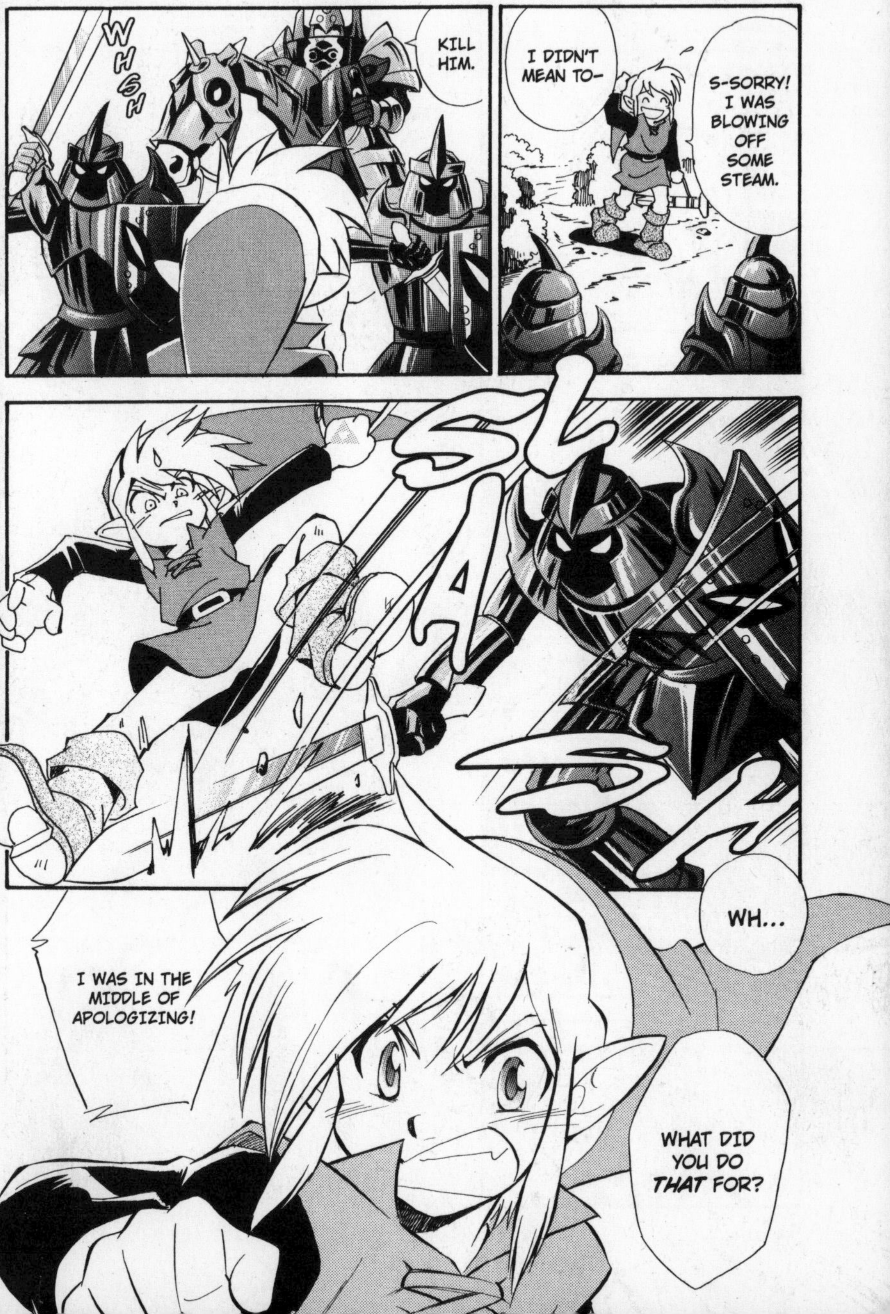
S-SORRY! I WAS BLOWING OFF SOME STEAM.
I DIDN'T MEAN TO–
KILL HIM.
WHSH
SLASH
WH...
WHAT DID YOU DO *THAT* FOR?
I WAS IN THE MIDDLE OF APOLOGIZING!

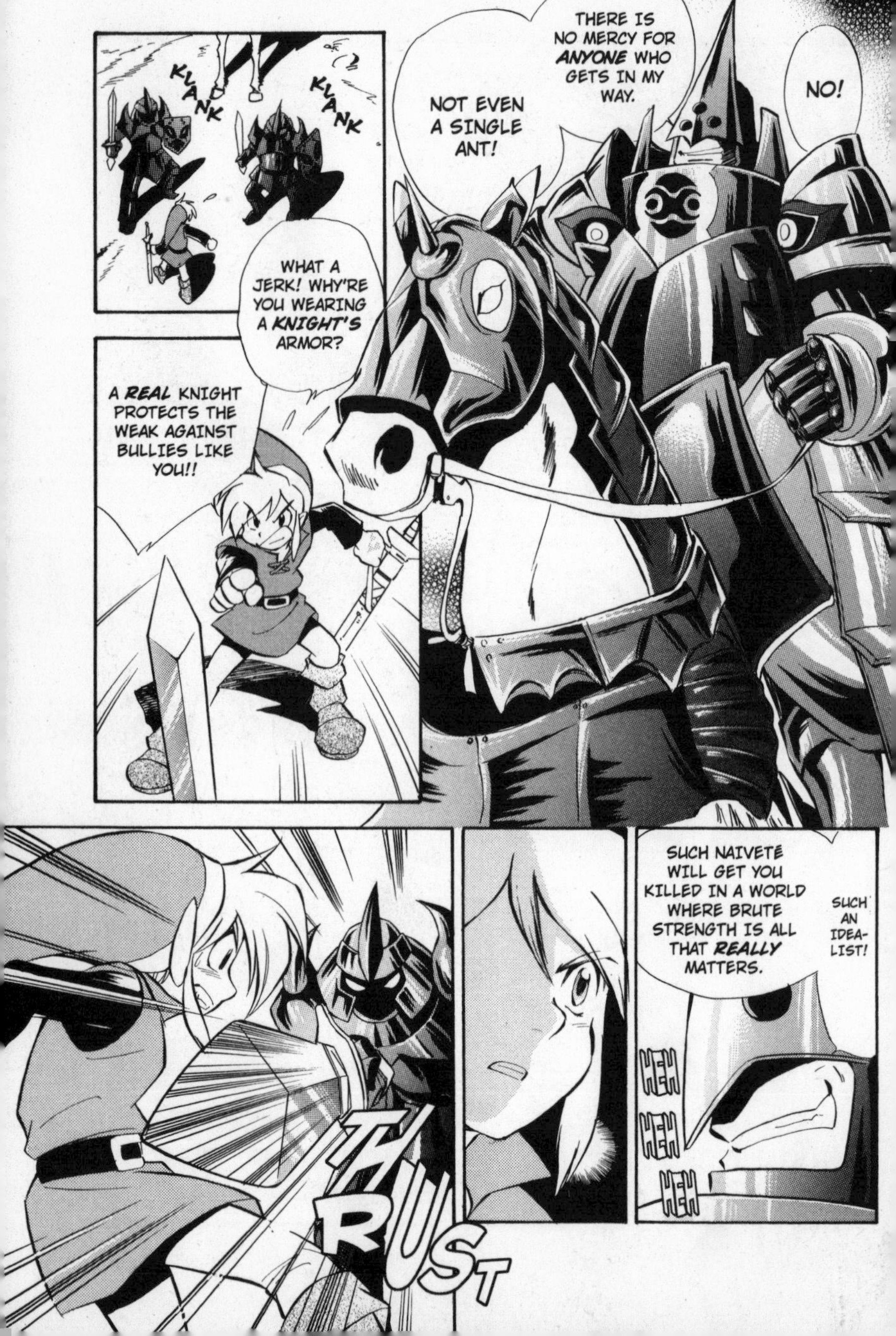
NO!
THERE IS NO MERCY FOR ANYONE WHO GETS IN MY WAY.
NOT EVEN A SINGLE ANT!
KLANK
KLANK
WHAT A JERK! WHY'RE YOU WEARING A KNIGHT'S ARMOR?
A REAL KNIGHT PROTECTS THE WEAK AGAINST BULLIES LIKE YOU!!
SUCH AN IDEALIST!
SUCH NAIVETÉ WILL GET YOU KILLED IN A WORLD WHERE BRUTE STRENGTH IS ALL THAT REALLY MATTERS.
HEH HEH HEH
THRUST

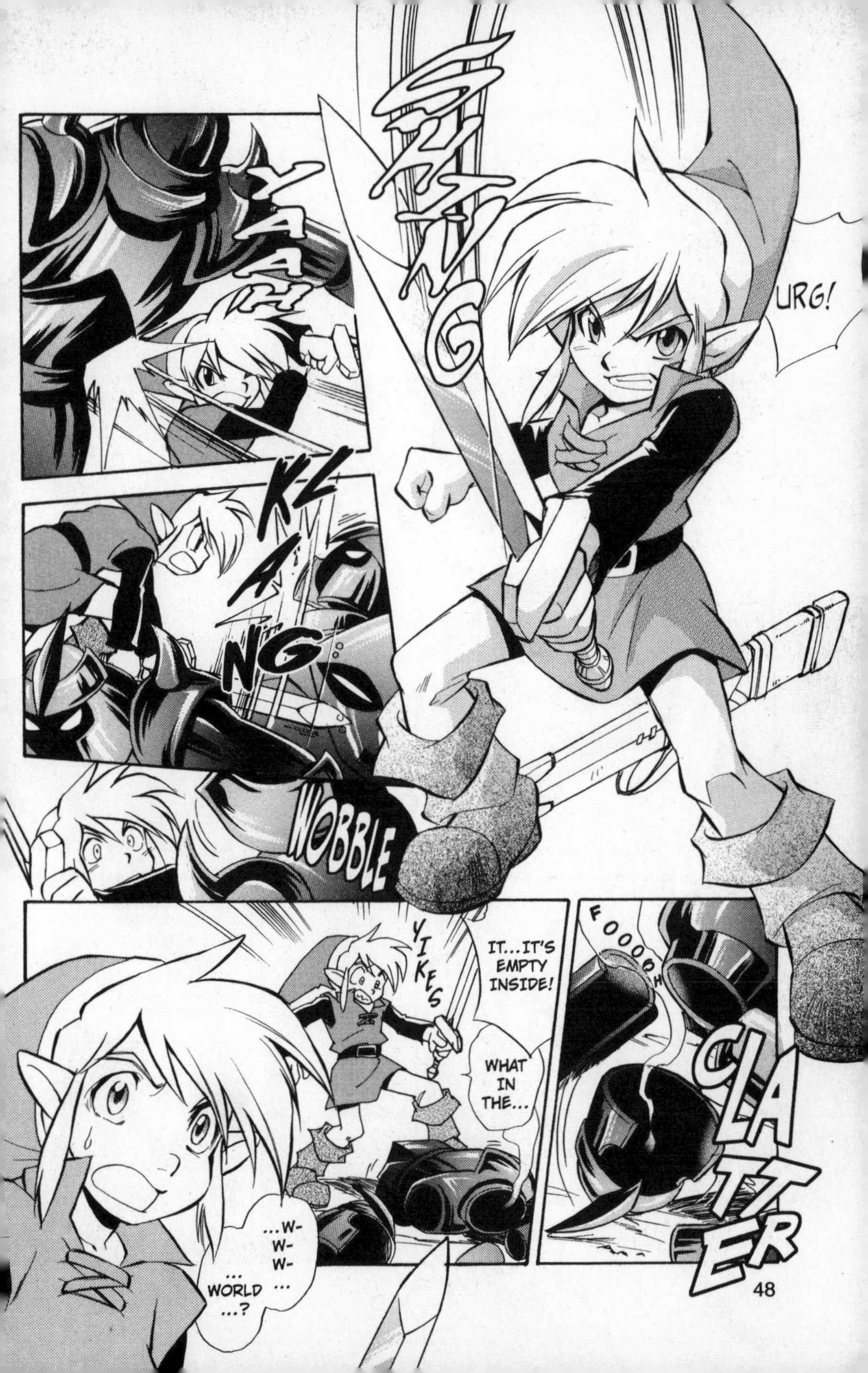
SCHING
URG!
YAAH
KLANG
WOBBLE
FOOOOH
CLATTER
YIKES
IT...IT'S EMPTY INSIDE!
WHAT IN THE...
...W- W- W- ...
... WORLD ...?

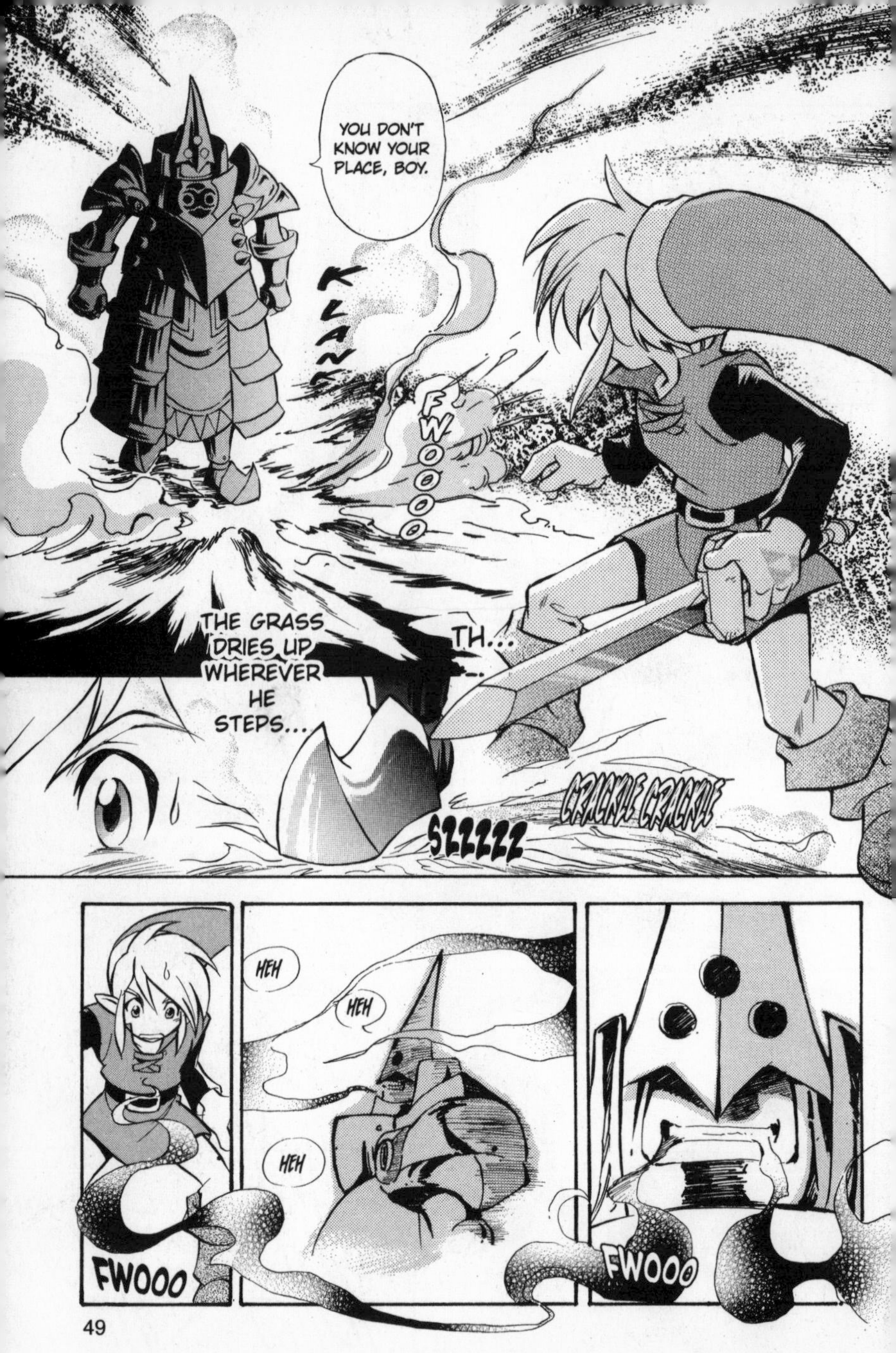

YOU DON'T KNOW YOUR PLACE, BOY.
KLANG
FWOOOOO
TH...
THE GRASS DRIES UP WHEREVER HE STEPS...
CRACKLE CRACKLE
SZZZZZ
FWOOO
HEH
HEH
HEH
FWOOO

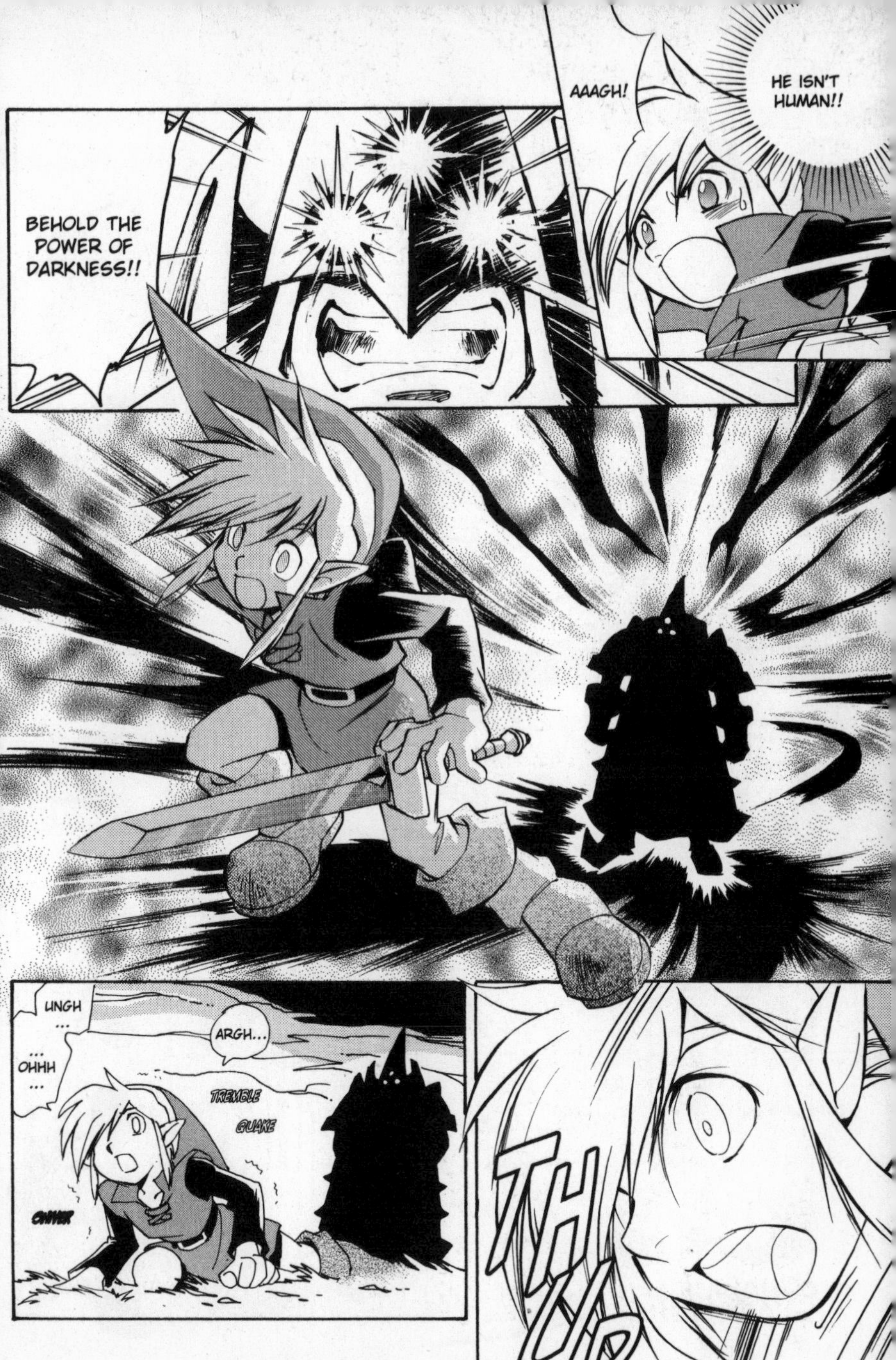
HE ISN'T HUMAN!!
AAAGH!
BEHOLD THE POWER OF DARKNESS!!
THUD
ARGH...
UNGH ...
... OHHH ...
TREMBLE
QUAKE
SHIVER

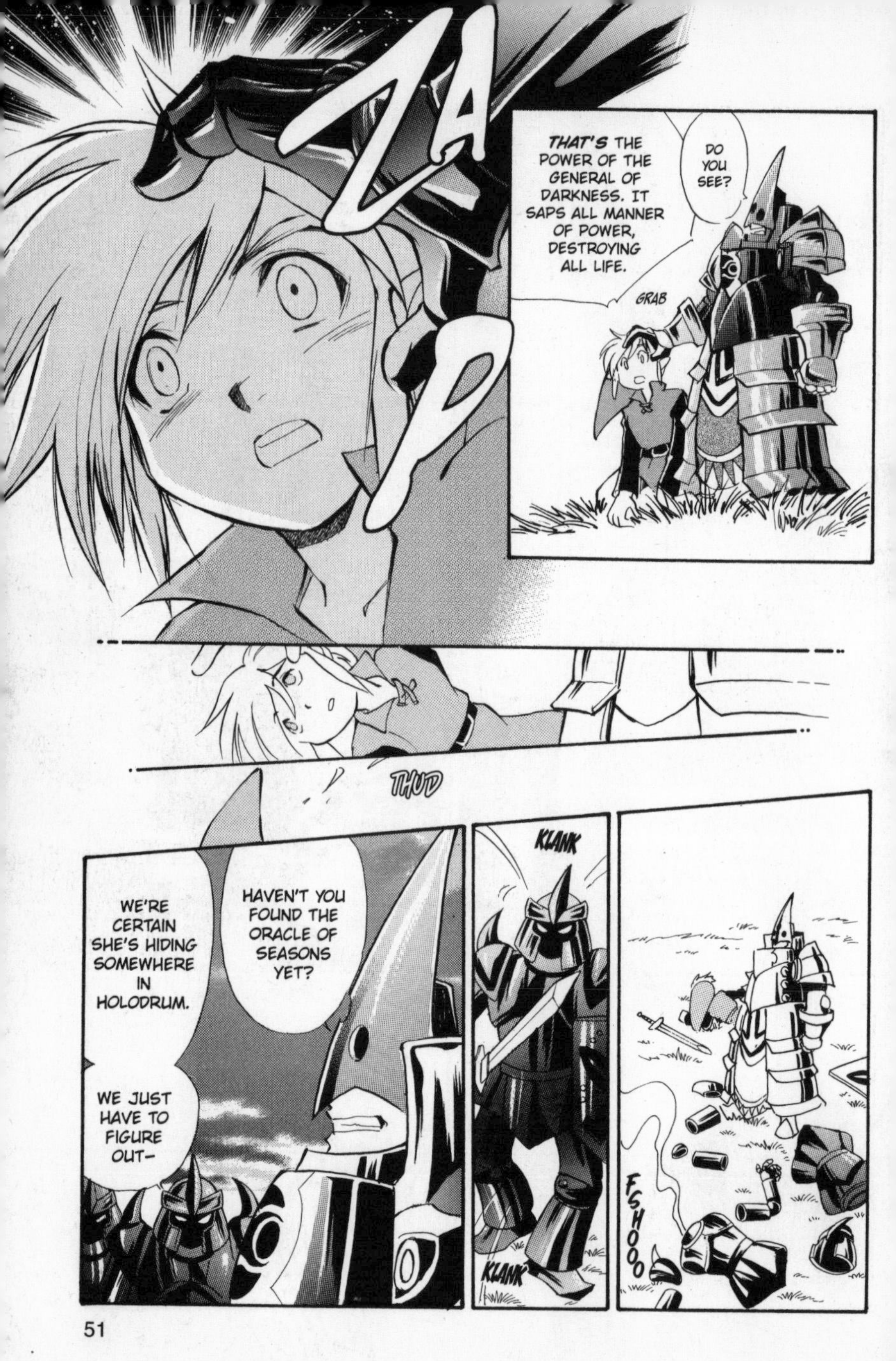

DO YOU SEE?
THAT'S THE POWER OF THE GENERAL OF DARKNESS. IT SAPS ALL MANNER OF POWER, DESTROYING ALL LIFE.
GRAB
ZA
THUD
FSHOOO
KLANK
KLANK
HAVEN'T YOU FOUND THE ORACLE OF SEASONS YET?
WE'RE CERTAIN SHE'S HIDING SOMEWHERE IN HOLODRUM.
WE JUST HAVE TO FIGURE OUT–

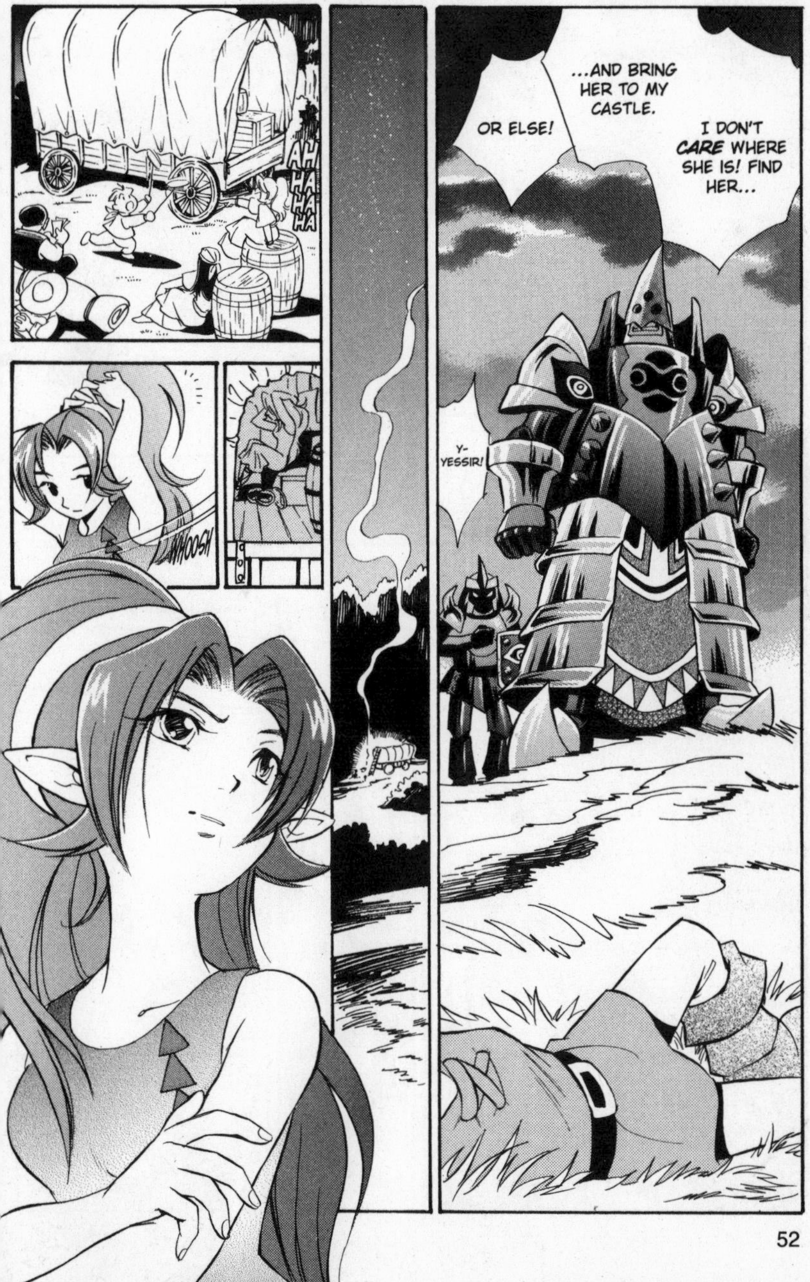
I DON'T **CARE** WHERE SHE IS! FIND HER...
...AND BRING HER TO MY CASTLE.
OR ELSE!
Y-YESSIR!
AH HA HA HA HA
WHOOSH

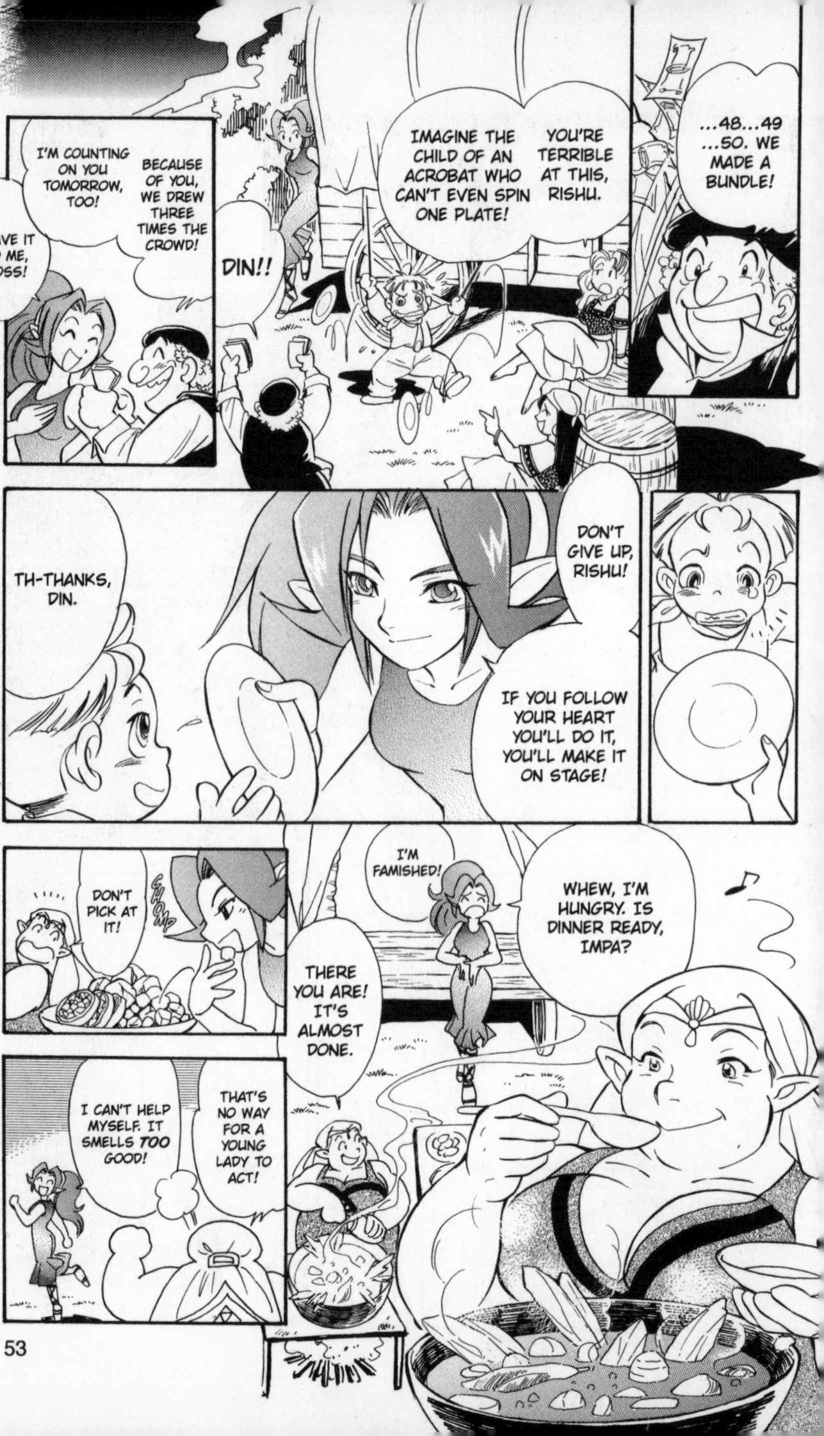
...48...49 ...50. WE MADE A BUNDLE!
YOU'RE TERRIBLE AT THIS, RISHU.
IMAGINE THE CHILD OF AN ACROBAT WHO CAN'T EVEN SPIN ONE PLATE!
DIN!!
BECAUSE OF YOU, WE DREW THREE TIMES THE CROWD!
I'M COUNTING ON YOU TOMORROW, TOO!
LEAVE IT TO ME, BOSS!
DON'T GIVE UP, RISHU!
IF YOU FOLLOW YOUR HEART YOU'LL DO IT, YOU'LL MAKE IT ON STAGE!
TH-THANKS, DIN.
WHEW, I'M HUNGRY. IS DINNER READY, IMPA?
I'M FAMISHED!
THERE YOU ARE! IT'S ALMOST DONE.
CHOMP
DON'T PICK AT IT!
THAT'S NO WAY FOR A YOUNG LADY TO ACT!
I CAN'T HELP MYSELF. IT SMELLS *TOO* GOOD!

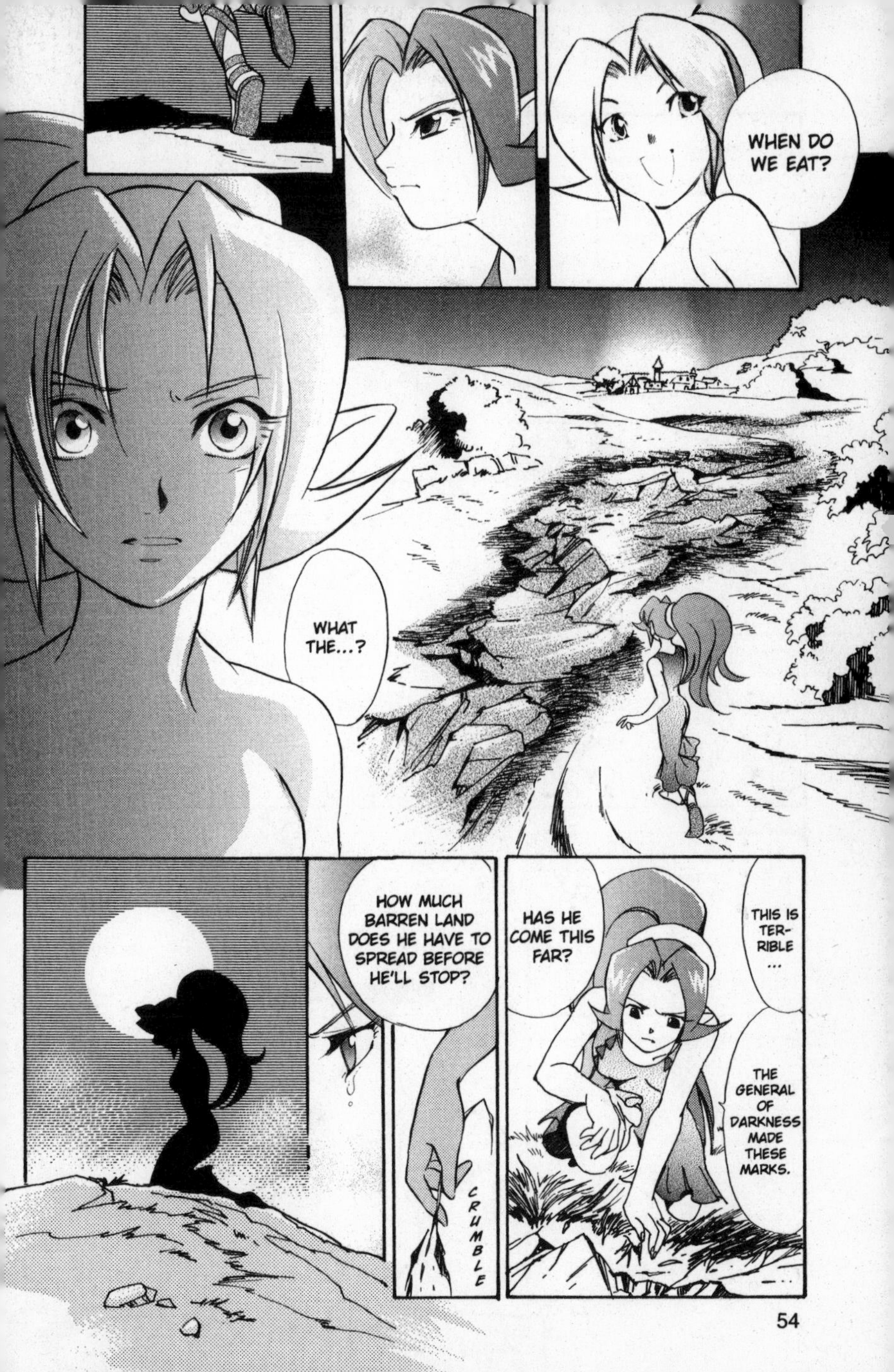
WHEN DO WE EAT?
WHAT THE...?
THIS IS TER-RIBLE ...
HAS HE COME THIS FAR?
THE GENERAL OF DARKNESS MADE THESE MARKS.
HOW MUCH BARREN LAND DOES HE HAVE TO SPREAD BEFORE HE'LL STOP?
CRUMBLE

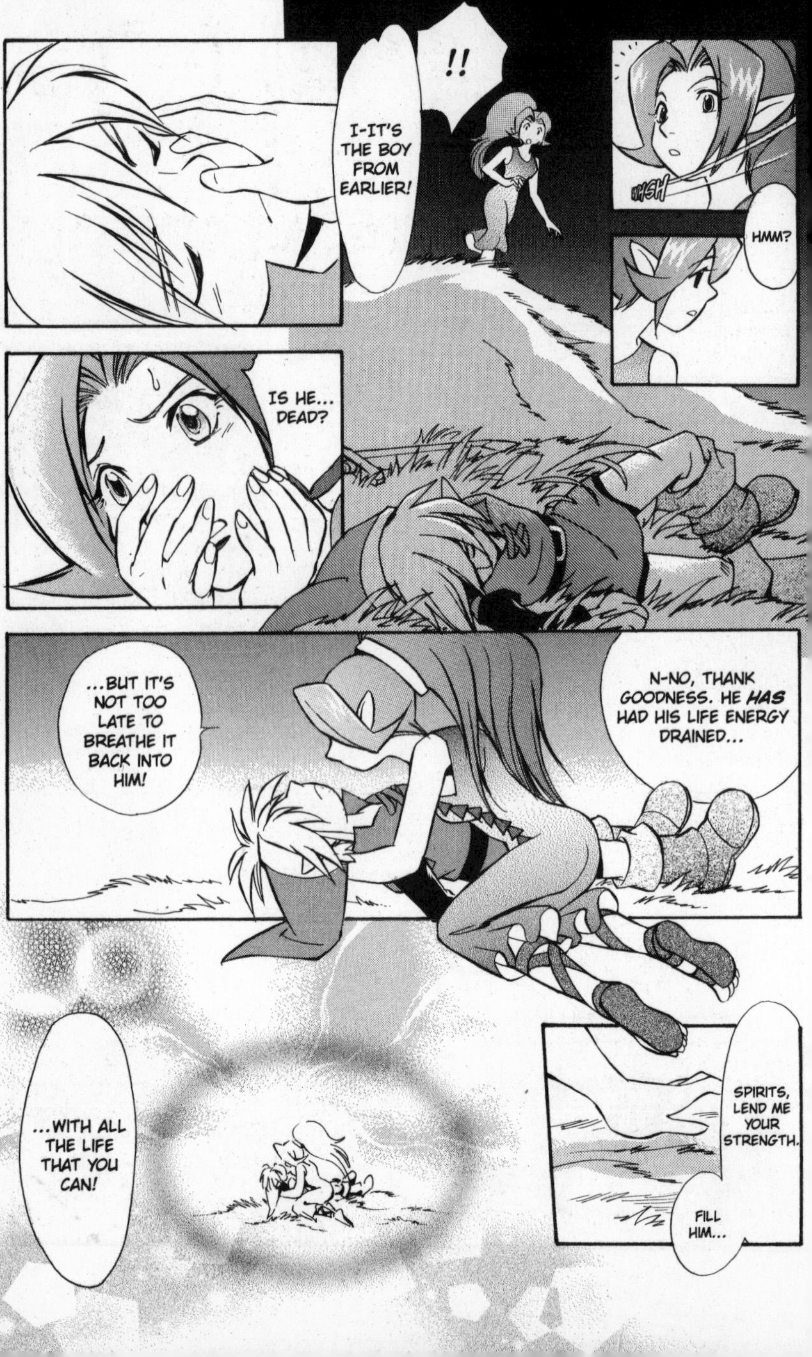
WHSH
HMM?
!!
I-IT'S THE BOY FROM EARLIER!
IS HE... DEAD?
N-NO, THANK GOODNESS. HE HAS HAD HIS LIFE ENERGY DRAINED...
...BUT IT'S NOT TOO LATE TO BREATHE IT BACK INTO HIM!
SPIRITS, LEND ME YOUR STRENGTH.
FILL HIM...
...WITH ALL THE LIFE THAT YOU CAN!

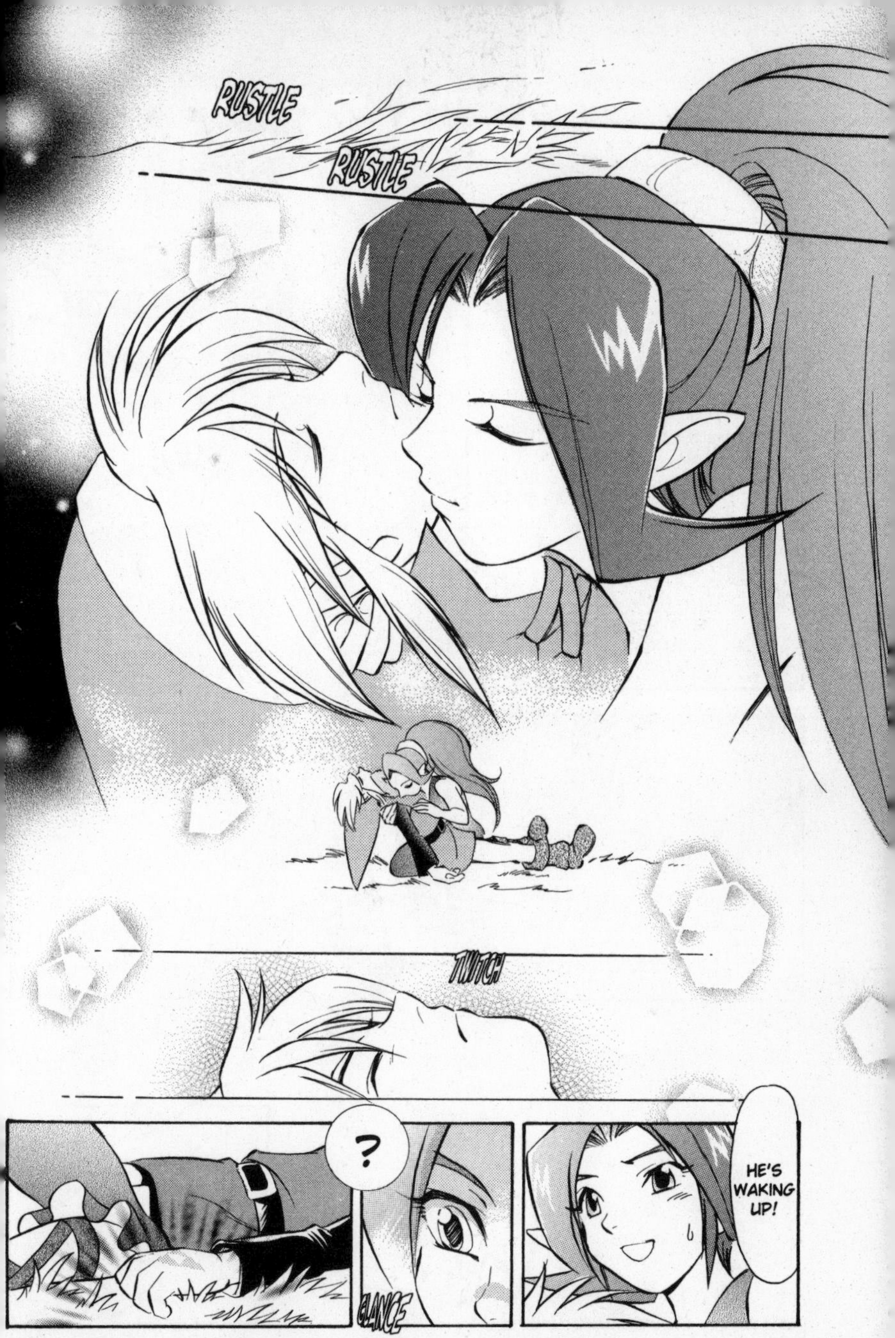
RUSTLE
RUSTLE
TWITCH
HE'S WAKING UP!
?
GLANCE

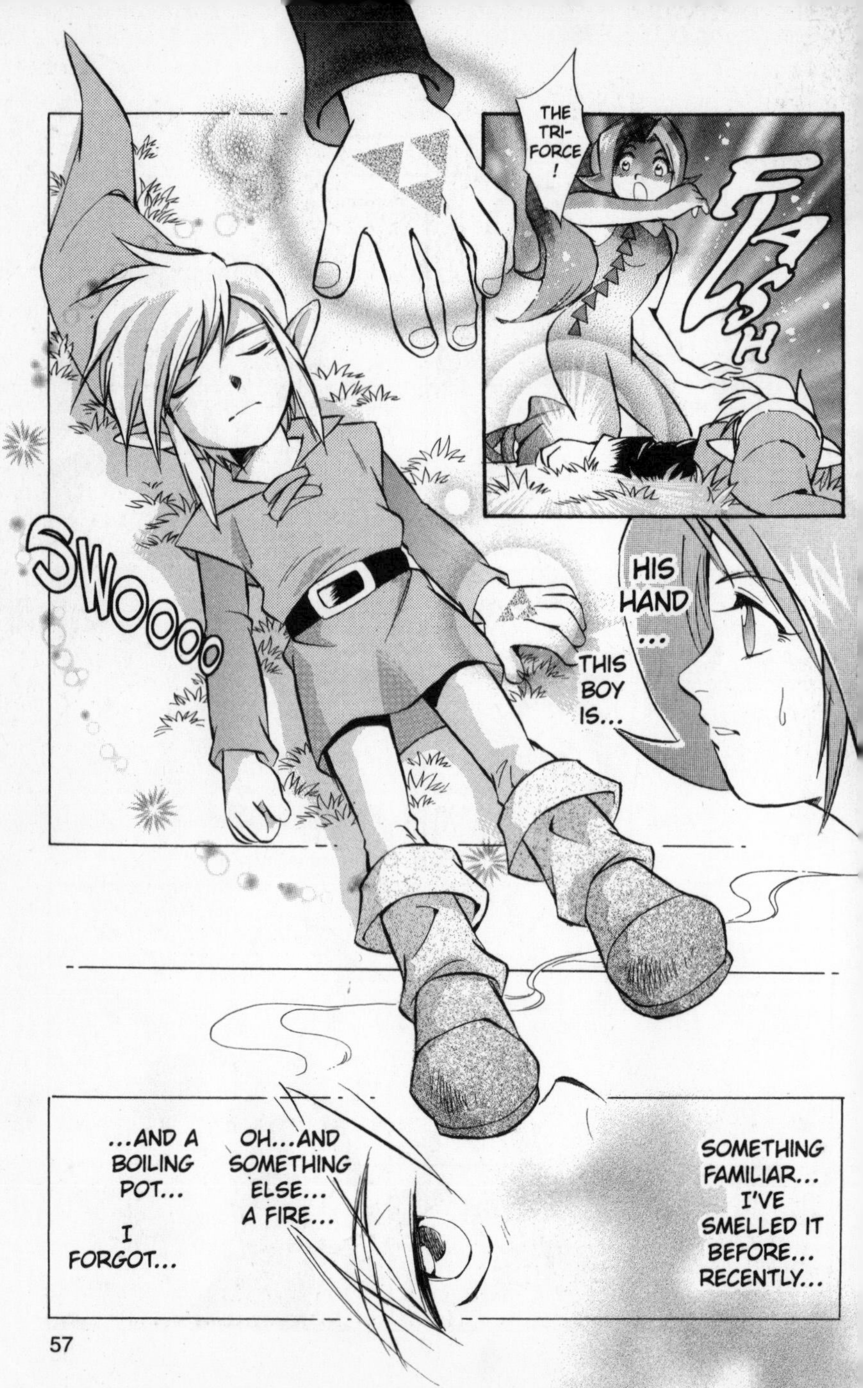
THE TRI-FORCE!
FLASH
HIS HAND... THIS BOY IS...
SWOOOO
SOMETHING FAMILIAR... I'VE SMELLED IT BEFORE... RECENTLY...
OH...AND SOMETHING ELSE... A FIRE...
...AND A BOILING POT...
I FORGOT...

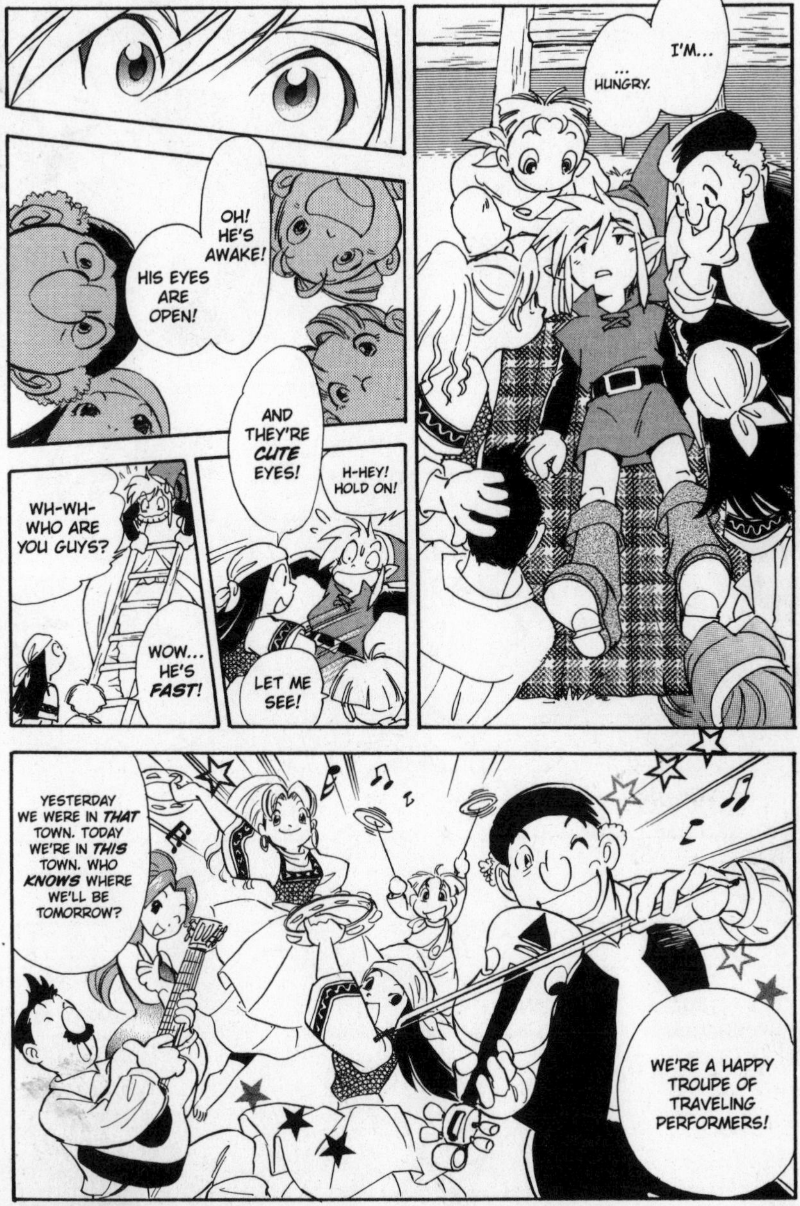
I'M...
... HUNGRY.
OH! HE'S AWAKE!
HIS EYES ARE OPEN!
AND THEY'RE *CUTE* EYES!
H-HEY! HOLD ON!
LET ME SEE!
WH-WH-WHO ARE YOU GUYS?
WOW... HE'S *FAST*!
WE'RE A HAPPY TROUPE OF TRAVELING PERFORMERS!
YESTERDAY WE WERE IN *THAT* TOWN. TODAY WE'RE IN *THIS* TOWN. WHO *KNOWS* WHERE WE'LL BE TOMORROW?

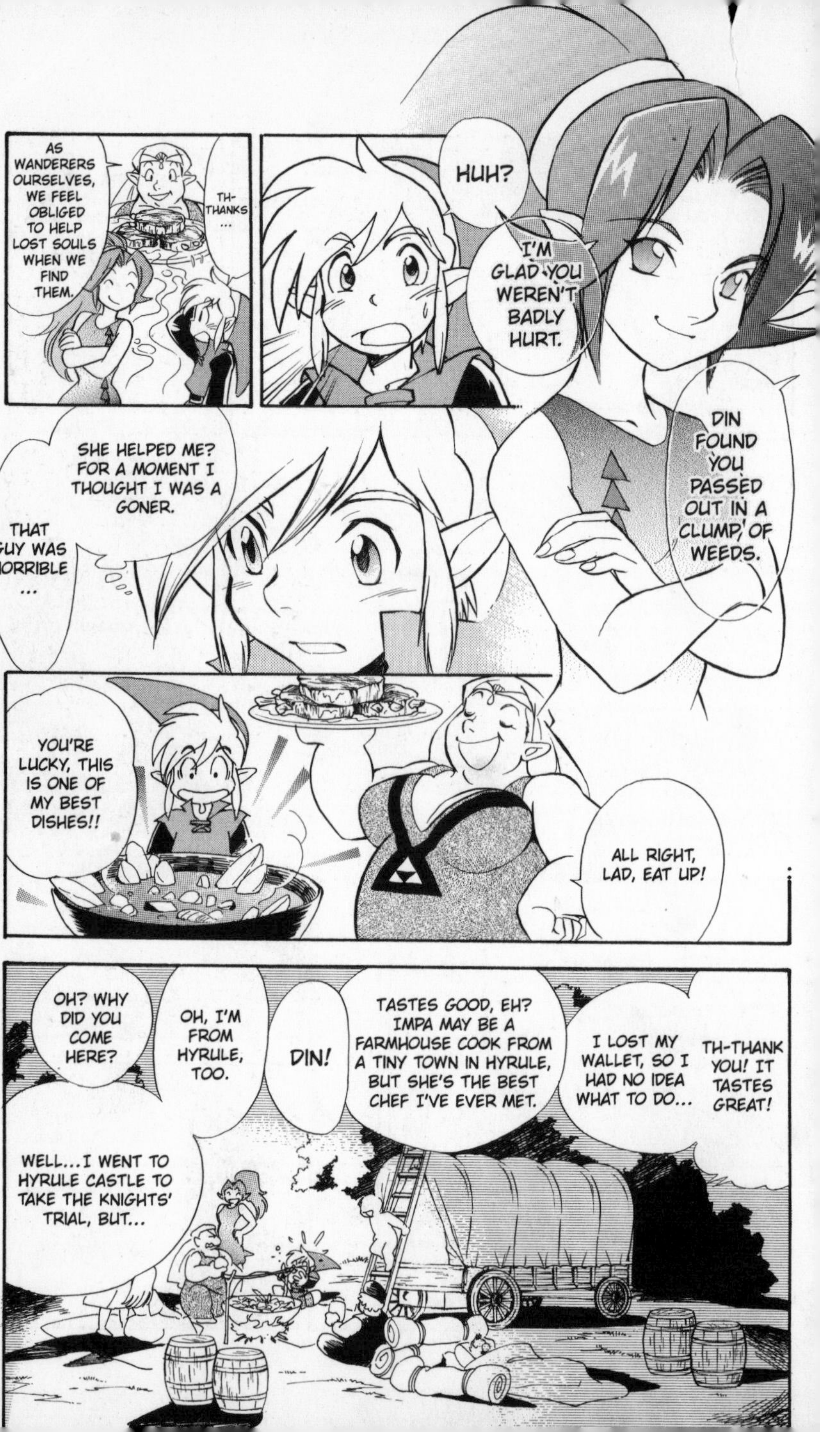
HUH?
I'M GLAD YOU WEREN'T BADLY HURT.
DIN FOUND YOU PASSED OUT IN A CLUMP OF WEEDS.
AS WANDERERS OURSELVES, WE FEEL OBLIGED TO HELP LOST SOULS WHEN WE FIND THEM.
TH-THANKS...
SHE HELPED ME? FOR A MOMENT I THOUGHT I WAS A GONER.
THAT GUY WAS HORRIBLE...
ALL RIGHT, LAD, EAT UP!
YOU'RE LUCKY, THIS IS ONE OF MY BEST DISHES!!
TH-THANK YOU! IT TASTES GREAT!
I LOST MY WALLET, SO I HAD NO IDEA WHAT TO DO...
TASTES GOOD, EH? IMPA MAY BE A FARMHOUSE COOK FROM A TINY TOWN IN HYRULE, BUT SHE'S THE BEST CHEF I'VE EVER MET.
DIN!
OH, I'M FROM HYRULE, TOO.
OH? WHY DID YOU COME HERE?
WELL...I WENT TO HYRULE CASTLE TO TAKE THE KNIGHTS' TRIAL, BUT...

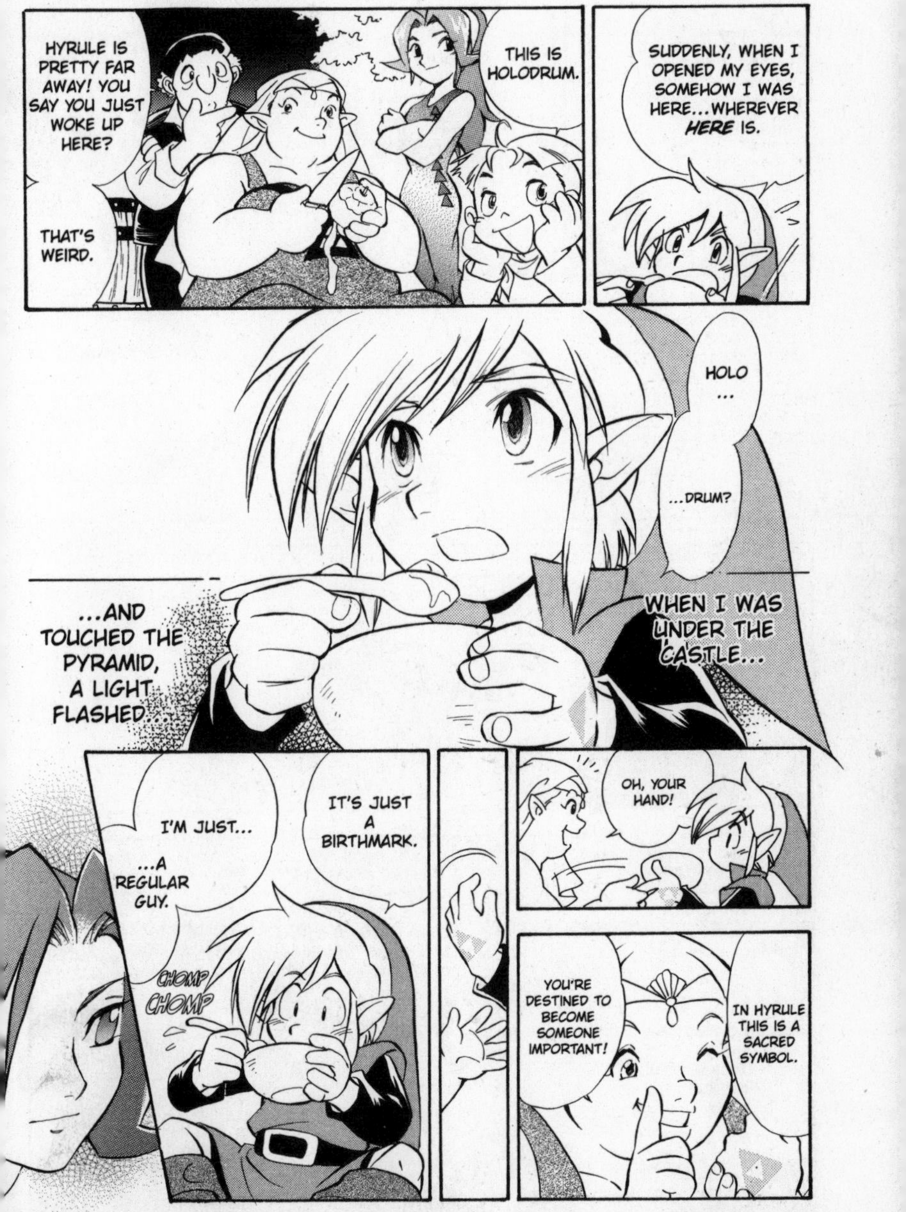
SUDDENLY, WHEN I OPENED MY EYES, SOMEHOW I WAS HERE...WHEREVER *HERE* IS.
THIS IS HOLODRUM.
HYRULE IS PRETTY FAR AWAY! YOU SAY YOU JUST WOKE UP HERE?
THAT'S WEIRD.
HOLO ...
...DRUM?
WHEN I WAS UNDER THE CASTLE...
...AND TOUCHED THE PYRAMID, A LIGHT FLASHED...
OH, YOUR HAND!
IN HYRULE THIS IS A SACRED SYMBOL.
YOU'RE DESTINED TO BECOME SOMEONE IMPORTANT!
IT'S JUST A BIRTHMARK.
I'M JUST...
...A REGULAR GUY.
CHOMP CHOMP

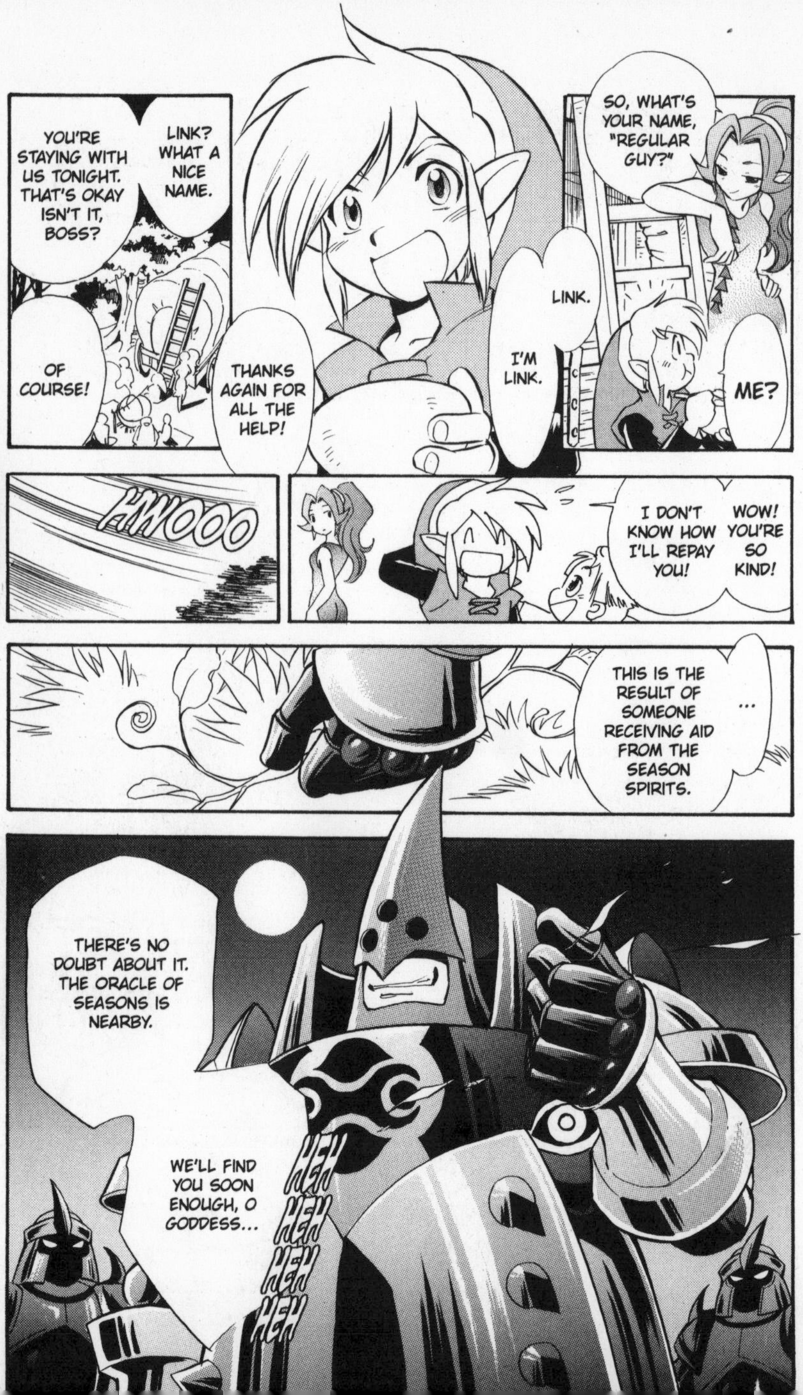
SO, WHAT'S YOUR NAME, "REGULAR GUY?"
ME?
LINK.
I'M LINK.
THANKS AGAIN FOR ALL THE HELP!
LINK? WHAT A NICE NAME.
YOU'RE STAYING WITH US TONIGHT. THAT'S OKAY ISN'T IT, BOSS?
OF COURSE!
WOW! YOU'RE SO KIND!
I DON'T KNOW HOW I'LL REPAY YOU!
HWOOO
...
THIS IS THE RESULT OF SOMEONE RECEIVING AID FROM THE SEASON SPIRITS.
THERE'S NO DOUBT ABOUT IT. THE ORACLE OF SEASONS IS NEARBY.
HEH HEH HEH HEH HEH
WE'LL FIND YOU SOON ENOUGH, O GODDESS...

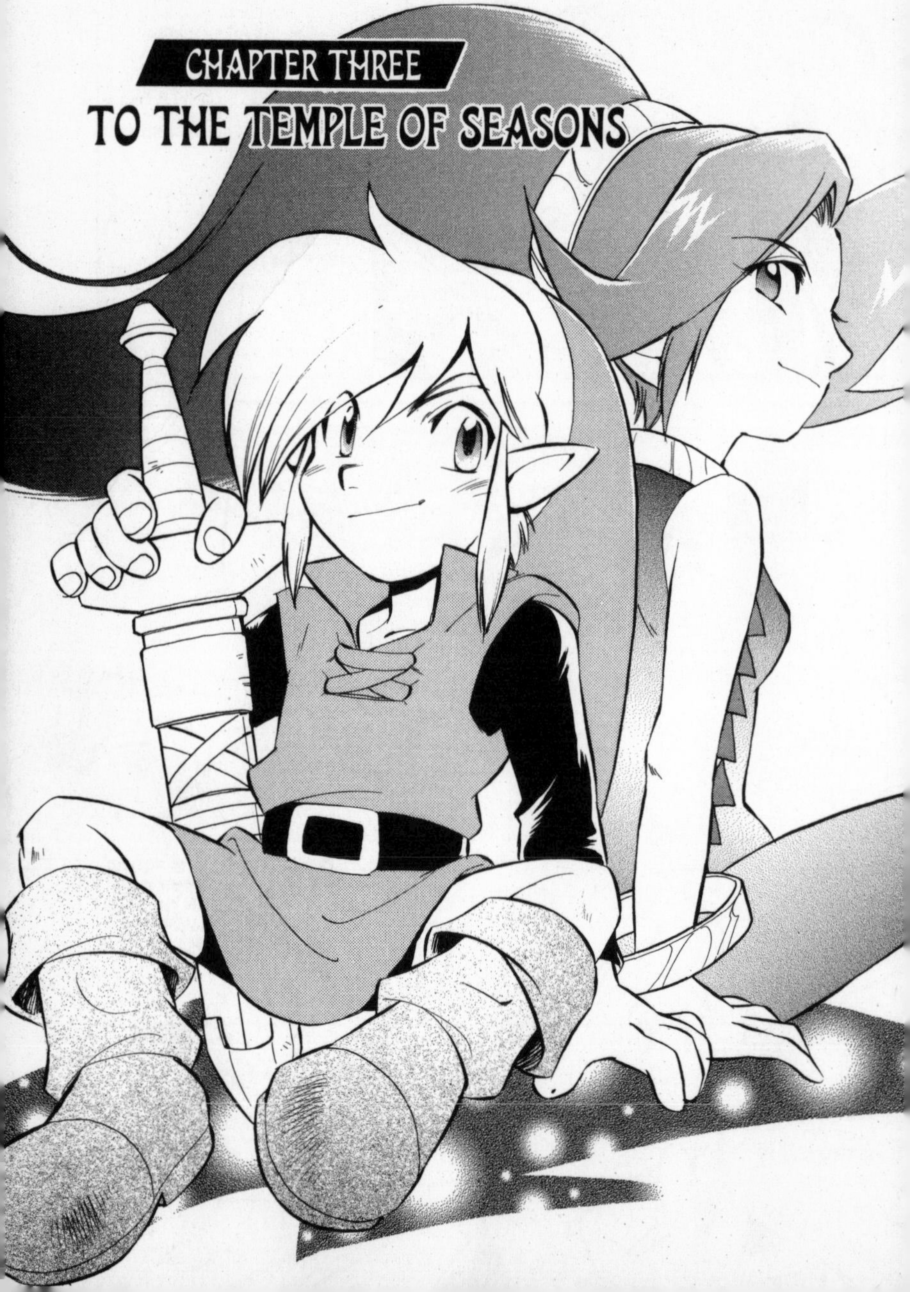
CHAPTER THREE
TO THE TEMPLE OF SEASONS

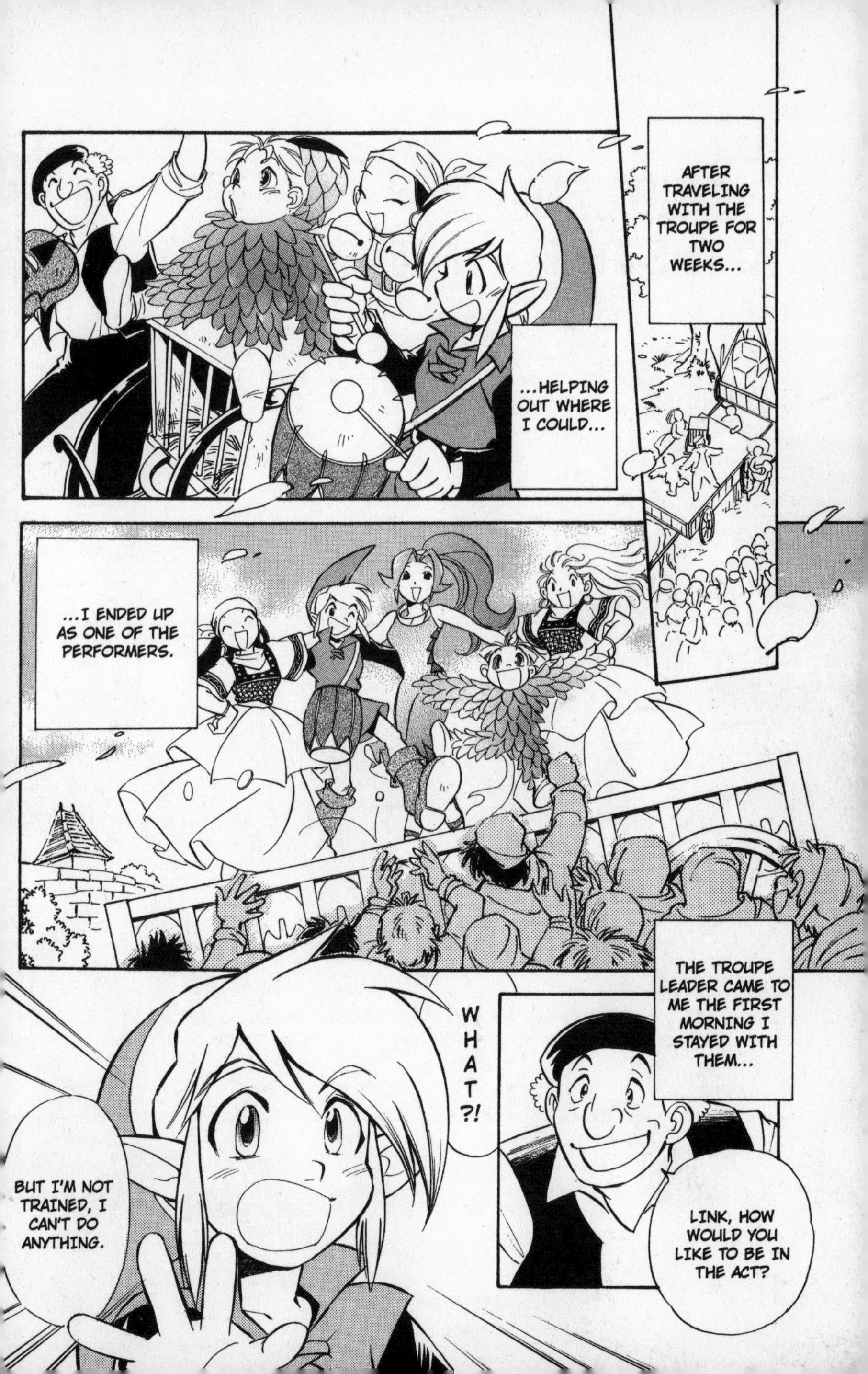
AFTER TRAVELING WITH THE TROUPE FOR TWO WEEKS...
...HELPING OUT WHERE I COULD...
...I ENDED UP AS ONE OF THE PERFORMERS.
THE TROUPE LEADER CAME TO ME THE FIRST MORNING I STAYED WITH THEM...
LINK, HOW WOULD YOU LIKE TO BE IN THE ACT?
WHAT?!
BUT I'M NOT TRAINED, I CAN'T DO ANYTHING.

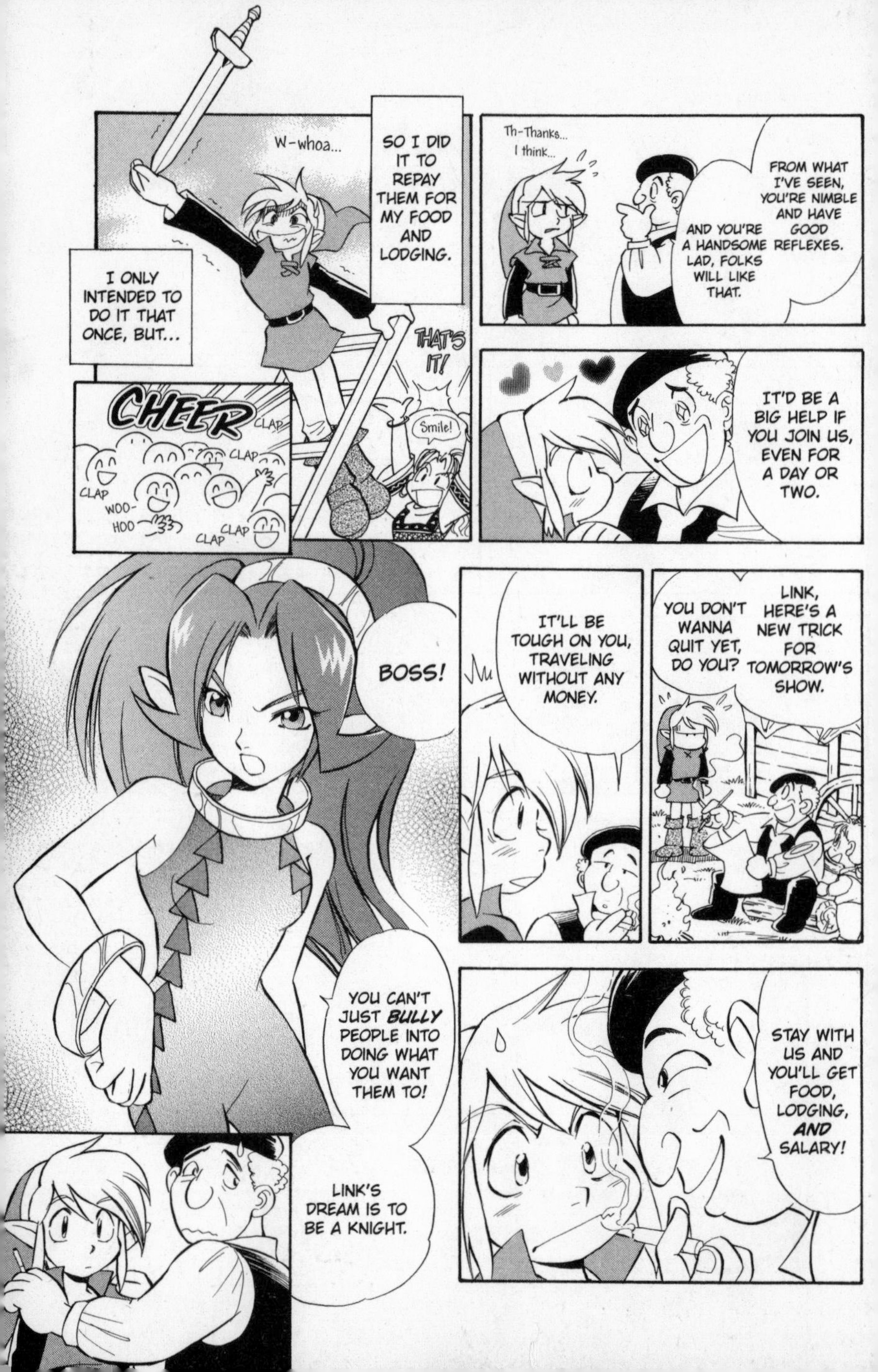

Th-Thanks... I think...
FROM WHAT I'VE SEEN, YOU'RE NIMBLE AND HAVE GOOD REFLEXES.
AND YOU'RE A HANDSOME LAD, FOLKS WILL LIKE THAT.
IT'D BE A BIG HELP IF YOU JOIN US, EVEN FOR A DAY OR TWO.
SO I DID IT TO REPAY THEM FOR MY FOOD AND LODGING.
W-whoa...
I ONLY INTENDED TO DO IT THAT ONCE, BUT...
THAT'S IT!
Smile!
CHEER
CLAP
CLAP
CLAP
WOO-HOO
CLAP
CLAP
LINK, HERE'S A NEW TRICK FOR TOMORROW'S SHOW.
YOU DON'T WANNA QUIT YET, DO YOU?
IT'LL BE TOUGH ON YOU, TRAVELING WITHOUT ANY MONEY.
STAY WITH US AND YOU'LL GET FOOD, LODGING, ***AND*** SALARY!
BOSS!
YOU CAN'T JUST ***BULLY*** PEOPLE INTO DOING WHAT YOU WANT THEM TO!
LINK'S DREAM IS TO BE A KNIGHT.

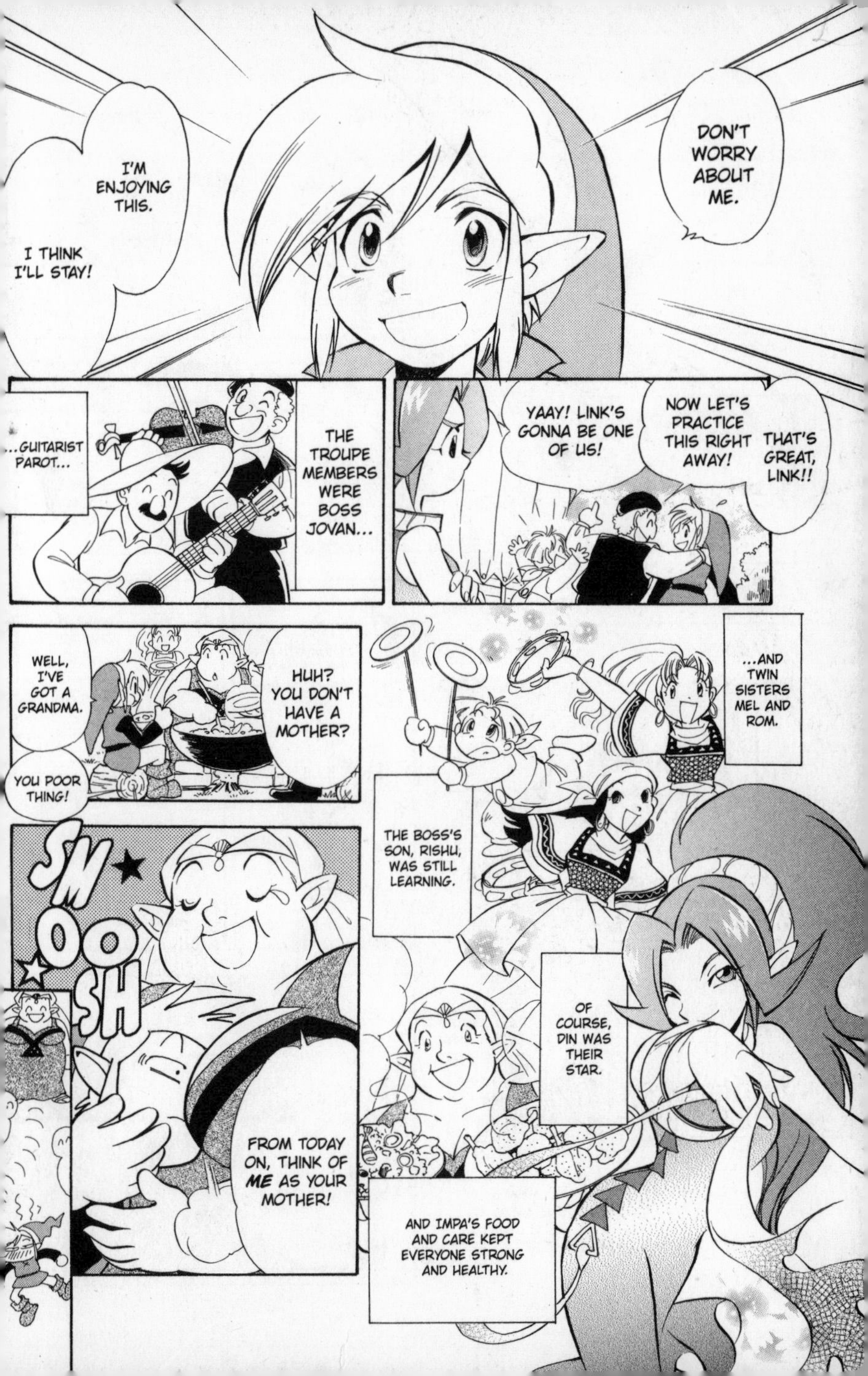
DON'T WORRY ABOUT ME.
I'M ENJOYING THIS.
I THINK I'LL STAY!
THAT'S GREAT, LINK!!
NOW LET'S PRACTICE THIS RIGHT AWAY!
YAAY! LINK'S GONNA BE ONE OF US!
THE TROUPE MEMBERS WERE BOSS JOVAN...
...GUITARIST PAROT...
...AND TWIN SISTERS MEL AND ROM.
THE BOSS'S SON, RISHU, WAS STILL LEARNING.
OF COURSE, DIN WAS THEIR STAR.
HUH? YOU DON'T HAVE A MOTHER?
WELL, I'VE GOT A GRANDMA.
YOU POOR THING!
SNOOSH
FROM TODAY ON, THINK OF *ME* AS YOUR MOTHER!
AND IMPA'S FOOD AND CARE KEPT EVERYONE STRONG AND HEALTHY.

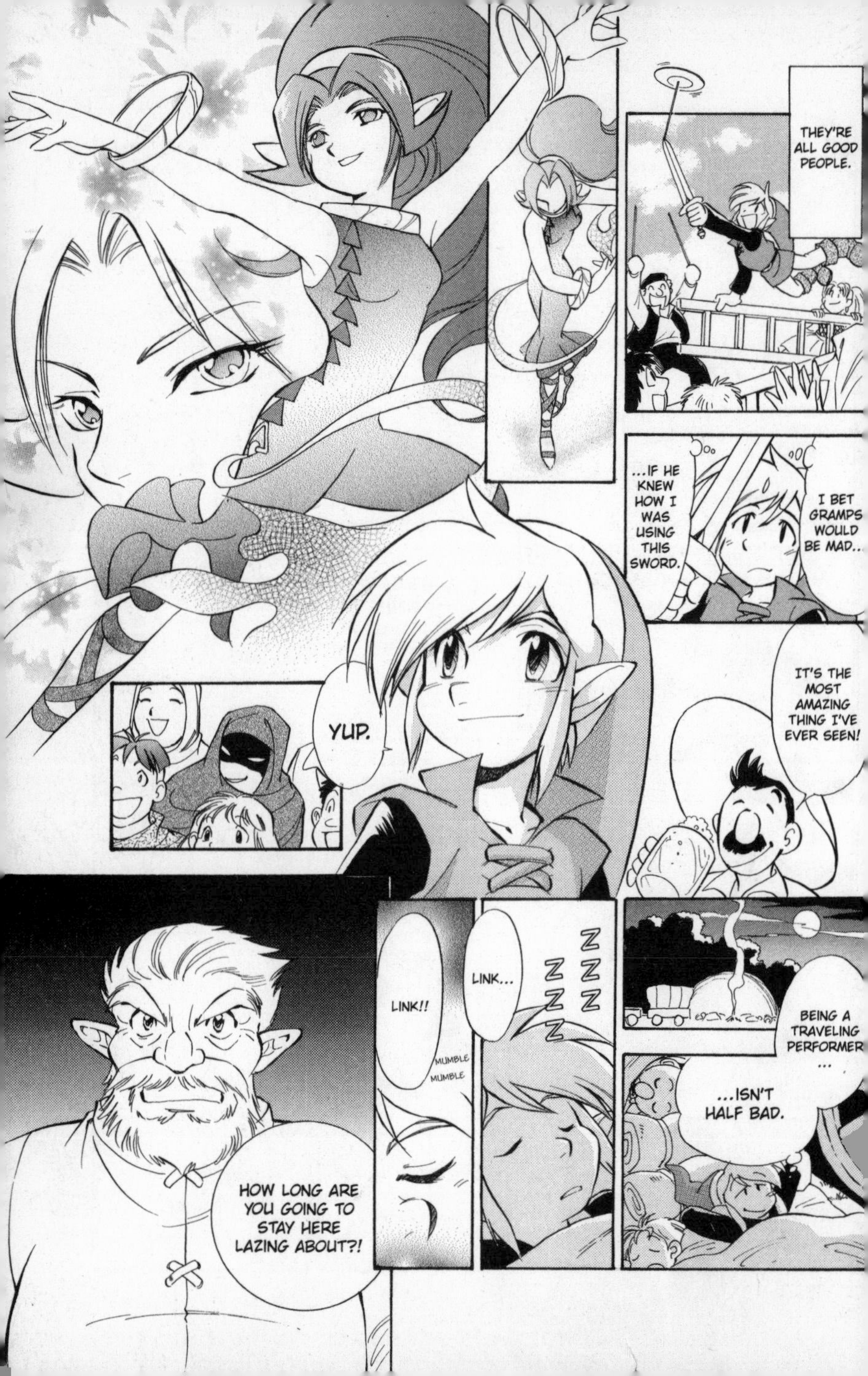
THEY'RE ALL GOOD PEOPLE.
I BET GRAMPS WOULD BE MAD...
...IF HE KNEW HOW I WAS USING THIS SWORD.
IT'S THE MOST AMAZING THING I'VE EVER SEEN!
YUP.
BEING A TRAVELING PERFORMER...
...ISN'T HALF BAD.
ZZZZZ
LINK...
LINK!!
MUMBLE MUMBLE
HOW LONG ARE YOU GOING TO STAY HERE LAZING ABOUT?!

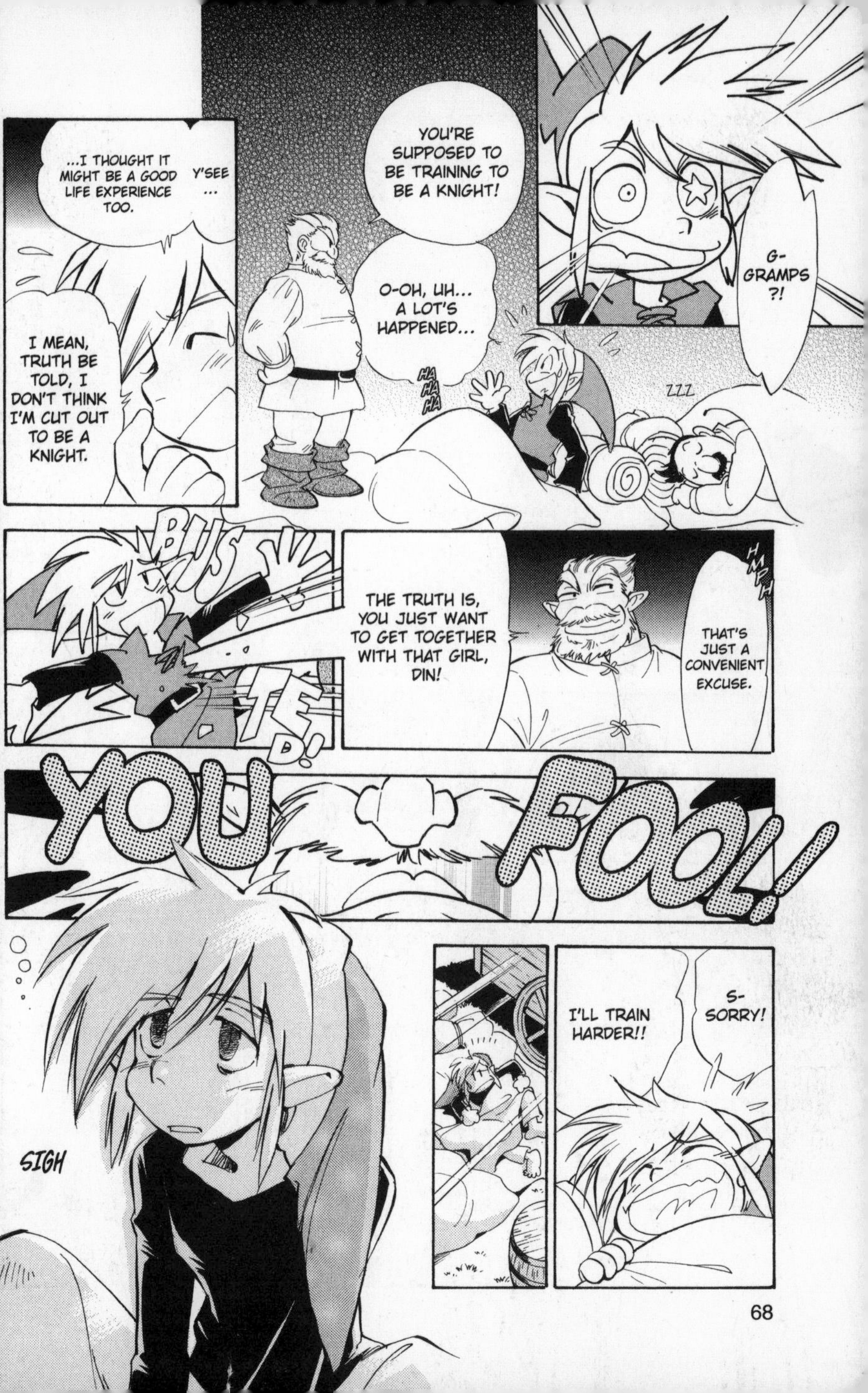
G-GRAMPS?!
YOU'RE SUPPOSED TO BE TRAINING TO BE A KNIGHT!
O-OH, UH... A LOT'S HAPPENED...
HA HA HA
ZZZ
Y'SEE...
...I THOUGHT IT MIGHT BE A GOOD LIFE EXPERIENCE TOO.
I MEAN, TRUTH BE TOLD, I DON'T THINK I'M CUT OUT TO BE A KNIGHT.
HMPH
THAT'S JUST A CONVENIENT EXCUSE.
THE TRUTH IS, YOU JUST WANT TO GET TOGETHER WITH THAT GIRL, DIN!
BUSTED!
YOU FOOL!!
S-SORRY!
I'LL TRAIN HARDER!!
SIGH

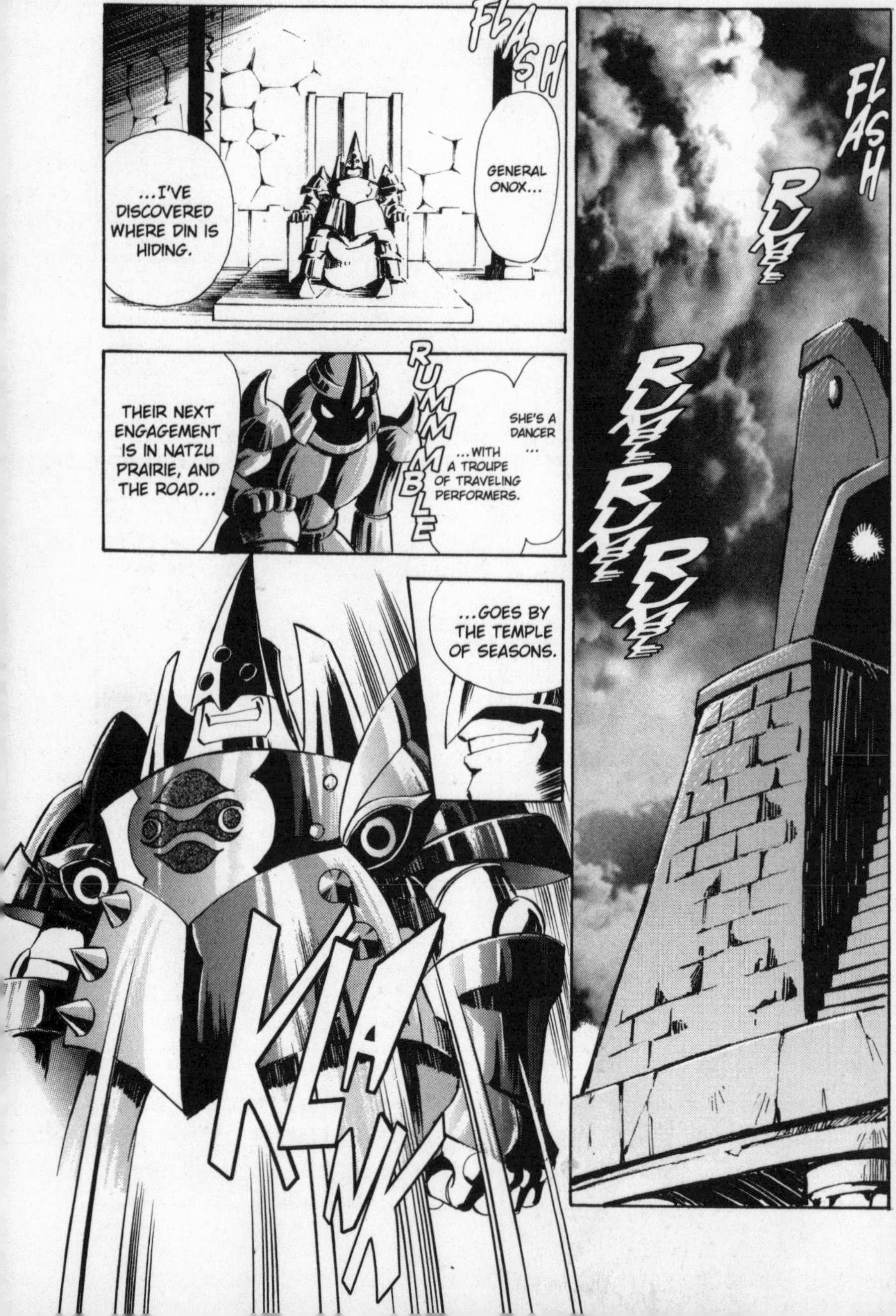
FLASH
RUM
RU RU RU
FLASH
GENERAL ONOX...
...I'VE DISCOVERED WHERE DIN IS HIDING.
SHE'S A DANCER ...
...WITH A TROUPE OF TRAVELING PERFORMERS.
RUMMMBLE
THEIR NEXT ENGAGEMENT IS IN NATZU PRAIRIE, AND THE ROAD...
...GOES BY THE TEMPLE OF SEASONS.
KLANK

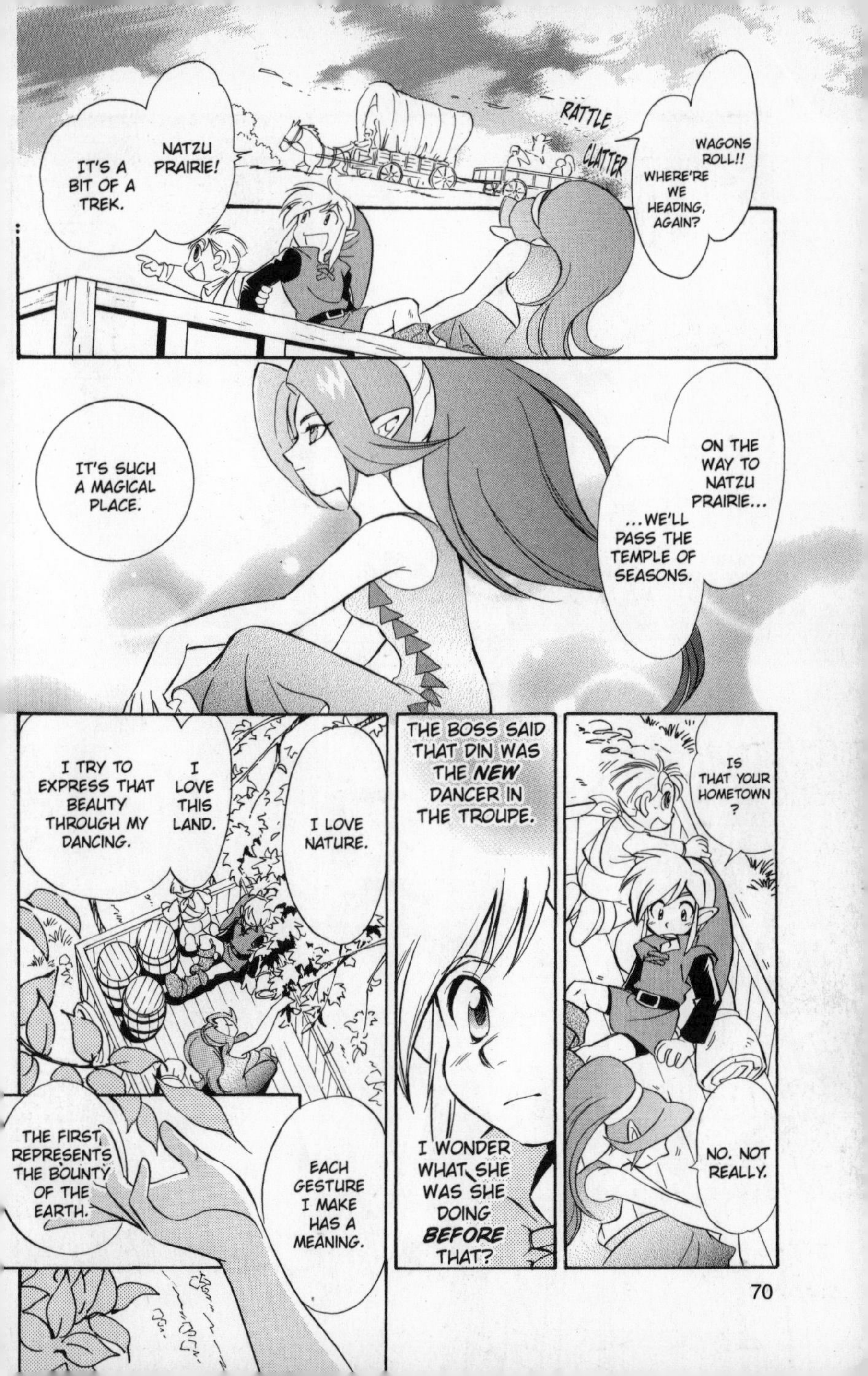
WAGONS ROLL!!
RATTLE
CLATTER
WHERE'RE WE HEADING, AGAIN?
NATZU PRAIRIE!
IT'S A BIT OF A TREK.
ON THE WAY TO NATZU PRAIRIE...
...WE'LL PASS THE TEMPLE OF SEASONS.
IT'S SUCH A MAGICAL PLACE.
IS THAT YOUR HOMETOWN?
NO. NOT REALLY.
THE BOSS SAID THAT DIN WAS THE *NEW* DANCER IN THE TROUPE.
I WONDER WHAT SHE WAS SHE DOING *BEFORE* THAT?
I LOVE NATURE.
I LOVE THIS LAND.
I TRY TO EXPRESS THAT BEAUTY THROUGH MY DANCING.
EACH GESTURE I MAKE HAS A MEANING.
THE FIRST REPRESENTS THE BOUNTY OF THE EARTH.

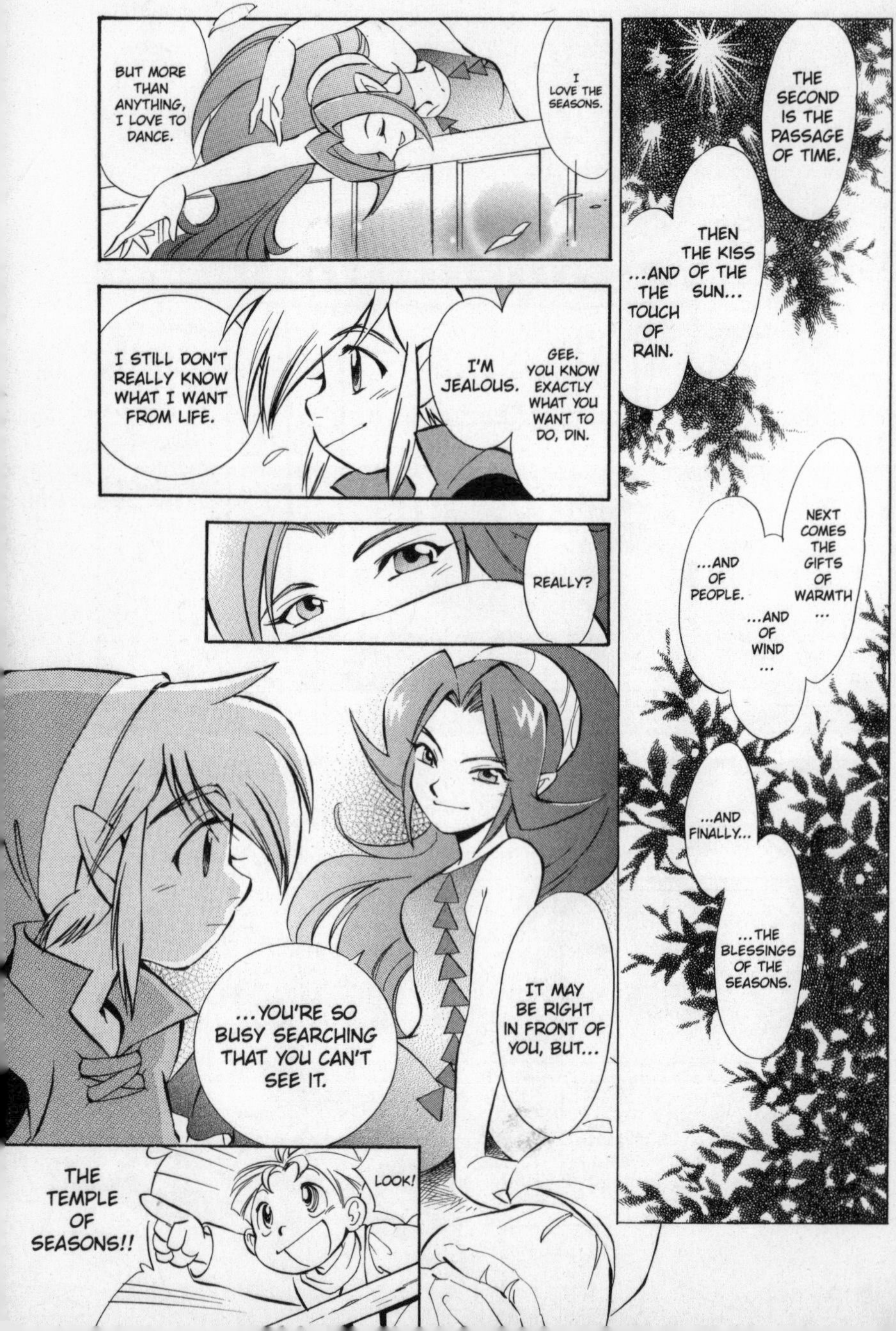
THE SECOND IS THE PASSAGE OF TIME.
THEN THE KISS OF THE SUN...
...AND THE TOUCH OF RAIN.
NEXT COMES THE GIFTS OF WARMTH...
...AND OF WIND...
...AND OF PEOPLE.
...AND FINALLY...
...THE BLESSINGS OF THE SEASONS.
I LOVE THE SEASONS.
BUT MORE THAN ANYTHING, I LOVE TO DANCE.
GEE. YOU KNOW EXACTLY WHAT YOU WANT TO DO, DIN.
I'M JEALOUS.
I STILL DON'T REALLY KNOW WHAT I WANT FROM LIFE.
REALLY?
IT MAY BE RIGHT IN FRONT OF YOU, BUT...
...YOU'RE SO BUSY SEARCHING THAT YOU CAN'T SEE IT.
LOOK!
THE TEMPLE OF SEASONS!!

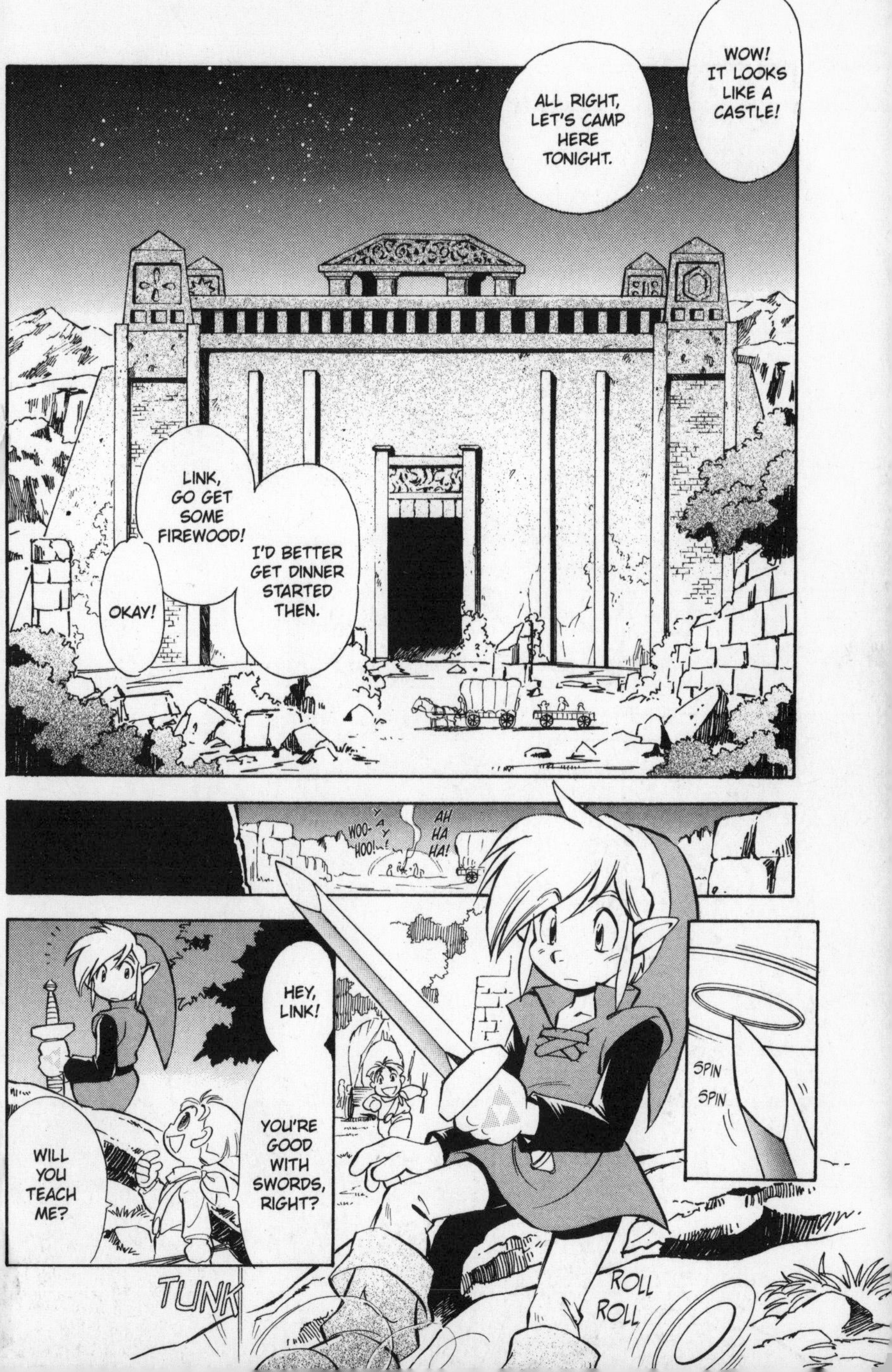
WOW! IT LOOKS LIKE A CASTLE!
ALL RIGHT, LET'S CAMP HERE TONIGHT.
LINK, GO GET SOME FIREWOOD!
OKAY!
I'D BETTER GET DINNER STARTED THEN.
AH HA HA!
YAY
WOO-HOO!
SPIN SPIN
ROLL ROLL
HEY, LINK!
YOU'RE GOOD WITH SWORDS, RIGHT?
WILL YOU TEACH ME?
TUNK

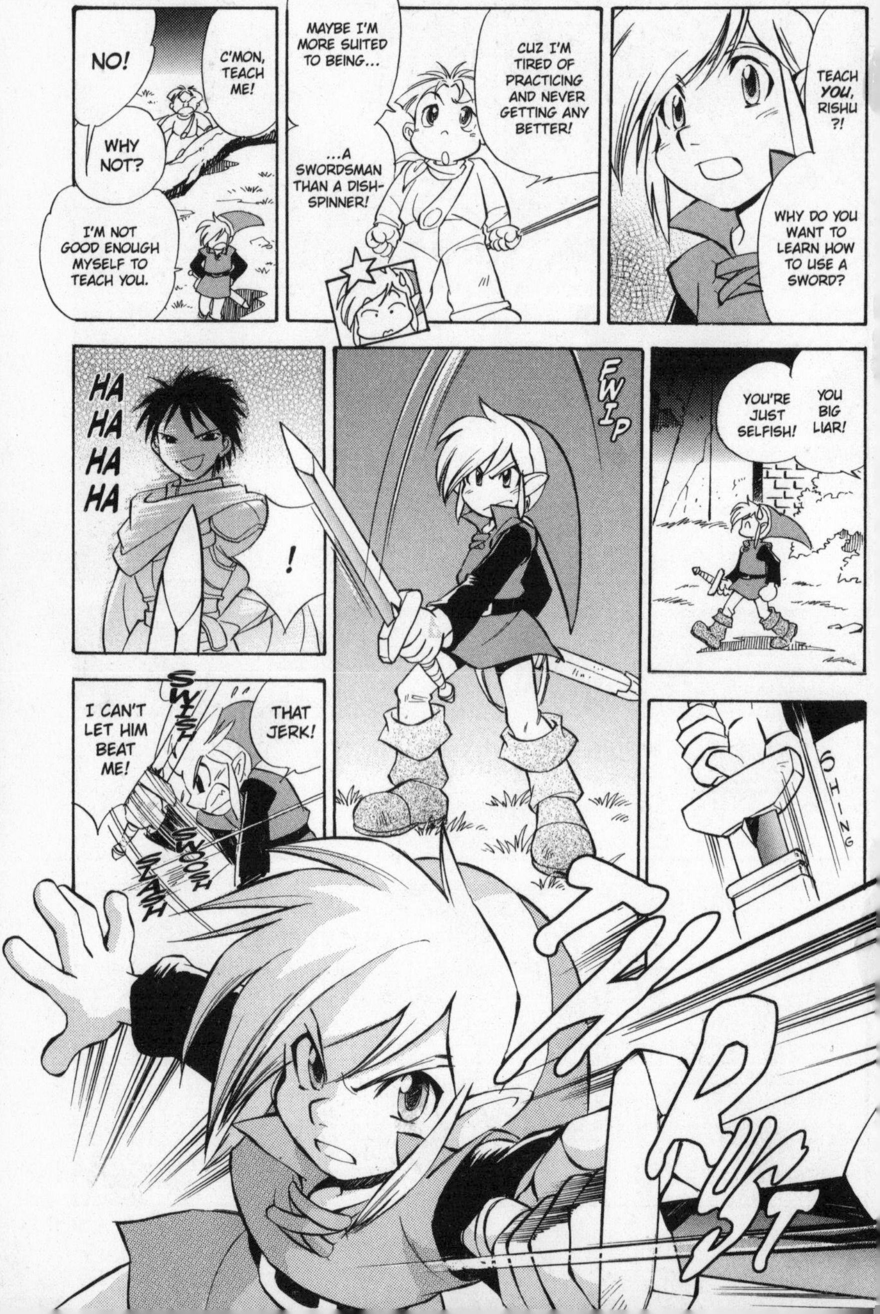
TEACH YOU, RISHU?!
WHY DO YOU WANT TO LEARN HOW TO USE A SWORD?
CUZ I'M TIRED OF PRACTICING AND NEVER GETTING ANY BETTER!
MAYBE I'M MORE SUITED TO BEING...
...A SWORDSMAN THAN A DISH-SPINNER!
C'MON, TEACH ME!
NO!
WHY NOT?
I'M NOT GOOD ENOUGH MYSELF TO TEACH YOU.
YOU BIG LIAR!
YOU'RE JUST SELFISH!
FWIP
HA HA HA HA
!
THAT JERK!
I CAN'T LET HIM BEAT ME!
SWISH
SWOOSH
SLASH
SHING

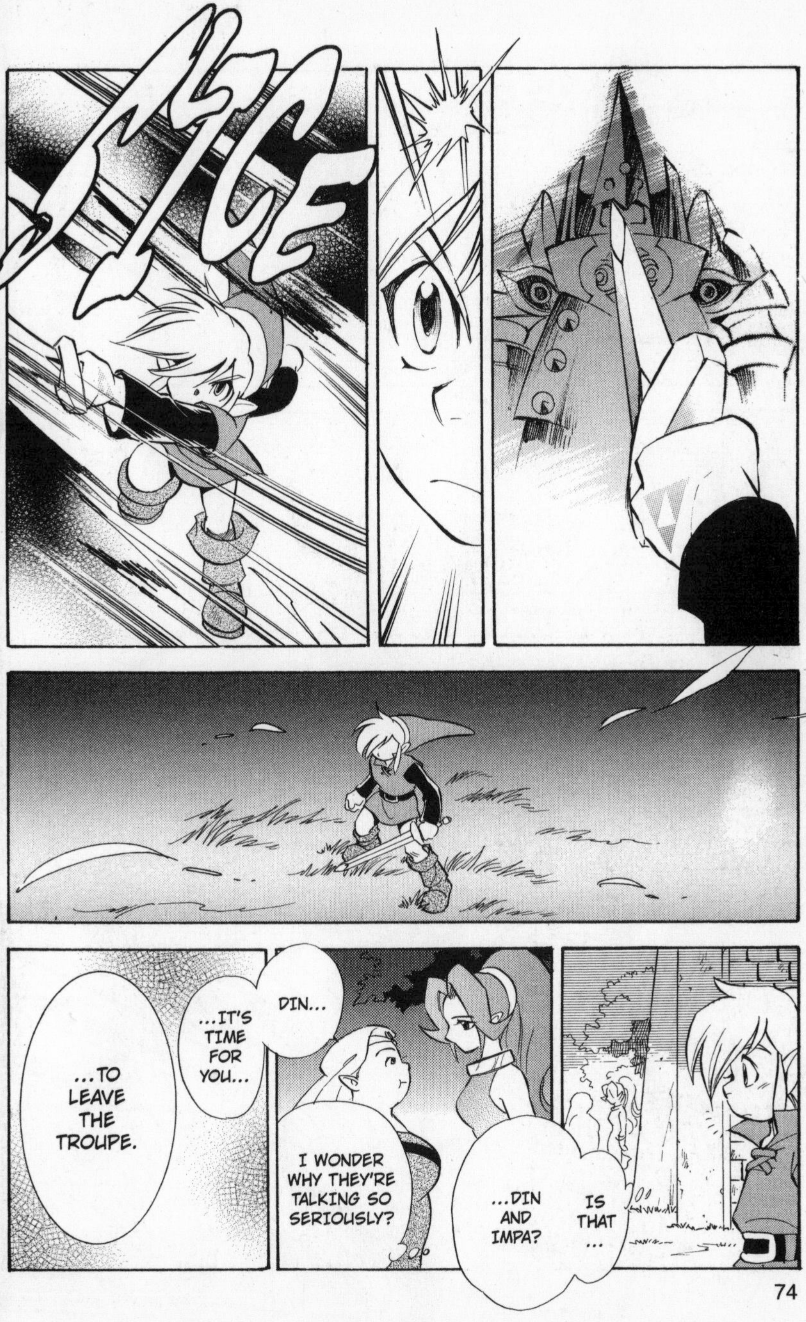
IS THAT ...
...DIN AND IMPA?
DIN...
...IT'S TIME FOR YOU...
I WONDER WHY THEY'RE TALKING SO SERIOUSLY?
...TO LEAVE THE TROUPE.

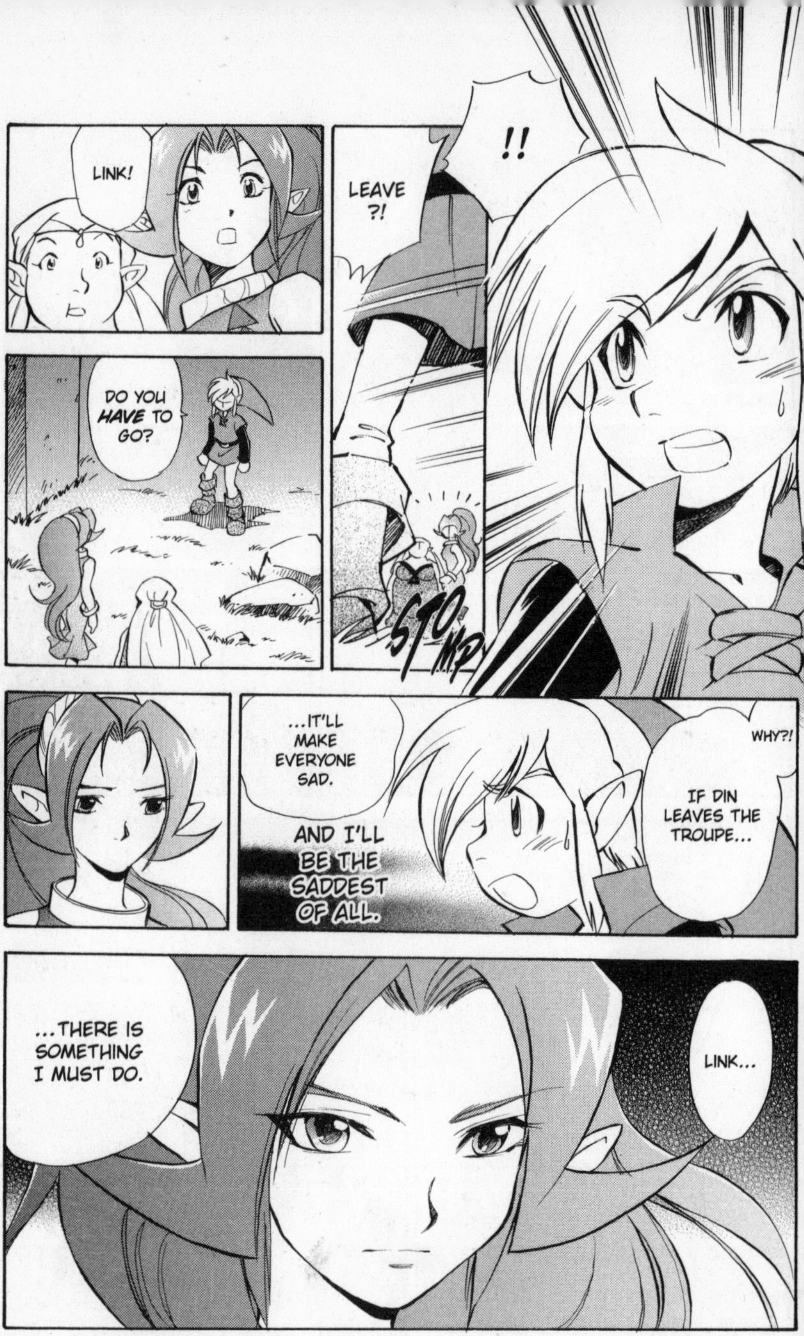
!!
LEAVE ?!
STOMP
LINK!
DO YOU *HAVE* TO GO?
WHY?!
IF DIN LEAVES THE TROUPE...
...IT'LL MAKE EVERYONE SAD.
AND I'LL BE THE SADDEST OF ALL.
LINK...
...THERE IS SOMETHING I MUST DO.

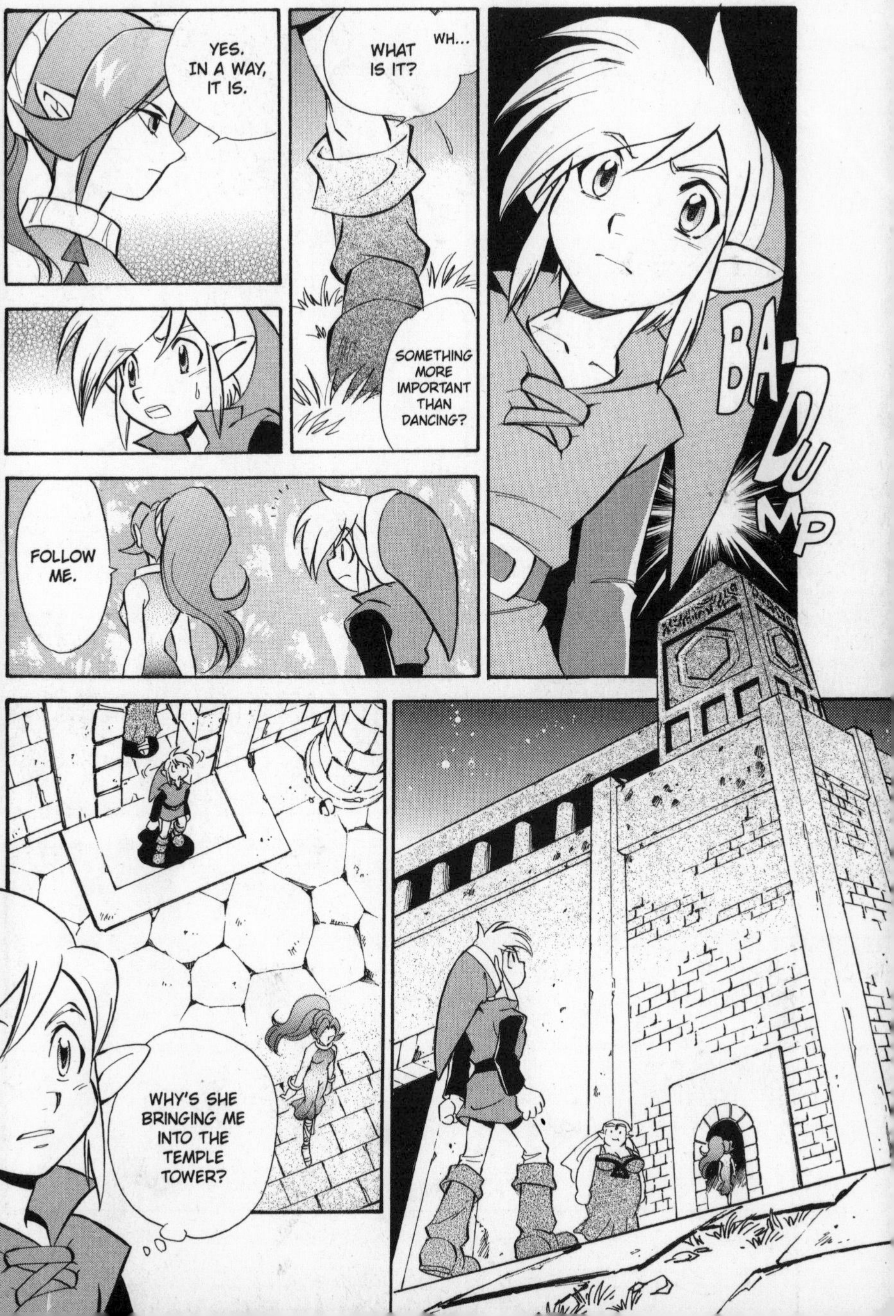
BA-DUMP
WH...
WHAT IS IT?
SOMETHING MORE IMPORTANT THAN DANCING?
YES. IN A WAY, IT IS.
FOLLOW ME.
WHY'S SHE BRINGING ME INTO THE TEMPLE TOWER?

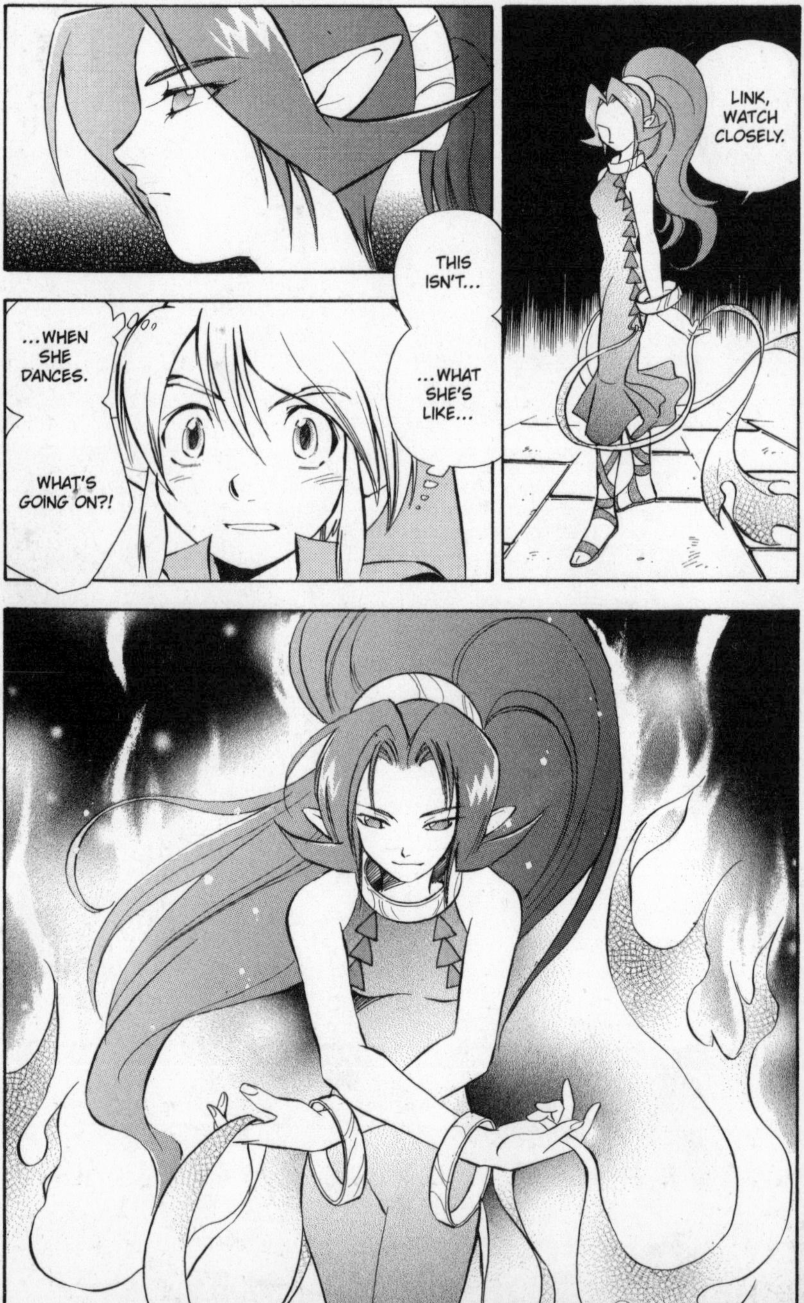
LINK, WATCH CLOSELY.
THIS ISN'T...
...WHAT SHE'S LIKE...
...WHEN SHE DANCES.
WHAT'S GOING ON?!

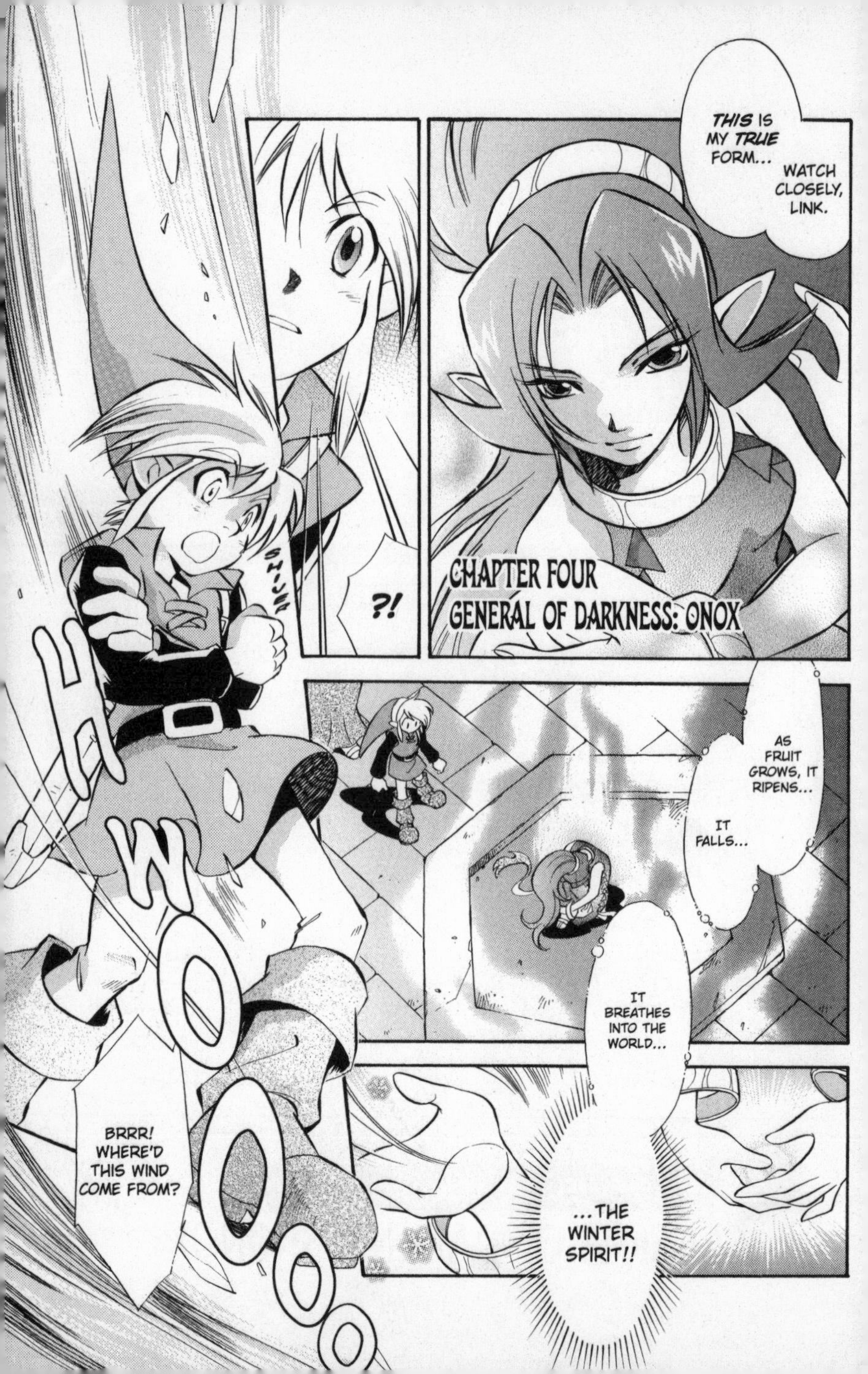
THIS IS MY TRUE FORM...
WATCH CLOSELY, LINK.
CHAPTER FOUR
GENERAL OF DARKNESS: ONOX
?!
AS FRUIT GROWS, IT RIPENS...
IT FALLS...
IT BREATHES INTO THE WORLD...
...THE WINTER SPIRIT!!
SHIVER
WHOOOOOO
BRRR! WHERE'D THIS WIND COME FROM?

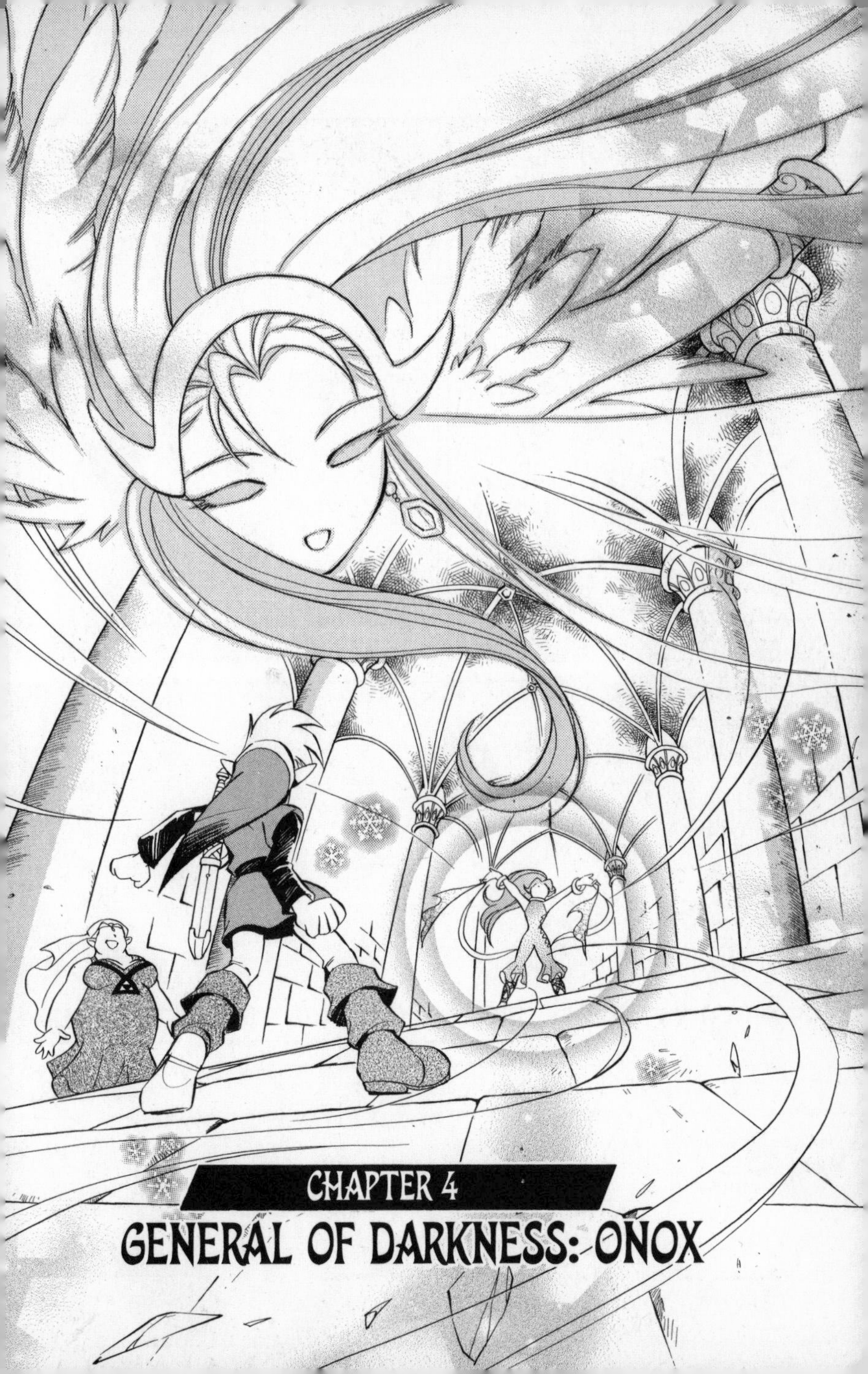

CHAPTER 4
GENERAL OF DARKNESS: ONOX

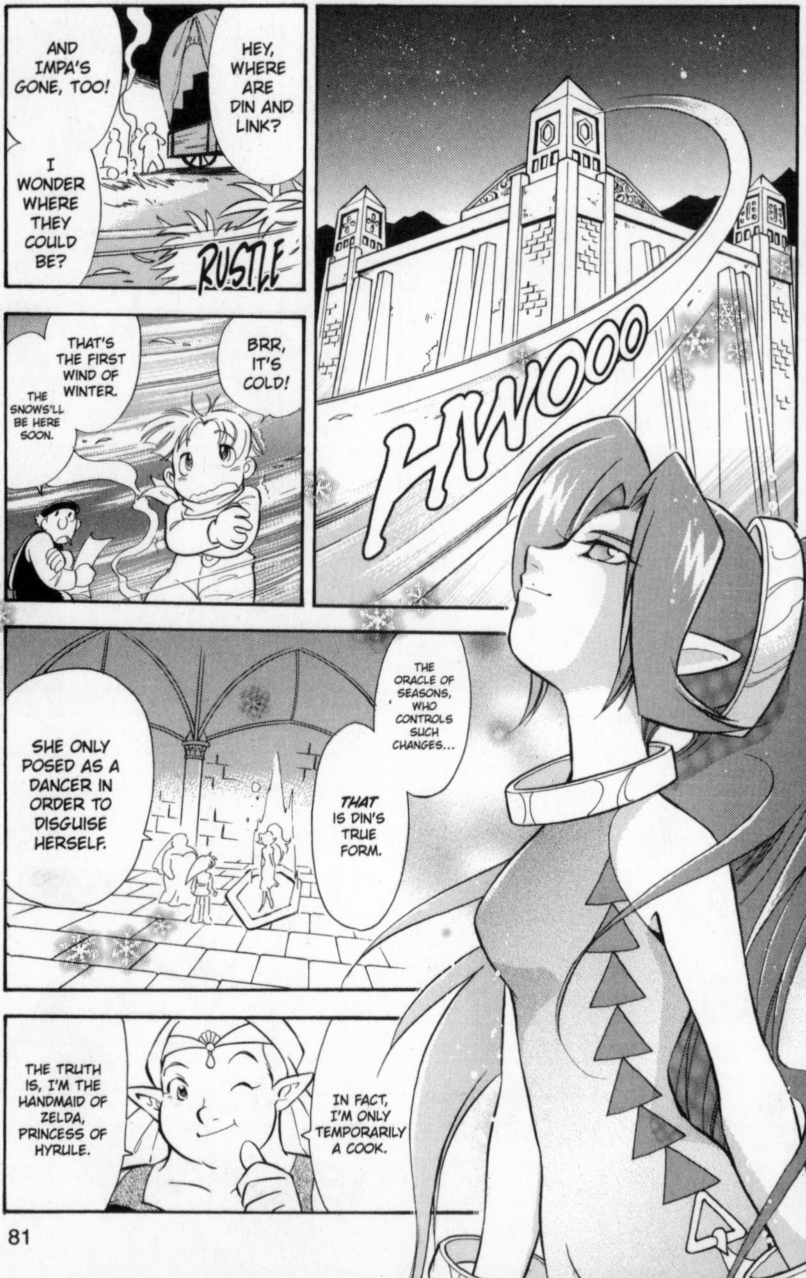

HWOOO
HEY, WHERE ARE DIN AND LINK?
AND IMPA'S GONE, TOO!
I WONDER WHERE THEY COULD BE?
RUSTLE
BRR, IT'S COLD!
THAT'S THE FIRST WIND OF WINTER.
THE SNOWS'LL BE HERE SOON.
THE ORACLE OF SEASONS, WHO CONTROLS SUCH CHANGES...
THAT IS DIN'S TRUE FORM.
SHE ONLY POSED AS A DANCER IN ORDER TO DISGUISE HERSELF.
IN FACT, I'M ONLY TEMPORARILY A COOK.
THE TRUTH IS, I'M THE HANDMAID OF ZELDA, PRINCESS OF HYRULE.

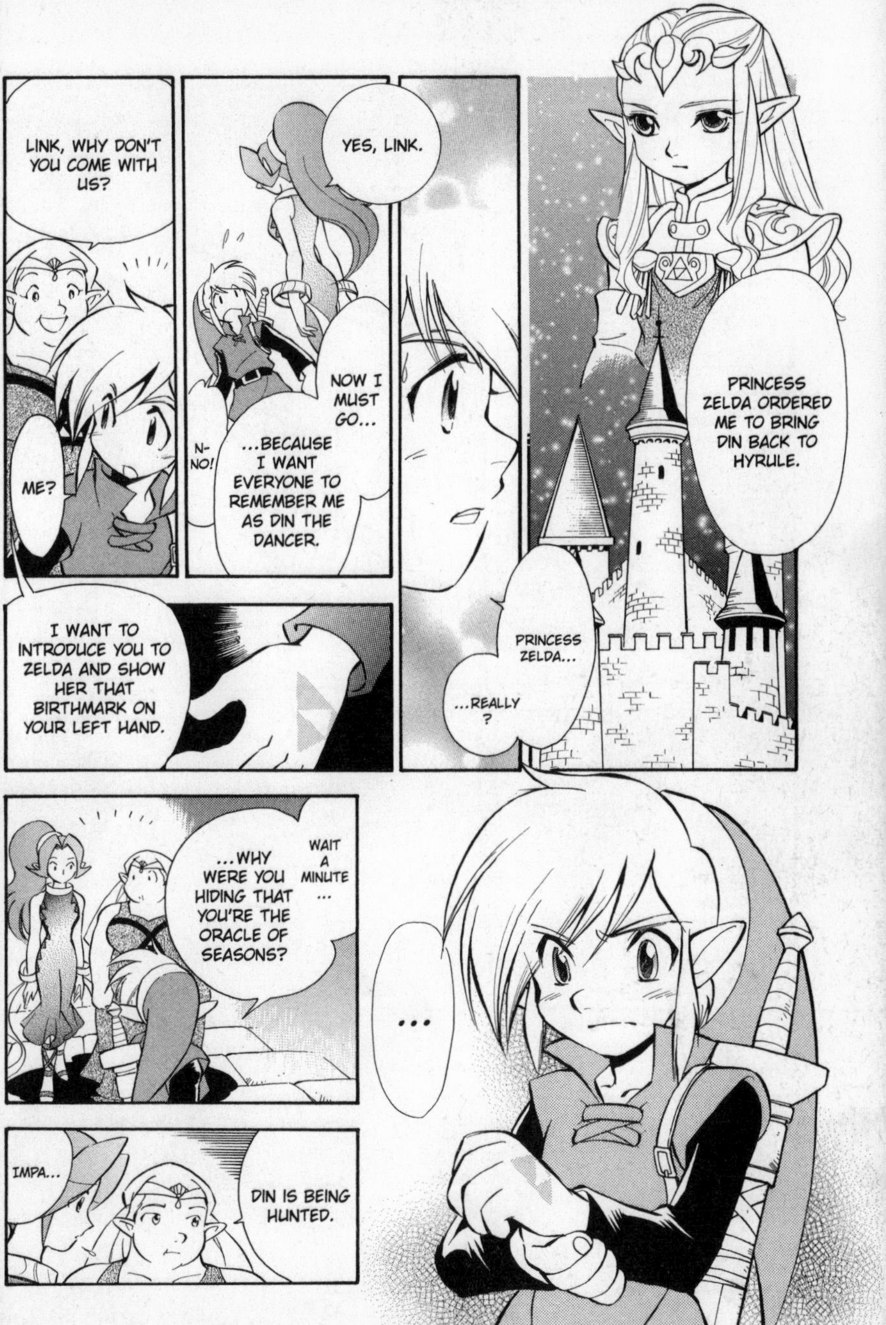
PRINCESS ZELDA ORDERED ME TO BRING DIN BACK TO HYRULE.
PRINCESS ZELDA...
...REALLY ?
YES, LINK.
NOW I MUST GO...
...BECAUSE I WANT EVERYONE TO REMEMBER ME AS DIN THE DANCER.
N-NO!
LINK, WHY DON'T YOU COME WITH US?
ME?
I WANT TO INTRODUCE YOU TO ZELDA AND SHOW HER THAT BIRTHMARK ON YOUR LEFT HAND.
...
WAIT A MINUTE ...
...WHY WERE YOU HIDING THAT YOU'RE THE ORACLE OF SEASONS?
DIN IS BEING HUNTED.
IMPA...

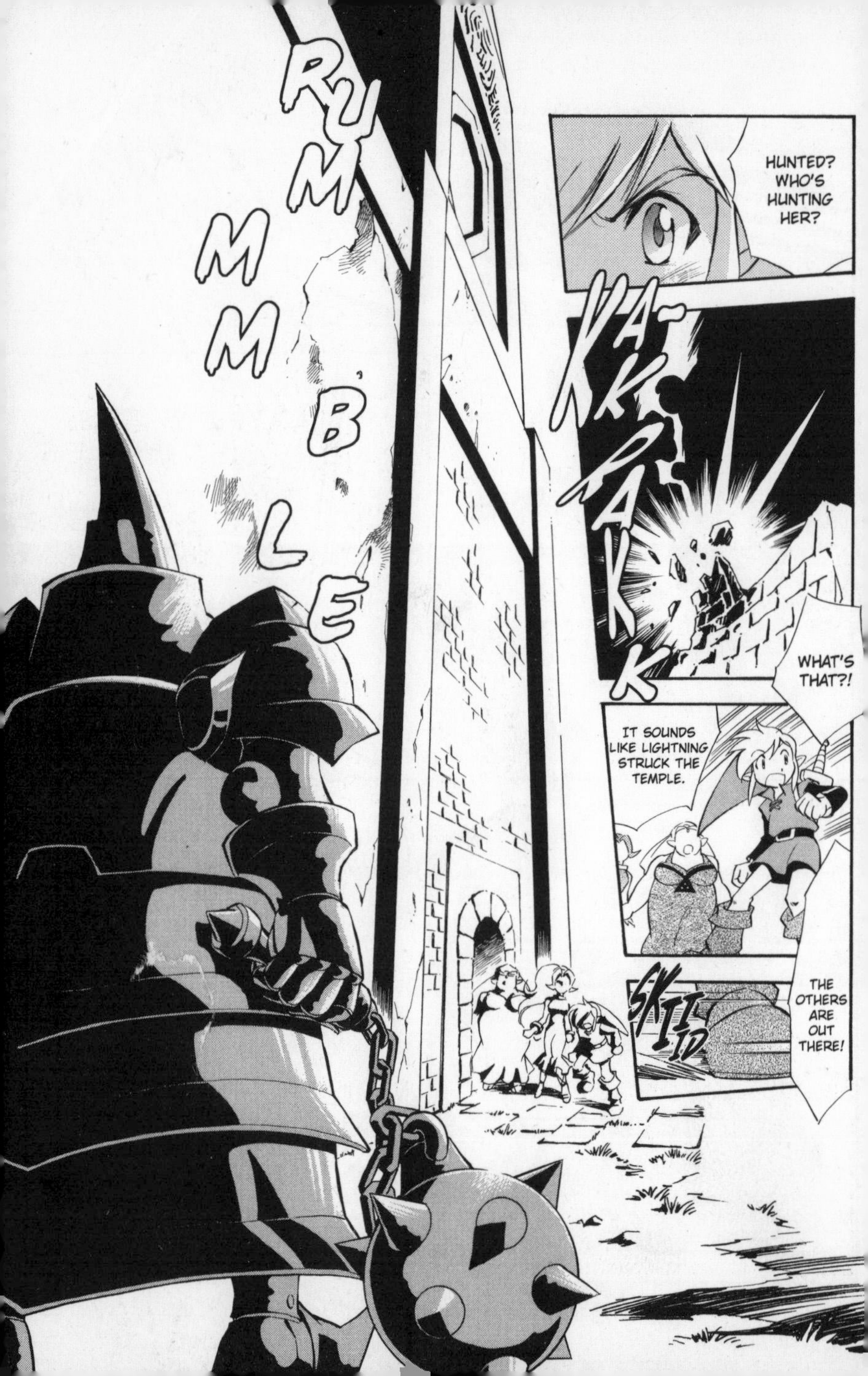
HUNTED? WHO'S HUNTING HER?
KA-KKRAKK
WHAT'S THAT?!
IT SOUNDS LIKE LIGHTNING STRUCK THE TEMPLE.
SKIID
THE OTHERS ARE OUT THERE!
RUMMMMBLE

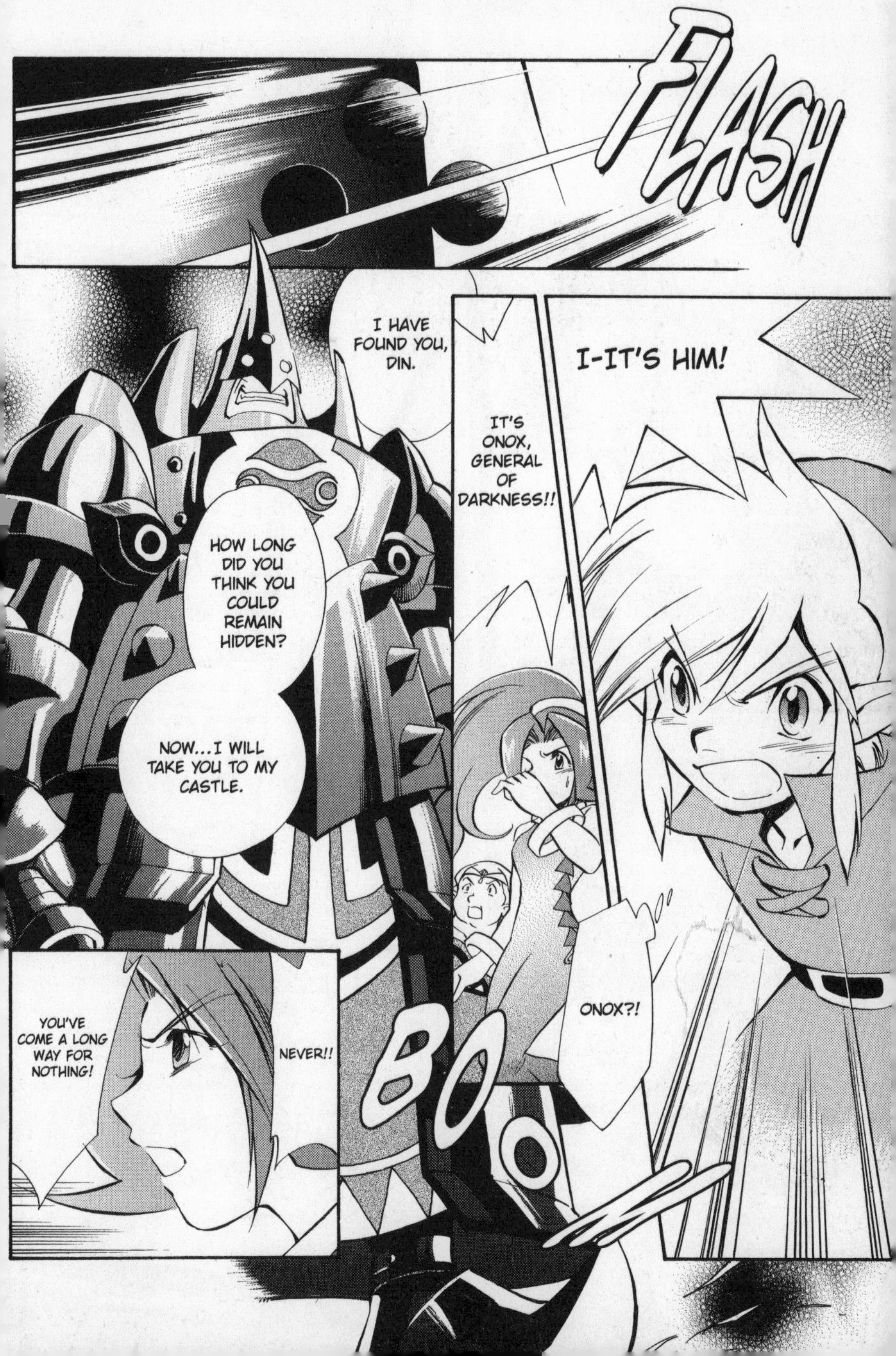
FLASH
I HAVE FOUND YOU, DIN.
HOW LONG DID YOU THINK YOU COULD REMAIN HIDDEN?
NOW...I WILL TAKE YOU TO MY CASTLE.
I-IT'S HIM!
IT'S ONOX, GENERAL OF DARKNESS!!
ONOX?!
NEVER!!
YOU'VE COME A LONG WAY FOR NOTHING!
BOOO

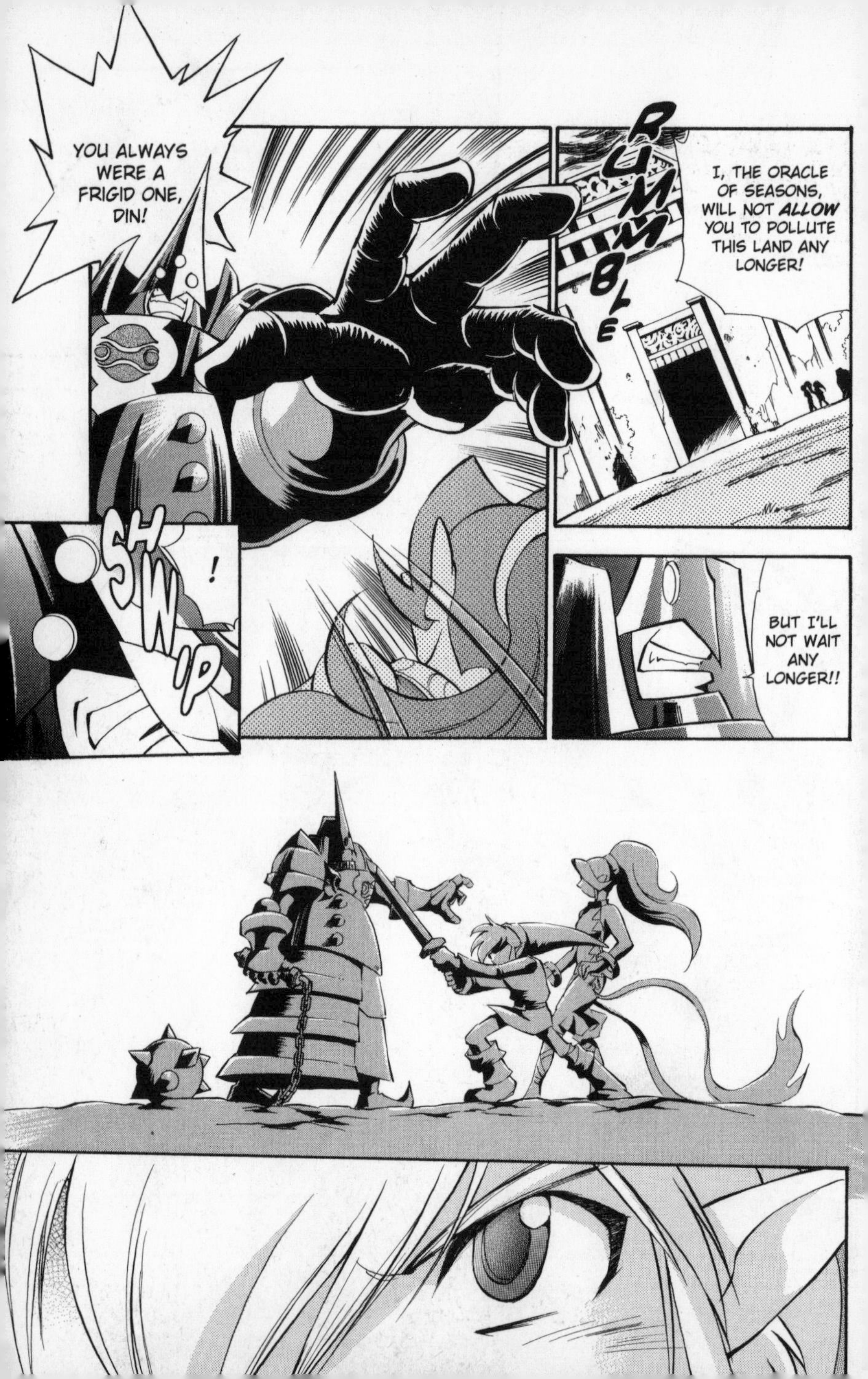
RUMMMBLE
I, THE ORACLE OF SEASONS, WILL NOT ***ALLOW*** YOU TO POLLUTE THIS LAND ANY LONGER!
BUT I'LL NOT WAIT ANY LONGER!!
YOU ALWAYS WERE A FRIGID ONE, DIN!
SHWIP
!

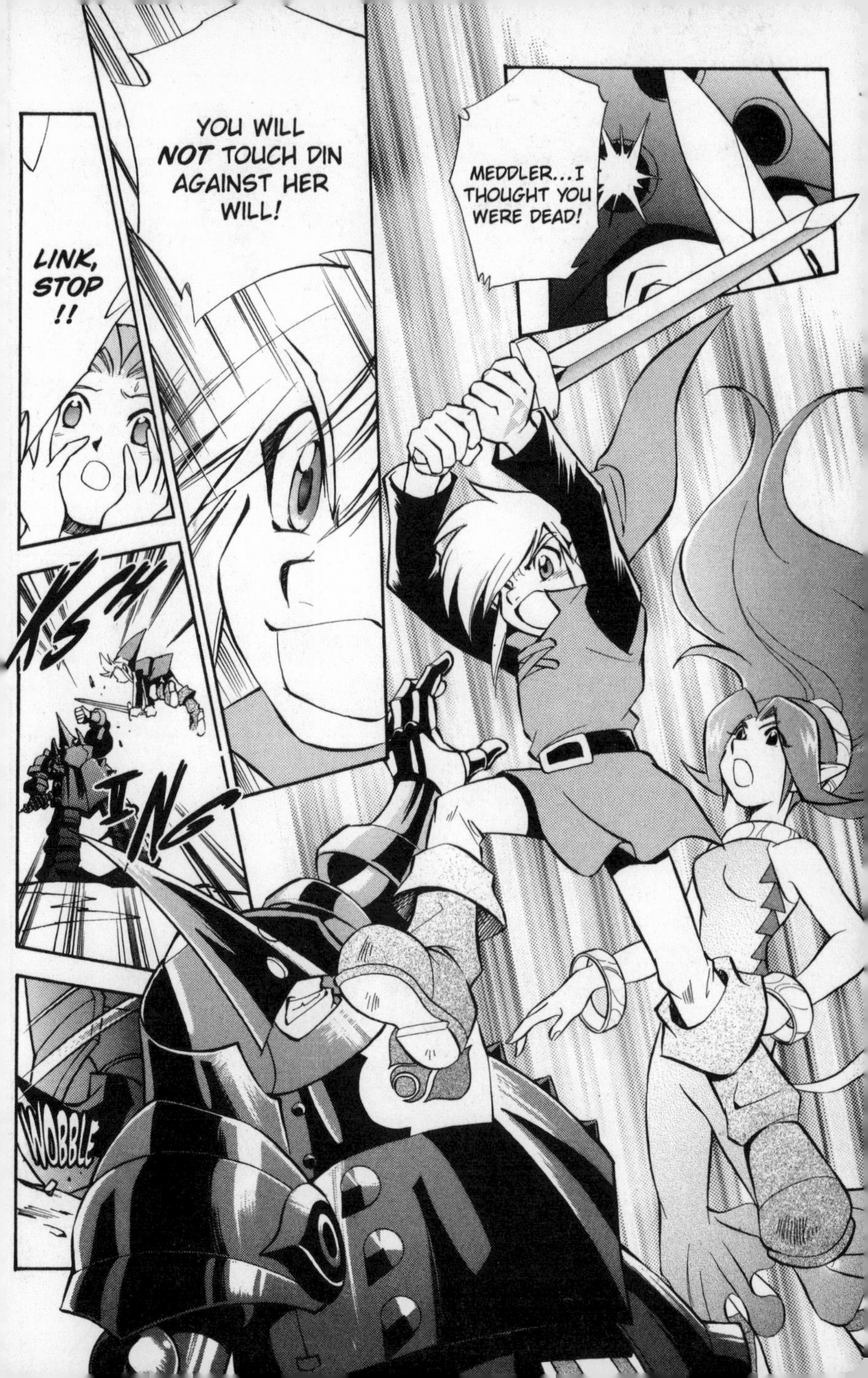
MEDDLER...I THOUGHT YOU WERE DEAD!
YOU WILL *NOT* TOUCH DIN AGAINST HER WILL!
LINK, STOP !!
TING
WOBBLE

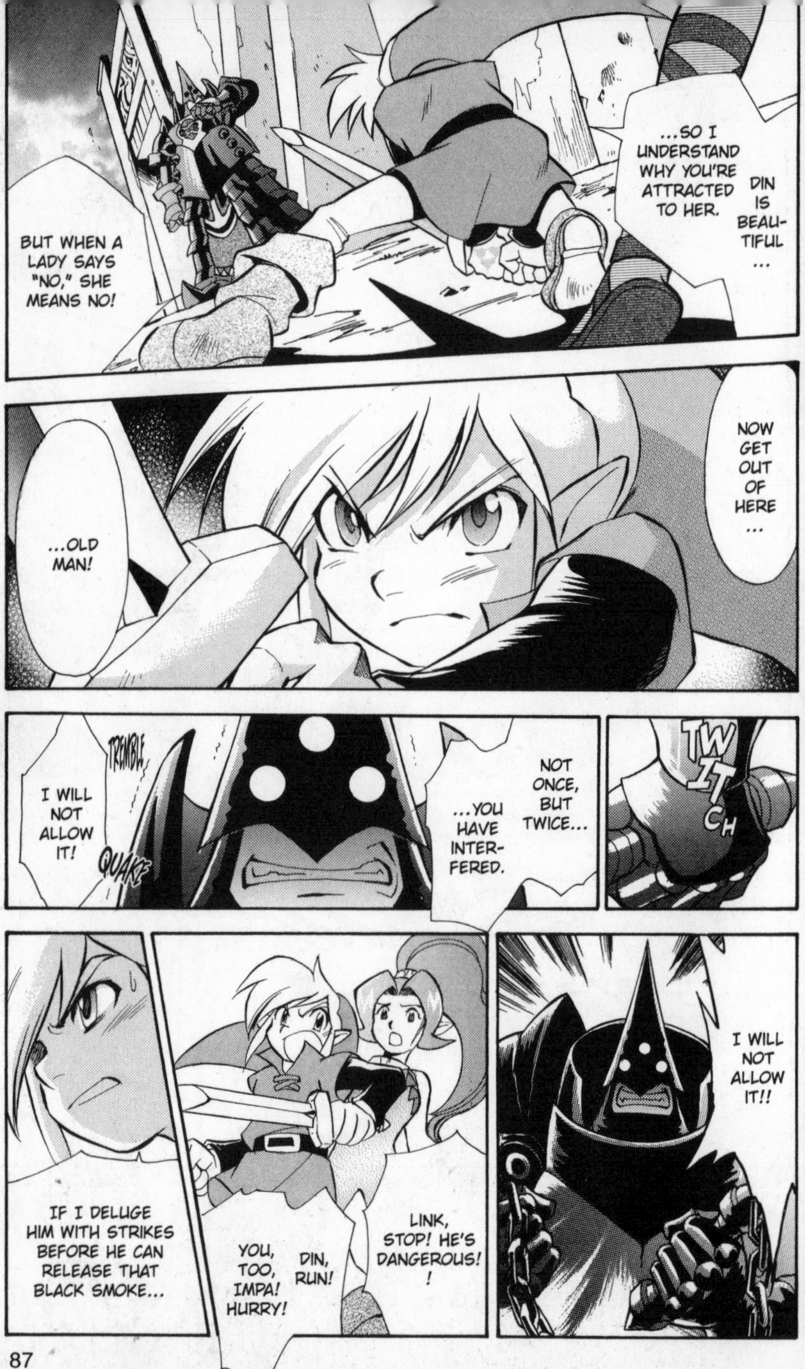
DIN IS BEAUTIFUL...
...SO I UNDERSTAND WHY YOU'RE ATTRACTED TO HER.
BUT WHEN A LADY SAYS "NO," SHE MEANS NO!
NOW GET OUT OF HERE...
...OLD MAN!
TWITCH
NOT ONCE, BUT TWICE...
...YOU HAVE INTERFERED.
TREMBLE
I WILL NOT ALLOW IT!
QUAKE
I WILL NOT ALLOW IT!!
LINK, STOP! HE'S DANGEROUS!!
DIN, RUN!
YOU, TOO, IMPA! HURRY!
IF I DELUGE HIM WITH STRIKES BEFORE HE CAN RELEASE THAT BLACK SMOKE...

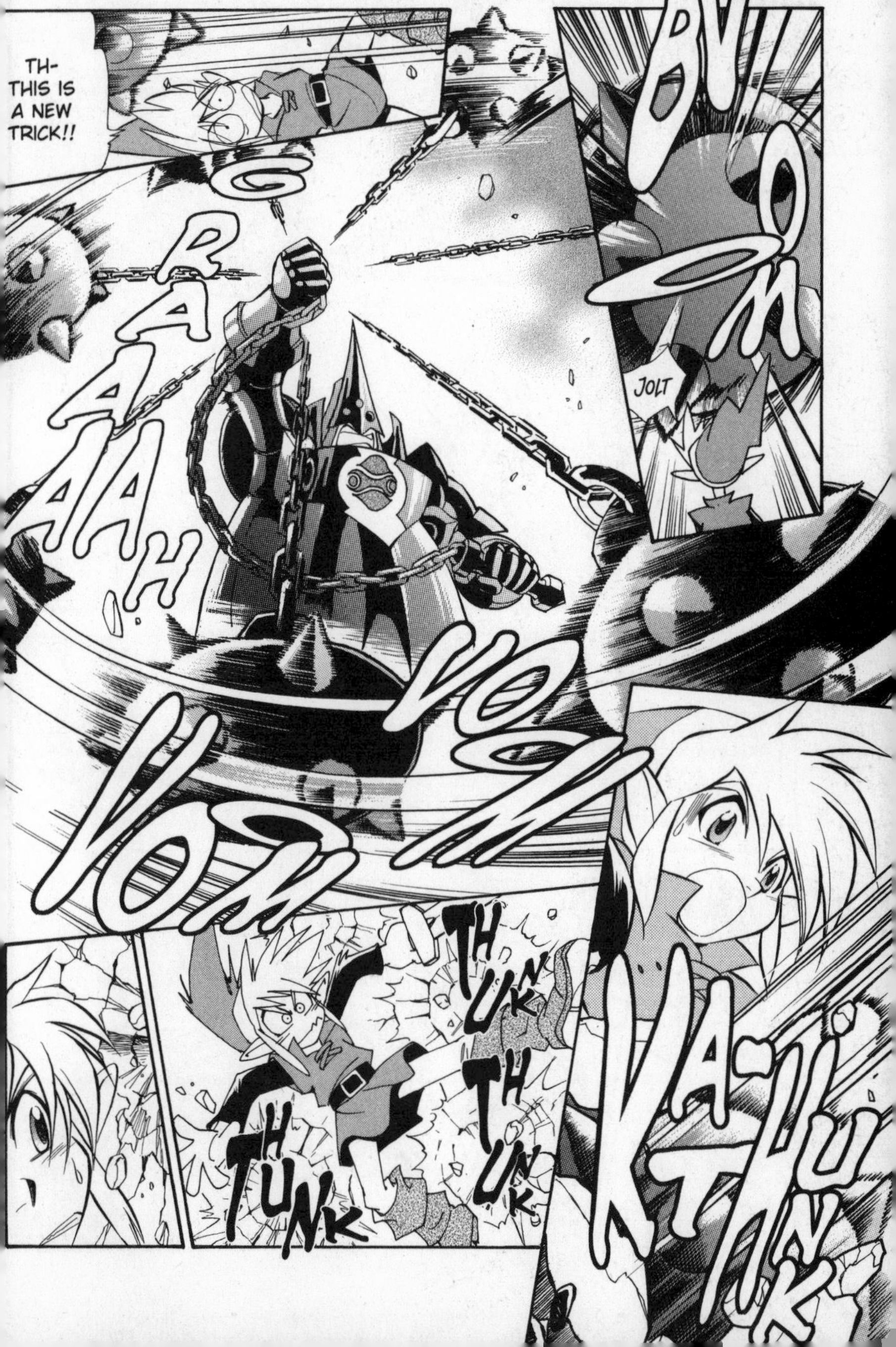

BVOOM
JOLT
TH-
THIS IS
A NEW
TRICK!!
GRAAAAH
VOOM
VOOM
KA-CHUNK
THUNK
THUNK
THUNK

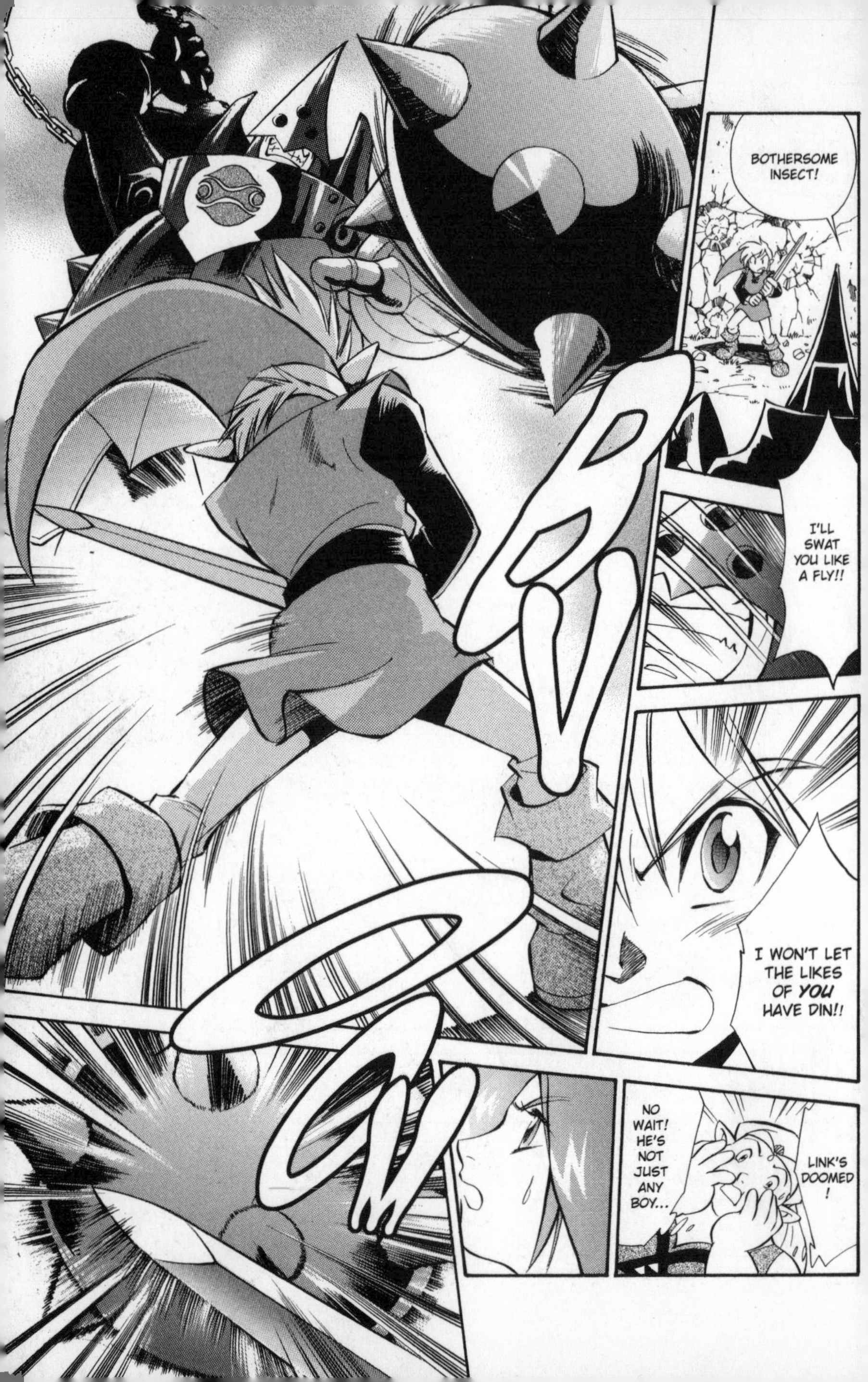
BOTHERSOME INSECT!
I'LL SWAT YOU LIKE A FLY!!
I WON'T LET THE LIKES OF *YOU* HAVE DIN!!
LINK'S DOOMED!
NO WAIT! HE'S NOT JUST ANY BOY...

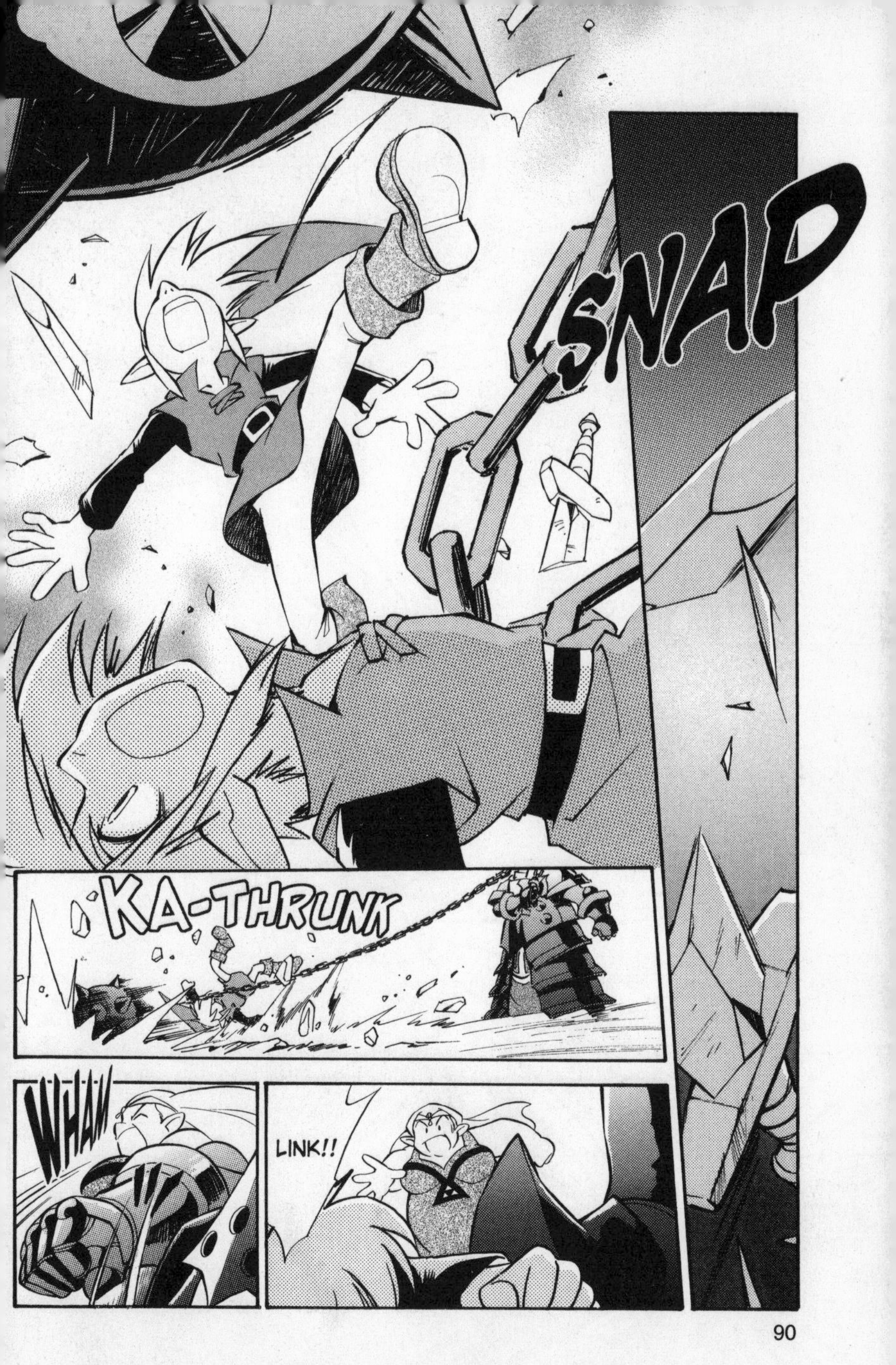
SNAP
KA-THRUNK
LINK!!
WHAM

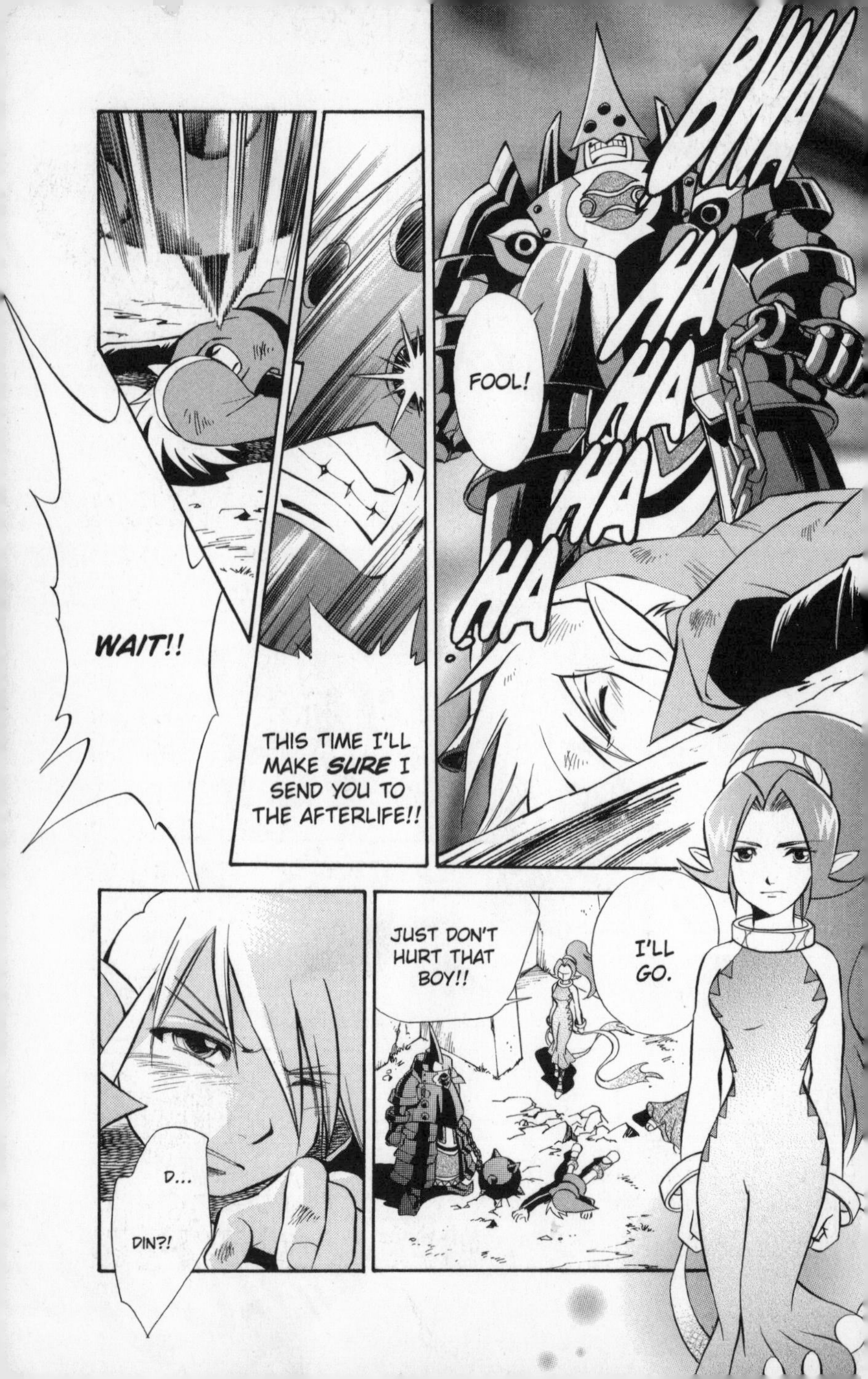
BWA HA HA HA HA
FOOL!
THIS TIME I'LL MAKE SURE I SEND YOU TO THE AFTERLIFE!!
WAIT!!
I'LL GO.
JUST DON'T HURT THAT BOY!!
D...
DIN?!

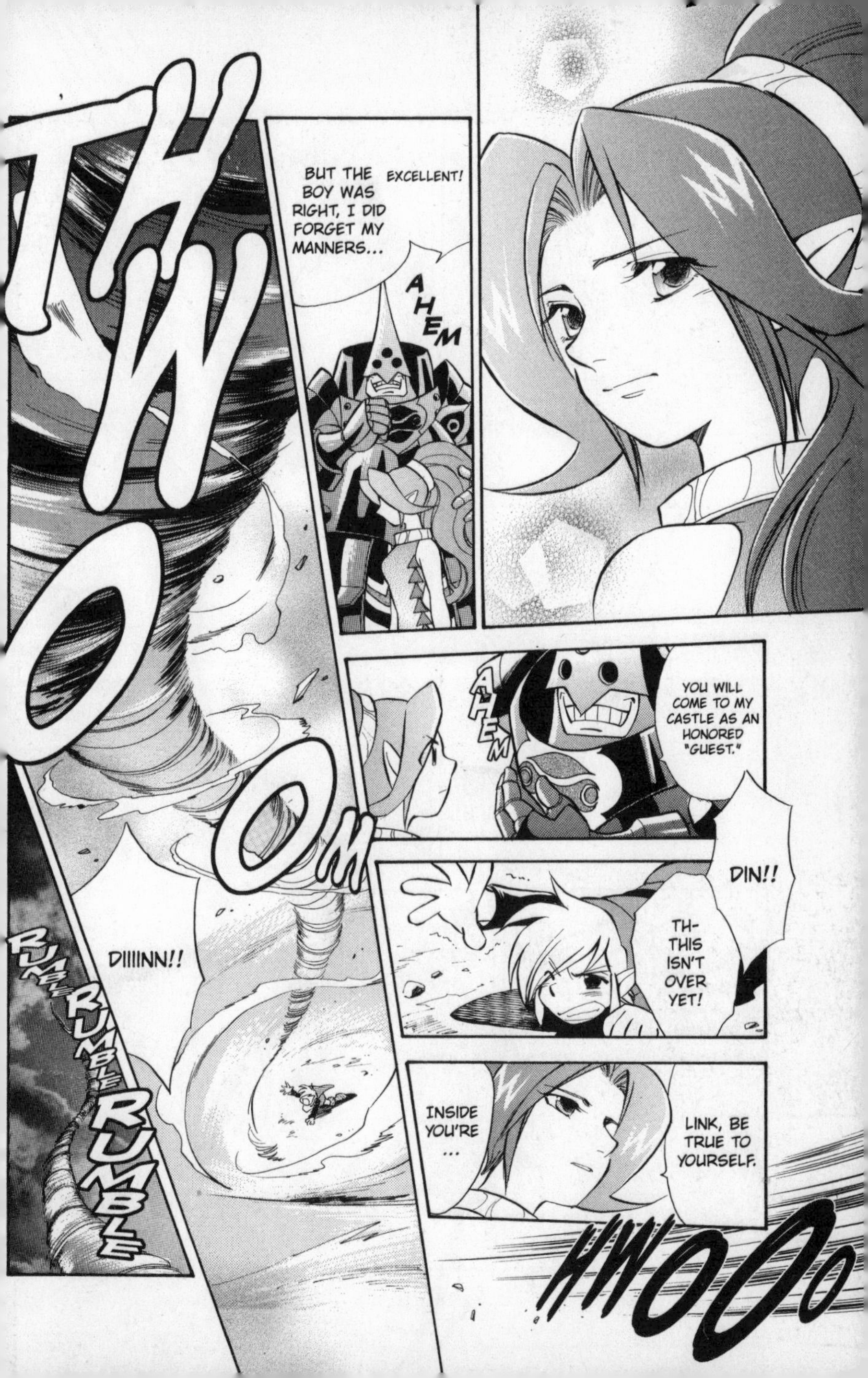
EXCELLENT!
BUT THE BOY WAS RIGHT, I DID FORGET MY MANNERS...
AHEM
AHEM
YOU WILL COME TO MY CASTLE AS AN HONORED "GUEST."
DIN!!
TH-THIS ISN'T OVER YET!
LINK, BE TRUE TO YOURSELF.
INSIDE YOU'RE ...
HWOOOO
THWOOOM
DIIIINN!!
RUMBLE RUMBLE RUMBLE

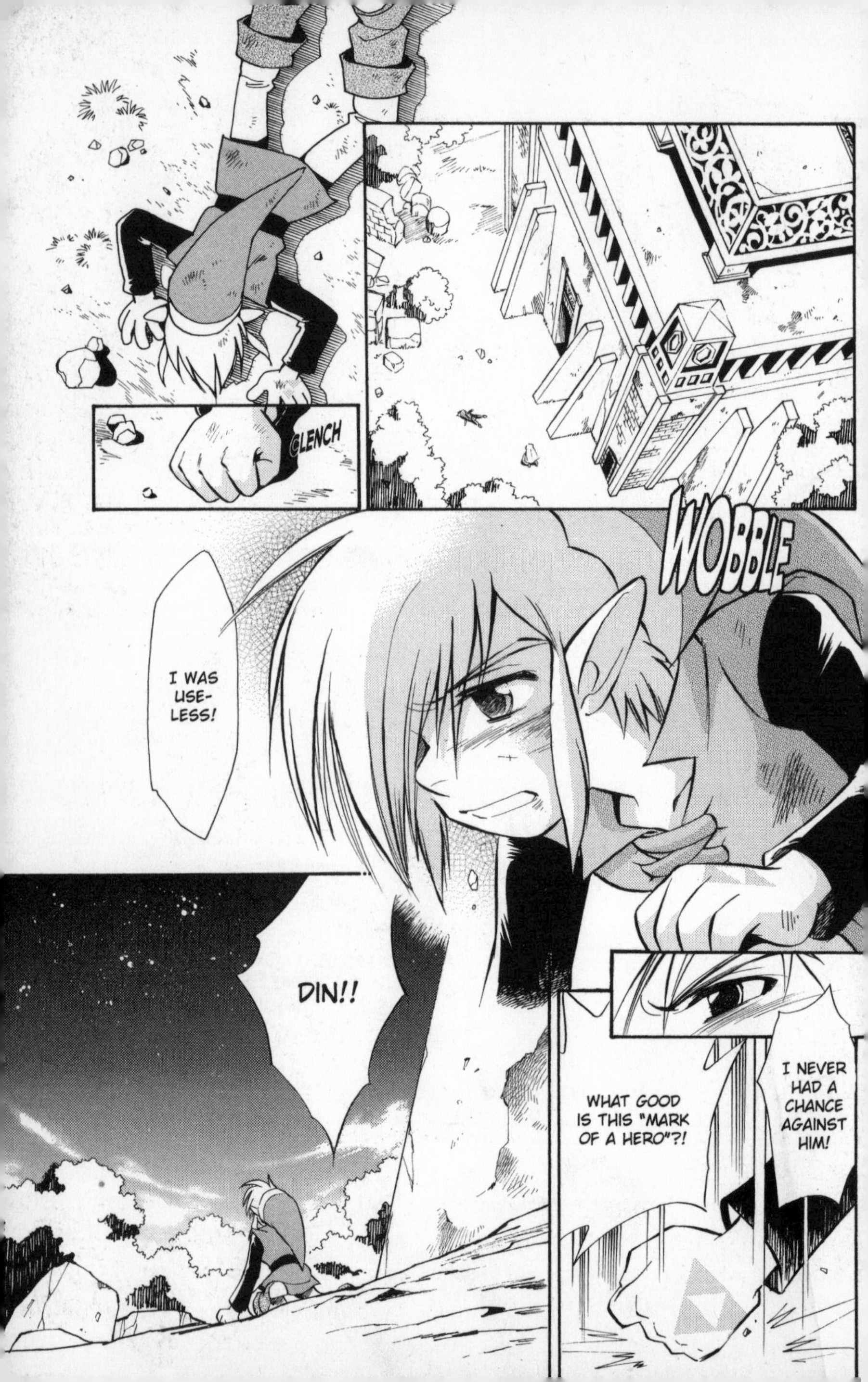
CLENCH
WOBBLE
I WAS USE-LESS!
I NEVER HAD A CHANCE AGAINST HIM!
WHAT GOOD IS THIS "MARK OF A HERO"?!
DIN!!

CHAPTER 5
SACRED PYRAMID: THE TRIFORCE

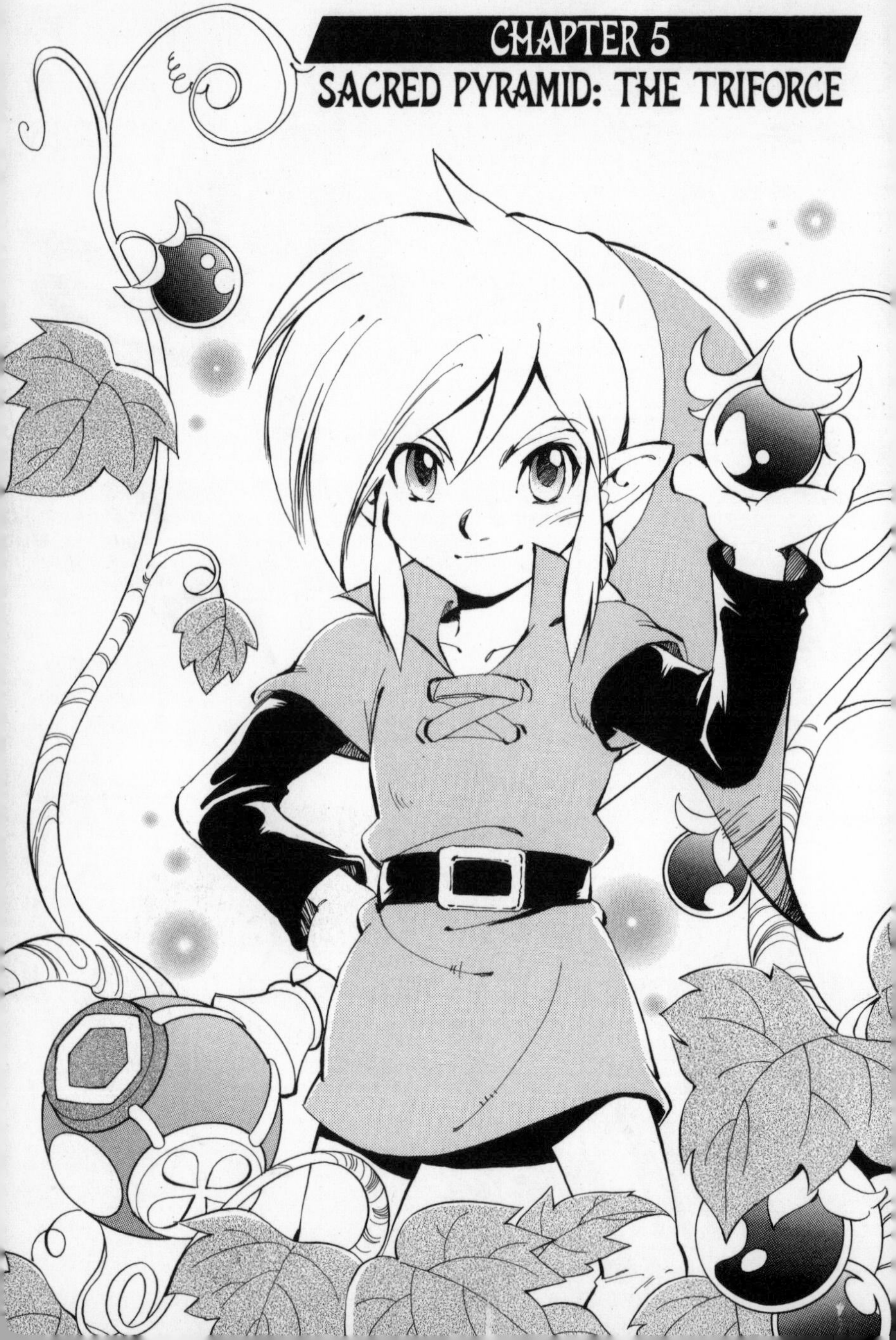

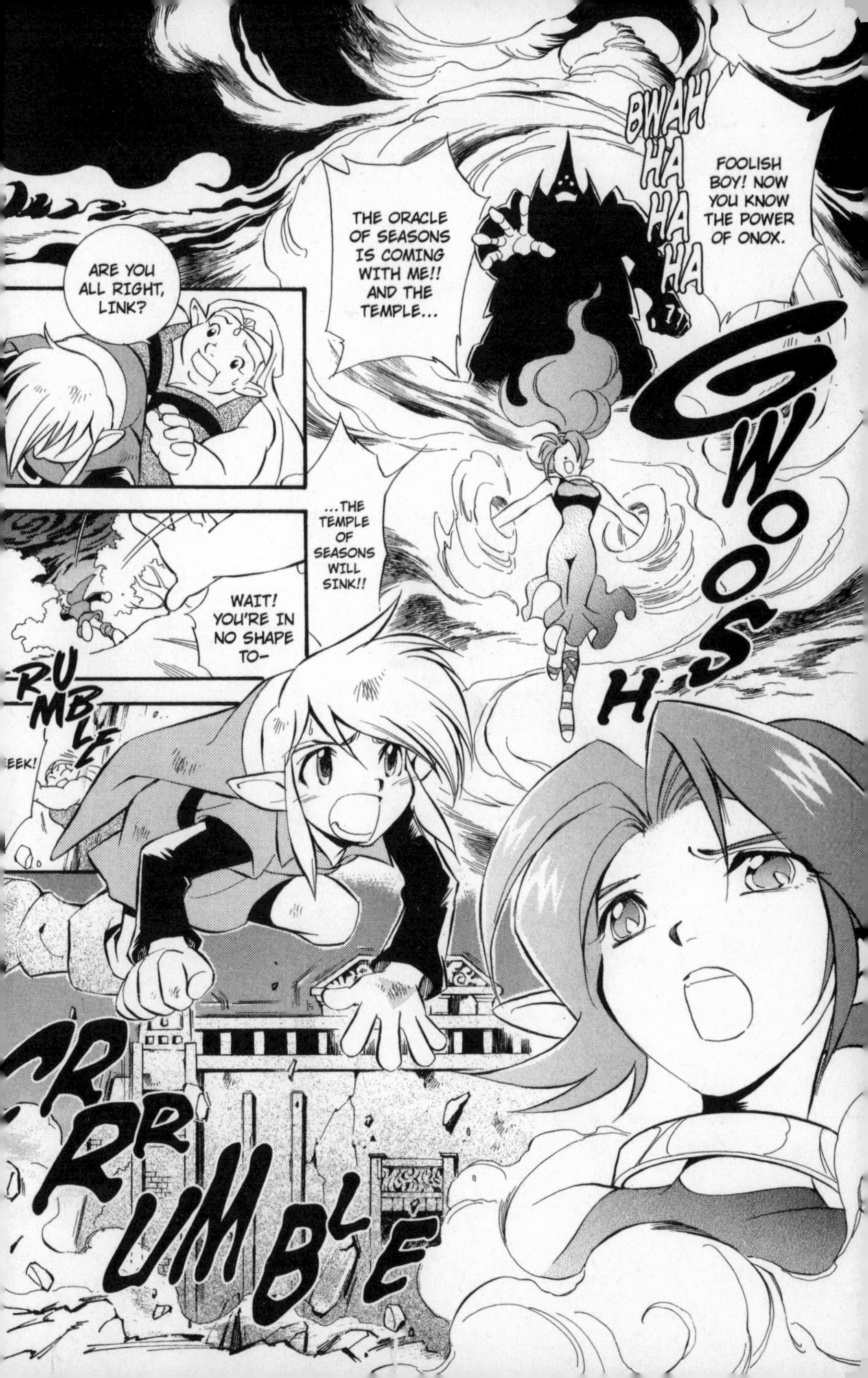
BWAH HA HA HA HA
FOOLISH BOY! NOW YOU KNOW THE POWER OF ONOX.
THE ORACLE OF SEASONS IS COMING WITH ME!! AND THE TEMPLE...
ARE YOU ALL RIGHT, LINK?
GWOOSH
...THE TEMPLE OF SEASONS WILL SINK!!
WAIT! YOU'RE IN NO SHAPE TO-
RUMBLE
EEK!
CRRRUMBLE

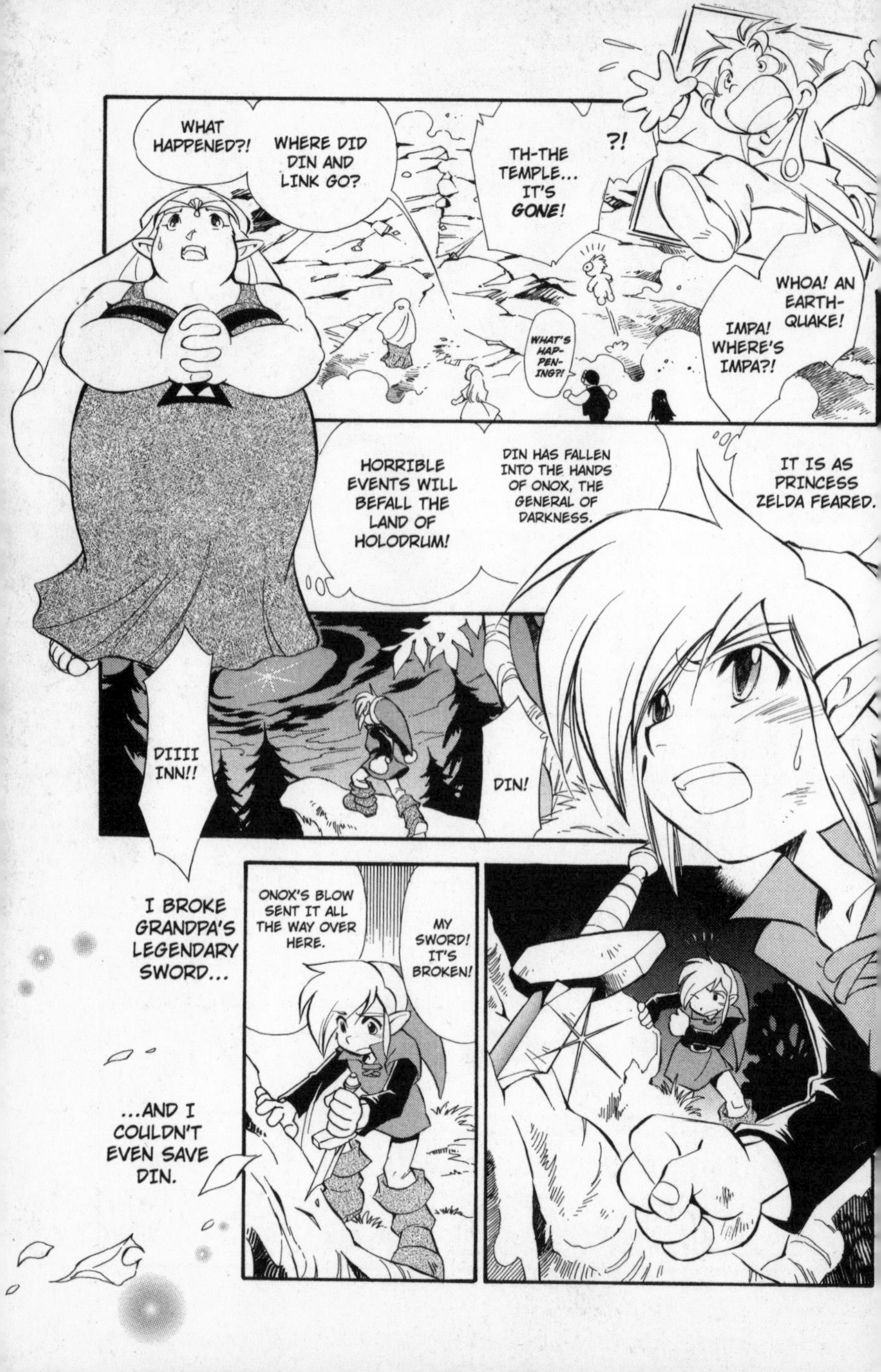
WHOA! AN EARTH-QUAKE!
IMPA! WHERE'S IMPA?!
?!
TH-THE TEMPLE... IT'S GONE!
WHAT'S HAP-PEN-ING?!
WHERE DID DIN AND LINK GO?
WHAT HAPPENED?!
IT IS AS PRINCESS ZELDA FEARED.
DIN HAS FALLEN INTO THE HANDS OF ONOX, THE GENERAL OF DARKNESS.
HORRIBLE EVENTS WILL BEFALL THE LAND OF HOLODRUM!
DIN!
DIIII INN!!
MY SWORD! IT'S BROKEN!
ONOX'S BLOW SENT IT ALL THE WAY OVER HERE.
I BROKE GRANDPA'S LEGENDARY SWORD...
...AND I COULDN'T EVEN SAVE DIN.

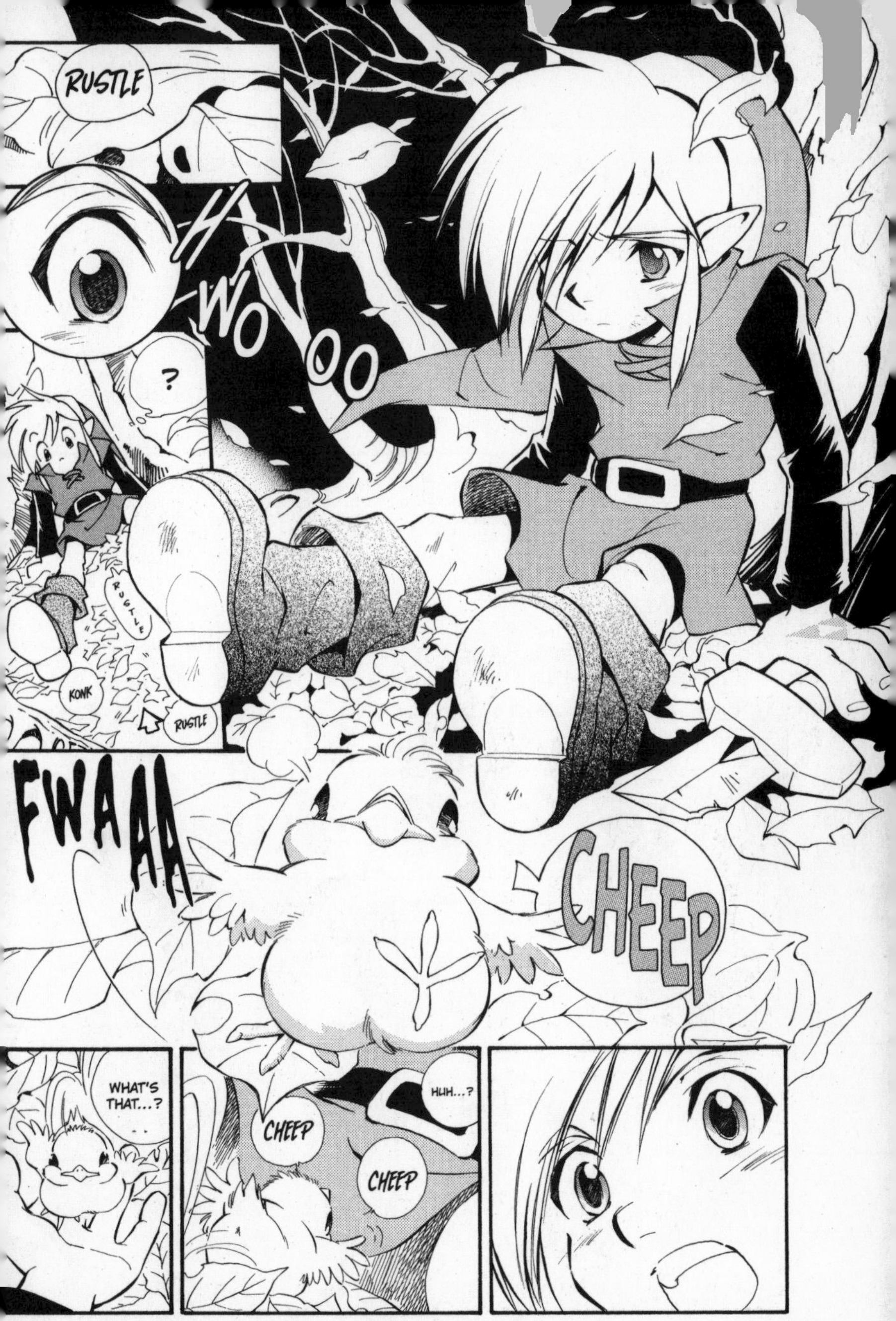
HWOOO
RUSTLE
?
RUSTLE
KONK
RUSTLE
CHEEP
FWAAA
HUH...?
CHEEP
CHEEP
WHAT'S THAT...?
..

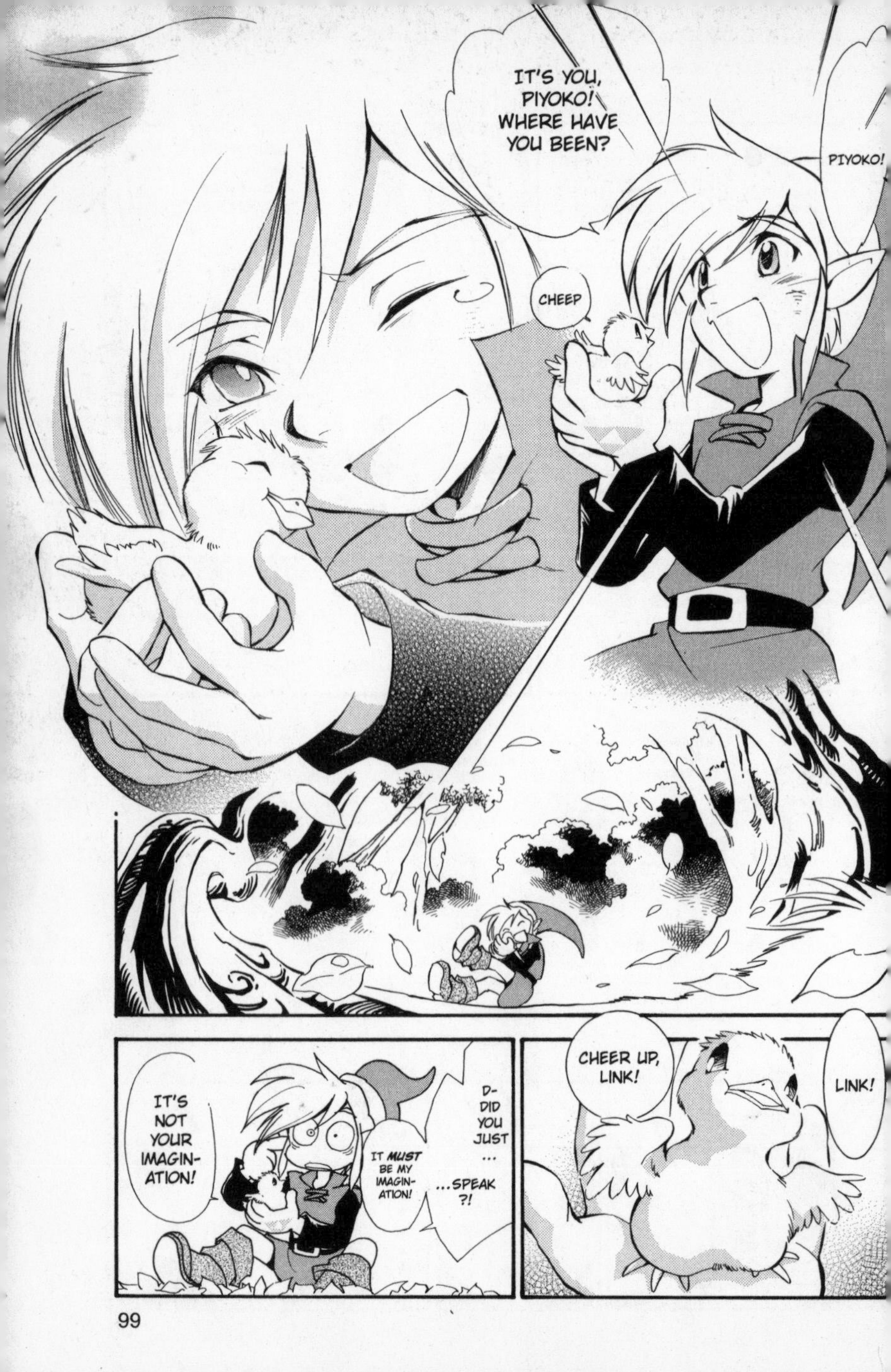
PIYOKO!
IT'S YOU, PIYOKO! WHERE HAVE YOU BEEN?
CHEEP
LINK!
CHEER UP, LINK!
D-DID YOU JUST...
...SPEAK?!
IT *MUST* BE MY IMAGINATION!
IT'S NOT YOUR IMAGINATION!

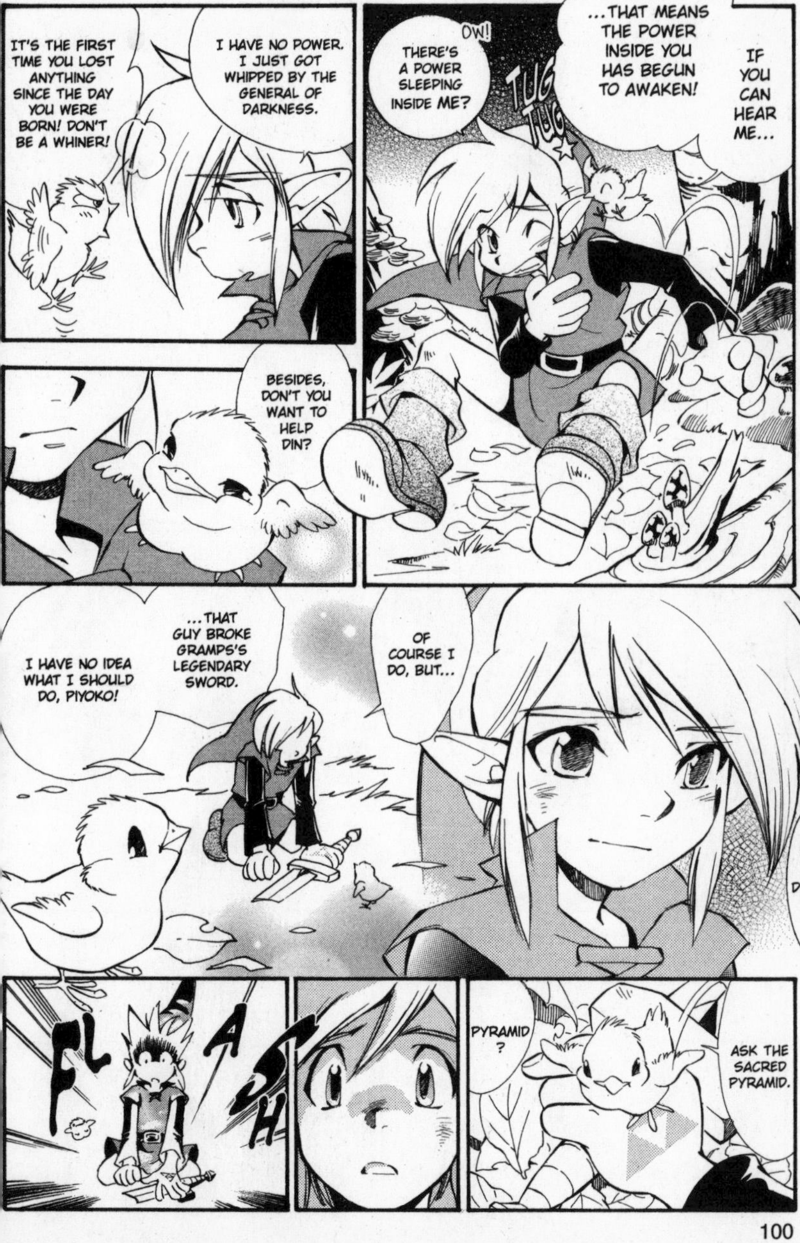
IF YOU CAN HEAR ME...
...THAT MEANS THE POWER INSIDE YOU HAS BEGUN TO AWAKEN!
OW!
TUG TUG
THERE'S A POWER SLEEPING INSIDE ME?
I HAVE NO POWER. I JUST GOT WHIPPED BY THE GENERAL OF DARKNESS.
IT'S THE FIRST TIME YOU LOST ANYTHING SINCE THE DAY YOU WERE BORN! DON'T BE A WHINER!
BESIDES, DON'T YOU WANT TO HELP DIN?
DIN...
OF COURSE I DO, BUT...
...THAT GUY BROKE GRAMPS'S LEGENDARY SWORD.
I HAVE NO IDEA WHAT I SHOULD DO, PIYOKO!
ASK THE SACRED PYRAMID.
PYRAMID?
FLASH

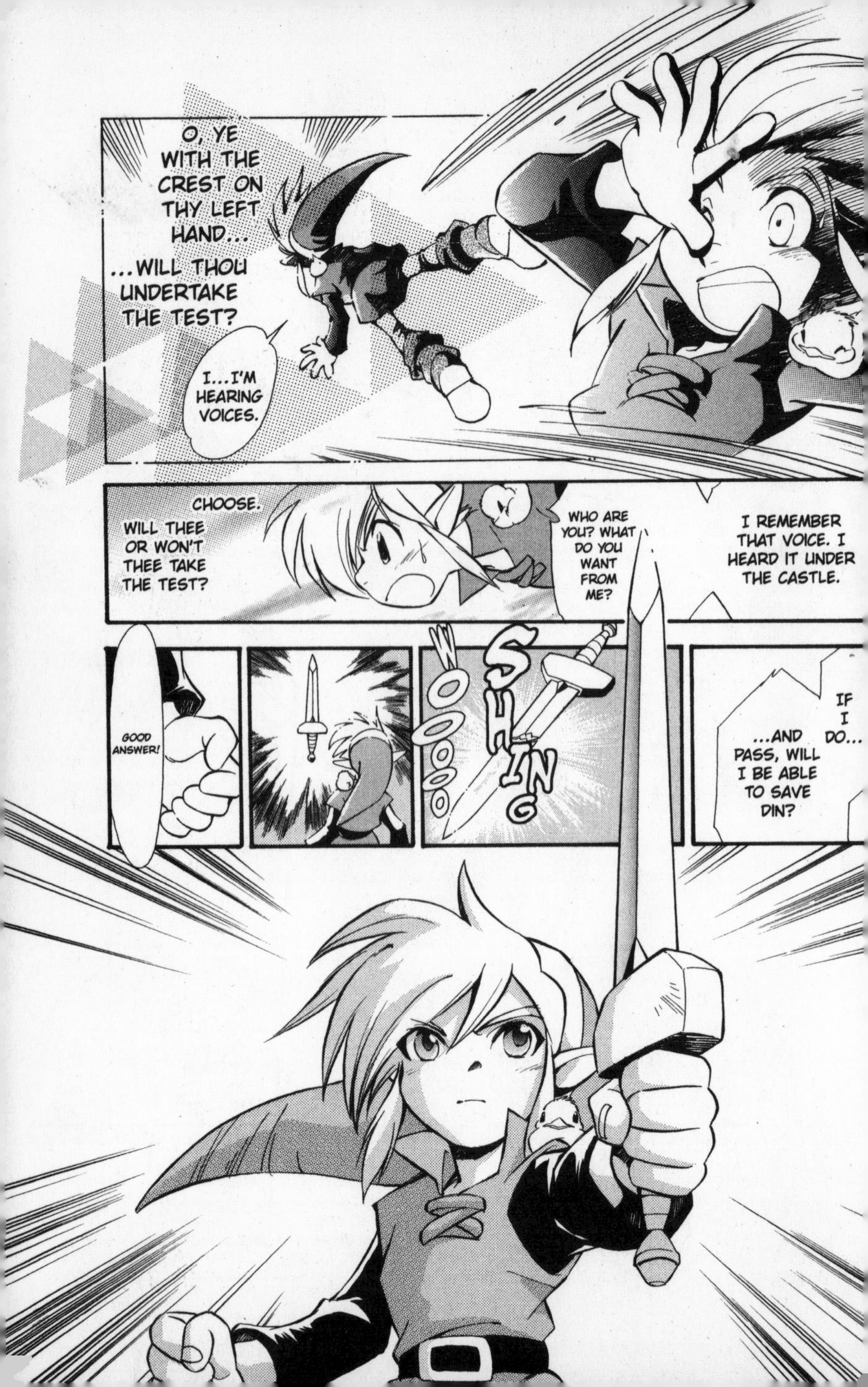
O, YE WITH THE CREST ON THY LEFT HAND... ...WILL THOU UNDERTAKE THE TEST?
I...I'M HEARING VOICES.
I REMEMBER THAT VOICE. I HEARD IT UNDER THE CASTLE.
WHO ARE YOU? WHAT DO YOU WANT FROM ME?
CHOOSE. WILL THEE OR WON'T THEE TAKE THE TEST?
IF I DO...
...AND PASS, WILL I BE ABLE TO SAVE DIN?
SHING
WOOOOO
GOOD ANSWER!

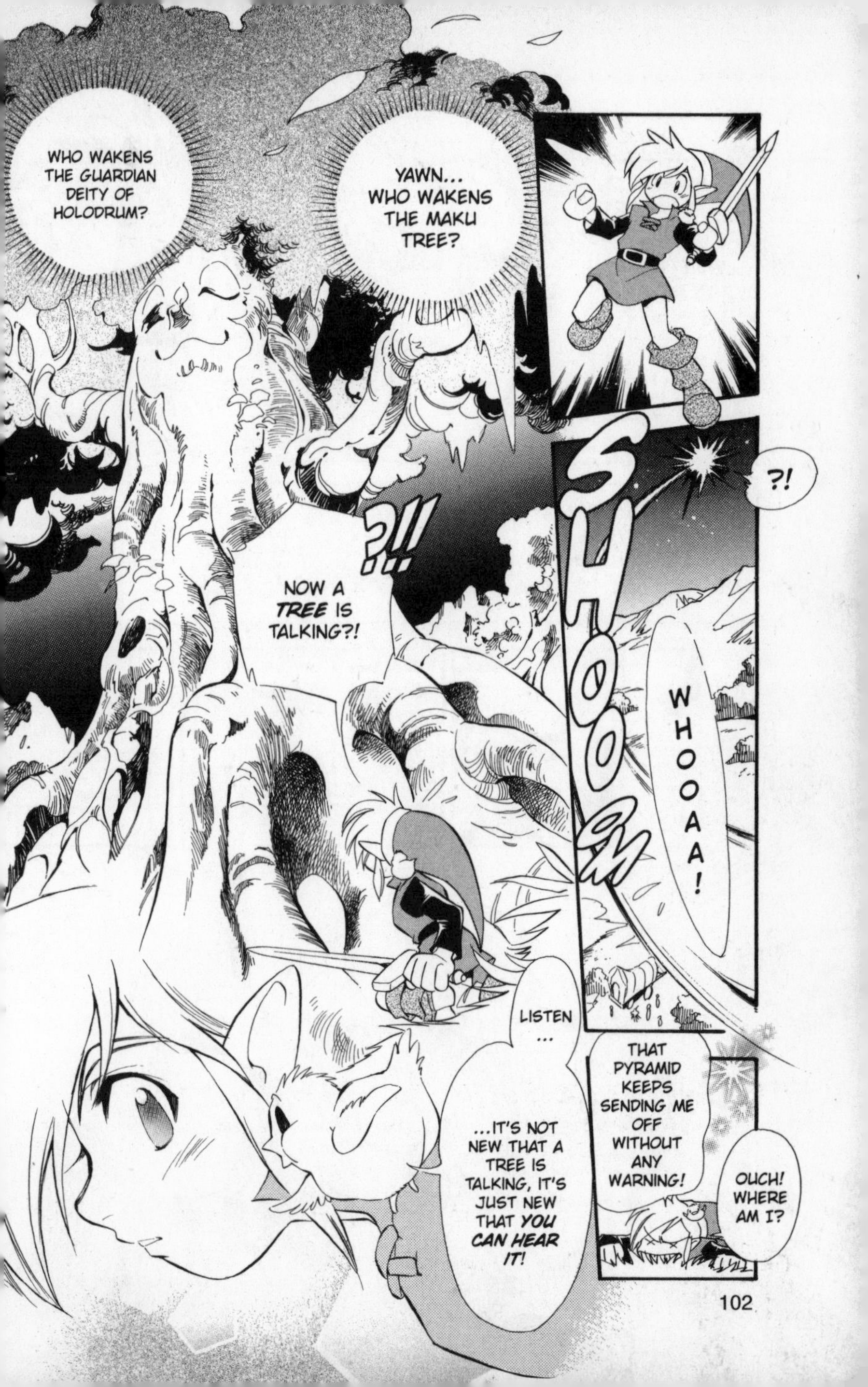
SHOOOOM
?!
WHOOAA!
OUCH! WHERE AM I?
THAT PYRAMID KEEPS SENDING ME OFF WITHOUT ANY WARNING!
YAWN... WHO WAKENS THE MAKU TREE?
WHO WAKENS THE GUARDIAN DEITY OF HOLODRUM?
?!!
NOW A *TREE* IS TALKING?!
LISTEN ...
...IT'S NOT NEW THAT A TREE IS TALKING, IT'S JUST NEW THAT *YOU CAN HEAR IT!*

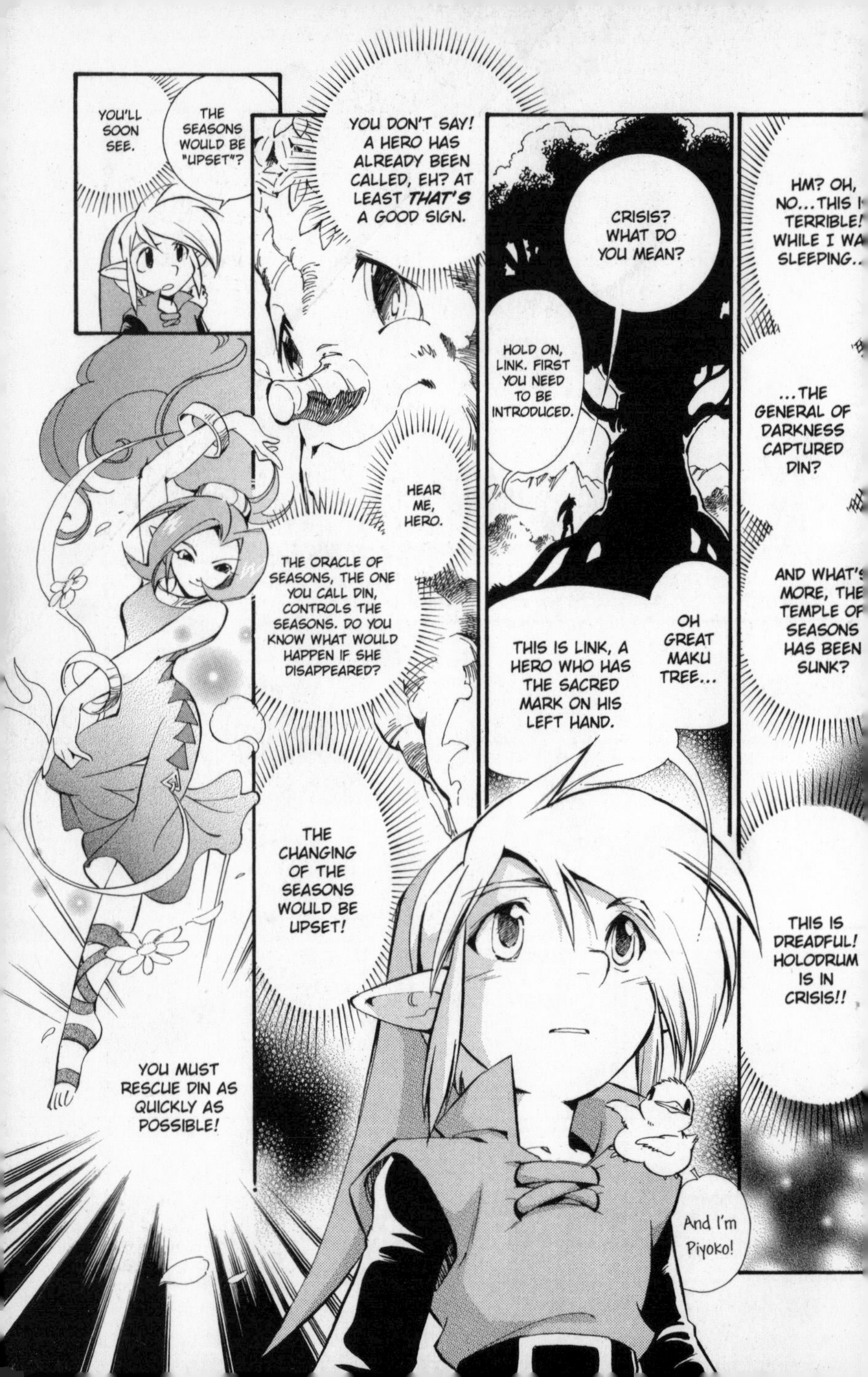
HM? OH, NO...THIS I TERRIBLE! WHILE I WA SLEEPING..
...THE GENERAL OF DARKNESS CAPTURED DIN?
AND WHAT'S MORE, THE TEMPLE OF SEASONS HAS BEEN SUNK?
THIS IS DREADFUL! HOLODRUM IS IN CRISIS!!
CRISIS? WHAT DO YOU MEAN?
HOLD ON, LINK. FIRST YOU NEED TO BE INTRODUCED.
OH GREAT MAKU TREE...
THIS IS LINK, A HERO WHO HAS THE SACRED MARK ON HIS LEFT HAND.
And I'm Piyoko!
YOU DON'T SAY! A HERO HAS ALREADY BEEN CALLED, EH? AT LEAST *THAT'S* A GOOD SIGN.
HEAR ME, HERO.
THE ORACLE OF SEASONS, THE ONE YOU CALL DIN, CONTROLS THE SEASONS. DO YOU KNOW WHAT WOULD HAPPEN IF SHE DISAPPEARED?
THE CHANGING OF THE SEASONS WOULD BE UPSET!
THE SEASONS WOULD BE "UPSET"?
YOU'LL SOON SEE.
YOU MUST RESCUE DIN AS QUICKLY AS POSSIBLE!

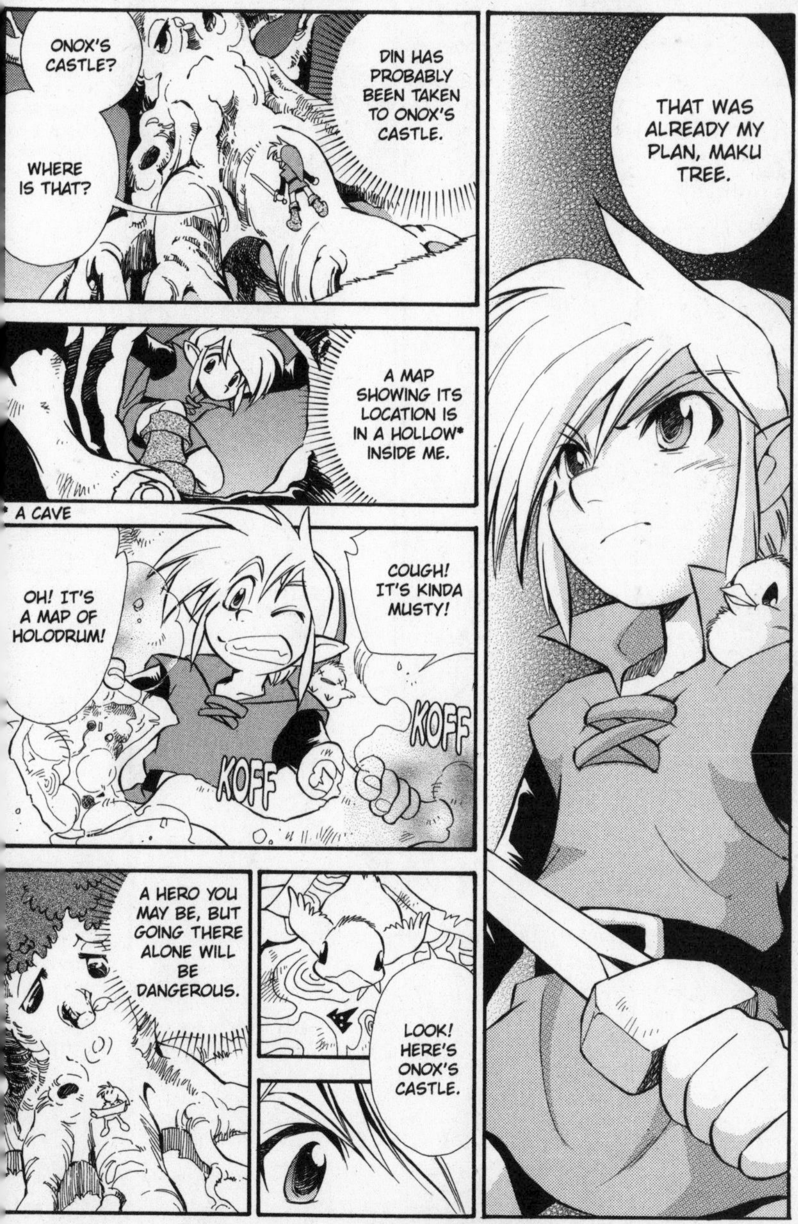
THAT WAS ALREADY MY PLAN, MAKU TREE.
DIN HAS PROBABLY BEEN TAKEN TO ONOX'S CASTLE.
ONOX'S CASTLE?
WHERE IS THAT?
A MAP SHOWING ITS LOCATION IS IN A HOLLOW* INSIDE ME.
COUGH! IT'S KINDA MUSTY!
KOFF
KOFF
OH! IT'S A MAP OF HOLODRUM!
LOOK! HERE'S ONOX'S CASTLE.
A HERO YOU MAY BE, BUT GOING THERE ALONE WILL BE DANGEROUS.

* A CAVE

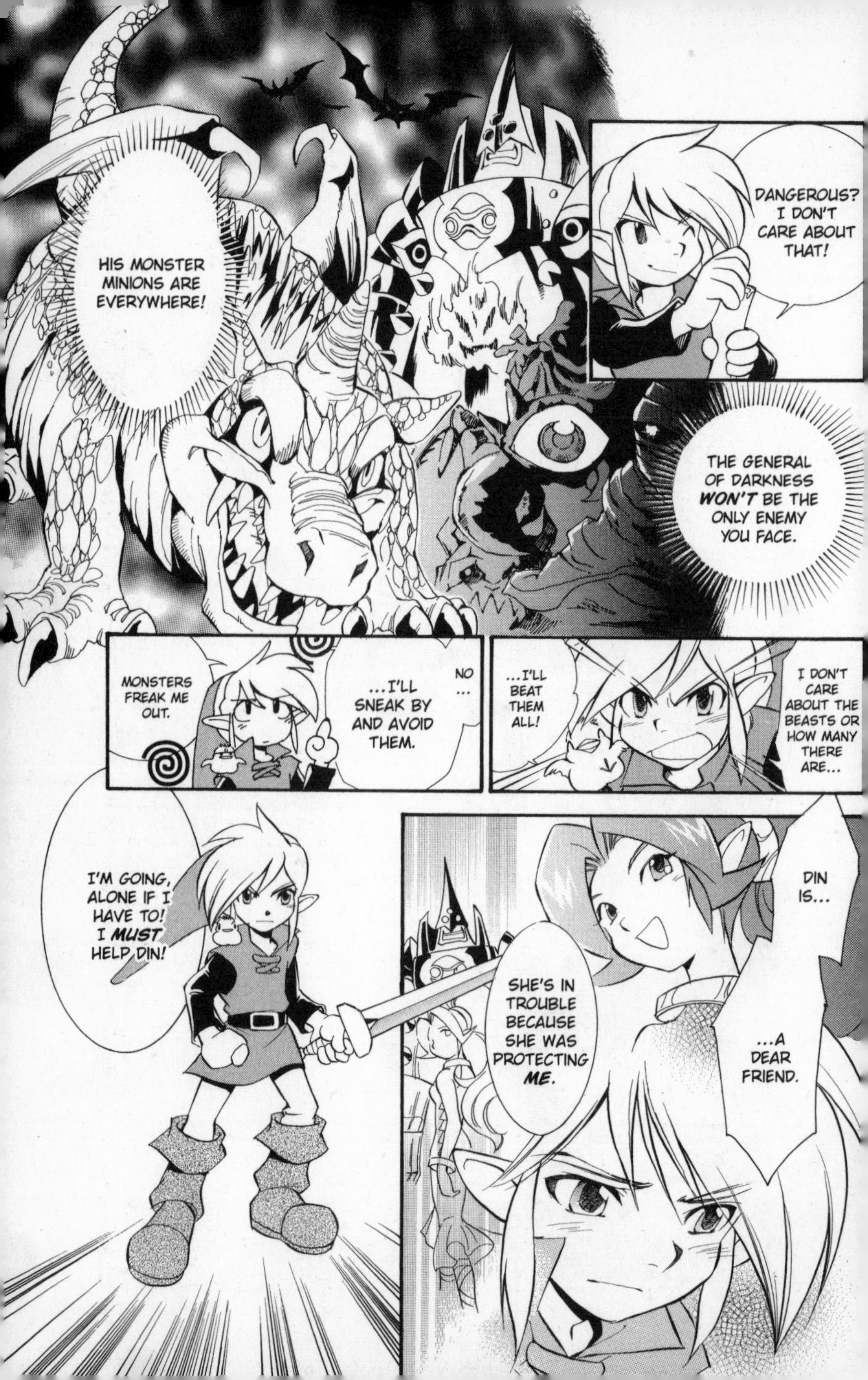
THE GENERAL OF DARKNESS *WON'T* BE THE ONLY ENEMY YOU FACE.
HIS MONSTER MINIONS ARE EVERYWHERE!
DANGEROUS? I DON'T CARE ABOUT THAT!
I DON'T CARE ABOUT THE BEASTS OR HOW MANY THERE ARE...
...I'LL BEAT THEM ALL!
NO ...
...I'LL SNEAK BY AND AVOID THEM.
MONSTERS FREAK ME OUT.
DIN IS...
...A DEAR FRIEND.
SHE'S IN TROUBLE BECAUSE SHE WAS PROTECTING *ME*.
I'M GOING, ALONE IF I HAVE TO! I *MUST* HELP DIN!

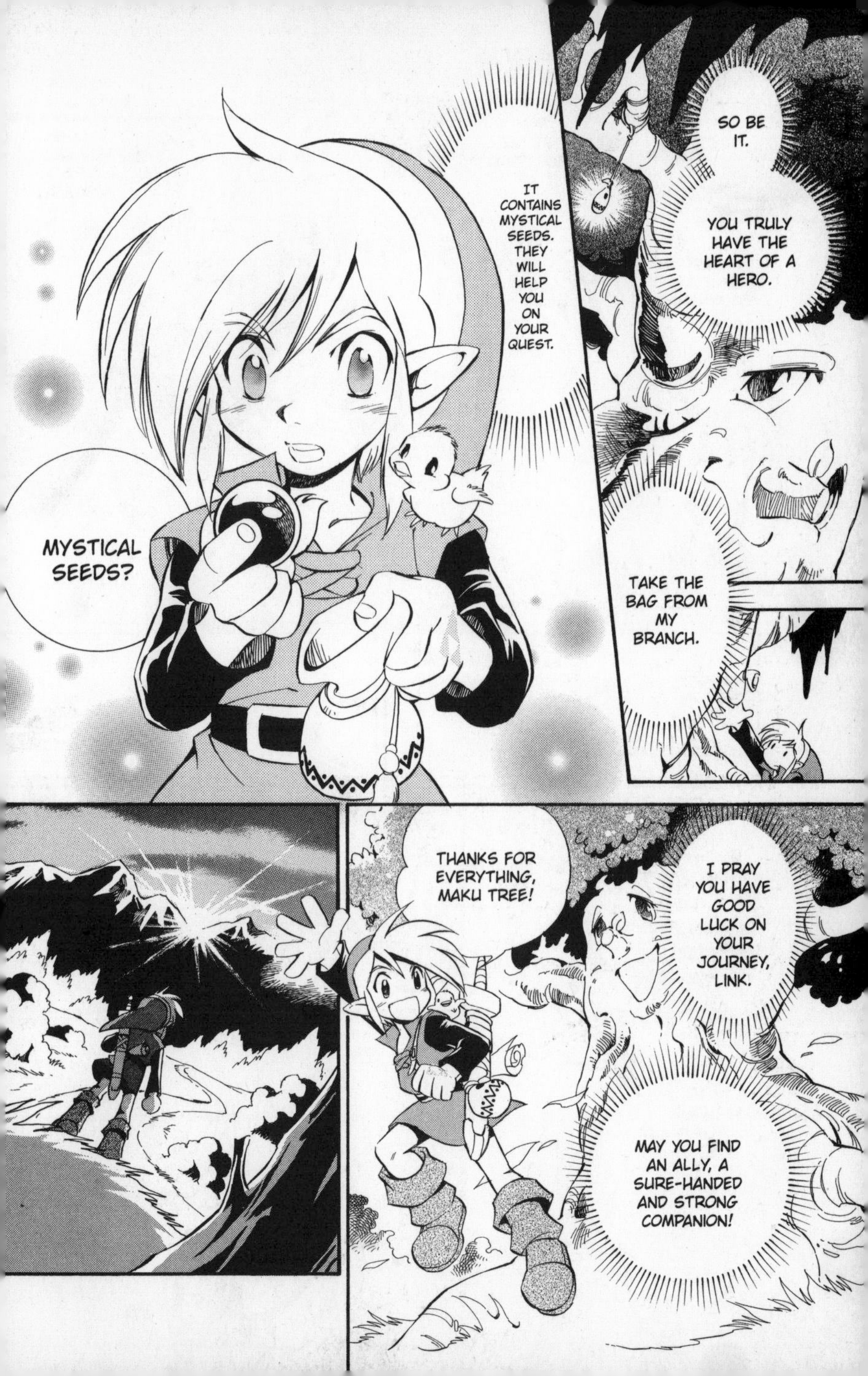
SO BE IT.
YOU TRULY HAVE THE HEART OF A HERO.
TAKE THE BAG FROM MY BRANCH.
IT CONTAINS MYSTICAL SEEDS. THEY WILL HELP YOU ON YOUR QUEST.
MYSTICAL SEEDS?
I PRAY YOU HAVE GOOD LUCK ON YOUR JOURNEY, LINK.
THANKS FOR EVERYTHING, MAKU TREE!
MAY YOU FIND AN ALLY, A SURE-HANDED AND STRONG COMPANION!

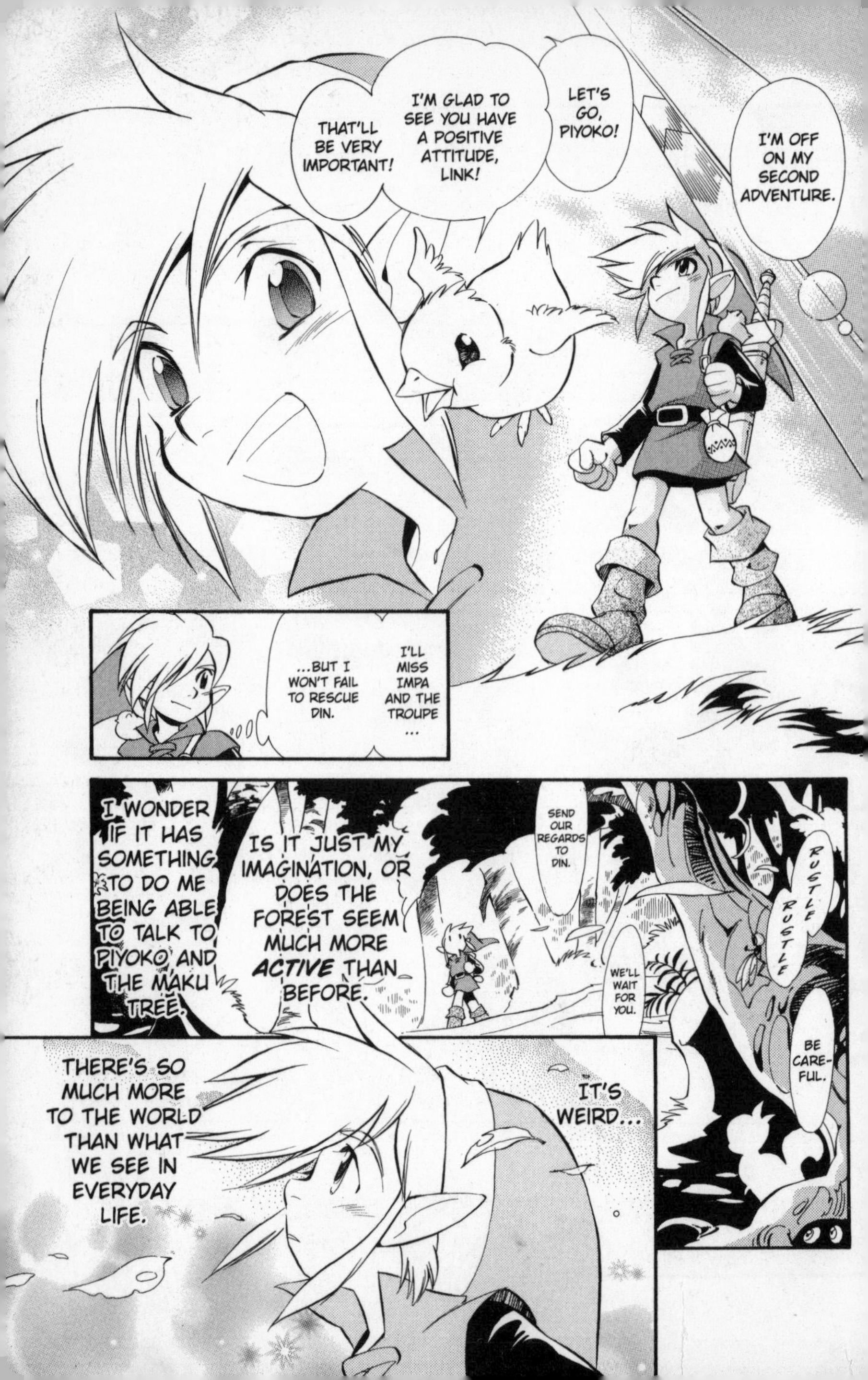
I'M OFF ON MY SECOND ADVENTURE.
LET'S GO, PIYOKO!
I'M GLAD TO SEE YOU HAVE A POSITIVE ATTITUDE, LINK!
THAT'LL BE VERY IMPORTANT!
I'LL MISS IMPA AND THE TROUPE ...
...BUT I WON'T FAIL TO RESCUE DIN.
RUSTLE
RUSTLE
SEND OUR REGARDS TO DIN.
WE'LL WAIT FOR YOU.
BE CARE-FUL.
IS IT JUST MY IMAGINATION, OR DOES THE FOREST SEEM MUCH MORE ACTIVE THAN BEFORE.
I WONDER IF IT HAS SOMETHING TO DO ME BEING ABLE TO TALK TO PIYOKO AND THE MAKU TREE.
IT'S WEIRD...
THERE'S SO MUCH MORE TO THE WORLD THAN WHAT WE SEE IN EVERYDAY LIFE.

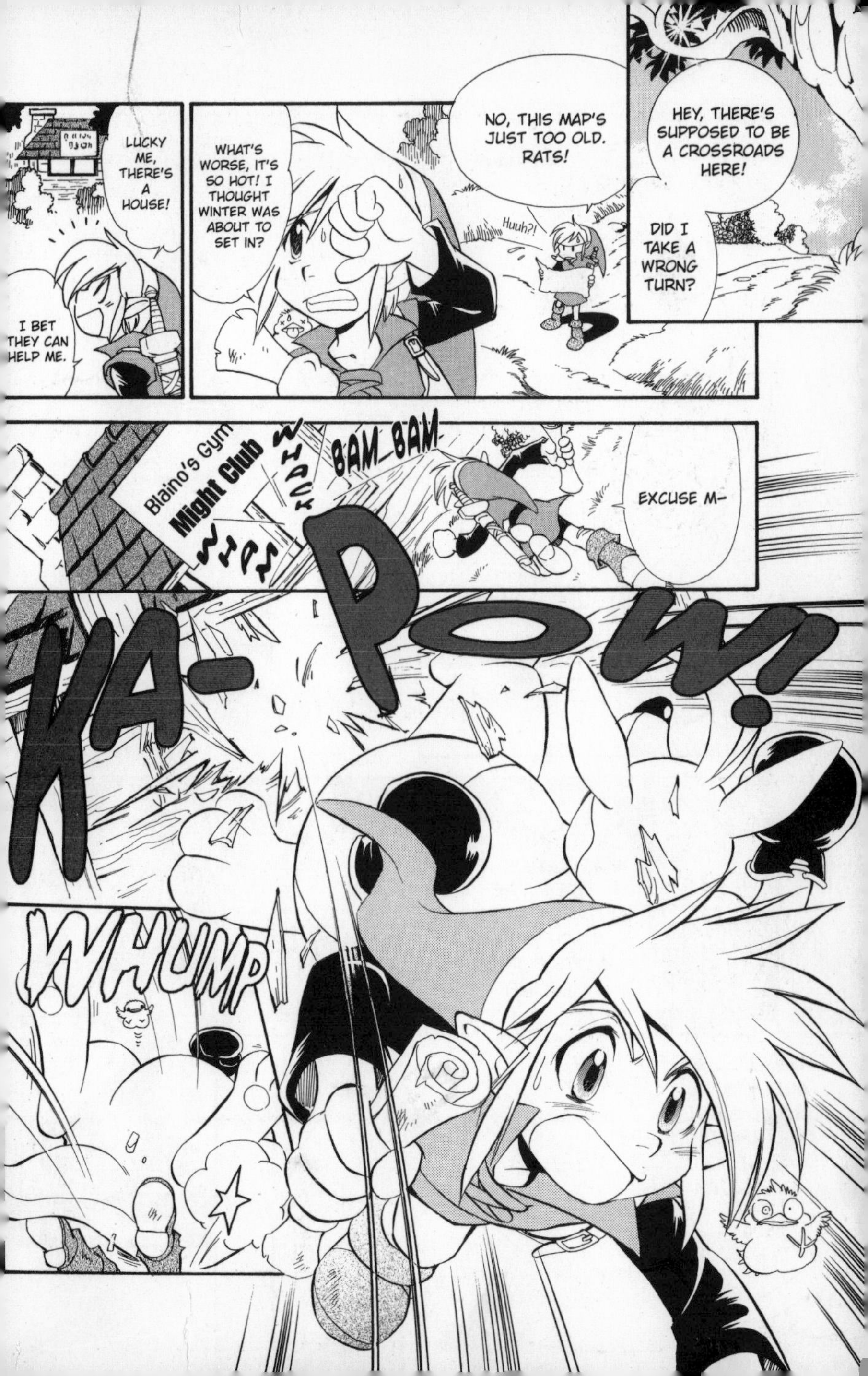
HEY, THERE'S SUPPOSED TO BE A CROSSROADS HERE!
DID I TAKE A WRONG TURN?
NO, THIS MAP'S JUST TOO OLD. RATS!
Huuh?!
WHAT'S WORSE, IT'S SO HOT! I THOUGHT WINTER WAS ABOUT TO SET IN?
LUCKY ME, THERE'S A HOUSE!
I BET THEY CAN HELP ME.
EXCUSE M-
BAM BAM
WHACK
Blaino's Gym
Might Club
KA-POW!
WHUMP

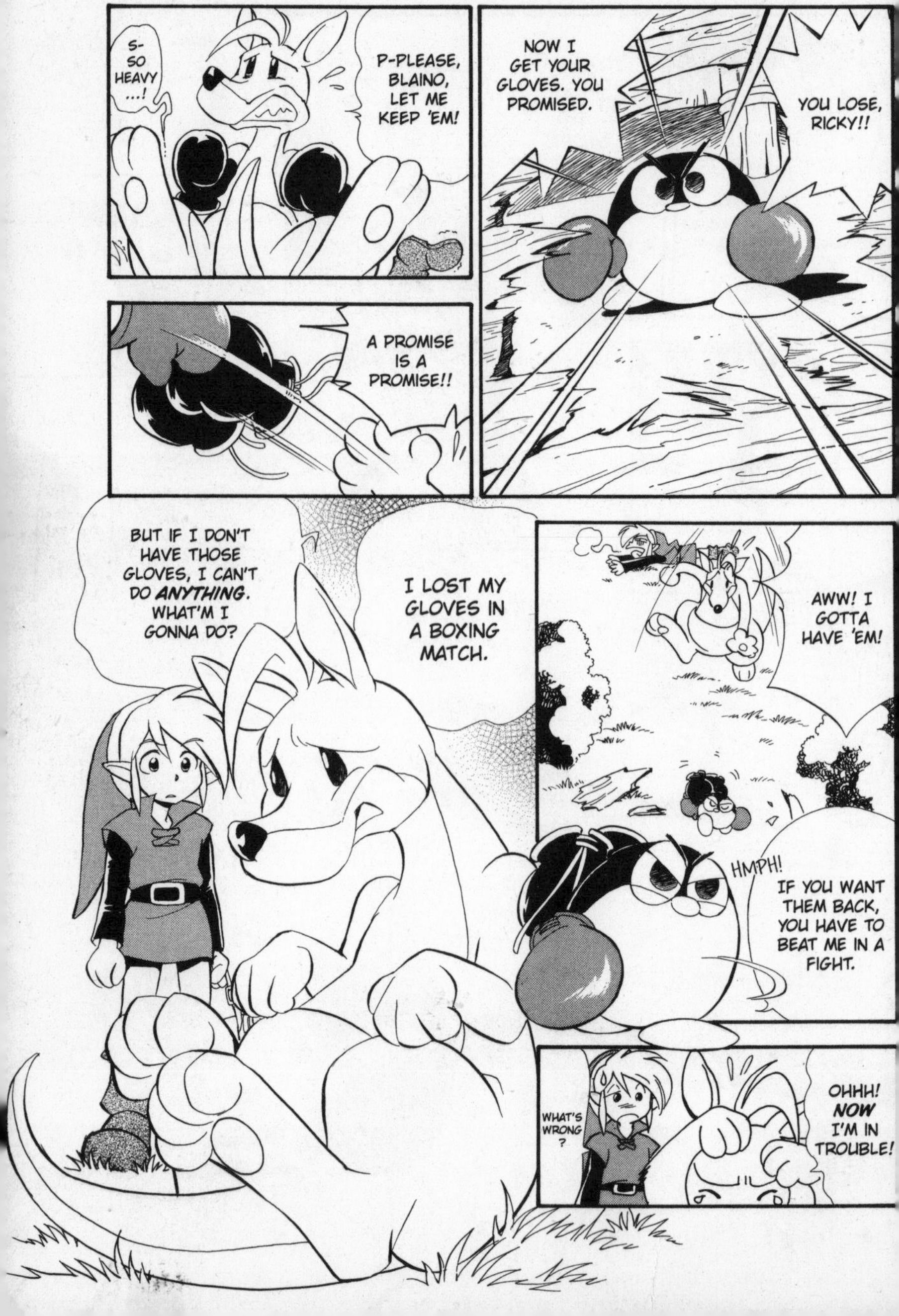
YOU LOSE, RICKY!!
NOW I GET YOUR GLOVES. YOU PROMISED.
P-PLEASE, BLAINO, LET ME KEEP 'EM!
S- SO HEAVY ...!
A PROMISE IS A PROMISE!!
AWW! I GOTTA HAVE 'EM!
HMPH!
IF YOU WANT THEM BACK, YOU HAVE TO BEAT ME IN A FIGHT.
OHHH! *NOW* I'M IN TROUBLE!
WHAT'S WRONG?
I LOST MY GLOVES IN A BOXING MATCH.
BUT IF I DON'T HAVE THOSE GLOVES, I CAN'T DO *ANYTHING*. WHAT'M I GONNA DO?

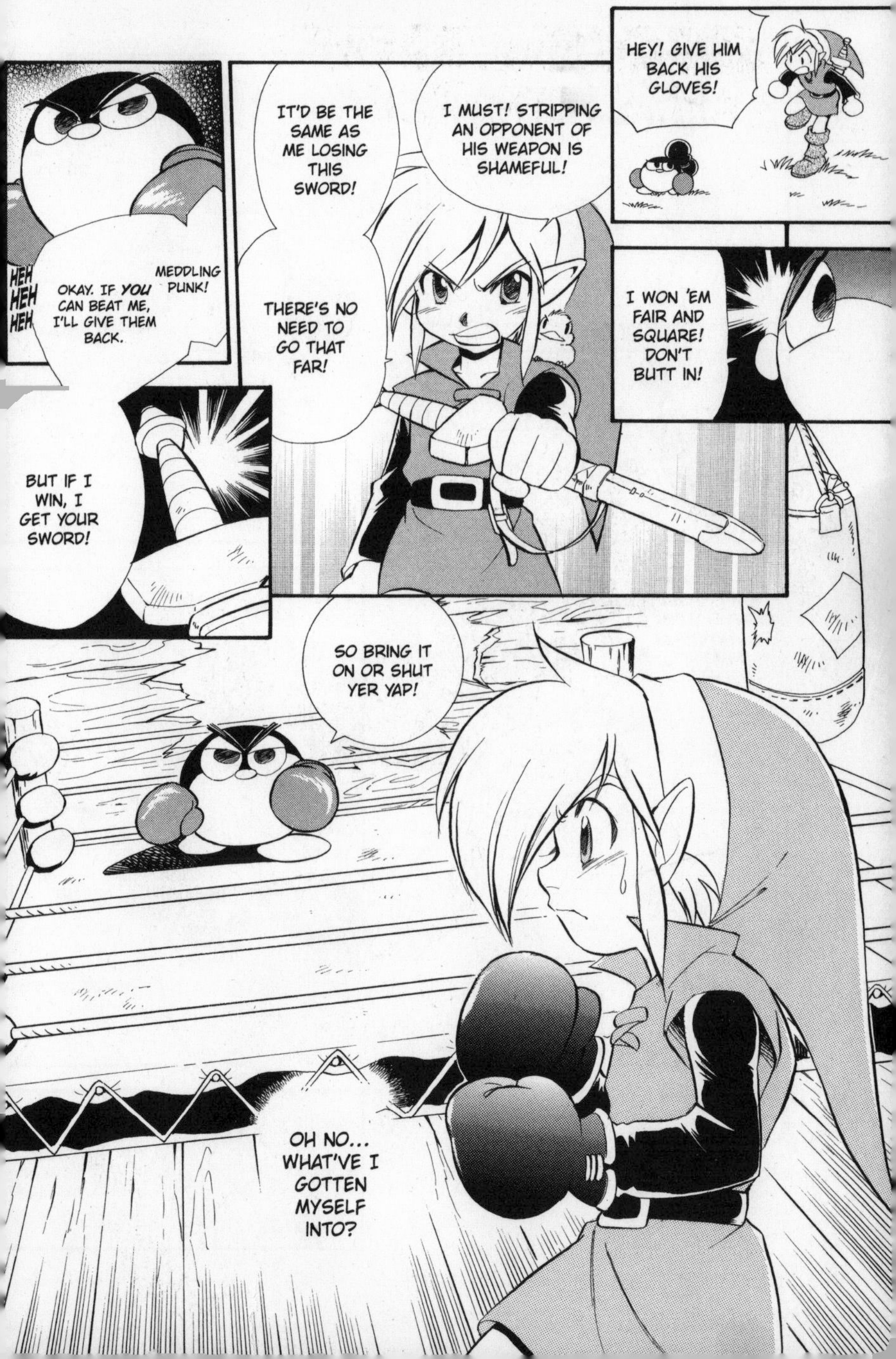
HEY! GIVE HIM BACK HIS GLOVES!
I WON 'EM FAIR AND SQUARE! DON'T BUTT IN!
HEH HEH HEH
MEDDLING PUNK!
OKAY. IF *YOU* CAN BEAT ME, I'LL GIVE THEM BACK.
BUT IF I WIN, I GET YOUR SWORD!
THERE'S NO NEED TO GO THAT FAR!
I MUST! STRIPPING AN OPPONENT OF HIS WEAPON IS SHAMEFUL!
IT'D BE THE SAME AS ME LOSING THIS SWORD!
SO BRING IT ON OR SHUT YER YAP!
OH NO... WHAT'VE I GOTTEN MYSELF INTO?

CHAPTER 6
A NEW FRIEND: RICKY

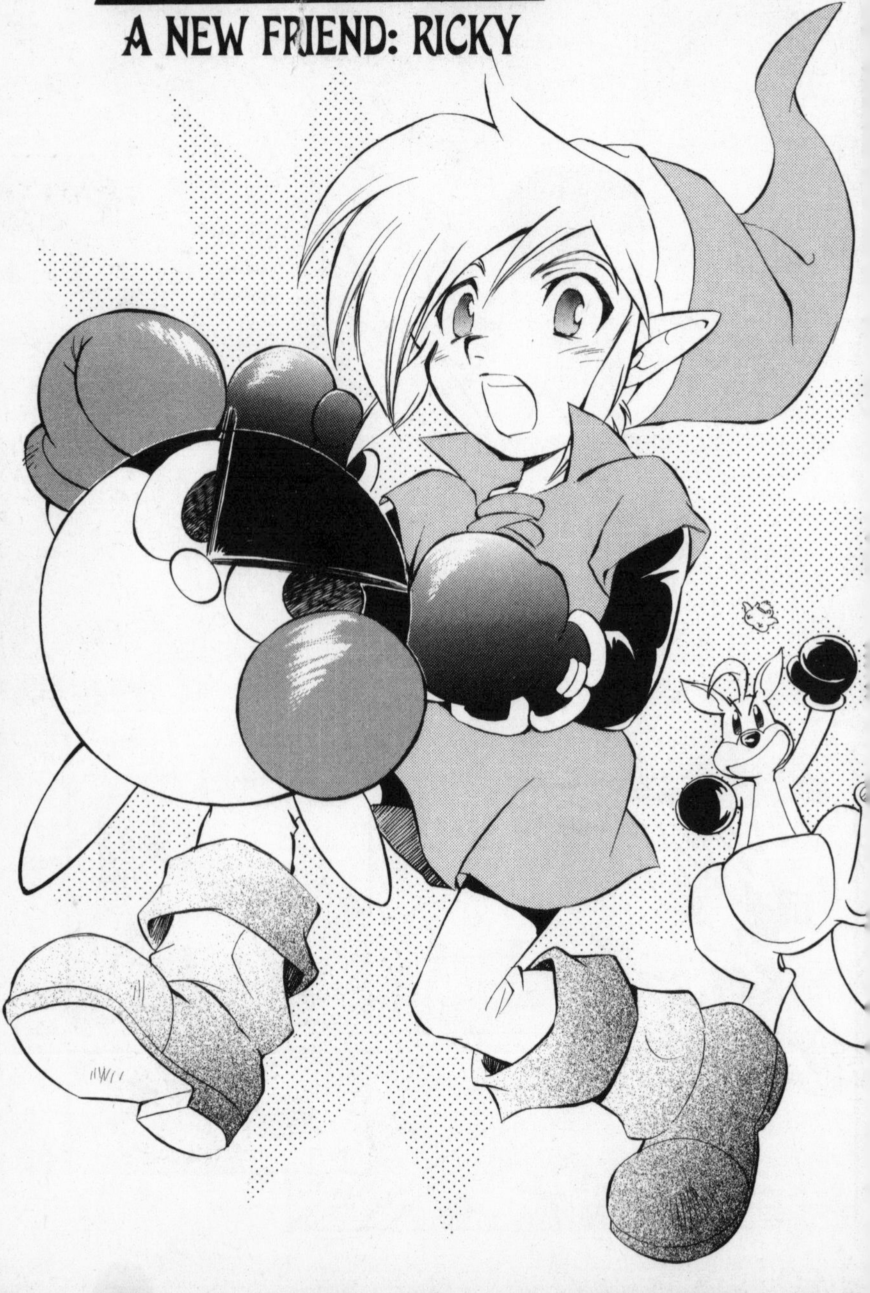

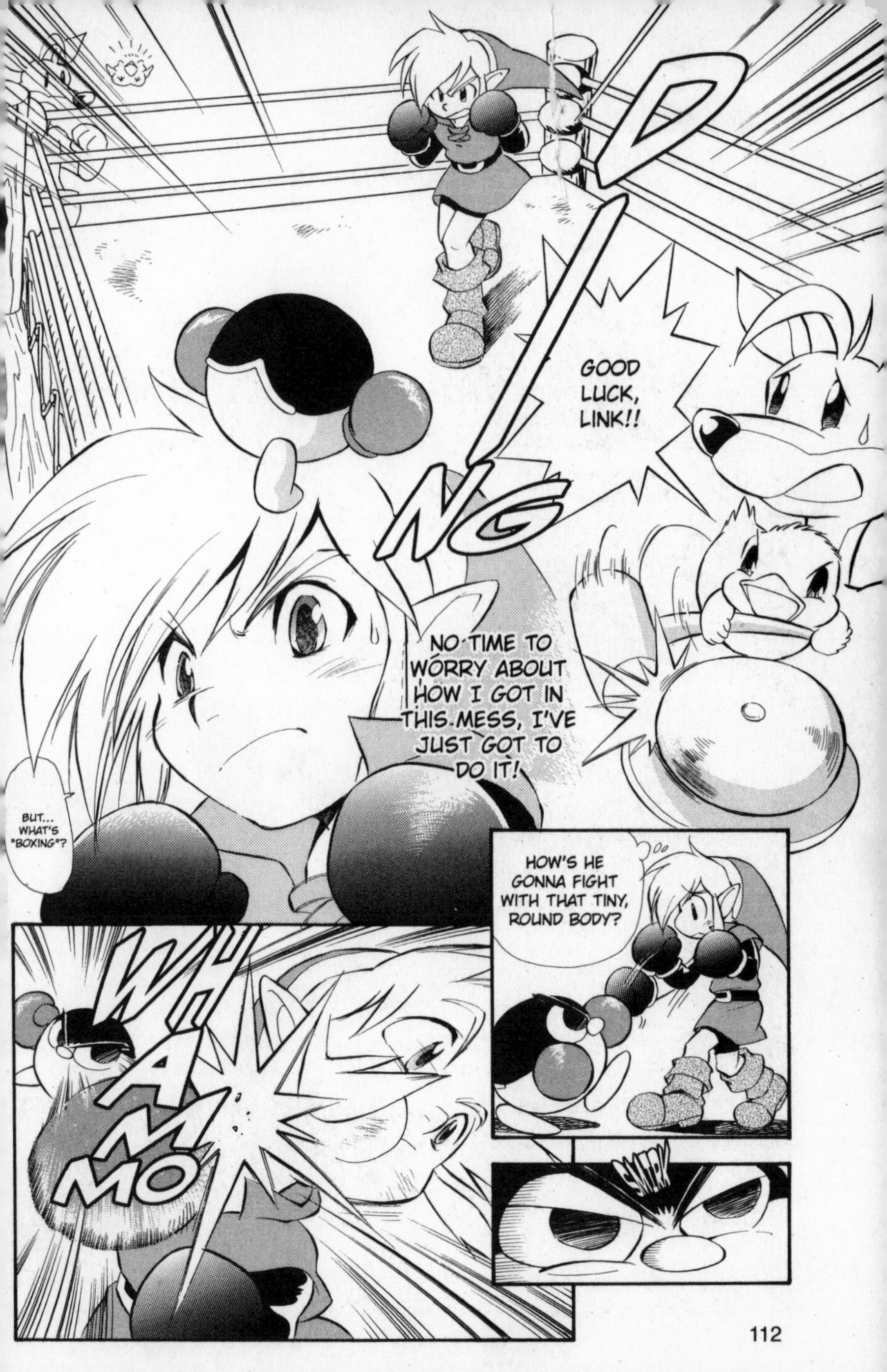
DING
GOOD LUCK, LINK!!
NO TIME TO WORRY ABOUT HOW I GOT IN THIS MESS, I'VE JUST GOT TO DO IT!
BUT... WHAT'S "BOXING"?
HOW'S HE GONNA FIGHT WITH THAT TINY, ROUND BODY?
WHAMMO

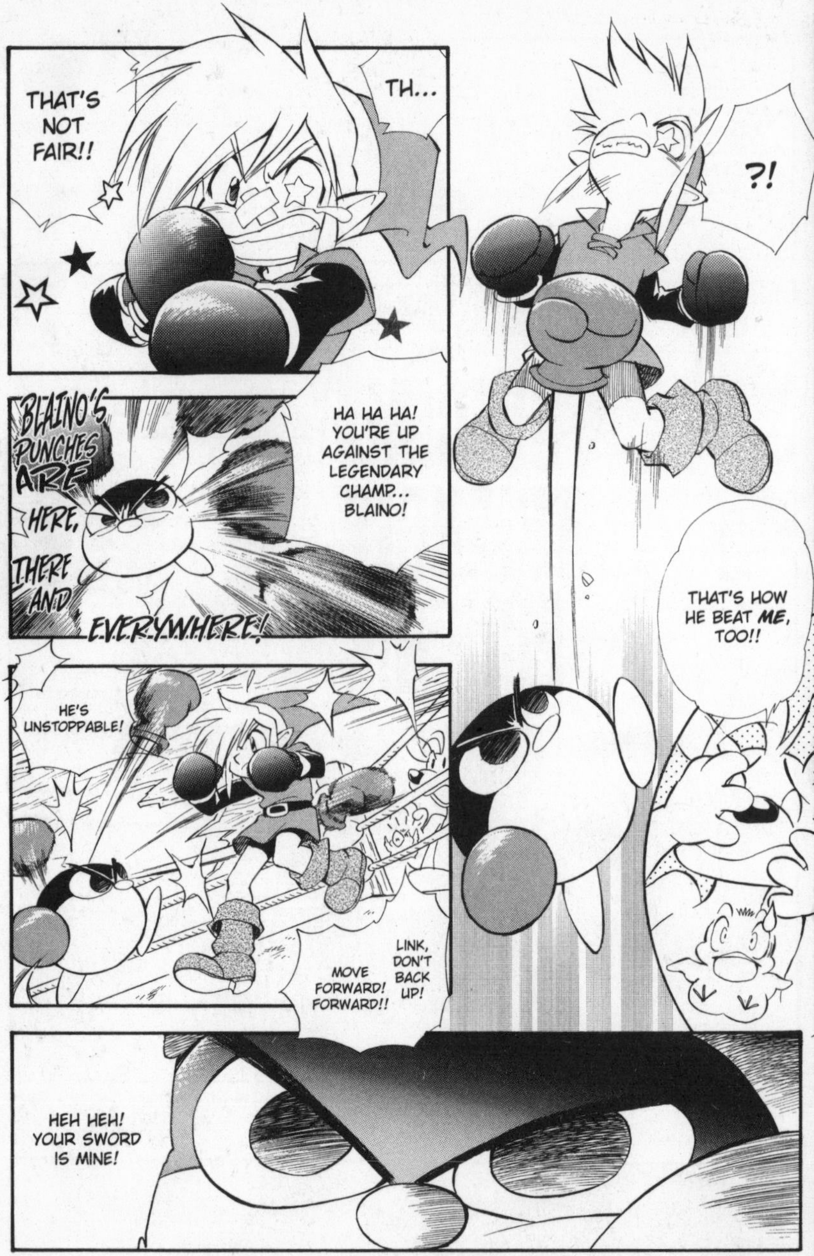
?!
THAT'S HOW HE BEAT ME, TOO!!
TH...
THAT'S NOT FAIR!!
HA HA HA! YOU'RE UP AGAINST THE LEGENDARY CHAMP... BLAINO!
BLAINO'S PUNCHES ARE HERE, THERE AND EVERYWHERE!
HE'S UNSTOPPABLE!
LINK, DON'T BACK UP!
MOVE FORWARD! FORWARD!!
HEH HEH! YOUR SWORD IS MINE!

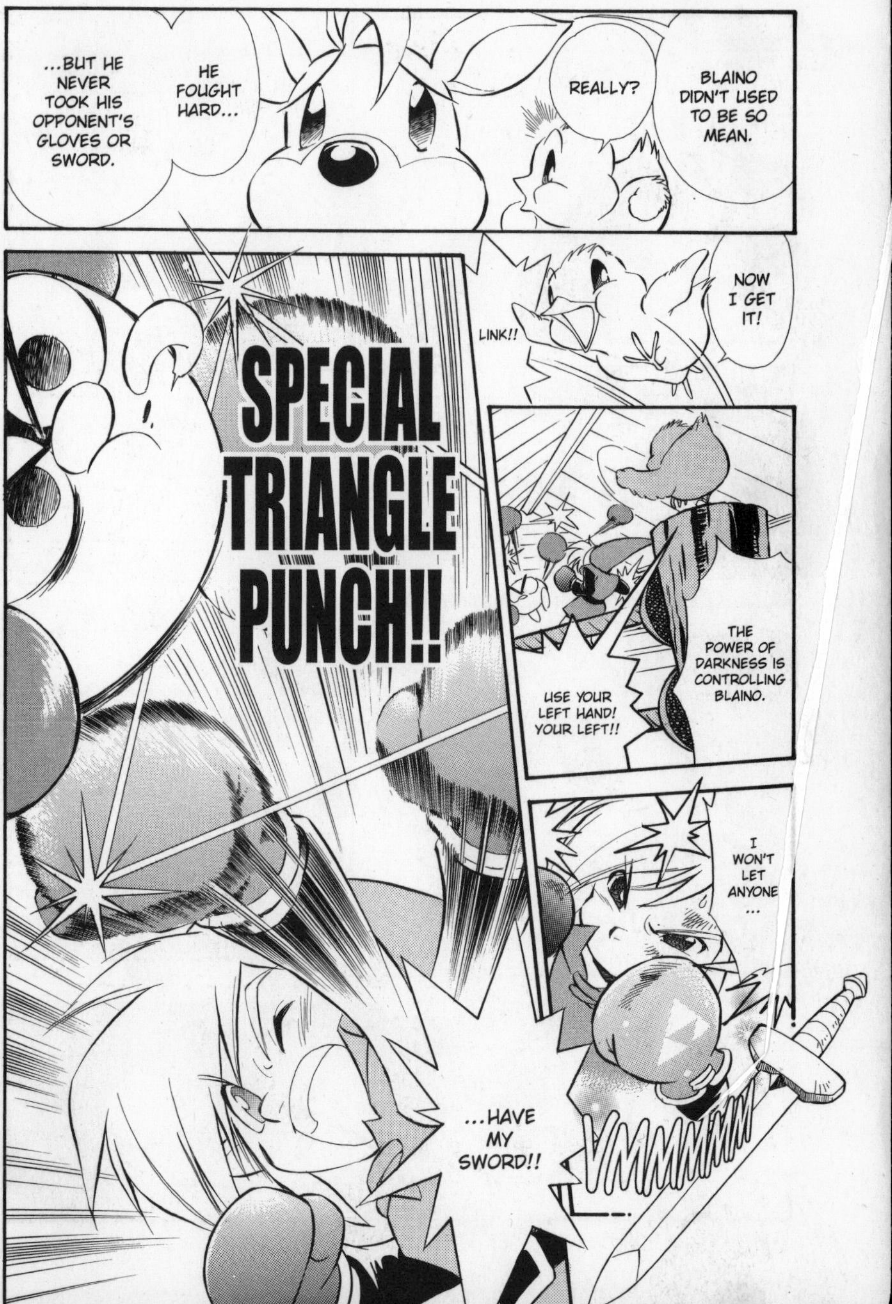
BLAINO DIDN'T USED TO BE SO MEAN.
REALLY?
HE FOUGHT HARD...
...BUT HE NEVER TOOK HIS OPPONENT'S GLOVES OR SWORD.
NOW I GET IT!
LINK!!
THE POWER OF DARKNESS IS CONTROLLING BLAINO.
USE YOUR LEFT HAND! YOUR LEFT!!
I WON'T LET ANYONE ...
...HAVE MY SWORD!!
VMMMMM
SPECIAL TRIANGLE PUNCH!!

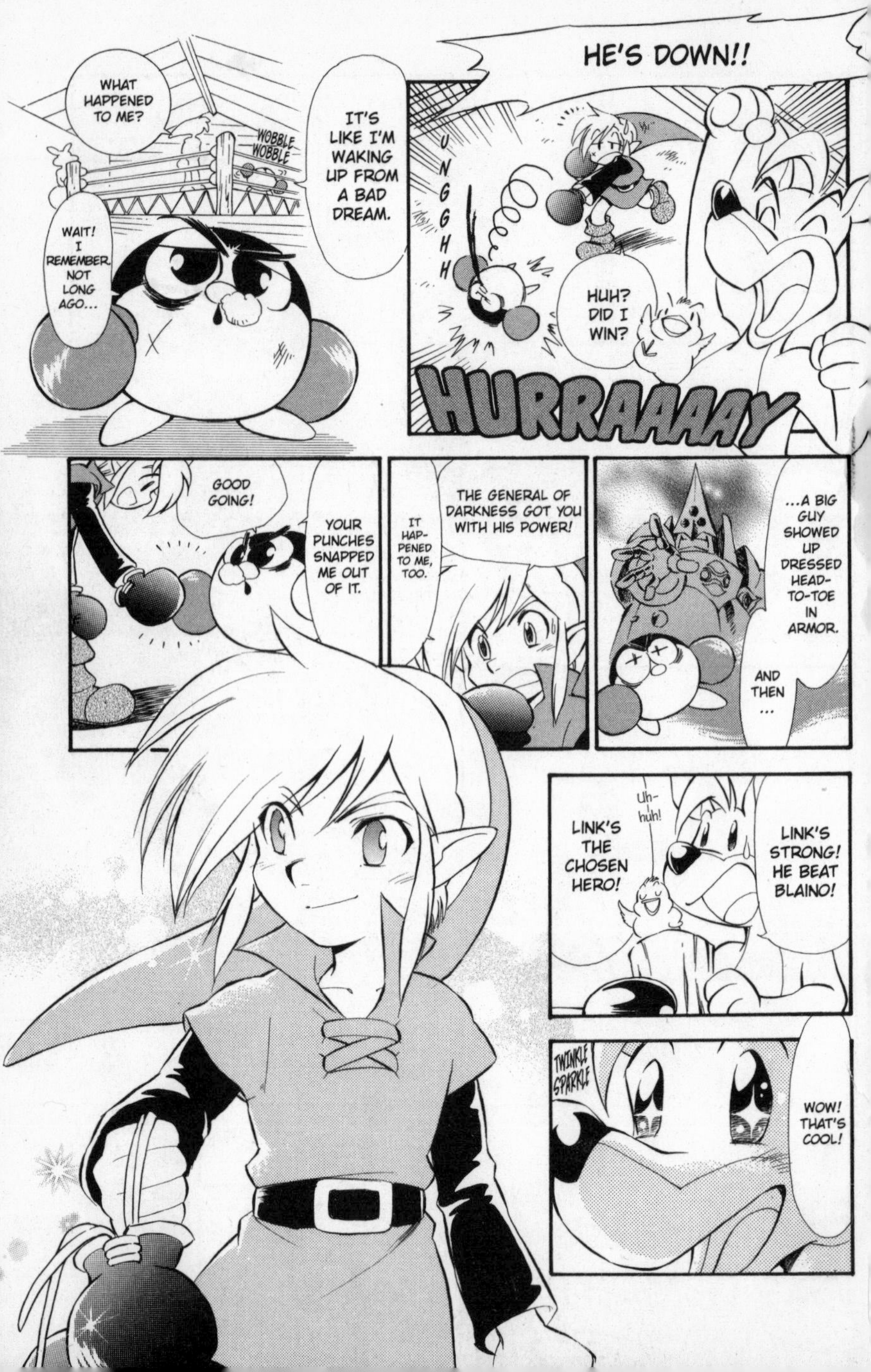
HE'S DOWN!!
UNGGHH
HUH? DID I WIN?
HURRAAAAY
IT'S LIKE I'M WAKING UP FROM A BAD DREAM.
WHAT HAPPENED TO ME?
WOBBLE WOBBLE
WAIT! I REMEMBER. NOT LONG AGO...
...A BIG GUY SHOWED UP DRESSED HEAD-TO-TOE IN ARMOR.
AND THEN ...
THE GENERAL OF DARKNESS GOT YOU WITH HIS POWER!
IT HAPPENED TO ME, TOO.
YOUR PUNCHES SNAPPED ME OUT OF IT.
GOOD GOING!
LINK'S STRONG! HE BEAT BLAINO!
Uh-huh!
LINK'S THE CHOSEN HERO!
WOW! THAT'S COOL!
TWINKLE SPARKLE

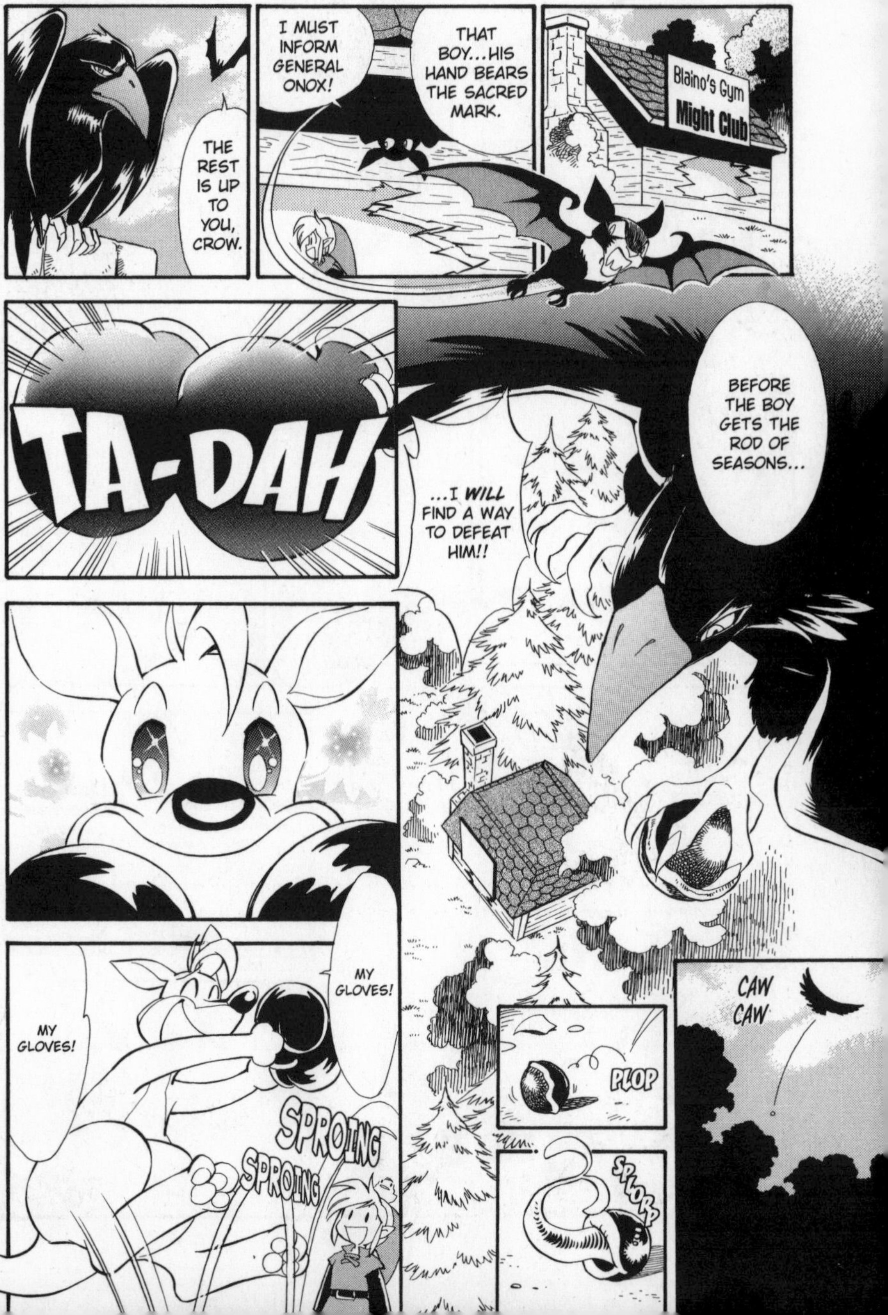
Blaino's Gym
Might Club
THAT BOY...HIS HAND BEARS THE SACRED MARK.
I MUST INFORM GENERAL ONOX!
THE REST IS UP TO YOU, CROW.
BEFORE THE BOY GETS THE ROD OF SEASONS...
...I *WILL* FIND A WAY TO DEFEAT HIM!!
TA-DAH
CAW CAW
PLOP
SPLORP
MY GLOVES!
MY GLOVES!
SPROING
SPROING

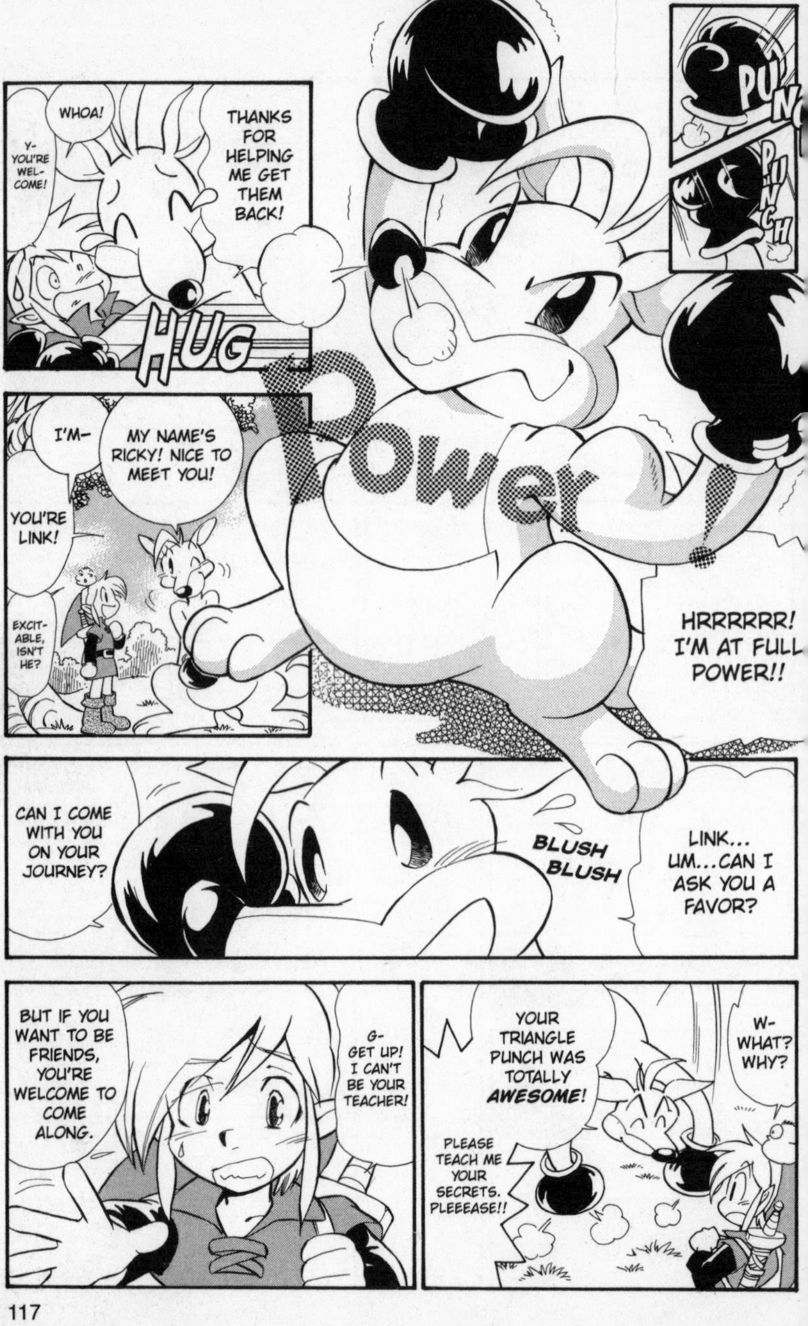
PUNCH
PUNCH
POWER!
HRRRRRR! I'M AT FULL POWER!!
THANKS FOR HELPING ME GET THEM BACK!
WHOA!
Y-YOU'RE WEL-COME!
HUG
MY NAME'S RICKY! NICE TO MEET YOU!
I'M-
YOU'RE LINK!
EXCIT-ABLE, ISN'T HE?
LINK... UM...CAN I ASK YOU A FAVOR?
BLUSH BLUSH
CAN I COME WITH YOU ON YOUR JOURNEY?
W-WHAT? WHY?
YOUR TRIANGLE PUNCH WAS TOTALLY AWESOME!
PLEASE TEACH ME YOUR SECRETS. PLEEEASE!!
G-GET UP! I CAN'T BE YOUR TEACHER!
BUT IF YOU WANT TO BE FRIENDS, YOU'RE WELCOME TO COME ALONG.

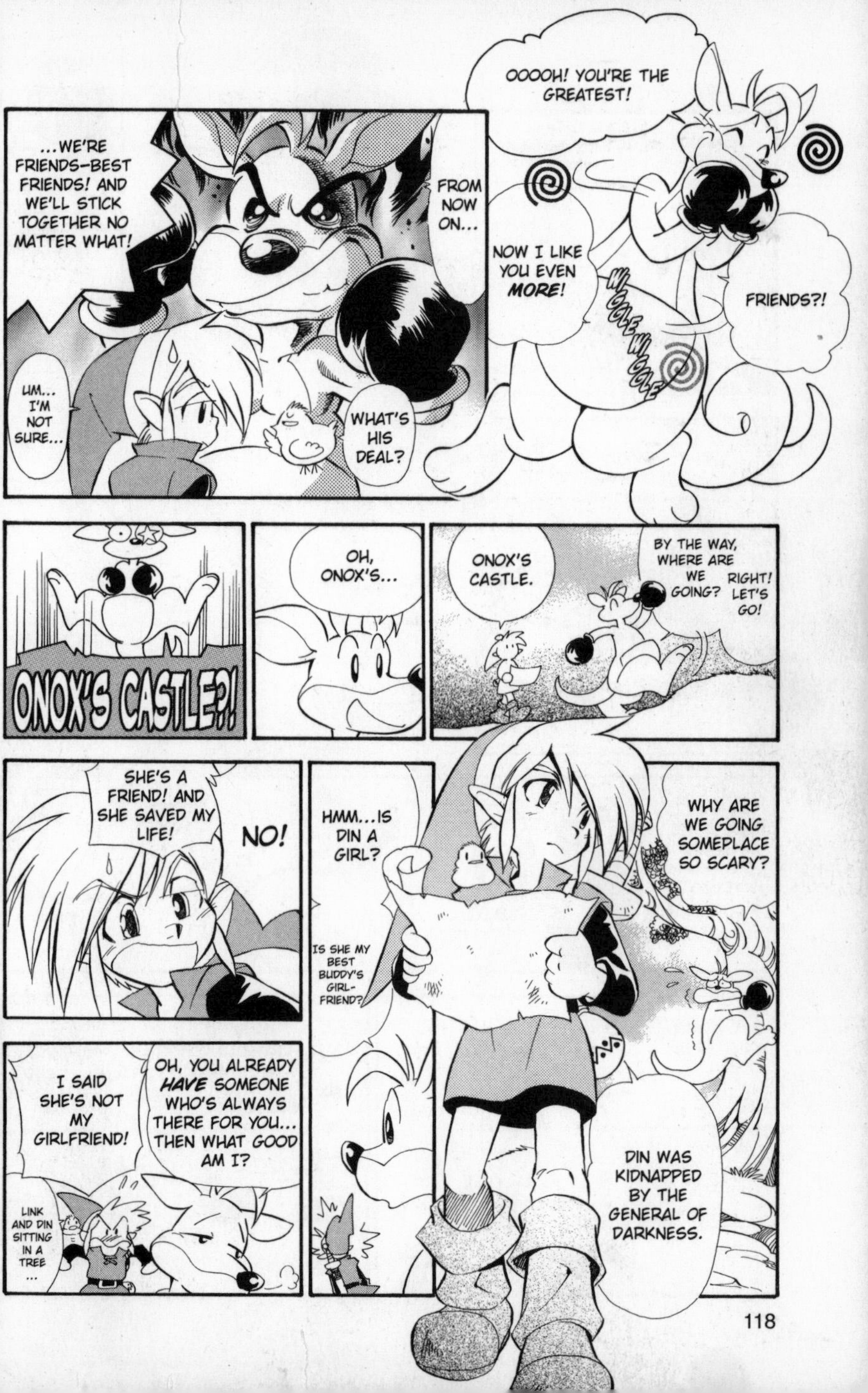
FROM NOW ON...
...WE'RE FRIENDS—BEST FRIENDS! AND WE'LL STICK TOGETHER NO MATTER WHAT!
WHAT'S HIS DEAL?
UM... I'M NOT SURE...
FRIENDS?!
NOW I LIKE YOU EVEN ***MORE!***
WIGGLE WIGGLE
OOOOH! YOU'RE THE GREATEST!
RIGHT! LET'S GO!
BY THE WAY, WHERE ARE WE GOING?
ONOX'S CASTLE.
OH, ONOX'S...
ONOX'S CASTLE?!
WHY ARE WE GOING SOMEPLACE SO SCARY?
DIN WAS KIDNAPPED BY THE GENERAL OF DARKNESS.
HMM...IS DIN A GIRL?
IS SHE MY BEST BUDDY'S GIRL-FRIEND?
NO!
SHE'S A FRIEND! AND SHE SAVED MY LIFE!
OH, YOU ALREADY ***HAVE*** SOMEONE WHO'S ALWAYS THERE FOR YOU... THEN WHAT GOOD AM I?
I SAID SHE'S NOT MY GIRLFRIEND!
LINK AND DIN SITTING IN A TREE ...

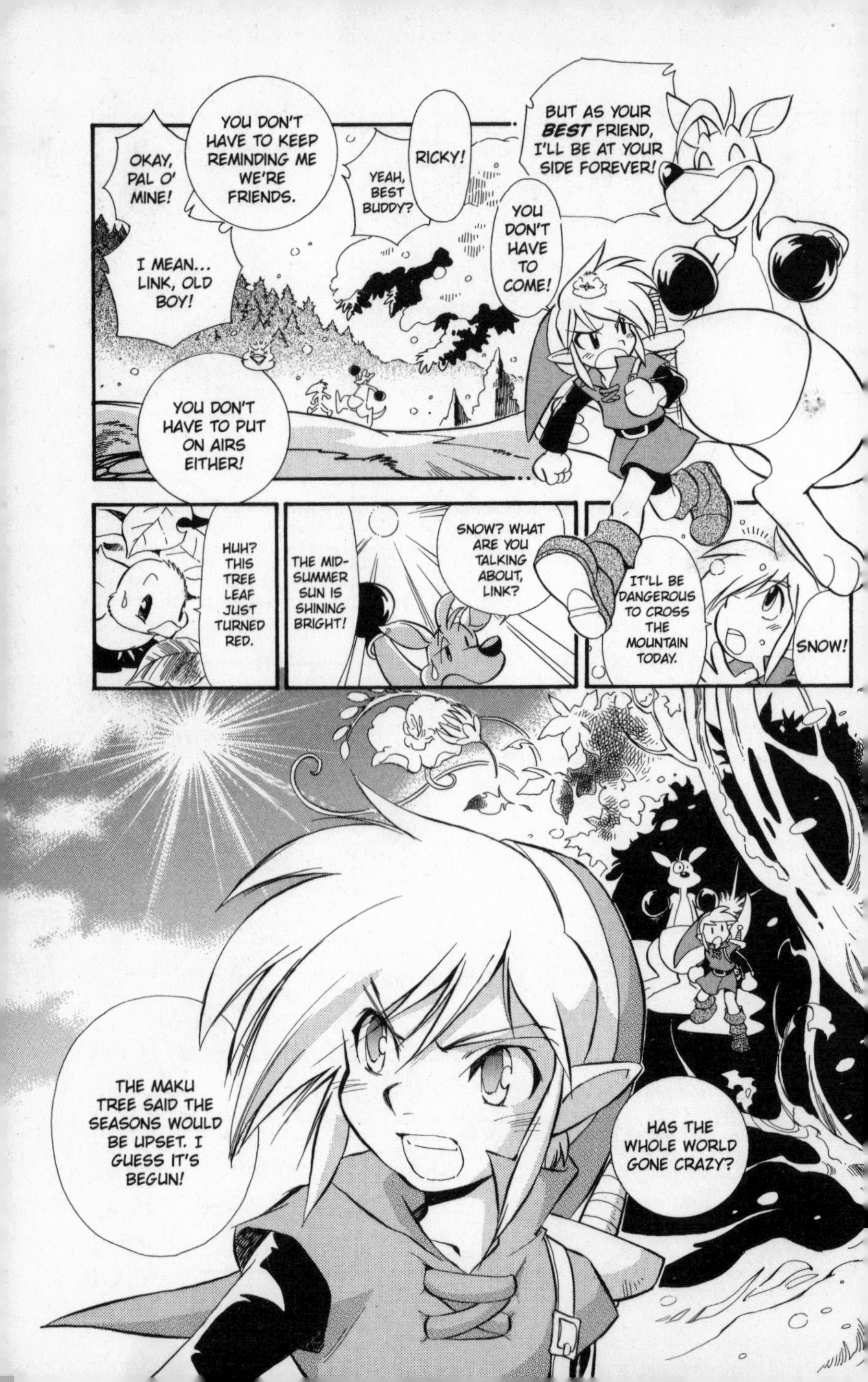
BUT AS YOUR **BEST** FRIEND, I'LL BE AT YOUR SIDE FOREVER!
YOU DON'T HAVE TO COME!
RICKY!
YEAH, BEST BUDDY?
YOU DON'T HAVE TO KEEP REMINDING ME WE'RE FRIENDS.
OKAY, PAL O' MINE!
I MEAN... LINK, OLD BOY!
YOU DON'T HAVE TO PUT ON AIRS EITHER!
SNOW!
IT'LL BE DANGEROUS TO CROSS THE MOUNTAIN TODAY.
SNOW? WHAT ARE YOU TALKING ABOUT, LINK?
THE MID-SUMMER SUN IS SHINING BRIGHT!
HUH? THIS TREE LEAF JUST TURNED RED.
HAS THE WHOLE WORLD GONE CRAZY?
THE MAKU TREE SAID THE SEASONS WOULD BE UPSET. I GUESS IT'S BEGUN!

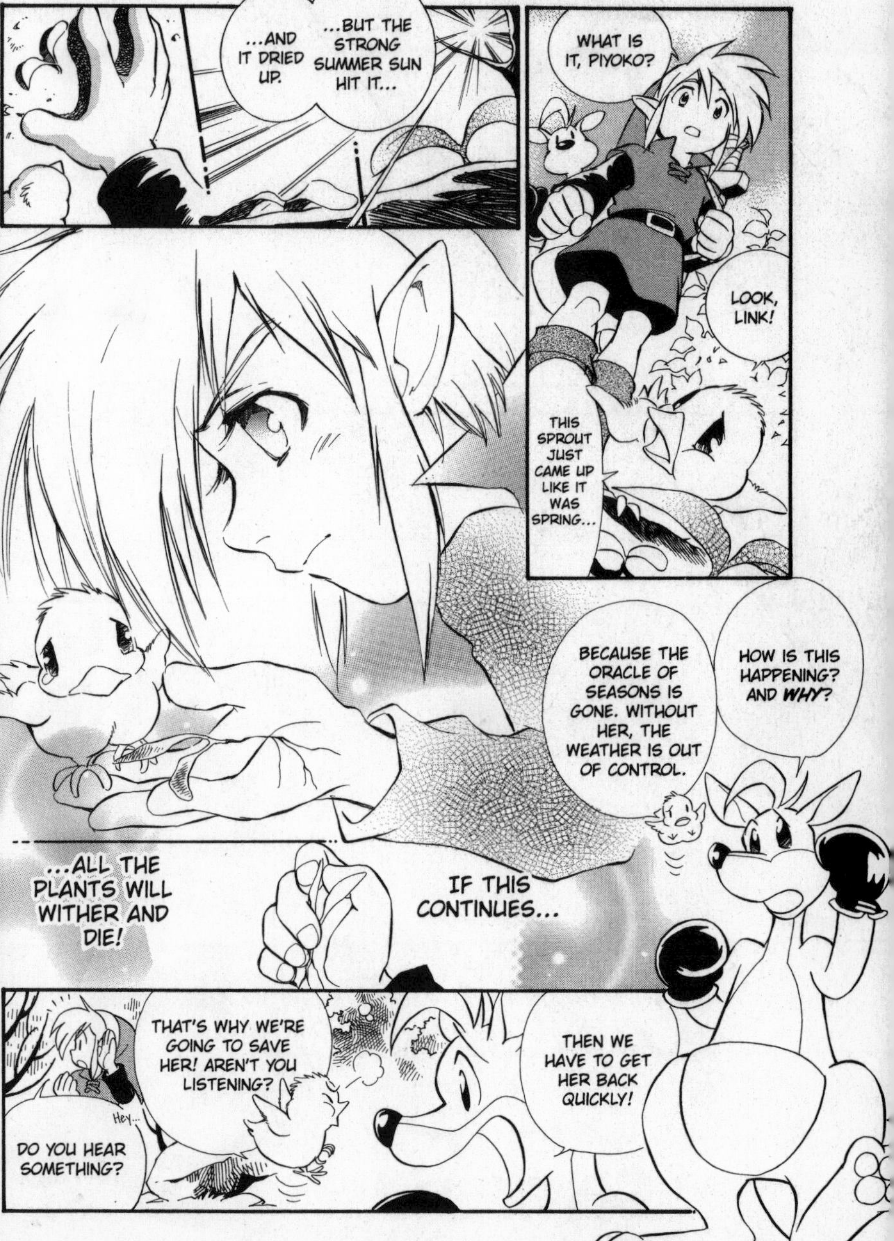
WHAT IS IT, PIYOKO?
LOOK, LINK!
THIS SPROUT JUST CAME UP LIKE IT WAS SPRING...
...BUT THE STRONG SUMMER SUN HIT IT...
...AND IT DRIED UP.
HOW IS THIS HAPPENING? AND WHY?
BECAUSE THE ORACLE OF SEASONS IS GONE. WITHOUT HER, THE WEATHER IS OUT OF CONTROL.
IF THIS CONTINUES...
...ALL THE PLANTS WILL WITHER AND DIE!
THEN WE HAVE TO GET HER BACK QUICKLY!
THAT'S WHY WE'RE GOING TO SAVE HER! AREN'T YOU LISTENING?
Hey...
DO YOU HEAR SOMETHING?

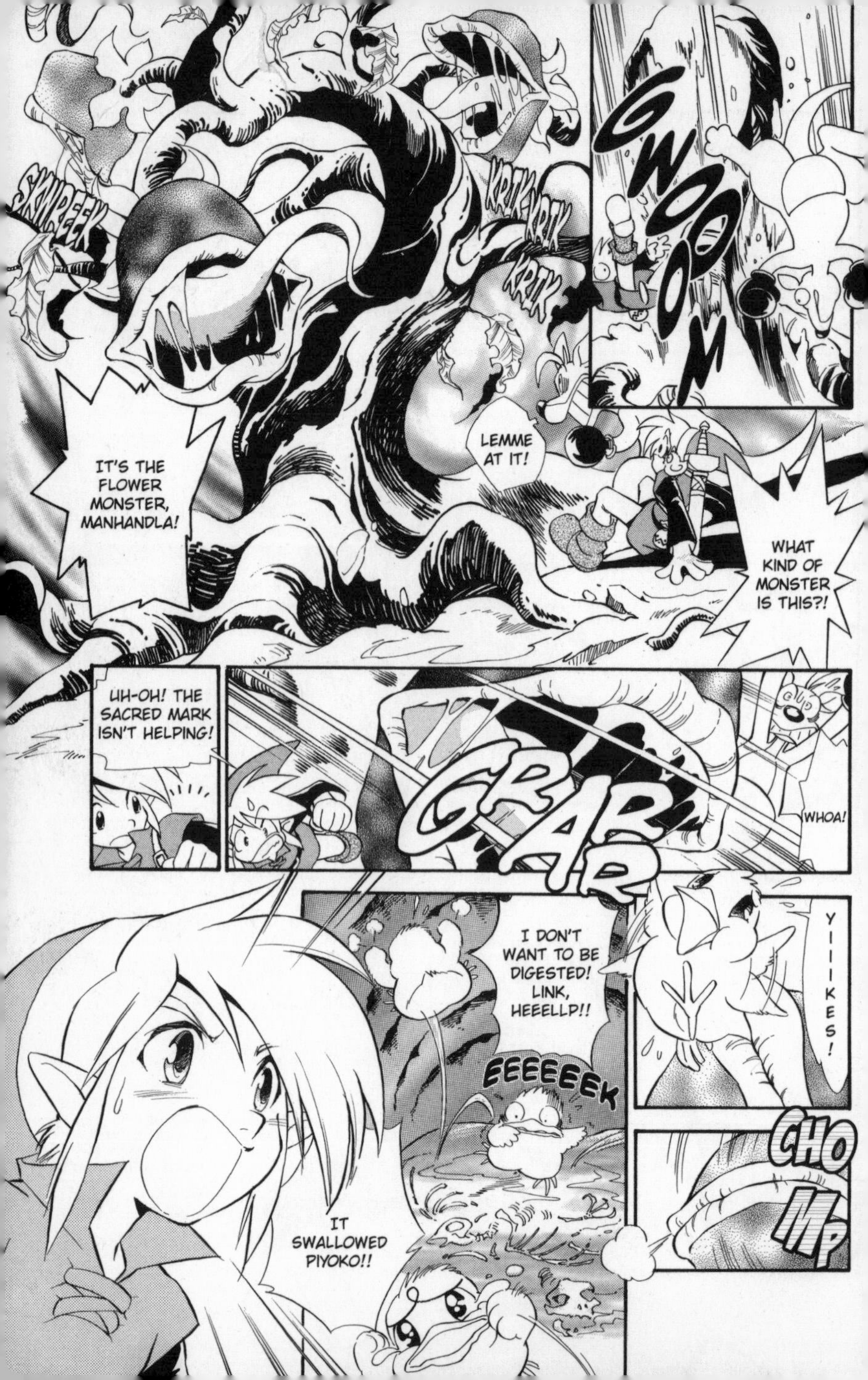
GWOOOOM
WHAT KIND OF MONSTER IS THIS?!
LEMME AT IT!
KRIK-KRIK
KRIK
SKWREEK
IT'S THE FLOWER MONSTER, MANHANDLA!
WHOA!
GRAR
UH-OH! THE SACRED MARK ISN'T HELPING!
YIIIKES!
CHOMP
I DON'T WANT TO BE DIGESTED! LINK, HEEELLLP!!
EEEEEEK
IT SWALLOWED PIYOKO!!

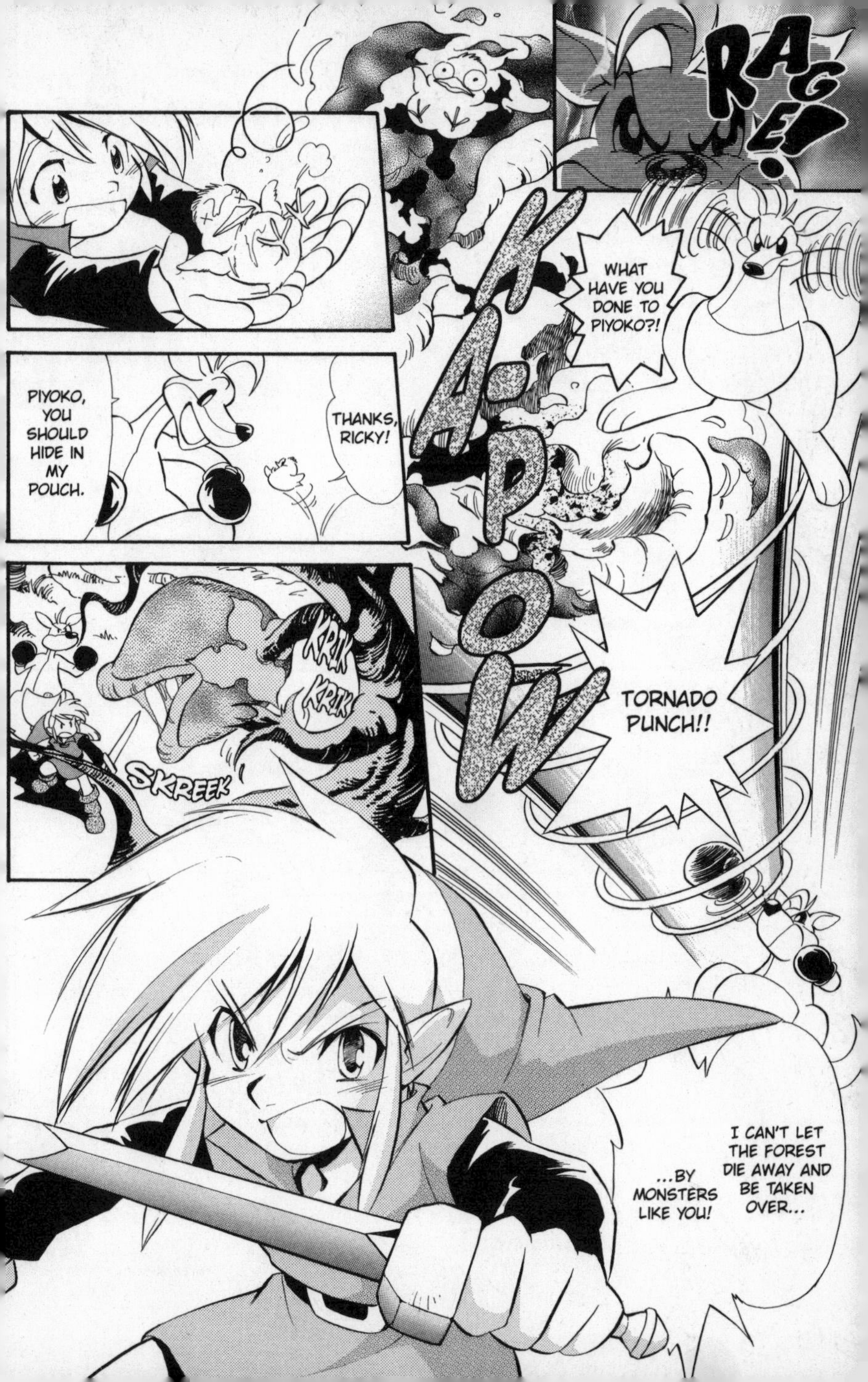
RAGE!
WHAT HAVE YOU DONE TO PIYOKO?!
KA-POW
TORNADO PUNCH!!
PIYOKO, YOU SHOULD HIDE IN MY POUCH.
THANKS, RICKY!
KRIK KRIK
SKREEK
I CAN'T LET THE FOREST DIE AWAY AND BE TAKEN OVER...
...BY MONSTERS LIKE YOU!

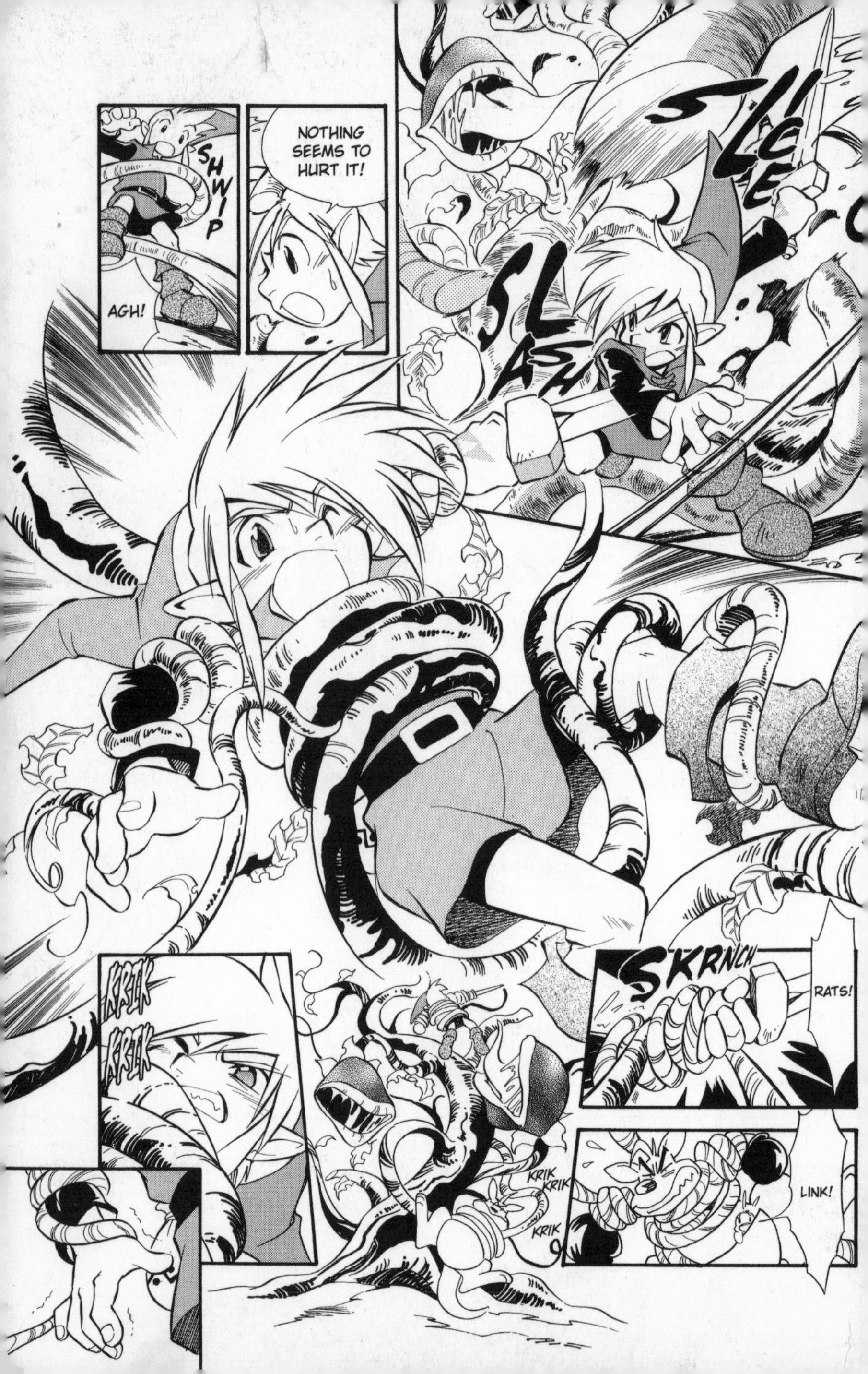
SHWIP
AGH!
NOTHING SEEMS TO HURT IT!
SLICE
SLASH
SKRNCH
RATS!
KRIK KRIK
KRIK
LINK!

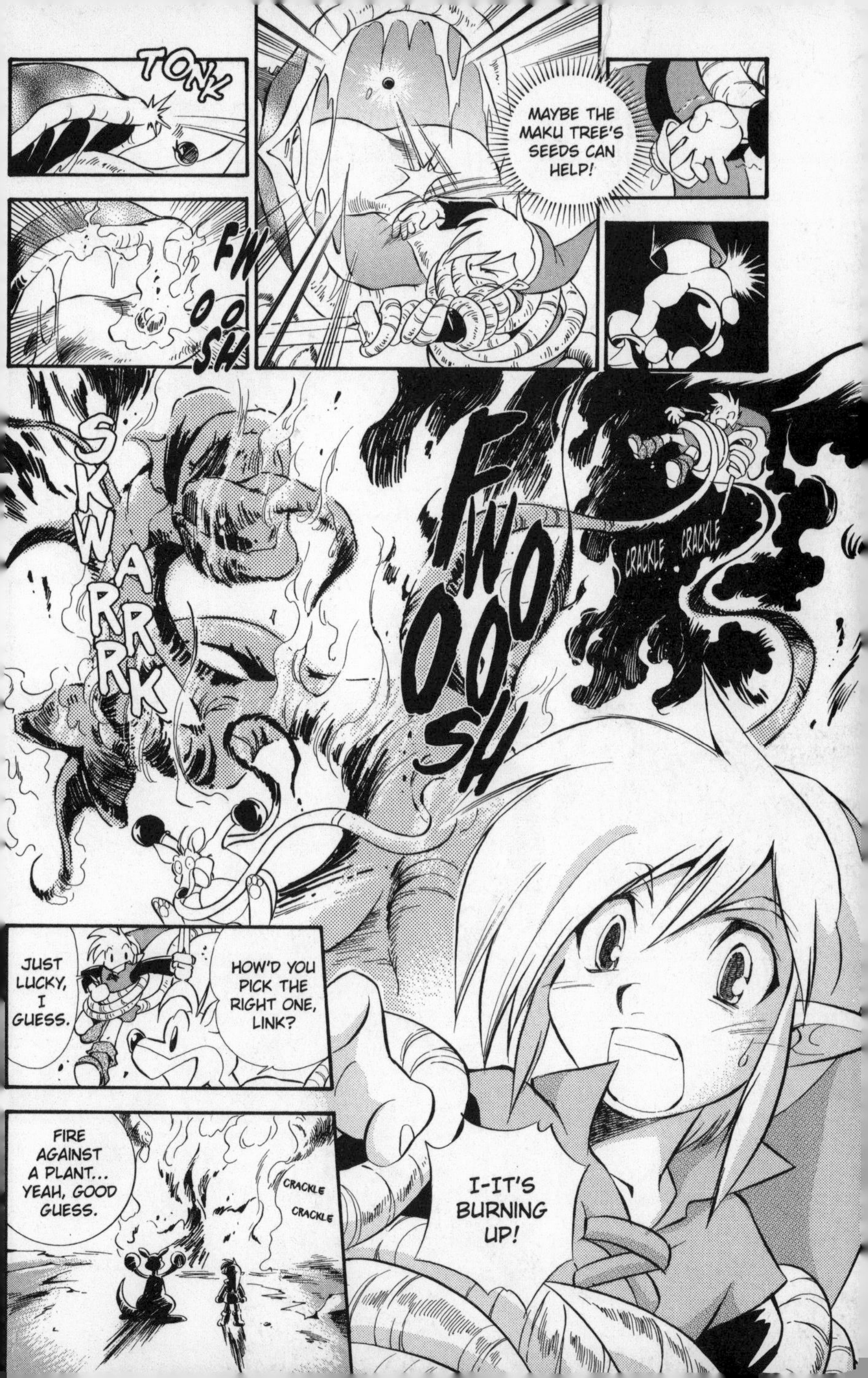
MAYBE THE MAKU TREE'S SEEDS CAN HELP!
TONK
FWOOSH
FWOOOOSH
CRACKLE CRACKLE
SKWARRRK
I-IT'S BURNING UP!
HOW'D YOU PICK THE RIGHT ONE, LINK?
JUST LUCKY, I GUESS.
CRACKLE CRACKLE
FIRE AGAINST A PLANT... YEAH, GOOD GUESS.

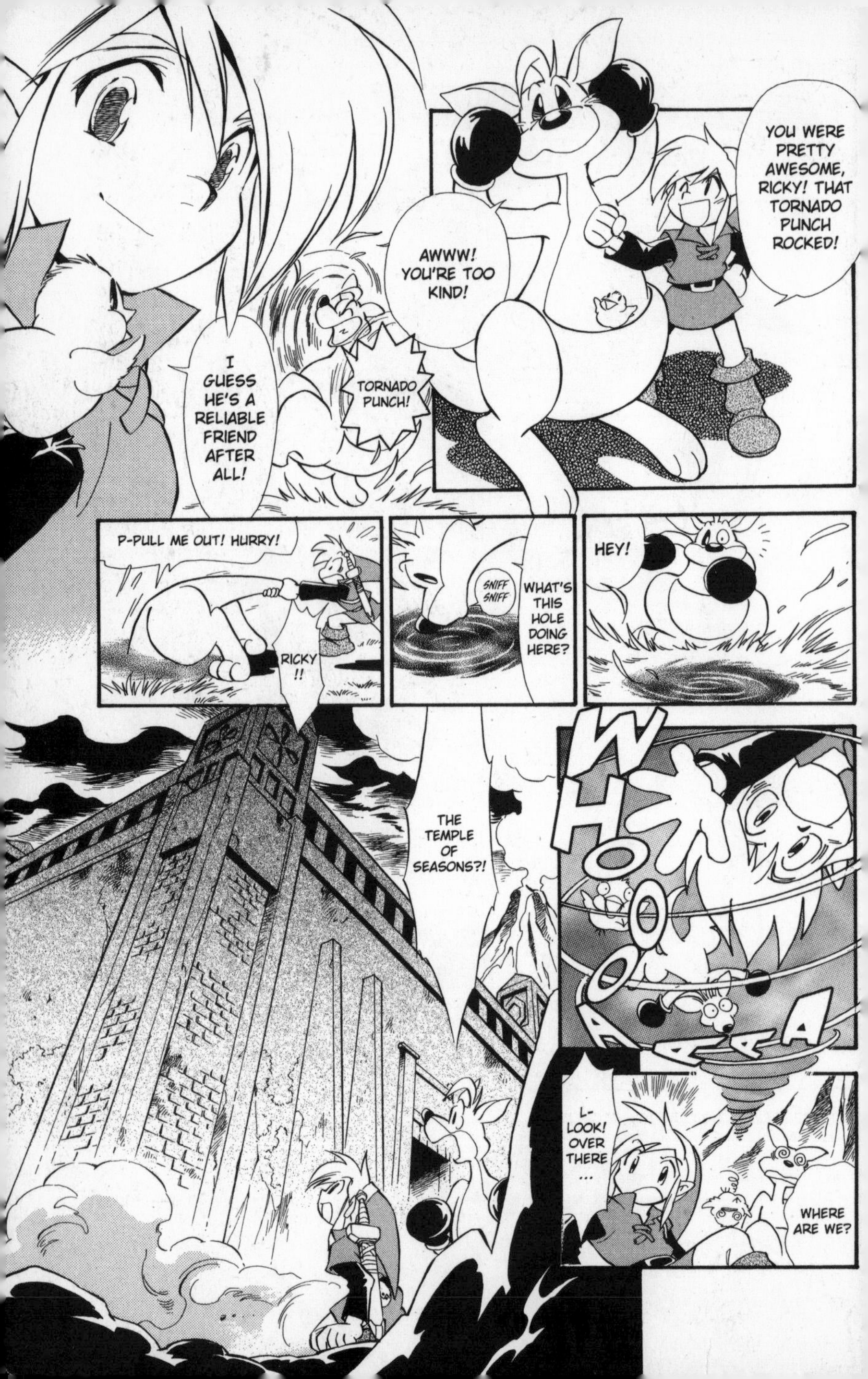
YOU WERE PRETTY AWESOME, RICKY! THAT TORNADO PUNCH ROCKED!
AWWW! YOU'RE TOO KIND!
TORNADO PUNCH!
I GUESS HE'S A RELIABLE FRIEND AFTER ALL!
HEY!
SNIFF SNIFF
WHAT'S THIS HOLE DOING HERE?
P-PULL ME OUT! HURRY!
RICKY!!
WHOOOOAAAA
WHERE ARE WE?
L-LOOK! OVER THERE...
THE TEMPLE OF SEASONS?!

CHAPTER 7
THE GREAT WITCH: MAPLE

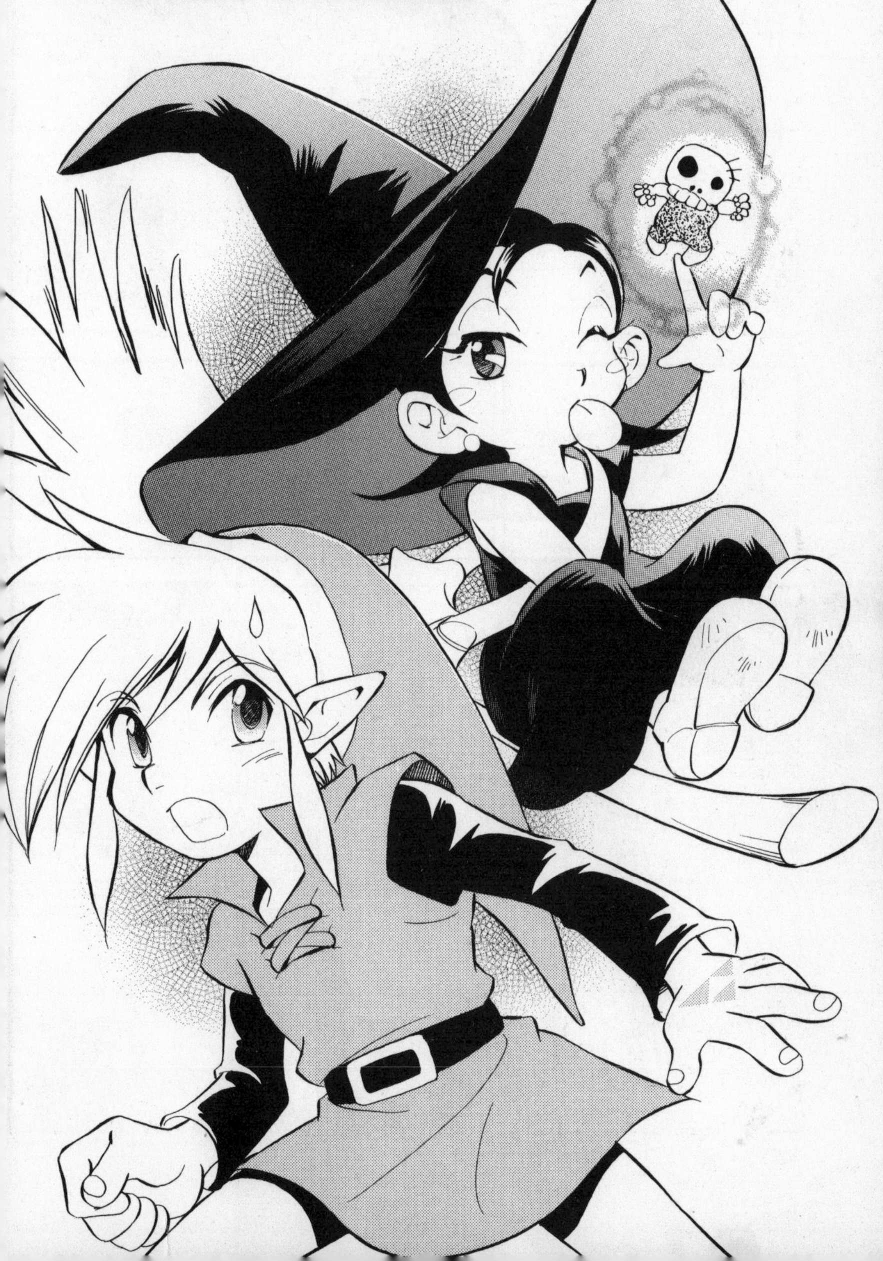

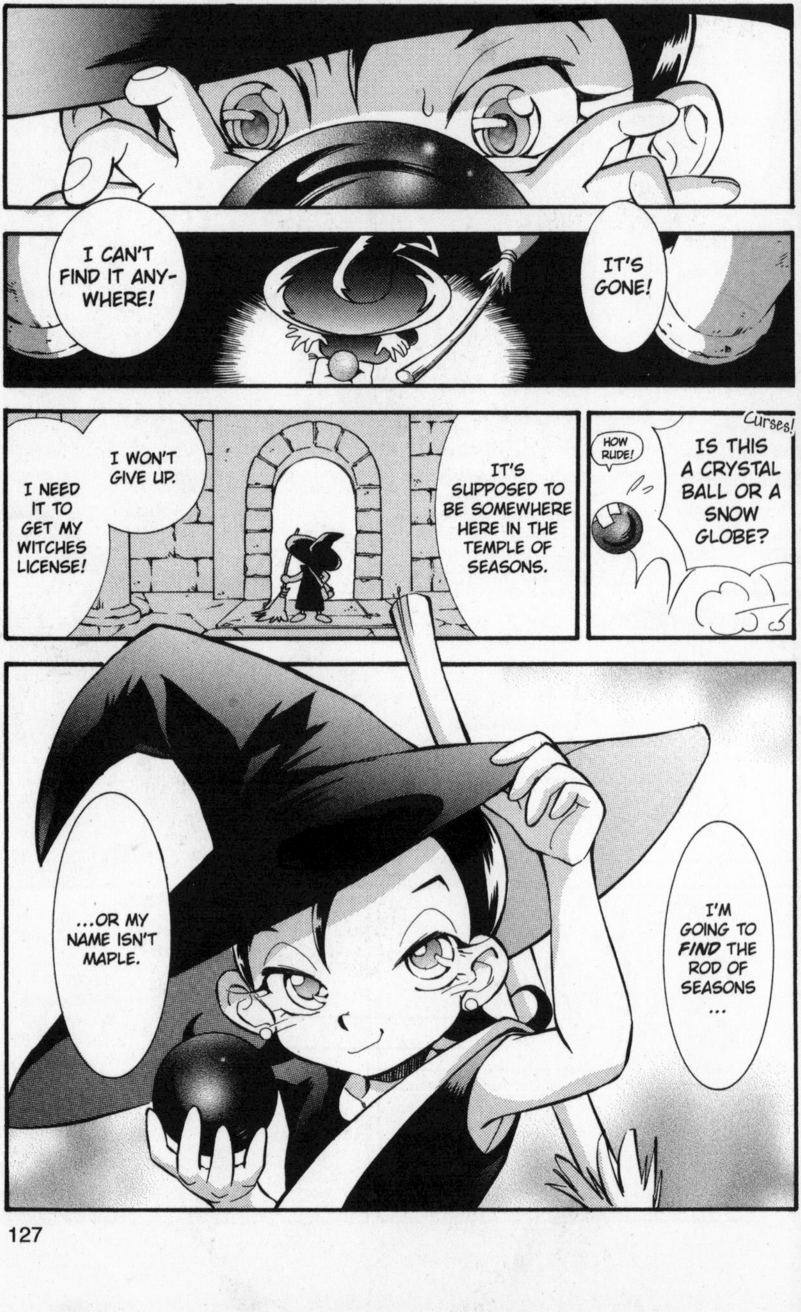
IT'S GONE!
I CAN'T FIND IT ANY-WHERE!
Curses!
IS THIS A CRYSTAL BALL OR A SNOW GLOBE?
HOW RUDE!
IT'S SUPPOSED TO BE SOMEWHERE HERE IN THE TEMPLE OF SEASONS.
I WON'T GIVE UP.
I NEED IT TO GET MY WITCHES LICENSE!
I'M GOING TO *FIND* THE ROD OF SEASONS ...
...OR MY NAME ISN'T MAPLE.

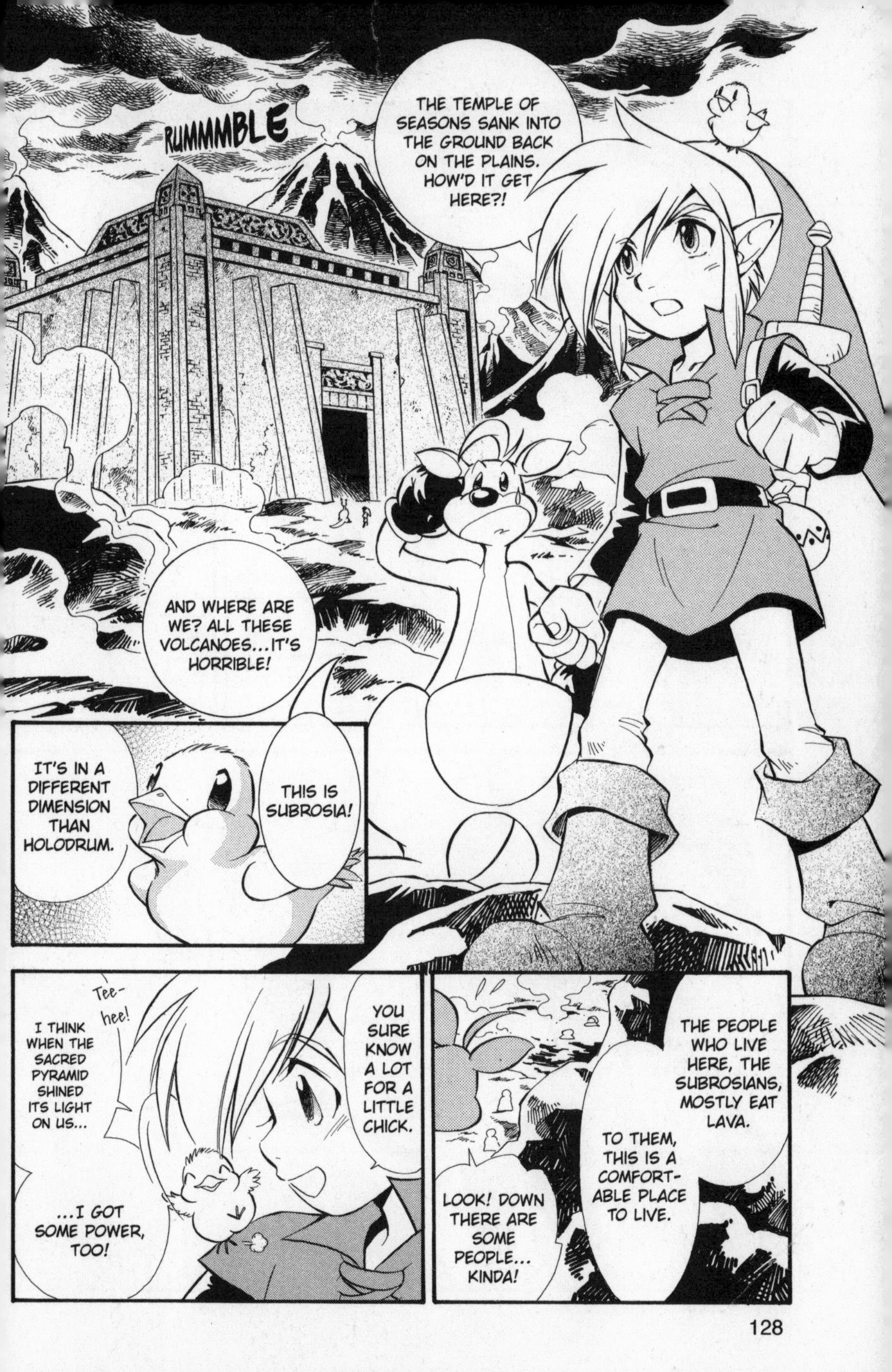
THE TEMPLE OF SEASONS SANK INTO THE GROUND BACK ON THE PLAINS. HOW'D IT GET HERE?!
RUMMMBLE
AND WHERE ARE WE? ALL THESE VOLCANOES...IT'S HORRIBLE!
THIS IS SUBROSIA!
IT'S IN A DIFFERENT DIMENSION THAN HOLODRUM.
THE PEOPLE WHO LIVE HERE, THE SUBROSIANS, MOSTLY EAT LAVA.
TO THEM, THIS IS A COMFORTABLE PLACE TO LIVE.
LOOK! DOWN THERE ARE SOME PEOPLE... KINDA!
YOU SURE KNOW A LOT FOR A LITTLE CHICK.
Tee-hee!
I THINK WHEN THE SACRED PYRAMID SHINED ITS LIGHT ON US...
...I GOT SOME POWER, TOO!

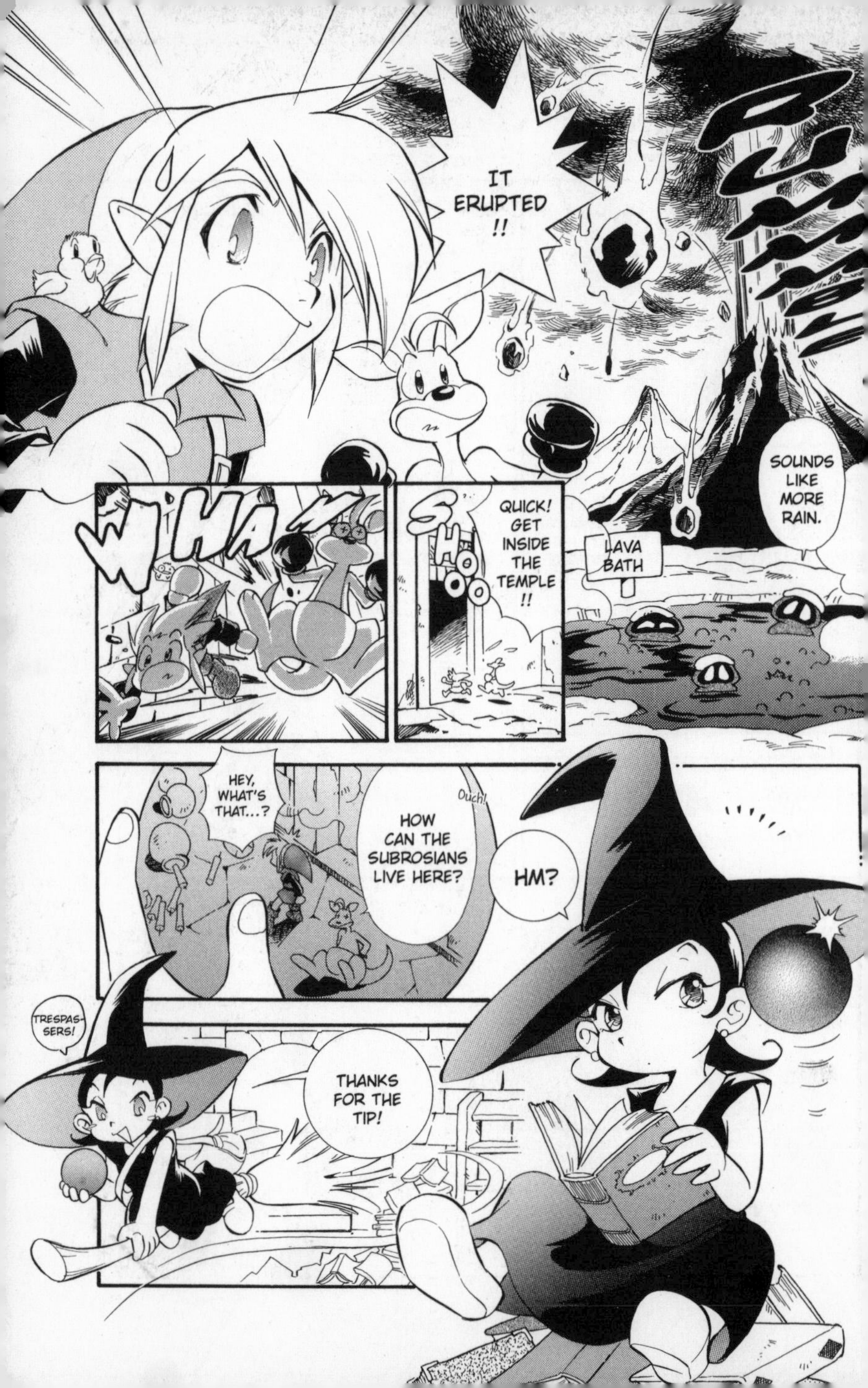

IT ERUPTED !!
SOUNDS LIKE MORE RAIN.
LAVA BATH
SHOOO
QUICK! GET INSIDE THE TEMPLE !!
WHAM
HM?
HOW CAN THE SUBROSIANS LIVE HERE?
Ouch!
HEY, WHAT'S THAT...?
THANKS FOR THE TIP!
TRESPASSERS!

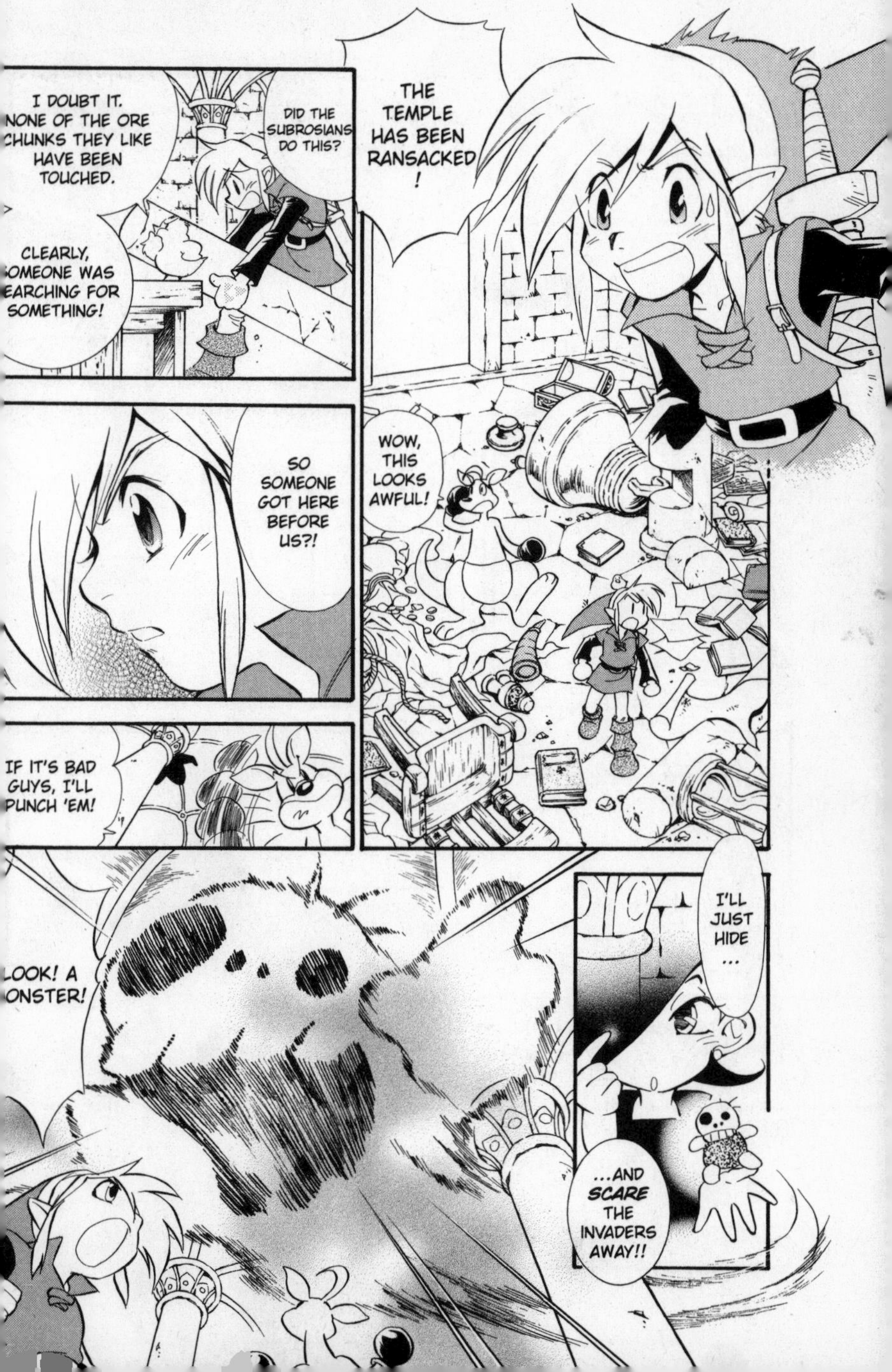

THE TEMPLE HAS BEEN RANSACKED!
WOW, THIS LOOKS AWFUL!
DID THE SUBROSIANS DO THIS?
I DOUBT IT. NONE OF THE ORE HUNKS THEY LIKE HAVE BEEN TOUCHED.
CLEARLY, OMEONE WAS EARCHING FOR SOMETHING!
SO SOMEONE GOT HERE BEFORE US?!
IF IT'S BAD GUYS, I'LL PUNCH 'EM!
I'LL JUST HIDE ...
...AND SCARE THE INVADERS AWAY!!
OOK! A ONSTER!

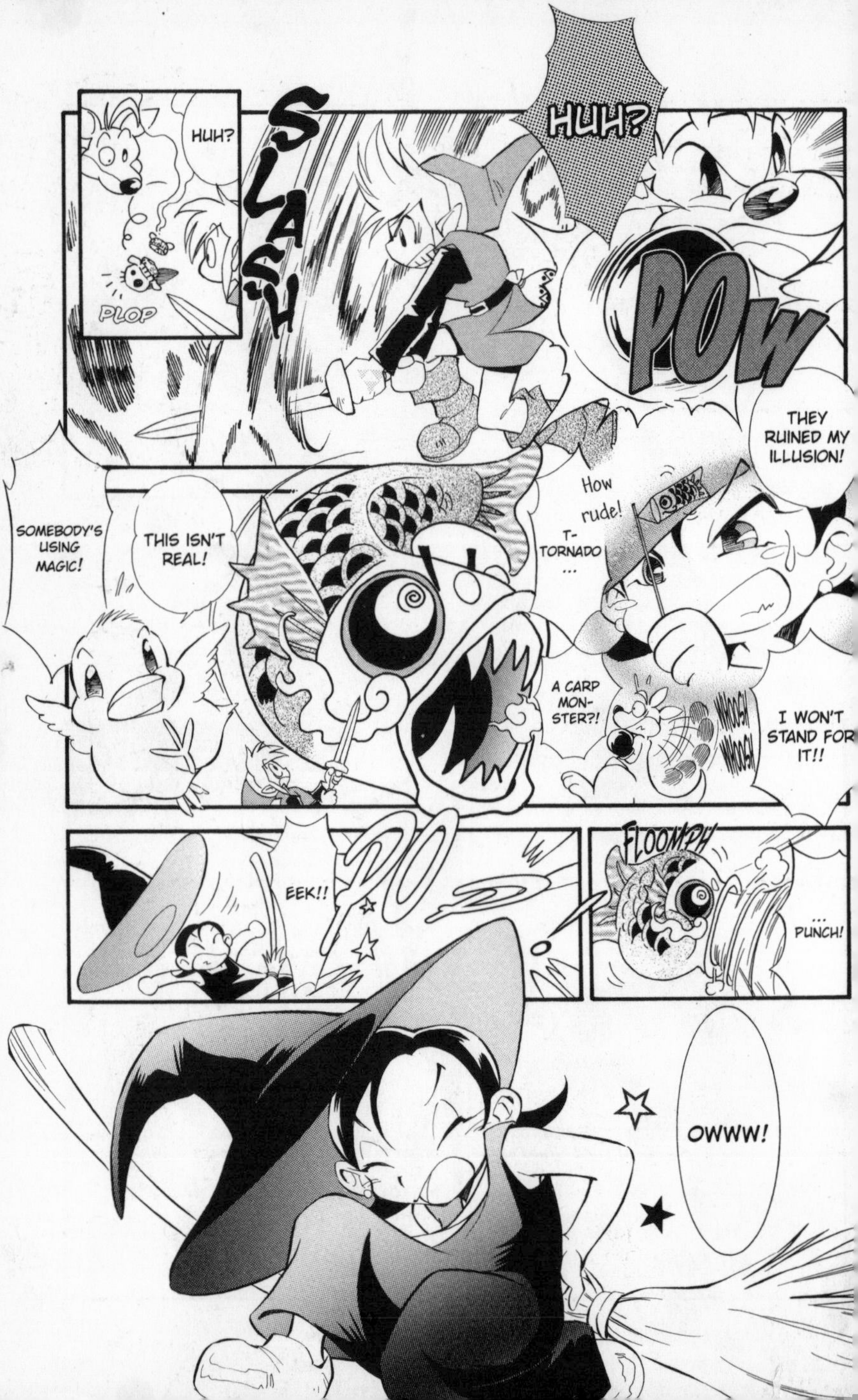
HUH?
POW
SLASH
HUH?
PLOP
THEY RUINED MY ILLUSION!
How rude!
T-TORNADO...
I WON'T STAND FOR IT!!
WHOOSH WHOOSH
A CARP MONSTER?!
THIS ISN'T REAL!
SOMEBODY'S USING MAGIC!
FLOOMPH
...PUNCH!
EEK!!
OWWW!

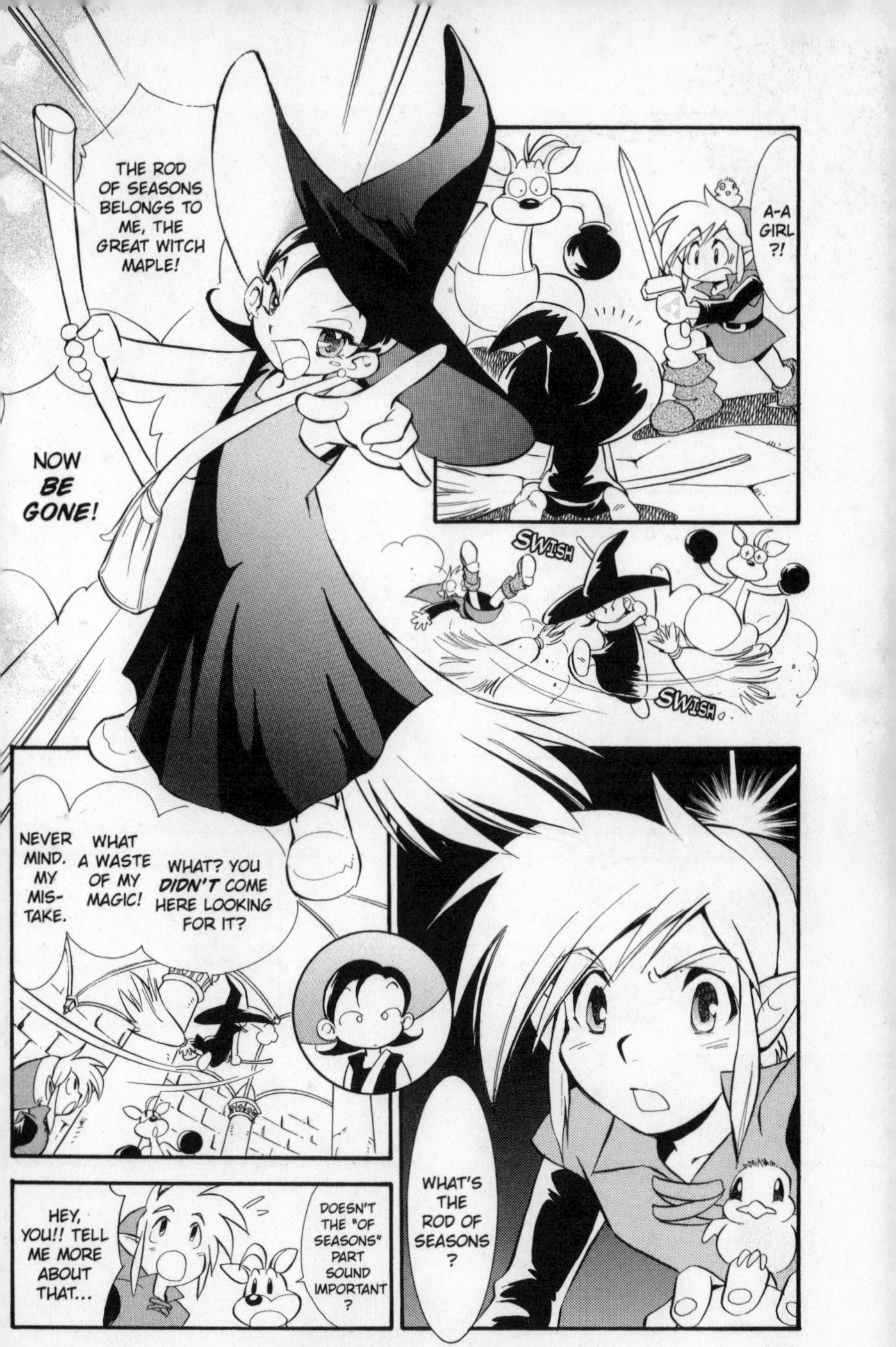
A-A GIRL ?!
THE ROD OF SEASONS BELONGS TO ME, THE GREAT WITCH MAPLE!
NOW *BE* *GONE!*
SWISH
SWISH
WHAT'S THE ROD OF SEASONS ?
WHAT? YOU *DIDN'T* COME HERE LOOKING FOR IT?
WHAT A WASTE OF MY MAGIC!
NEVER MIND. MY MIS-TAKE.
DOESN'T THE "OF SEASONS" PART SOUND IMPORTANT ?
HEY, YOU!! TELL ME MORE ABOUT THAT...

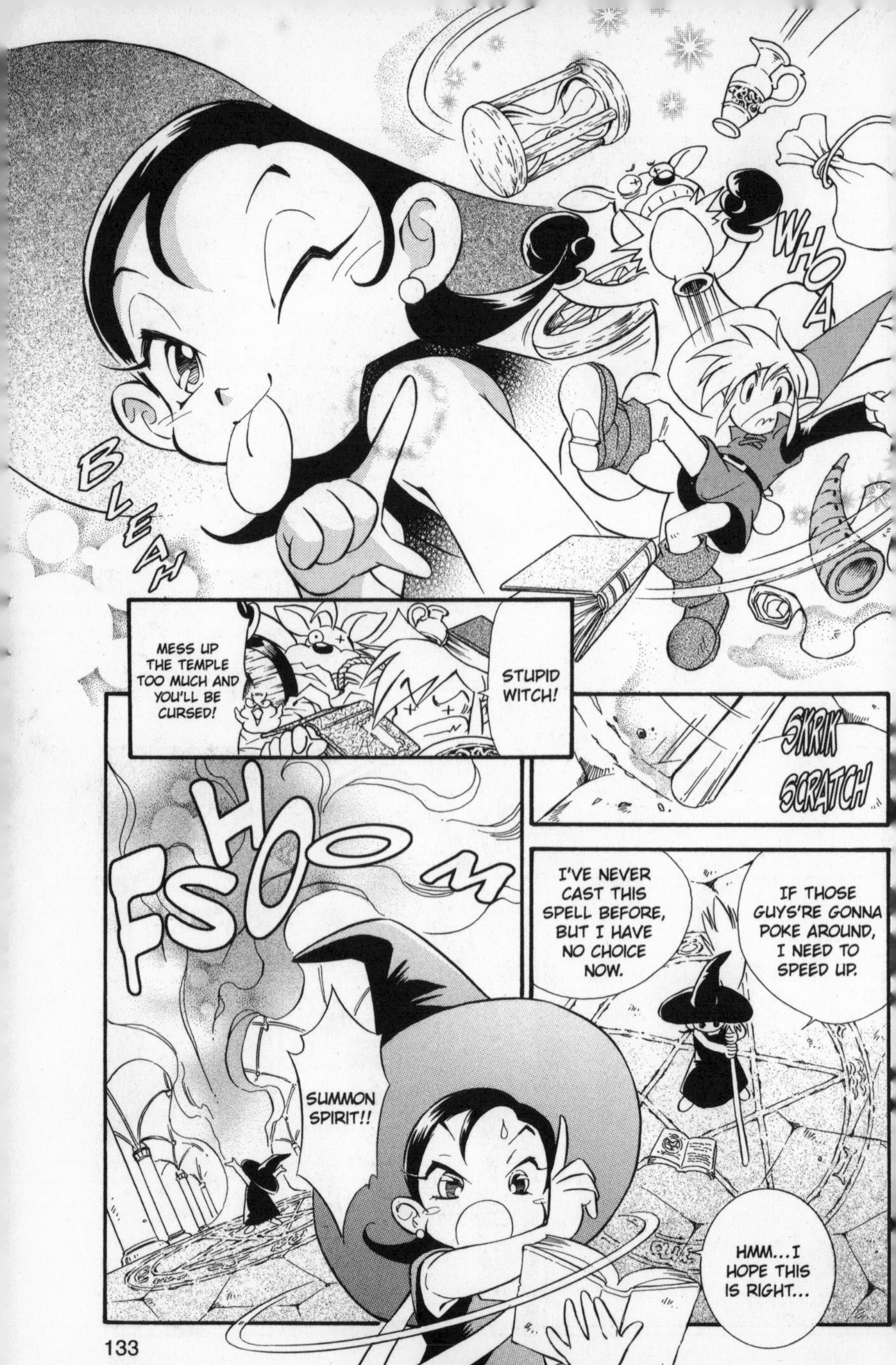
WHOA
BLEAH
STUPID WITCH!
MESS UP THE TEMPLE TOO MUCH AND YOU'LL BE CURSED!
SKRIK
SCRATCH
IF THOSE GUYS'RE GONNA POKE AROUND, I NEED TO SPEED UP.
I'VE NEVER CAST THIS SPELL BEFORE, BUT I HAVE NO CHOICE NOW.
HMM...I HOPE THIS IS RIGHT...
FSHOOM
SUMMON SPIRIT!!

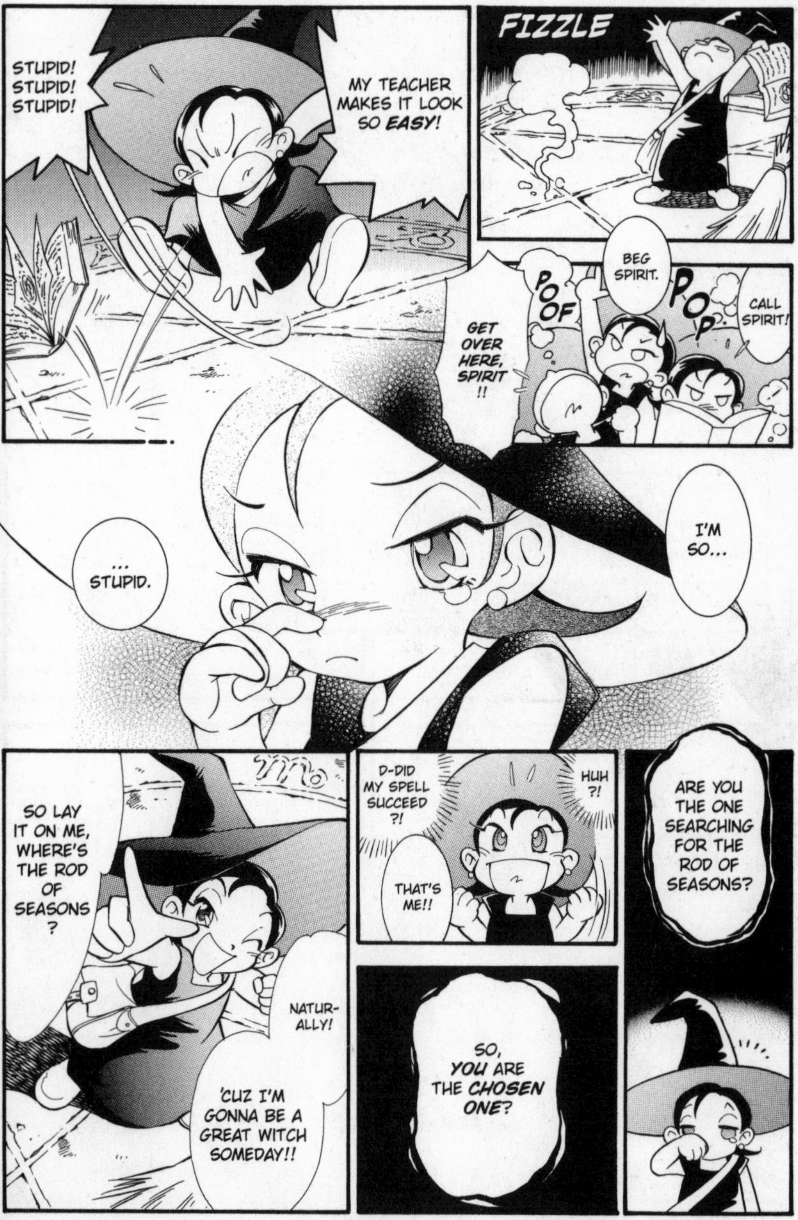
FIZZLE
CALL SPIRIT!
POP
BEG SPIRIT.
POOF
GET OVER HERE, SPIRIT!!
MY TEACHER MAKES IT LOOK SO *EASY*!
STUPID! STUPID! STUPID!
I'M SO...
... STUPID.
ARE YOU THE ONE SEARCHING FOR THE ROD OF SEASONS?
HUH?!
D-DID MY SPELL SUCCEED?!
THAT'S ME!!
SO, *YOU* ARE THE *CHOSEN ONE*?
NATUR-ALLY!
'CUZ I'M GONNA BE A GREAT WITCH SOMEDAY!!
SO LAY IT ON ME, WHERE'S THE ROD OF SEASONS?

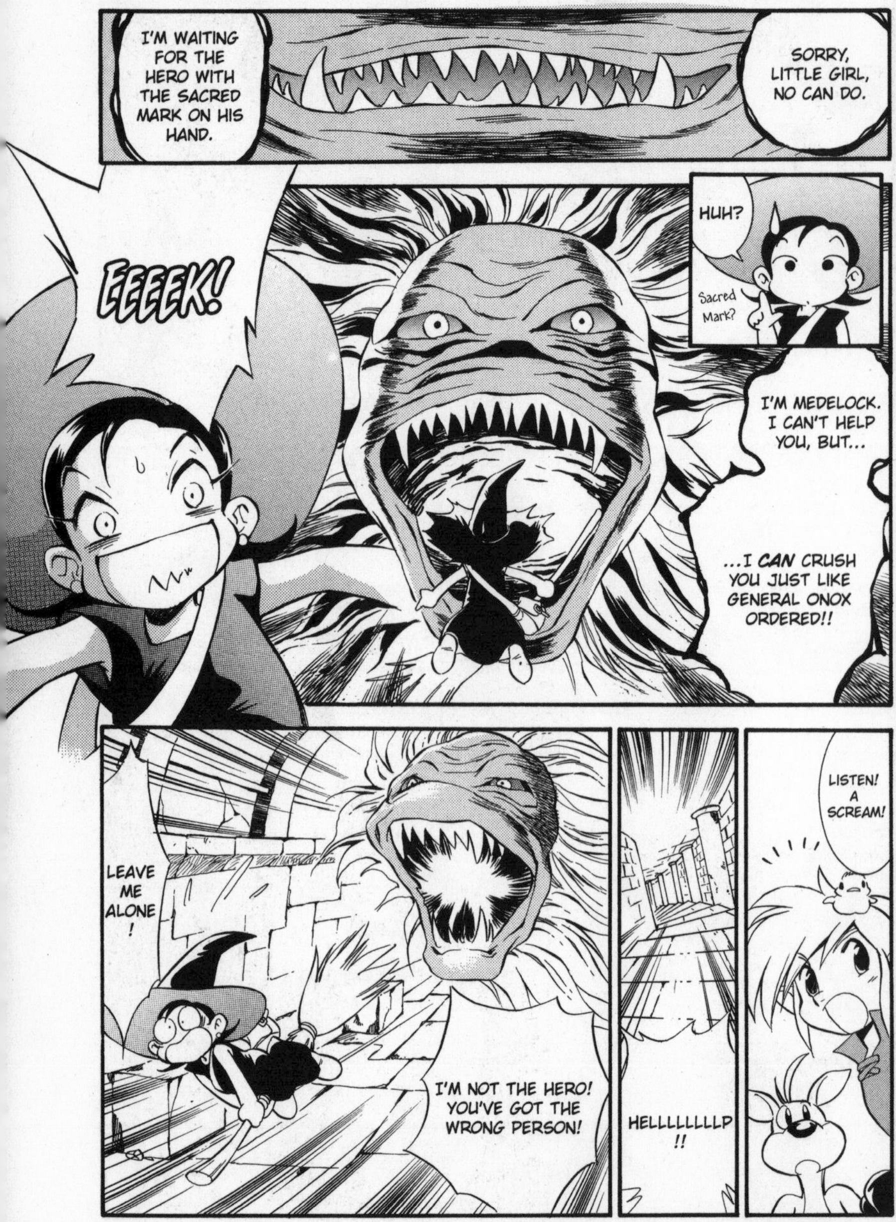
SORRY, LITTLE GIRL, NO CAN DO.
I'M WAITING FOR THE HERO WITH THE SACRED MARK ON HIS HAND.
HUH?
Sacred Mark?
I'M MEDELOCK. I CAN'T HELP YOU, BUT...
...I *CAN* CRUSH YOU JUST LIKE GENERAL ONOX ORDERED!!
EEEEK!
LISTEN! A SCREAM!
HELLLLLLLLP!!
I'M NOT THE HERO! YOU'VE GOT THE WRONG PERSON!
LEAVE ME ALONE!

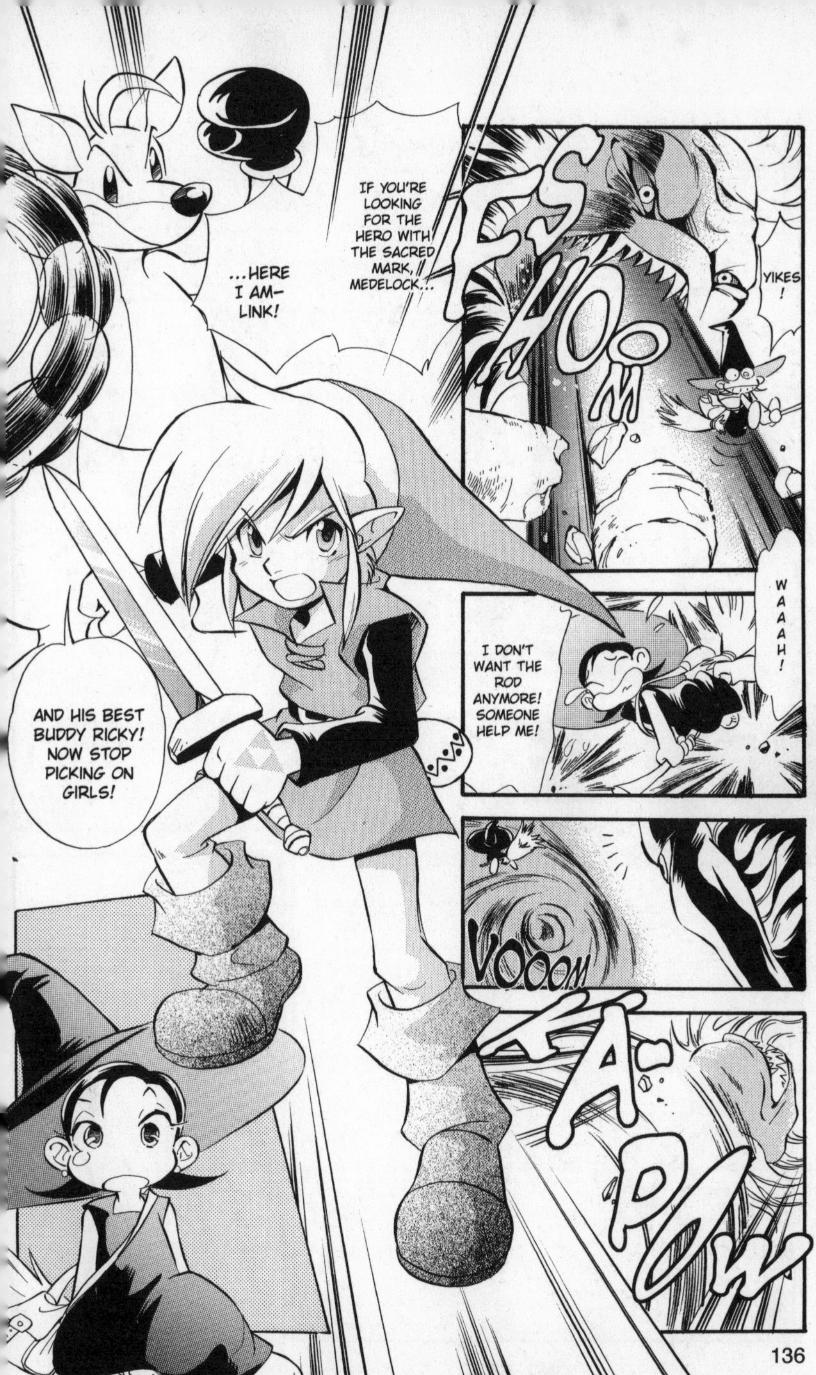

IF YOU'RE LOOKING FOR THE HERO WITH THE SACRED MARK, MEDELOCK...
...HERE I AM- LINK!
AND HIS BEST BUDDY RICKY! NOW STOP PICKING ON GIRLS!
FSHOOM
YIKES!
WAAAH!
I DON'T WANT THE ROD ANYMORE! SOMEONE HELP ME!
VOOOM
KA-POW

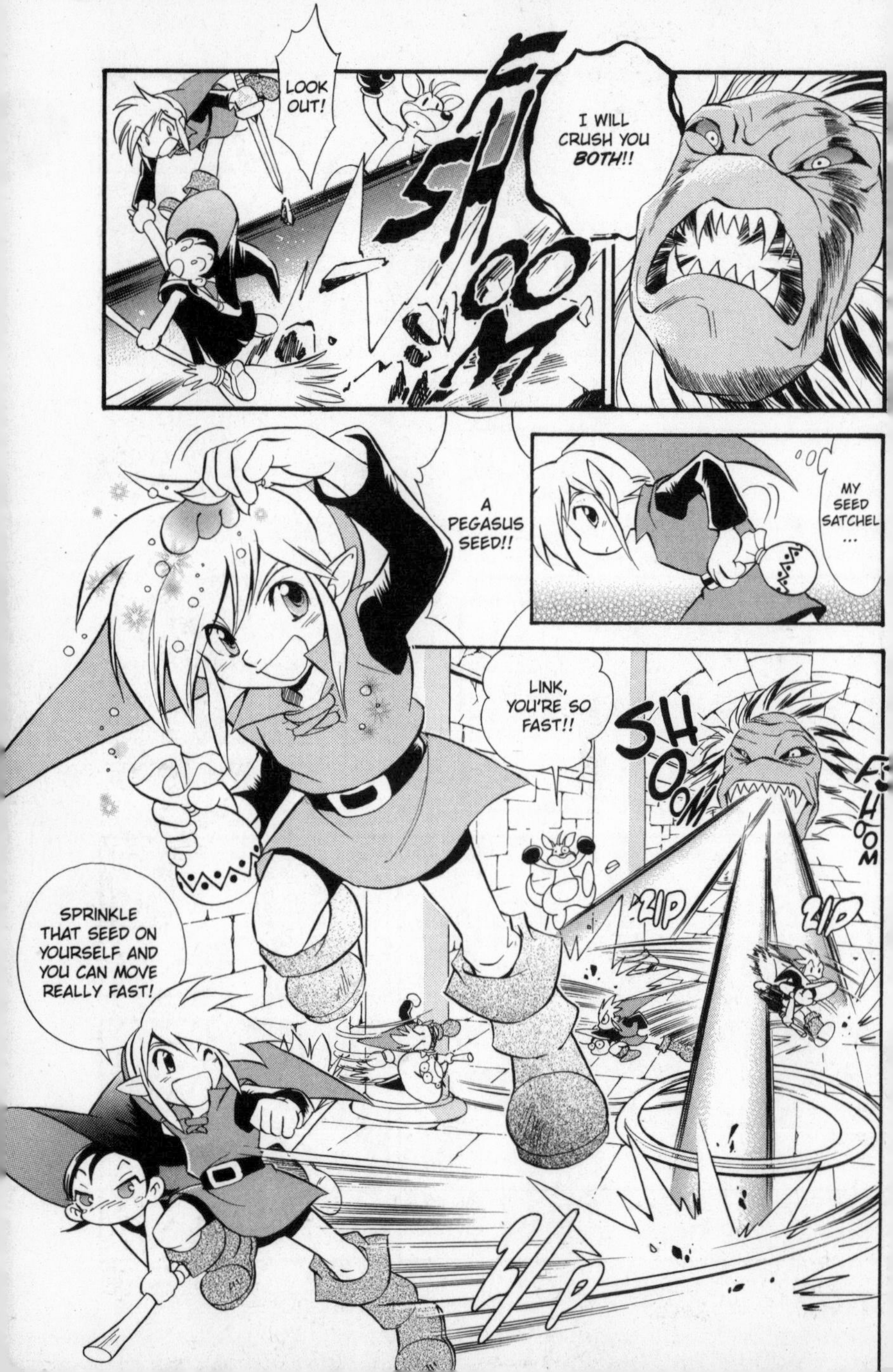
I WILL CRUSH YOU *BOTH!!*
SHOOOM
LOOK OUT!
MY SEED SATCHEL ...
A PEGASUS SEED!!
LINK, YOU'RE SO FAST!!
SHOOOM
ZIP
ZIP
SPRINKLE THAT SEED ON YOURSELF AND YOU CAN MOVE REALLY FAST!
ZIP

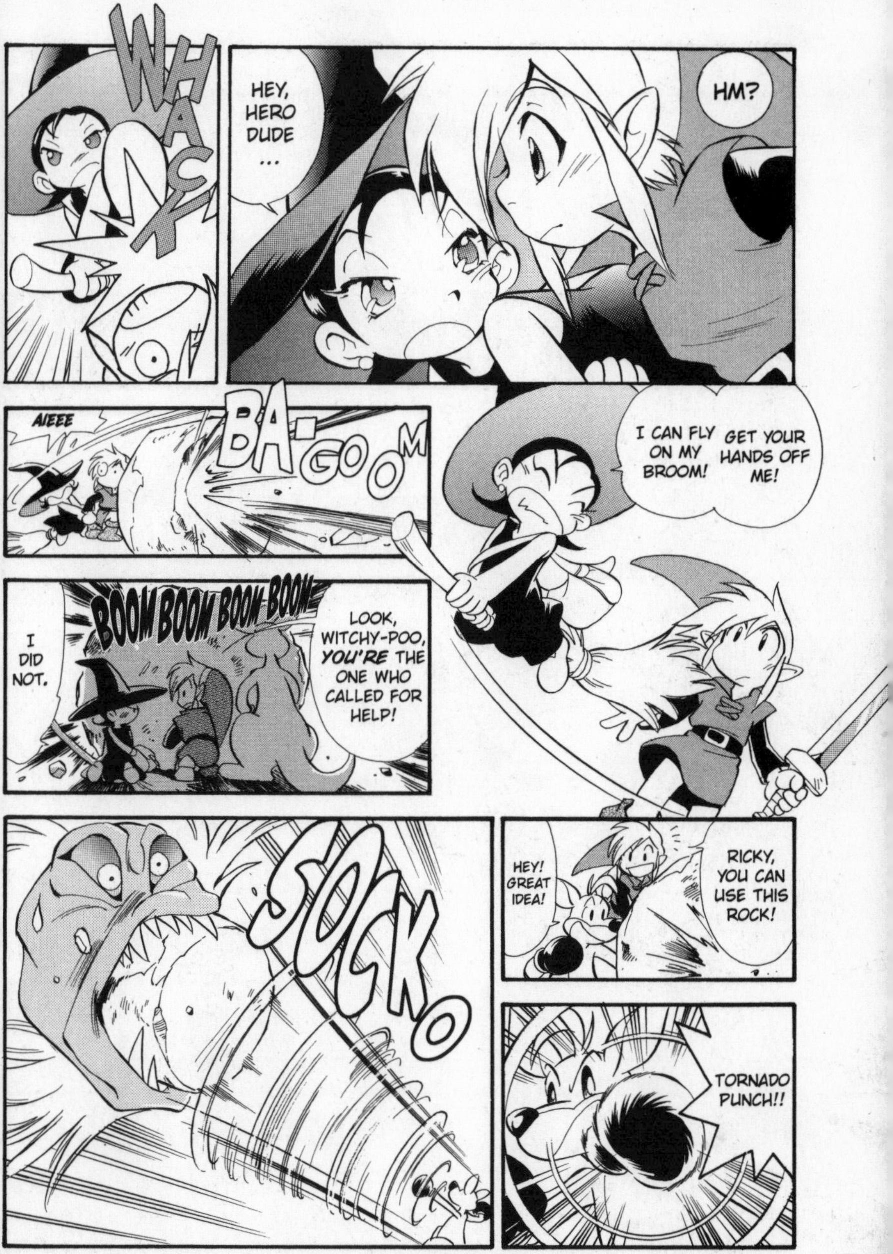
HM?
HEY, HERO DUDE ...
WHACK
GET YOUR HANDS OFF ME!
I CAN FLY ON MY BROOM!
AIEEE
BA-GOOOM
BOOM BOOM BOOM BOOM
LOOK, WITCHY-POO, *YOU'RE* THE ONE WHO CALLED FOR HELP!
I DID NOT.
RICKY, YOU CAN USE THIS ROCK!
HEY! GREAT IDEA!
TORNADO PUNCH!!
SOCKO

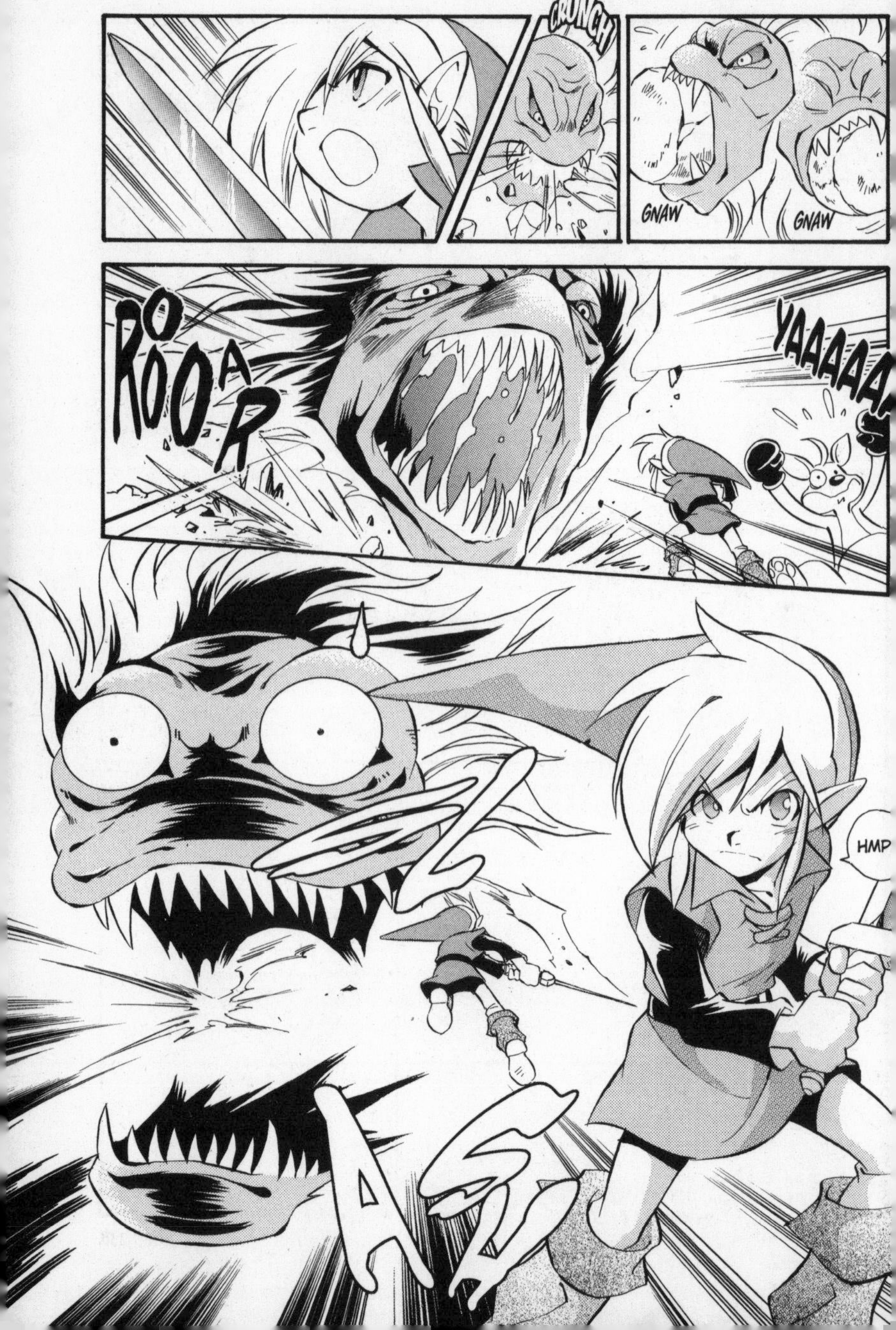
GNAW
GNAW
CRUNCH
YAAAAA
ROOOAR
HMP
ZASH

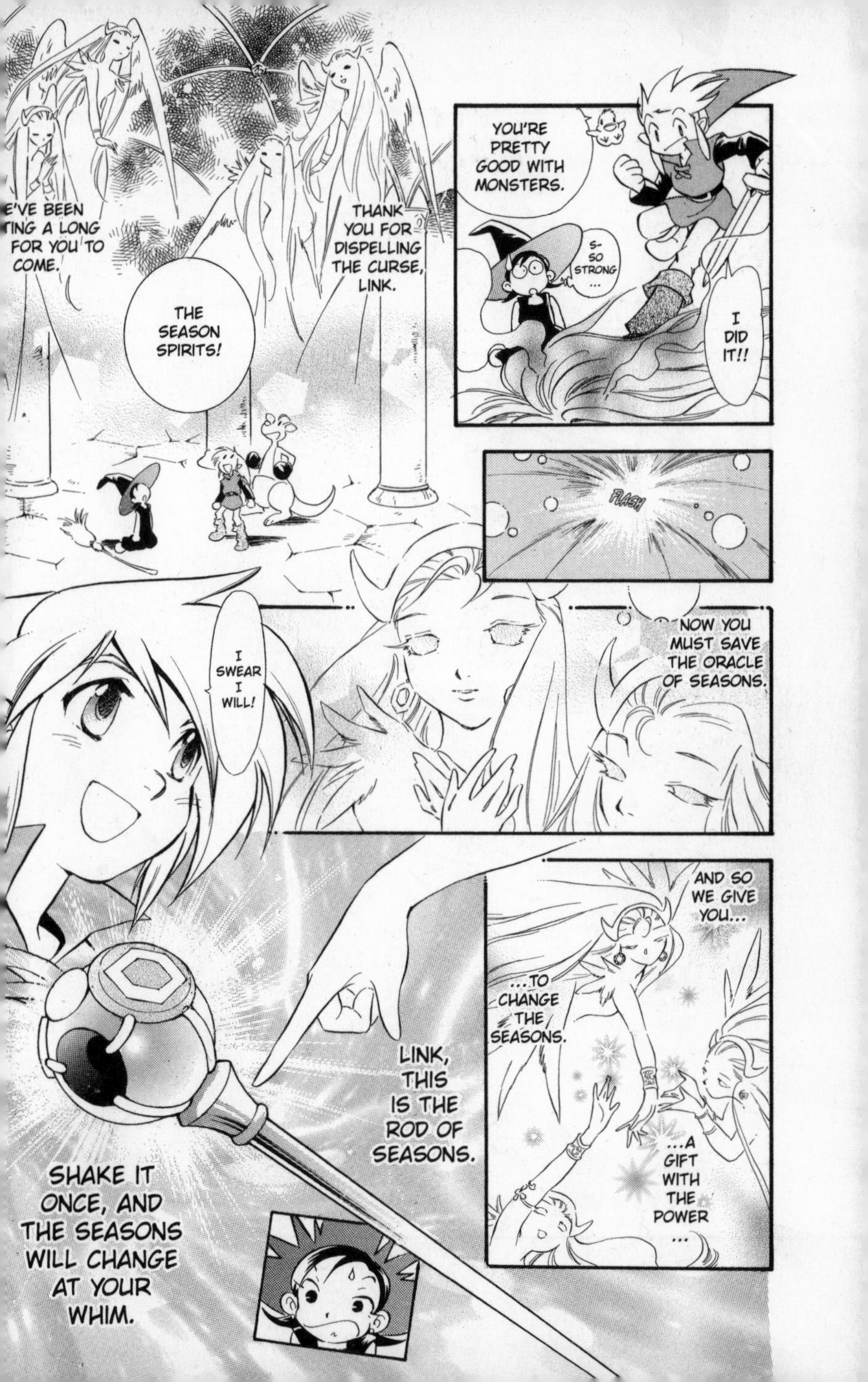
YOU'RE PRETTY GOOD WITH MONSTERS.
S-SO STRONG ...
I DID IT!!
FLASH
THANK YOU FOR DISPELLING THE CURSE, LINK.
E'VE BEEN TING A LONG FOR YOU TO COME.
THE SEASON SPIRITS!
NOW YOU MUST SAVE THE ORACLE OF SEASONS.
I SWEAR I WILL!
AND SO WE GIVE YOU...
...A GIFT WITH THE POWER ...
...TO CHANGE THE SEASONS.
LINK, THIS IS THE ROD OF SEASONS.
SHAKE IT ONCE, AND THE SEASONS WILL CHANGE AT YOUR WHIM.

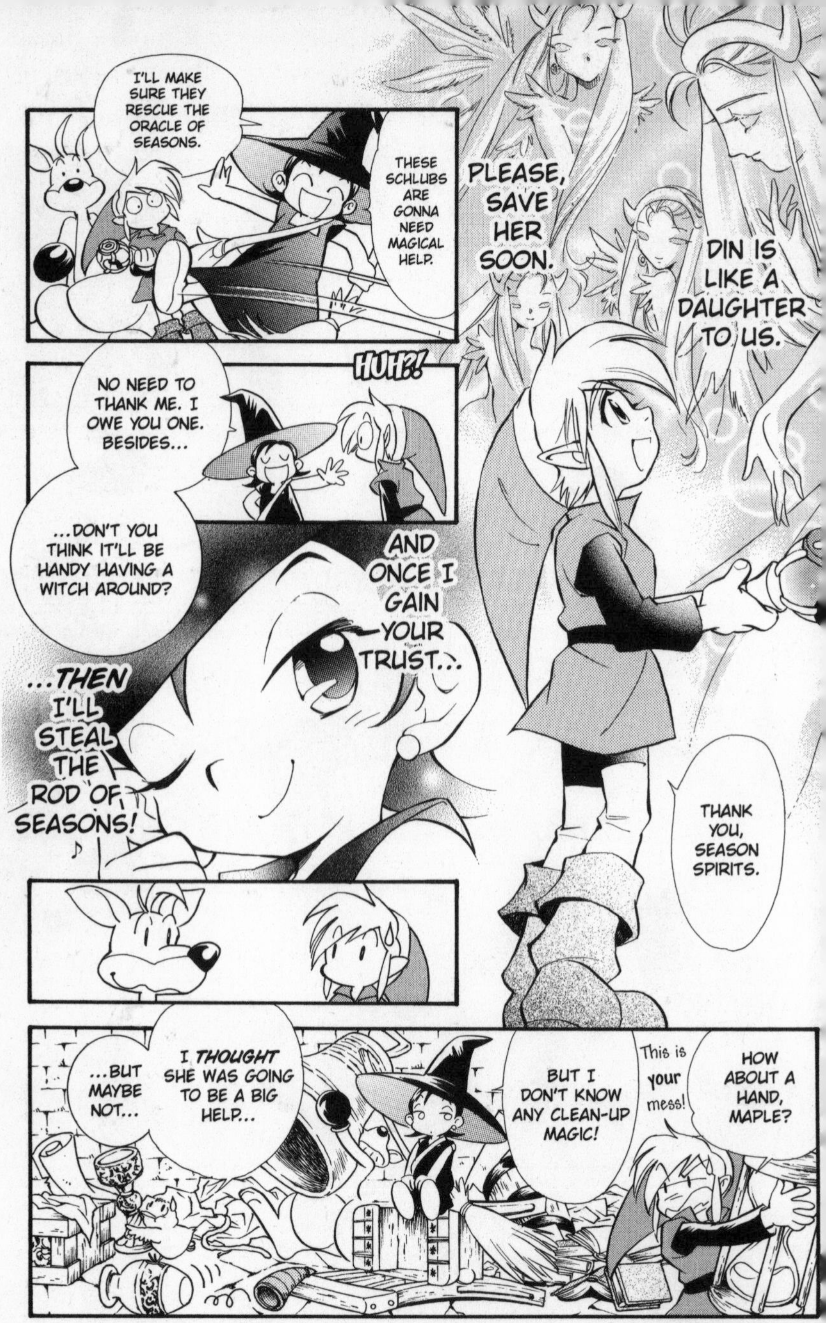
DIN IS LIKE A DAUGHTER TO US.
PLEASE, SAVE HER SOON.
THANK YOU, SEASON SPIRITS.
THESE SCHLUBS ARE GONNA NEED MAGICAL HELP.
I'LL MAKE SURE THEY RESCUE THE ORACLE OF SEASONS.
HUH?!
NO NEED TO THANK ME. I OWE YOU ONE. BESIDES...
...DON'T YOU THINK IT'LL BE HANDY HAVING A WITCH AROUND?
AND ONCE I GAIN YOUR TRUST...
...THEN I'LL STEAL THE ROD OF SEASONS! ♪
HOW ABOUT A HAND, MAPLE?
This is your mess!
BUT I DON'T KNOW ANY CLEAN-UP MAGIC!
I THOUGHT SHE WAS GOING TO BE A BIG HELP...
...BUT MAYBE NOT...

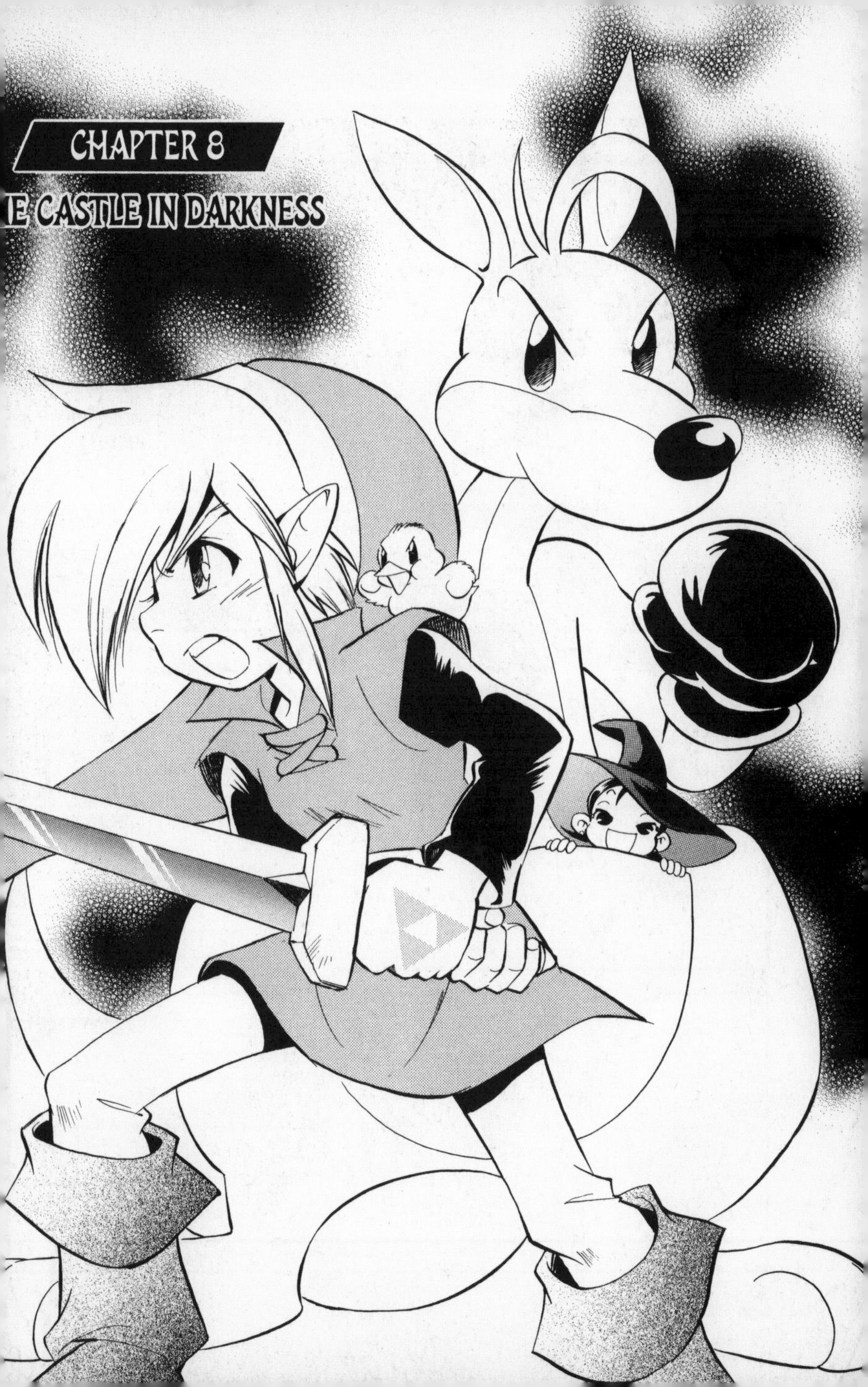
CHAPTER 8
E CASTLE IN DARKNESS

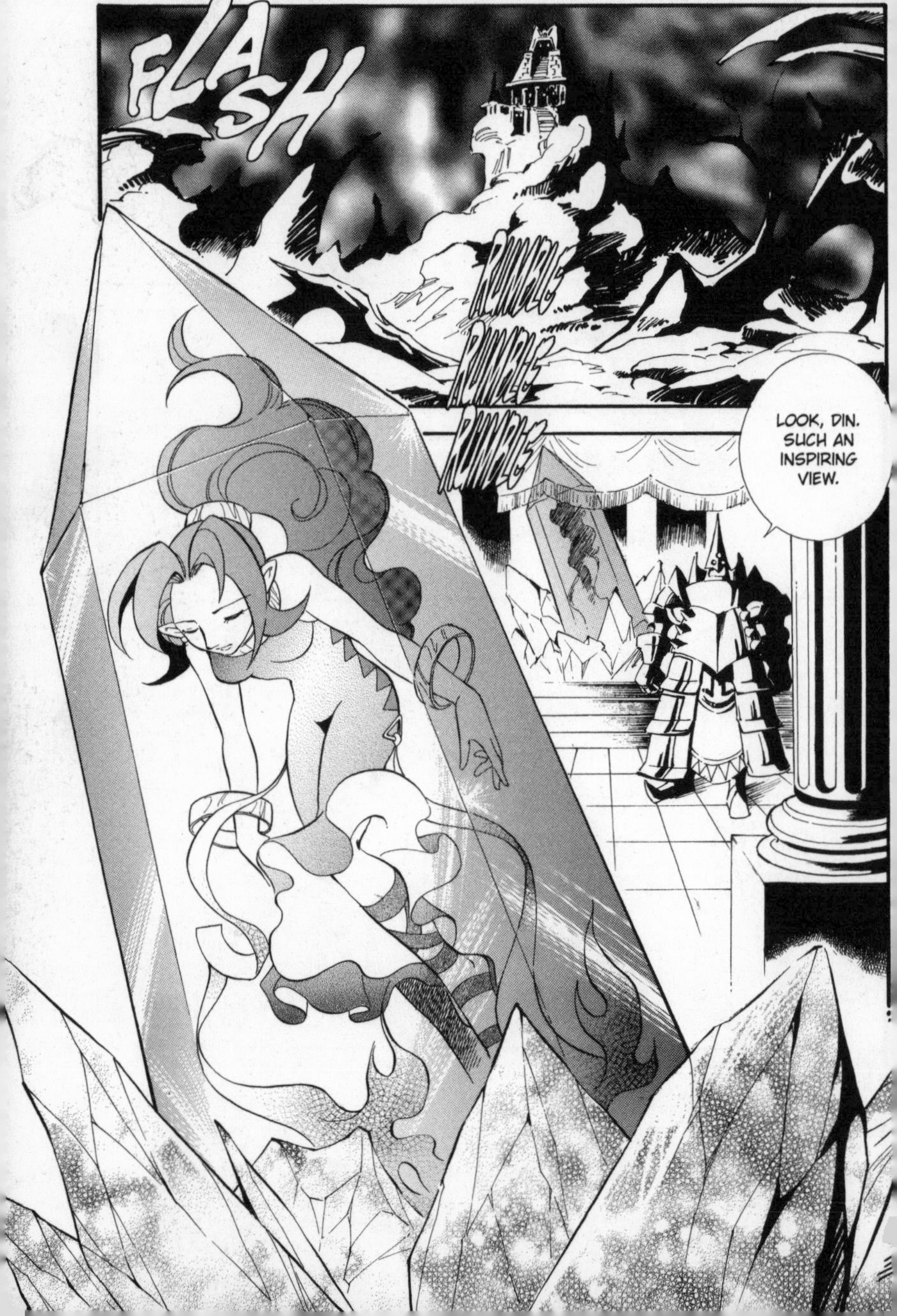
FLASH
RUMBLE
RUMBLE
RUMBLE
LOOK, DIN. SUCH AN INSPIRING VIEW.

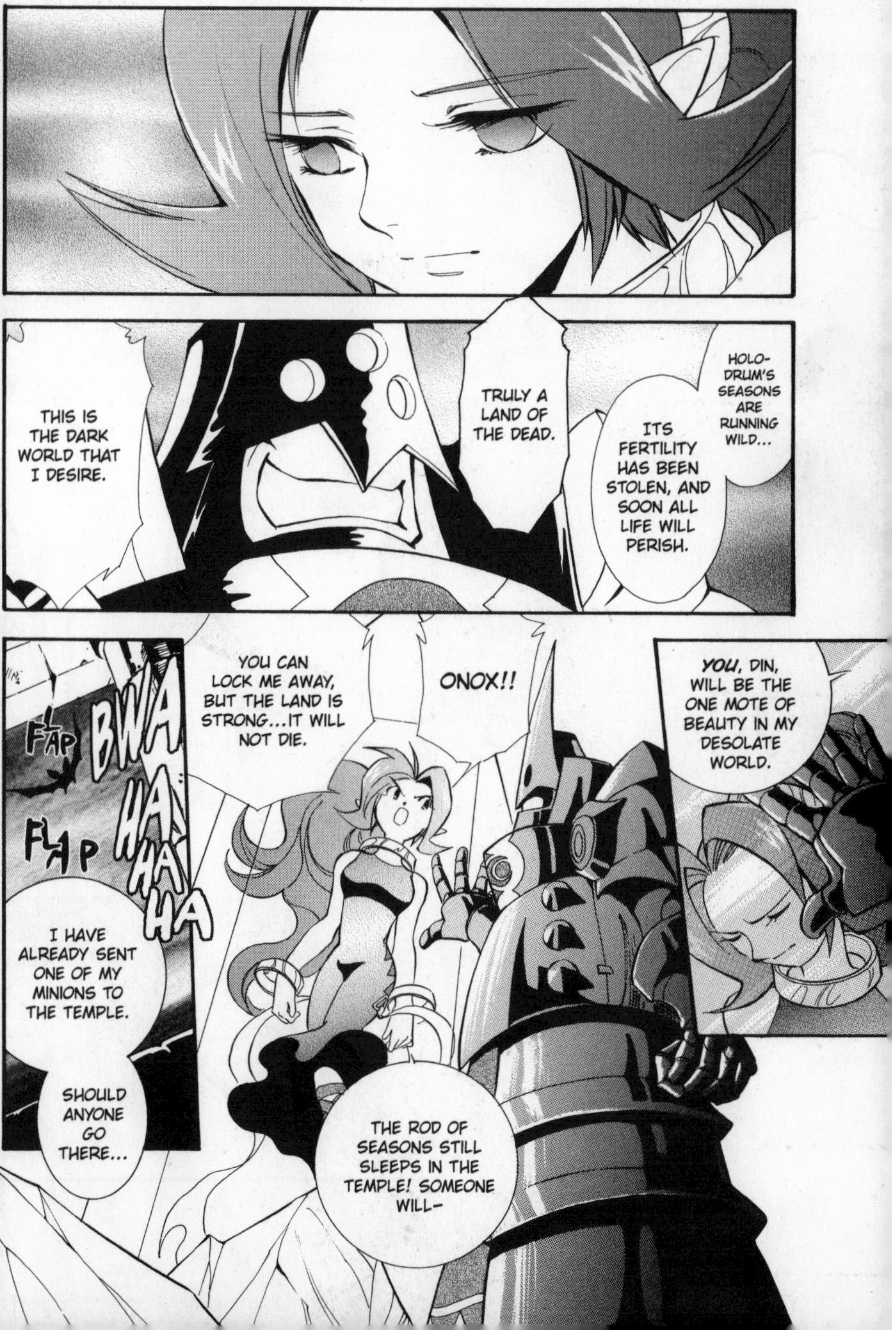
HOLO-DRUM'S SEASONS ARE RUNNING WILD...
ITS FERTILITY HAS BEEN STOLEN, AND SOON ALL LIFE WILL PERISH.
TRULY A LAND OF THE DEAD.
THIS IS THE DARK WORLD THAT I DESIRE.
YOU, DIN, WILL BE THE ONE MOTE OF BEAUTY IN MY DESOLATE WORLD.
ONOX!!
YOU CAN LOCK ME AWAY, BUT THE LAND IS STRONG...IT WILL NOT DIE.
THE ROD OF SEASONS STILL SLEEPS IN THE TEMPLE! SOMEONE WILL-
I HAVE ALREADY SENT ONE OF MY MINIONS TO THE TEMPLE.
SHOULD ANYONE GO THERE...
BWA HA HA HA HA
FLAP
FLAP

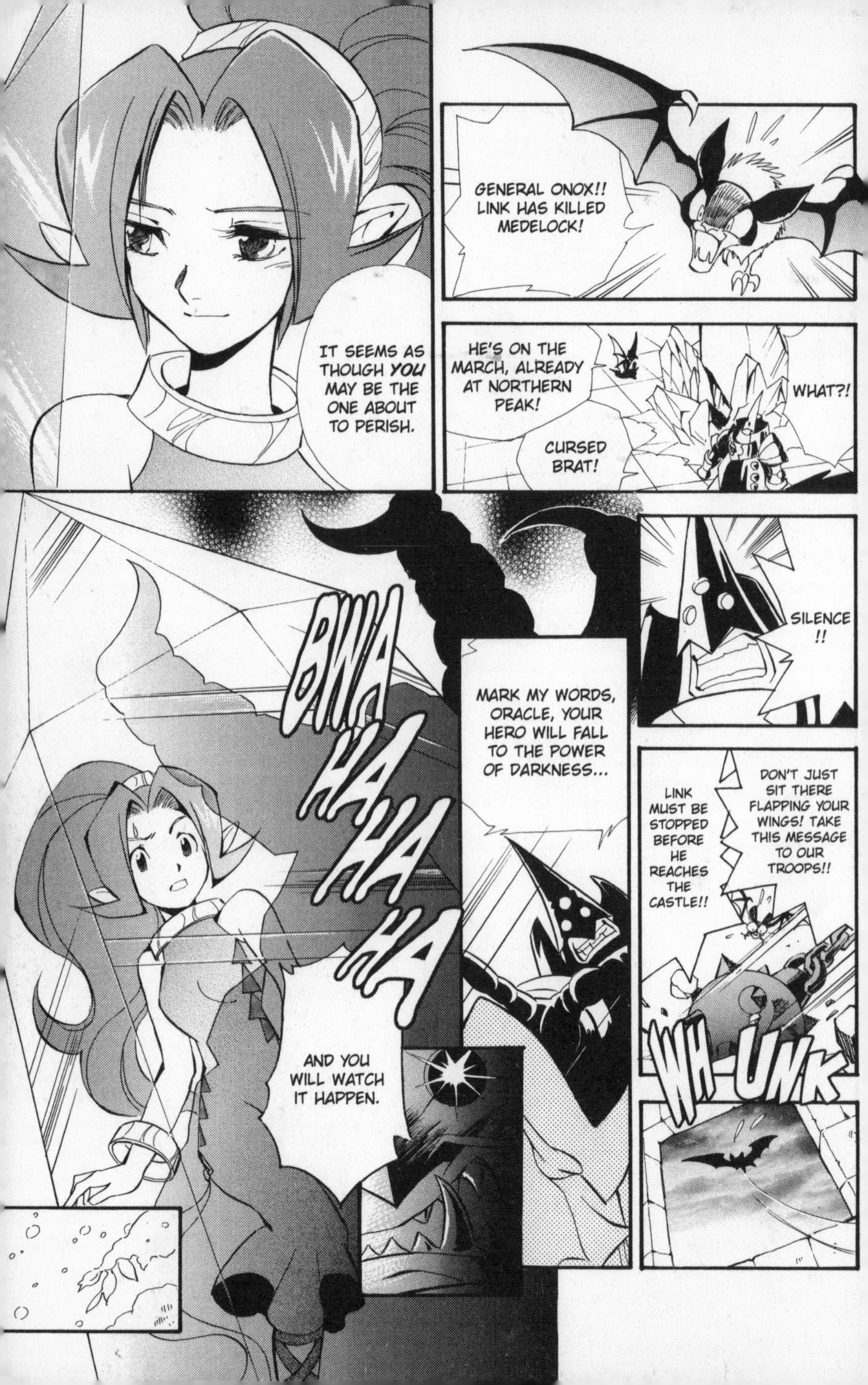

GENERAL ONOX!! LINK HAS KILLED MEDELOCK!
HE'S ON THE MARCH, ALREADY AT NORTHERN PEAK!
WHAT?!
CURSED BRAT!
IT SEEMS AS THOUGH *YOU* MAY BE THE ONE ABOUT TO PERISH.
SILENCE!!
DON'T JUST SIT THERE FLAPPING YOUR WINGS! TAKE THIS MESSAGE TO OUR TROOPS!!
LINK MUST BE STOPPED BEFORE HE REACHES THE CASTLE!!
WH-UNK
MARK MY WORDS, ORACLE, YOUR HERO WILL FALL TO THE POWER OF DARKNESS...
BWA HA HA HA
AND YOU WILL WATCH IT HAPPEN.

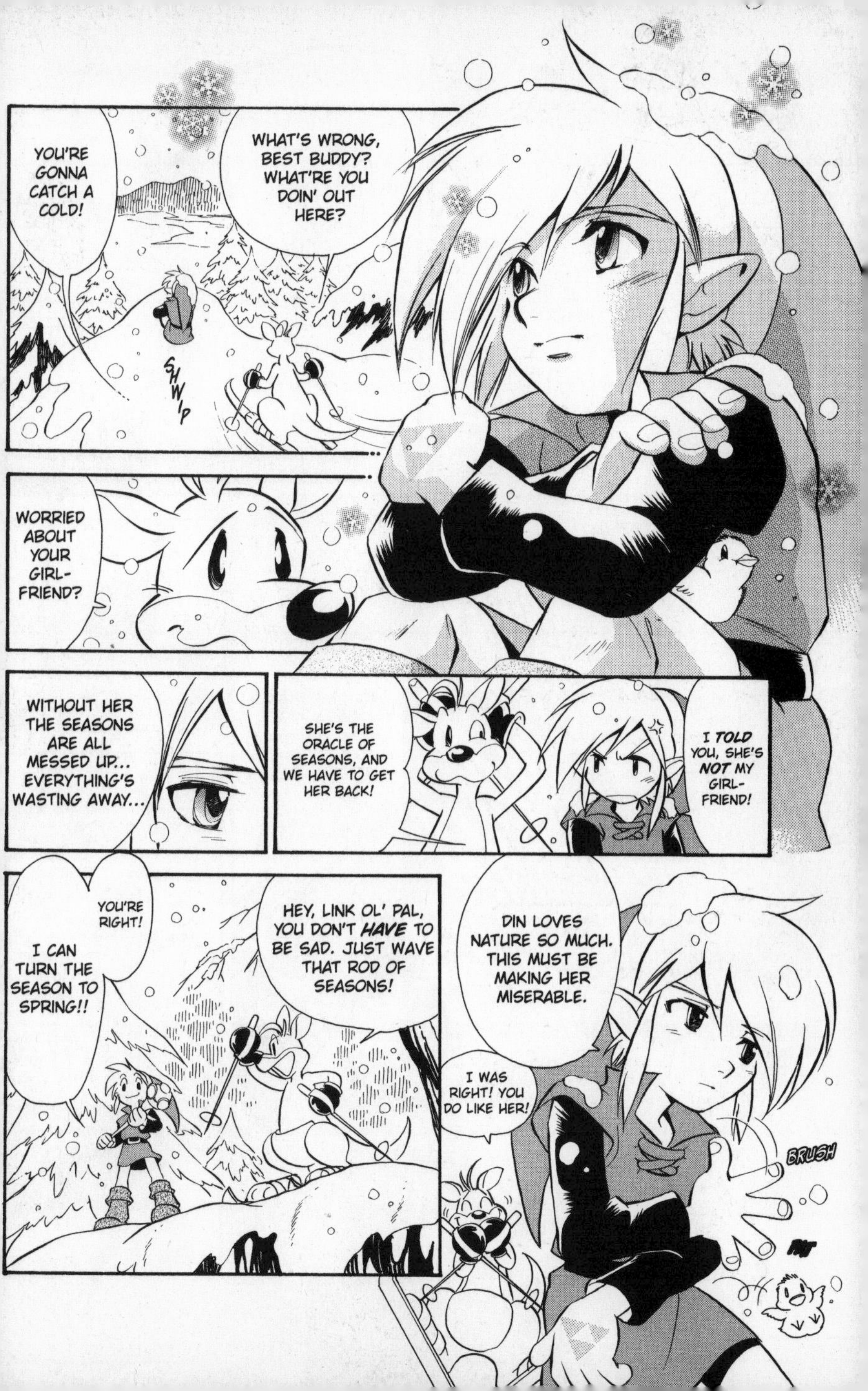
WHAT'S WRONG, BEST BUDDY? WHAT'RE YOU DOIN' OUT HERE?
YOU'RE GONNA CATCH A COLD!
SHWIP
WORRIED ABOUT YOUR GIRL-FRIEND?
I *TOLD* YOU, SHE'S *NOT* MY GIRL-FRIEND!
SHE'S THE ORACLE OF SEASONS, AND WE HAVE TO GET HER BACK!
WITHOUT HER THE SEASONS ARE ALL MESSED UP... EVERYTHING'S WASTING AWAY...
DIN LOVES NATURE SO MUCH. THIS MUST BE MAKING HER MISERABLE.
I WAS RIGHT! YOU DO LIKE HER!
BRUSH
HEY, LINK OL' PAL, YOU DON'T *HAVE* TO BE SAD. JUST WAVE THAT ROD OF SEASONS!
YOU'RE RIGHT!
I CAN TURN THE SEASON TO SPRING!!

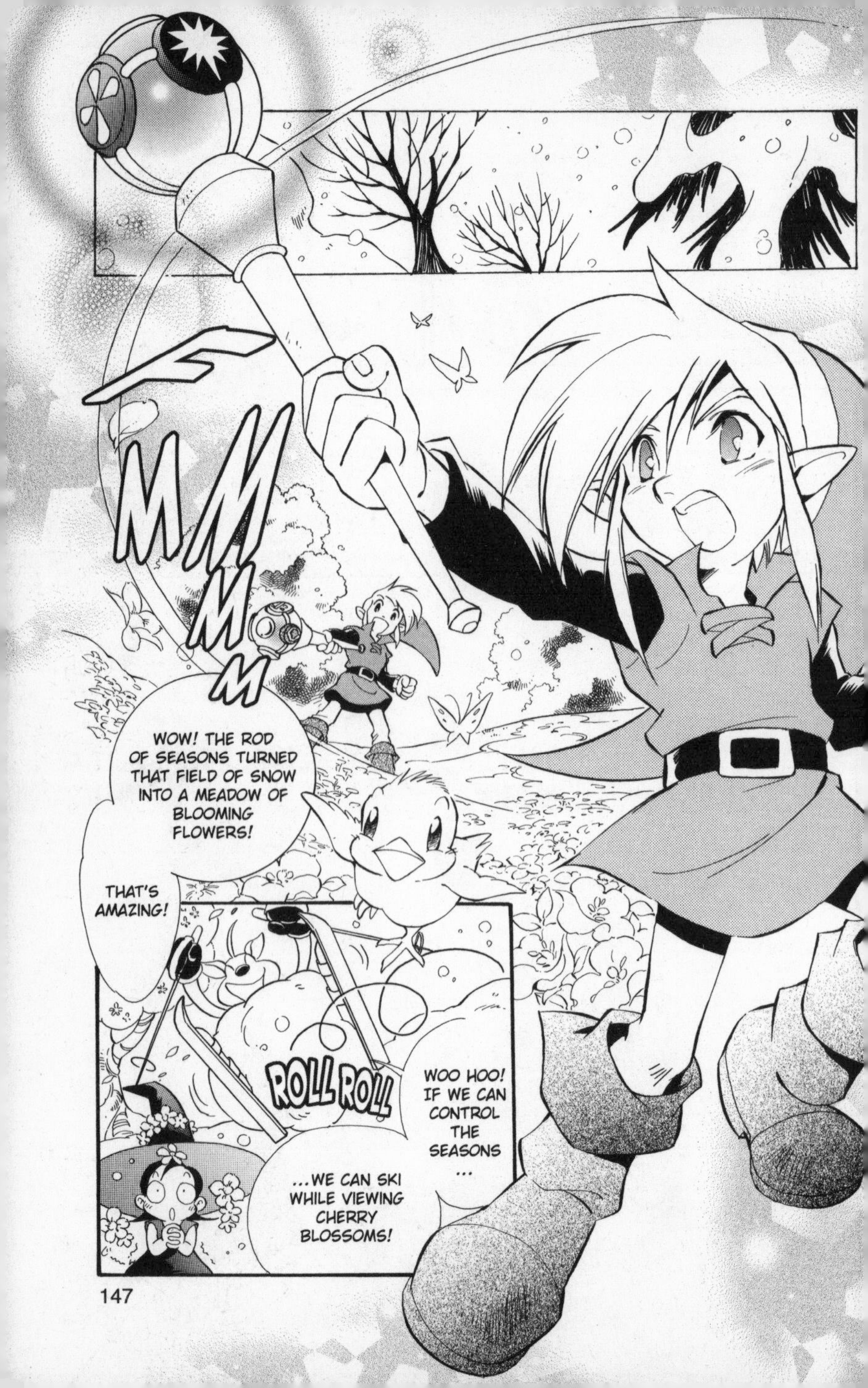
FMMMMM
WOW! THE ROD OF SEASONS TURNED THAT FIELD OF SNOW INTO A MEADOW OF BLOOMING FLOWERS!
THAT'S AMAZING!
ROLL ROLL
WOO HOO! IF WE CAN CONTROL THE SEASONS ...
...WE CAN SKI WHILE VIEWING CHERRY BLOSSOMS!

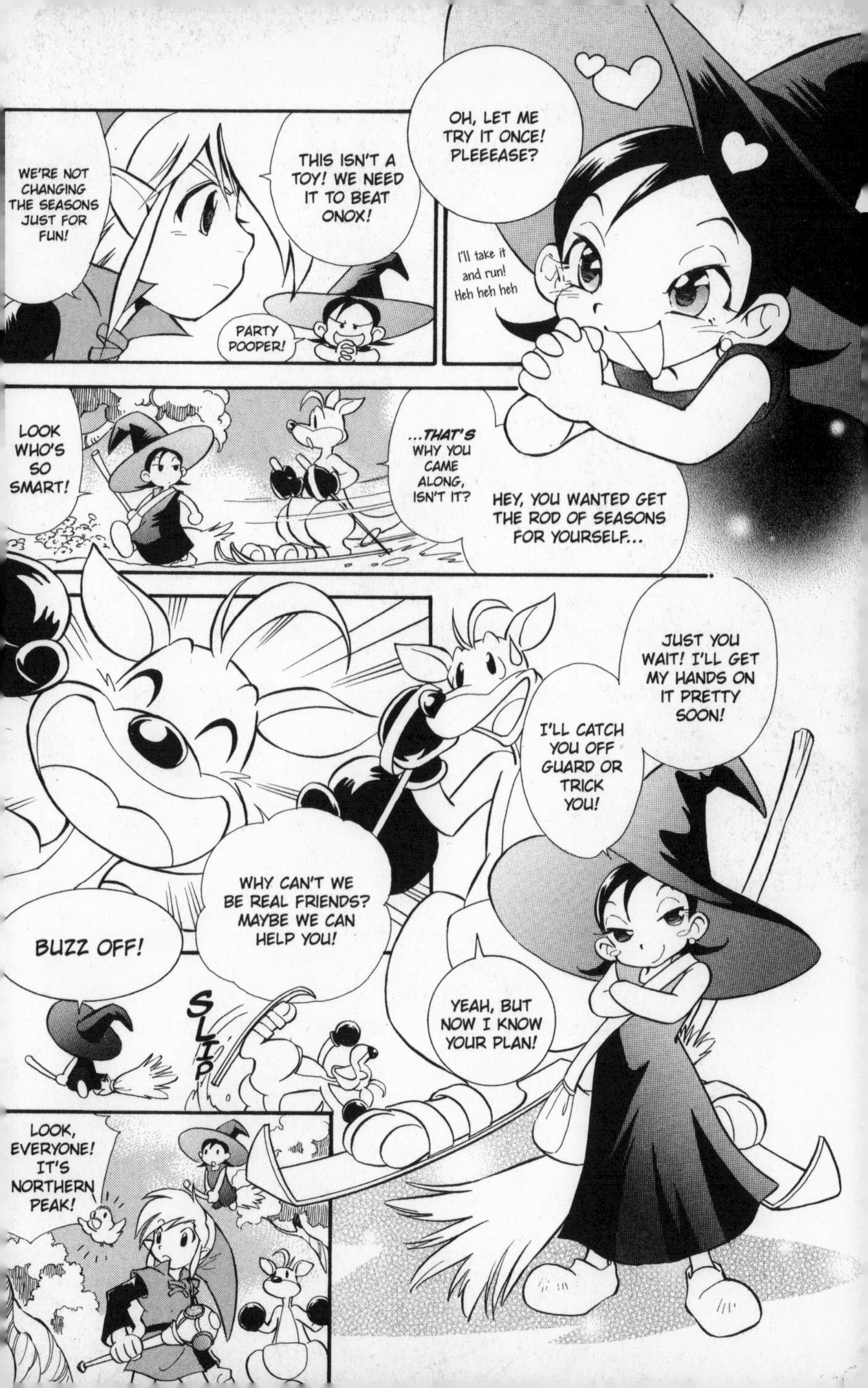
OH, LET ME TRY IT ONCE! PLEEEASE?
I'll take it and run! Heh heh heh
THIS ISN'T A TOY! WE NEED IT TO BEAT ONOX!
WE'RE NOT CHANGING THE SEASONS JUST FOR FUN!
PARTY POOPER!
HEY, YOU WANTED GET THE ROD OF SEASONS FOR YOURSELF...
...THAT'S WHY YOU CAME ALONG, ISN'T IT?
LOOK WHO'S SO SMART!
JUST YOU WAIT! I'LL GET MY HANDS ON IT PRETTY SOON!
I'LL CATCH YOU OFF GUARD OR TRICK YOU!
YEAH, BUT NOW I KNOW YOUR PLAN!
WHY CAN'T WE BE REAL FRIENDS? MAYBE WE CAN HELP YOU!
BUZZ OFF!
SLIP
LOOK, EVERYONE! IT'S NORTHERN PEAK!

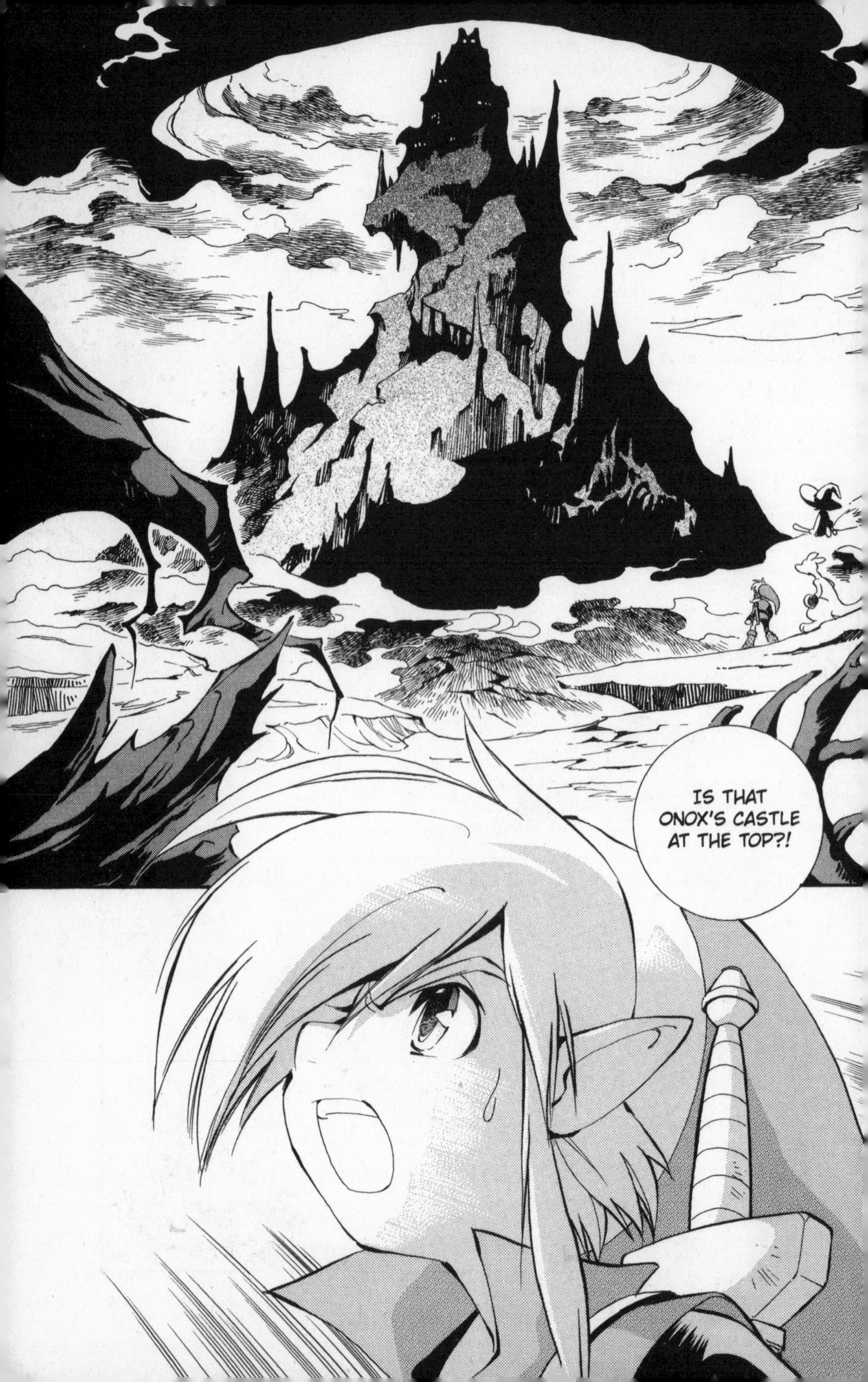
IS THAT ONOX'S CASTLE AT THE TOP?!

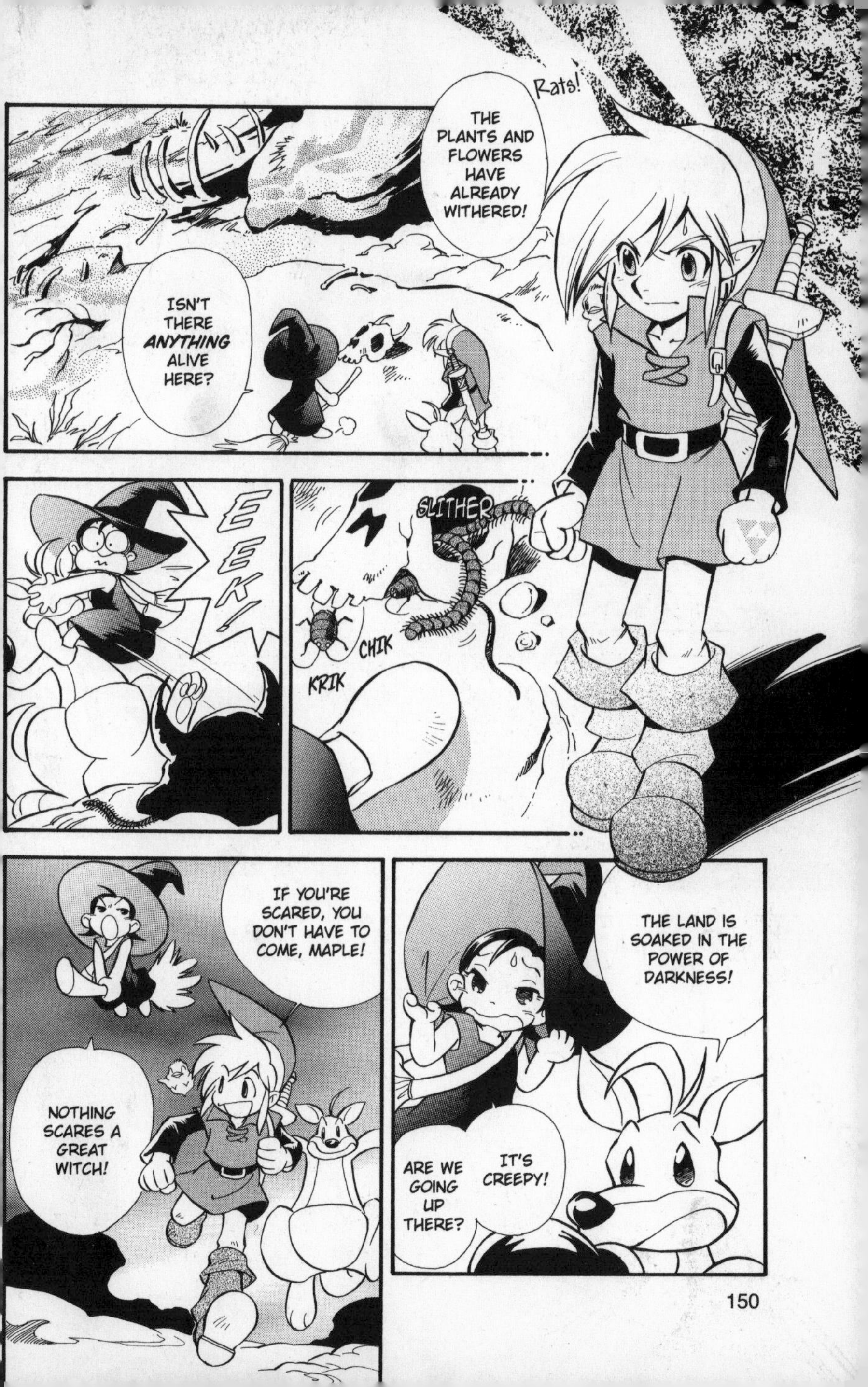
Rats!
THE PLANTS AND FLOWERS HAVE ALREADY WITHERED!
ISN'T THERE *ANYTHING* ALIVE HERE?
SLITHER
CHIK
KRIK
EEEK!
THE LAND IS SOAKED IN THE POWER OF DARKNESS!
IT'S CREEPY!
ARE WE GOING UP THERE?
IF YOU'RE SCARED, YOU DON'T HAVE TO COME, MAPLE!
NOTHING SCARES A GREAT WITCH!

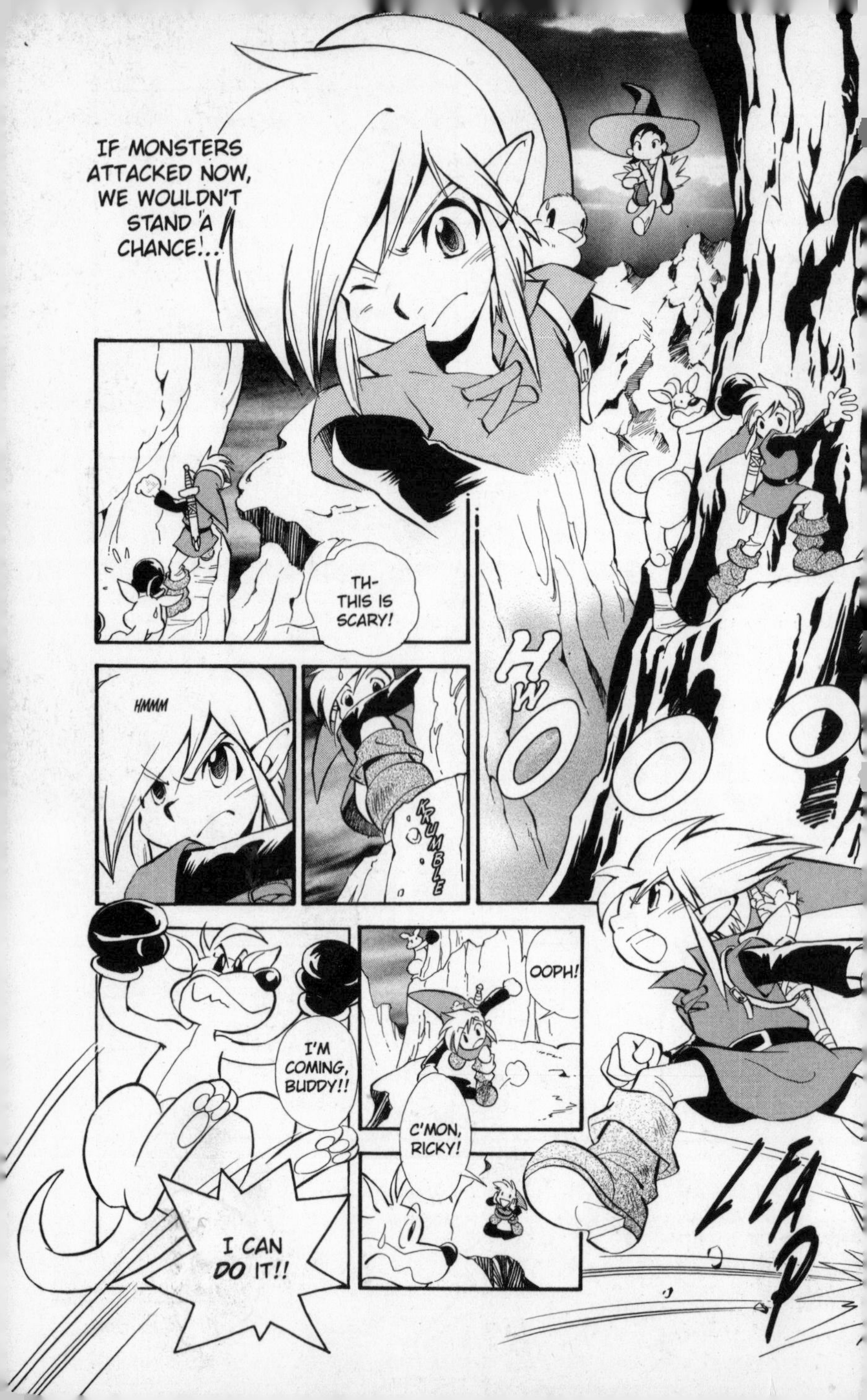
IF MONSTERS ATTACKED NOW, WE WOULDN'T STAND A CHANCE!...
HWOOOO
TH- THIS IS SCARY!
KRUMBLE
HMMM
LEAP
OOPH!
C'MON, RICKY!
I'M COMING, BUDDY!!
I CAN DO IT!!

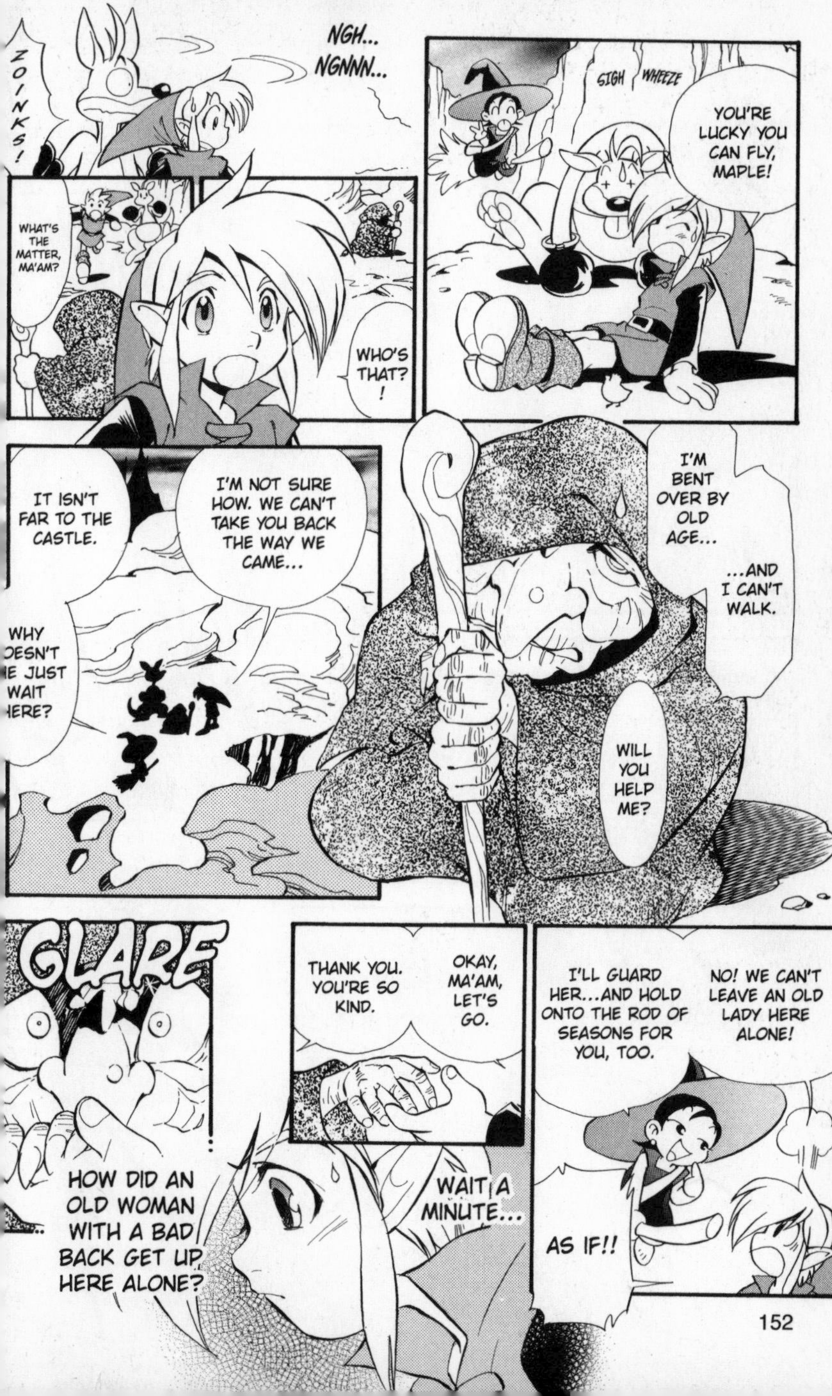
SIGH
WHEEZE
YOU'RE LUCKY YOU CAN FLY, MAPLE!
NGH... NGNNN...
ZOINKS!
WHO'S THAT?!
WHAT'S THE MATTER, MA'AM?
I'M BENT OVER BY OLD AGE...
...AND I CAN'T WALK.
WILL YOU HELP ME?
I'M NOT SURE HOW. WE CAN'T TAKE YOU BACK THE WAY WE CAME...
IT ISN'T FAR TO THE CASTLE.
WHY OESN'T E JUST WAIT ERE?
NO! WE CAN'T LEAVE AN OLD LADY HERE ALONE!
I'LL GUARD HER...AND HOLD ONTO THE ROD OF SEASONS FOR YOU, TOO.
AS IF!!
OKAY, MA'AM, LET'S GO.
THANK YOU. YOU'RE SO KIND.
WAIT A MINUTE...
GLARE
HOW DID AN OLD WOMAN WITH A BAD BACK GET UP HERE ALONE?

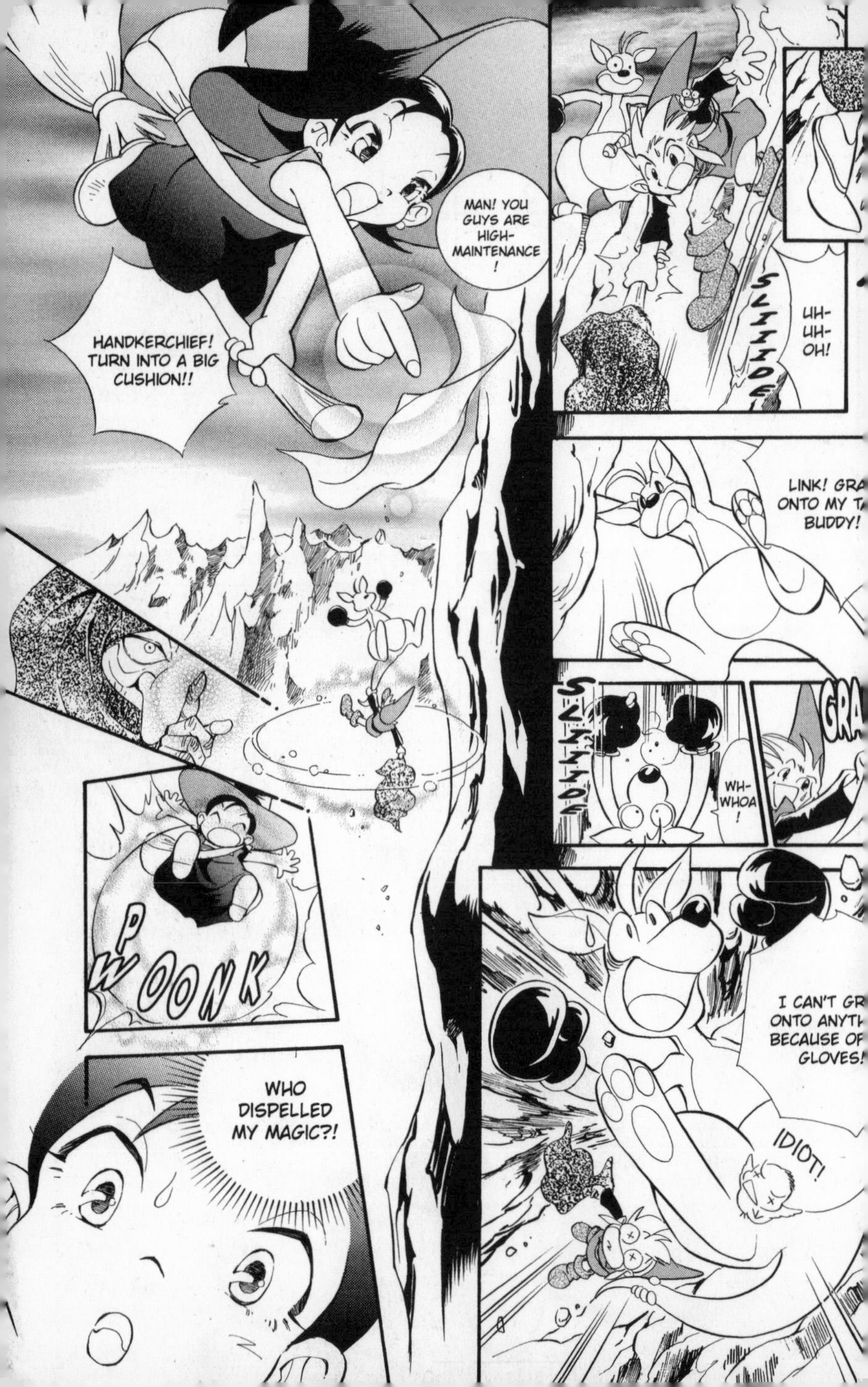
UH-UH-OH!
SLIIIIDE
LINK! GRA
ONTO MY TA
BUDDY!
GRA
WH-WHOA!
SLIIIIDE
I CAN'T GR
ONTO ANYTH
BECAUSE OF
GLOVES!
IDIOT!
MAN! YOU GUYS ARE HIGH-MAINTENANCE!
HANDKERCHIEF! TURN INTO A BIG CUSHION!!
PWOONK
WHO DISPELLED MY MAGIC?!

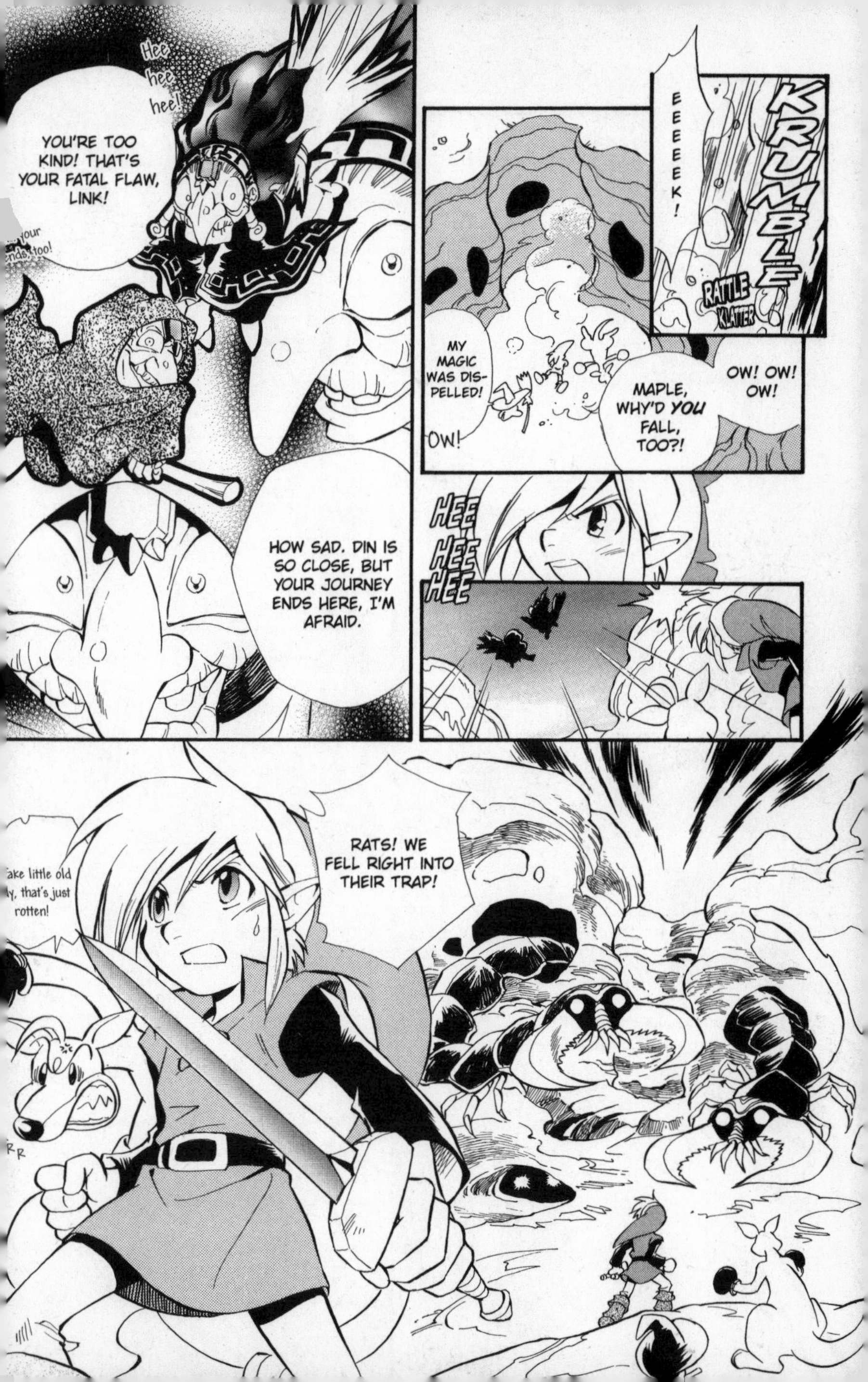
EEEEEEK!
KRUMBLE
RATTLE
KLATTER
OW! OW! OW!
MAPLE, WHY'D YOU FALL, TOO?!
MY MAGIC WAS DIS-PELLED!
OW!
HEE HEE HEE
Hee hee hee!
YOU'RE TOO KIND! THAT'S YOUR FATAL FLAW, LINK!
HOW SAD. DIN IS SO CLOSE, BUT YOUR JOURNEY ENDS HERE, I'M AFRAID.
RATS! WE FELL RIGHT INTO THEIR TRAP!

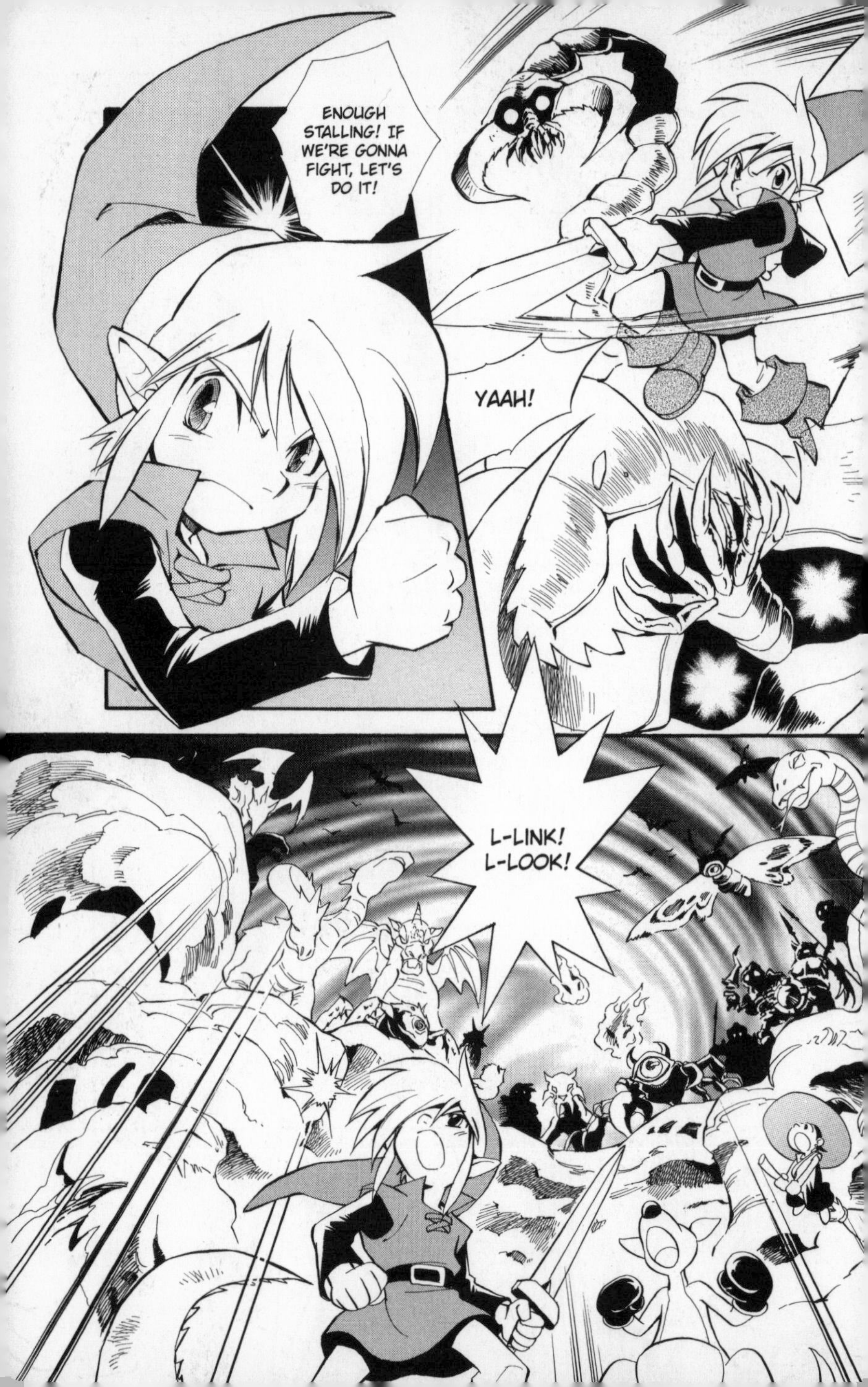
YAAH!
ENOUGH STALLING! IF WE'RE GONNA FIGHT, LET'S DO IT!
L-LINK! L-LOOK!

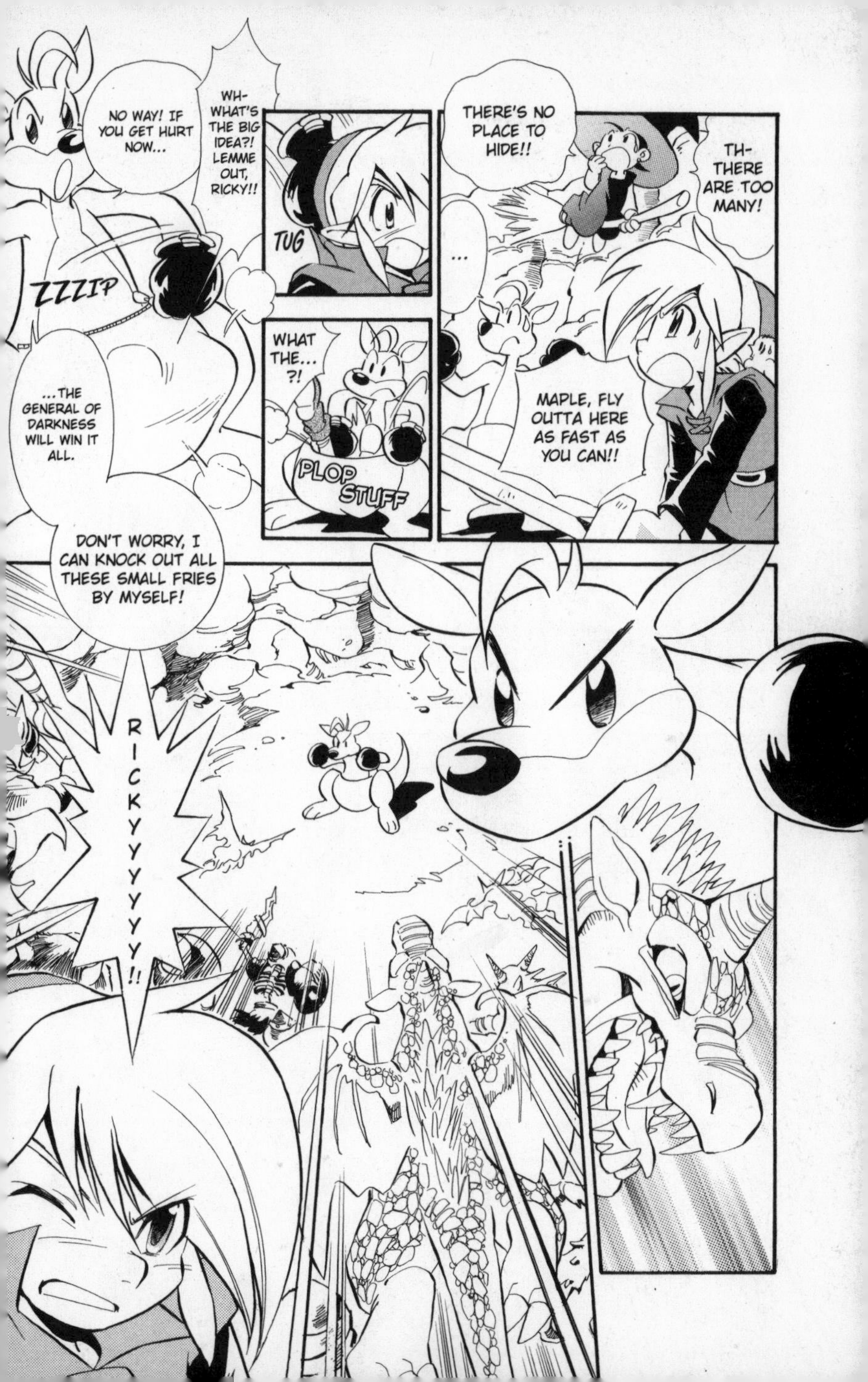
THERE'S NO PLACE TO HIDE!!
TH- THERE ARE TOO MANY!
...
MAPLE, FLY OUTTA HERE AS FAST AS YOU CAN!!
WH- WHAT'S THE BIG IDEA?! LEMME OUT, RICKY!!
TUG
WHAT THE... ?!
PLOP
STUFF
NO WAY! IF YOU GET HURT NOW...
ZZZIP
...THE GENERAL OF DARKNESS WILL WIN IT ALL.
DON'T WORRY, I CAN KNOCK OUT ALL THESE SMALL FRIES BY MYSELF!
RICKYYYYYY!!

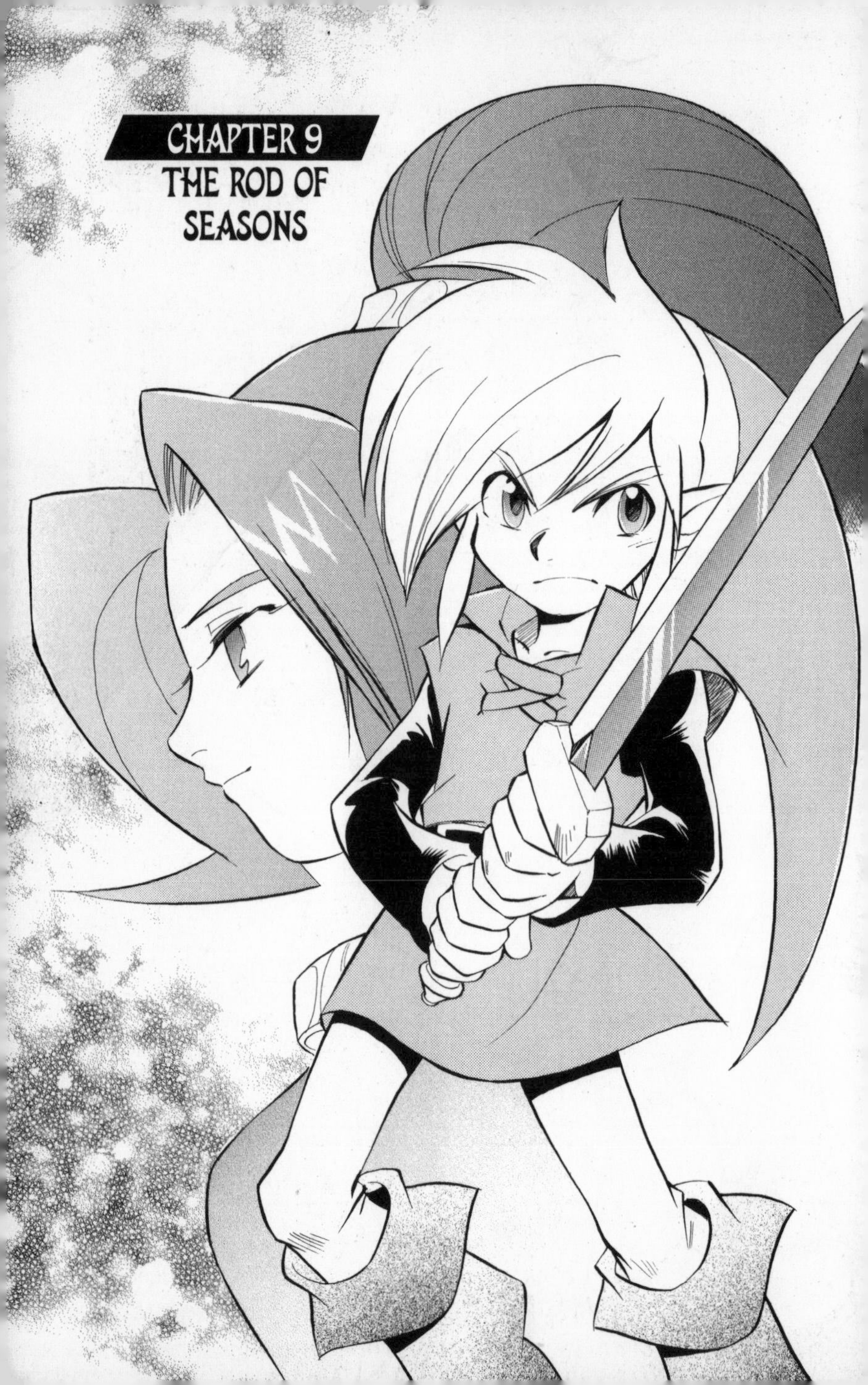
CHAPTER 9
THE ROD OF SEASONS

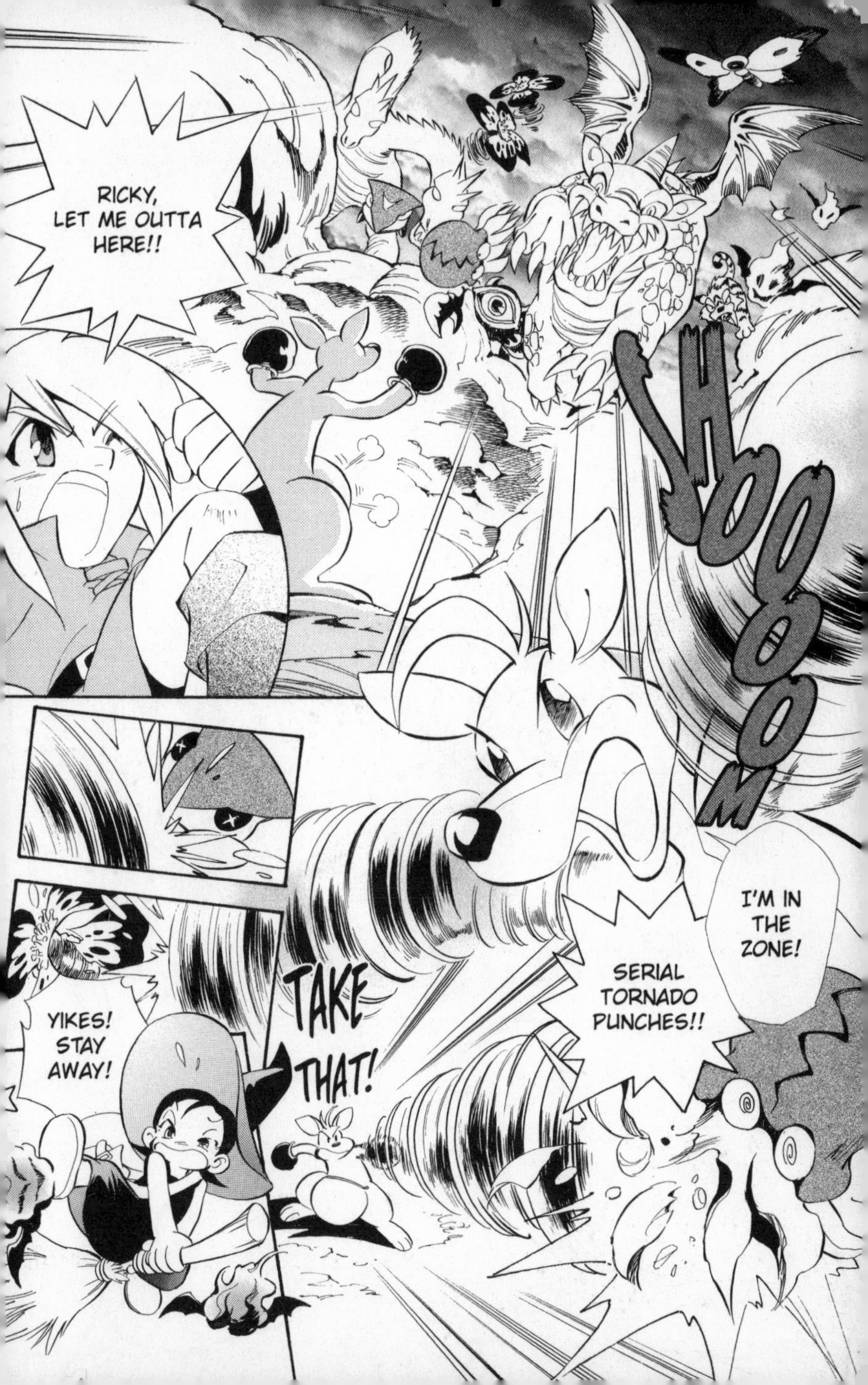
RICKY, LET ME OUTTA HERE!!
SHOOOOM
I'M IN THE ZONE!
SERIAL TORNADO PUNCHES!!
TAKE THAT!
YIKES! STAY AWAY!

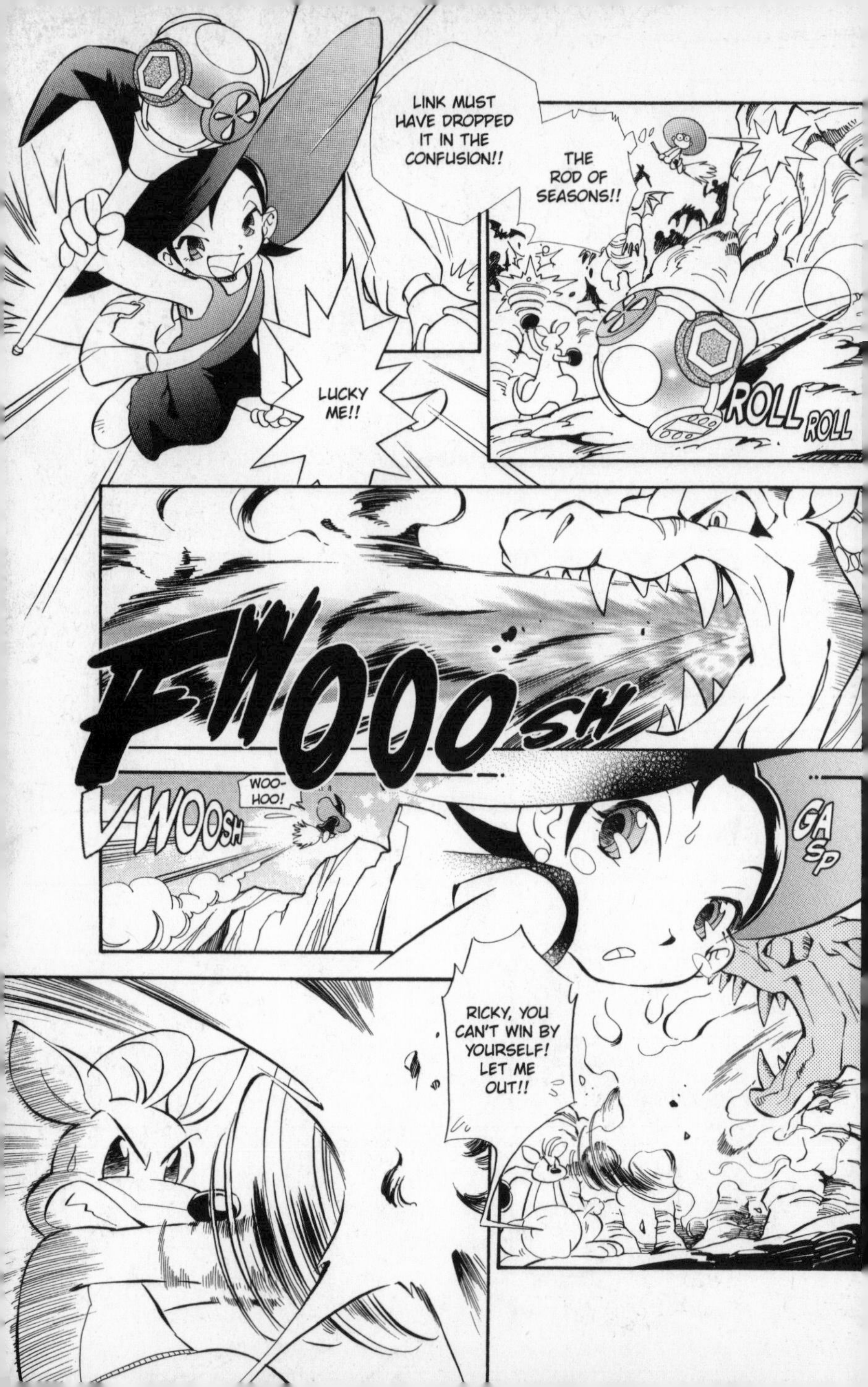
THE ROD OF SEASONS!!
ROLL ROLL
LINK MUST HAVE DROPPED IT IN THE CONFUSION!!
LUCKY ME!!
FWOOOSH
GASP
WOO-HOO!
VWOOSH
RICKY, YOU CAN'T WIN BY YOURSELF! LET ME OUT!!

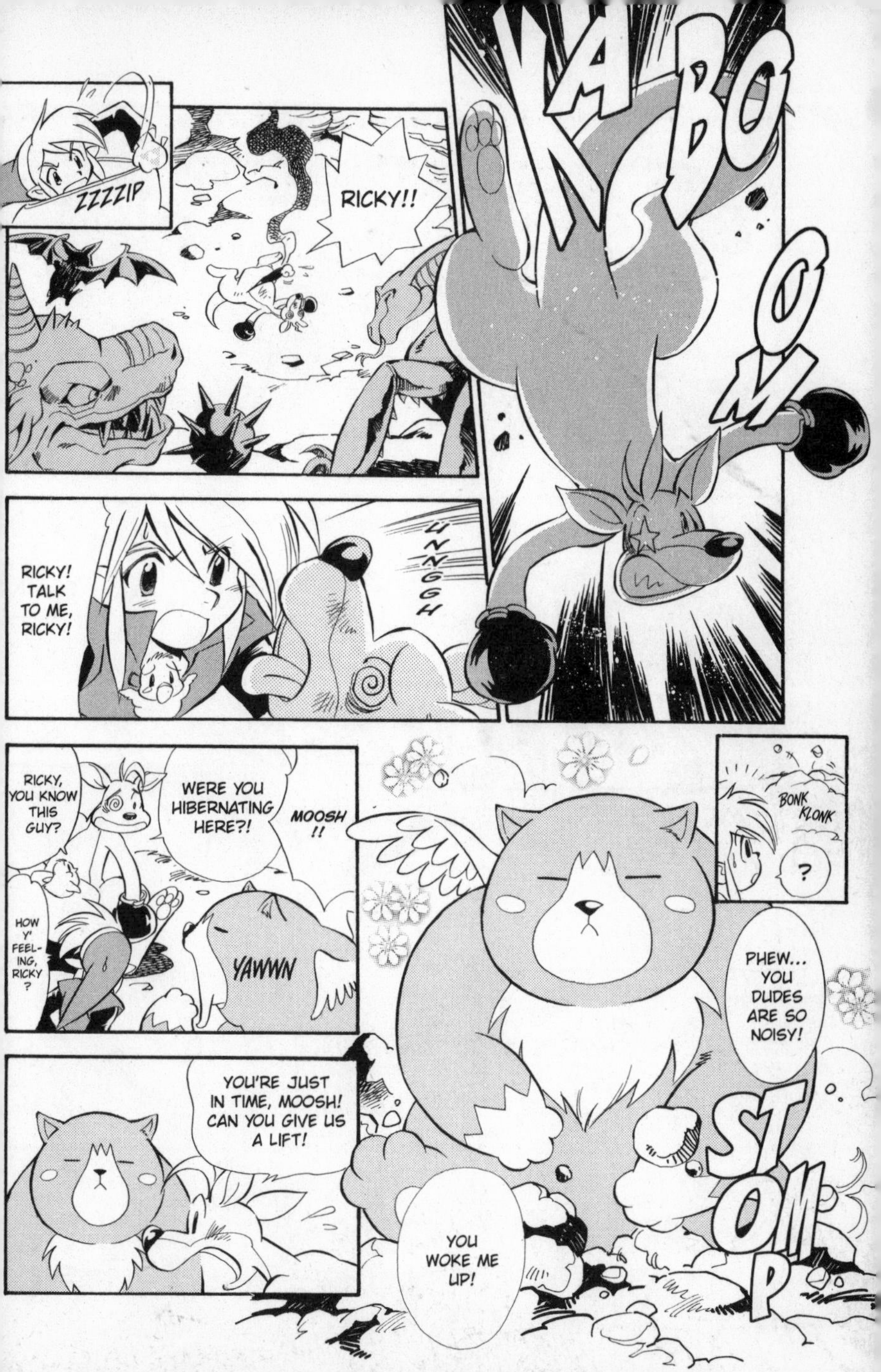
WA-BOOM
UNNNGGH
RICKY!!
ZZZZIP
RICKY! TALK TO ME, RICKY!
BONK
KLONK
?
PHEW... YOU DUDES ARE SO NOISY!
STOMP
YOU WOKE ME UP!
MOOSH!!
WERE YOU HIBERNATING HERE?!
RICKY, YOU KNOW THIS GUY?
HOW Y' FEELING, RICKY?
YAWWN
YOU'RE JUST IN TIME, MOOSH! CAN YOU GIVE US A LIFT!

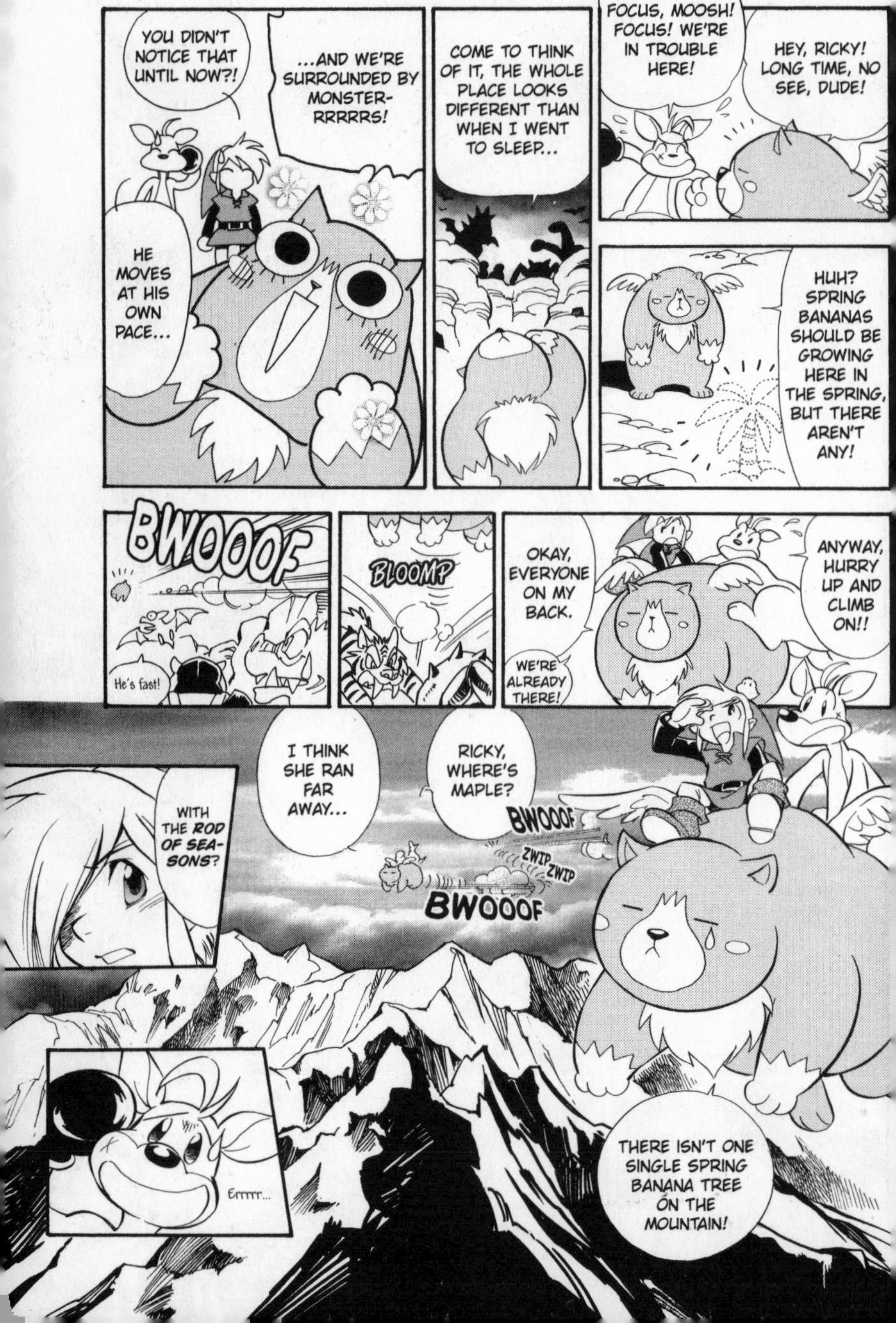
HEY, RICKY! LONG TIME, NO SEE, DUDE!
FOCUS, MOOSH! FOCUS! WE'RE IN TROUBLE HERE!
HUH? SPRING BANANAS SHOULD BE GROWING HERE IN THE SPRING, BUT THERE AREN'T ANY!
COME TO THINK OF IT, THE WHOLE PLACE LOOKS DIFFERENT THAN WHEN I WENT TO SLEEP...
...AND WE'RE SURROUNDED BY MONSTER-RRRRRS!
YOU DIDN'T NOTICE THAT UNTIL NOW?!
HE MOVES AT HIS OWN PACE...
ANYWAY, HURRY UP AND CLIMB ON!!
OKAY, EVERYONE ON MY BACK.
WE'RE ALREADY THERE!
BLOOMP
BWOOOF
He's fast!
RICKY, WHERE'S MAPLE?
I THINK SHE RAN FAR AWAY...
BWOOOF
ZWIP ZWIP
BWOOOF
WITH THE *ROD OF SEASONS*?
Errrrr...
THERE ISN'T ONE SINGLE SPRING BANANA TREE ON THE MOUNTAIN!

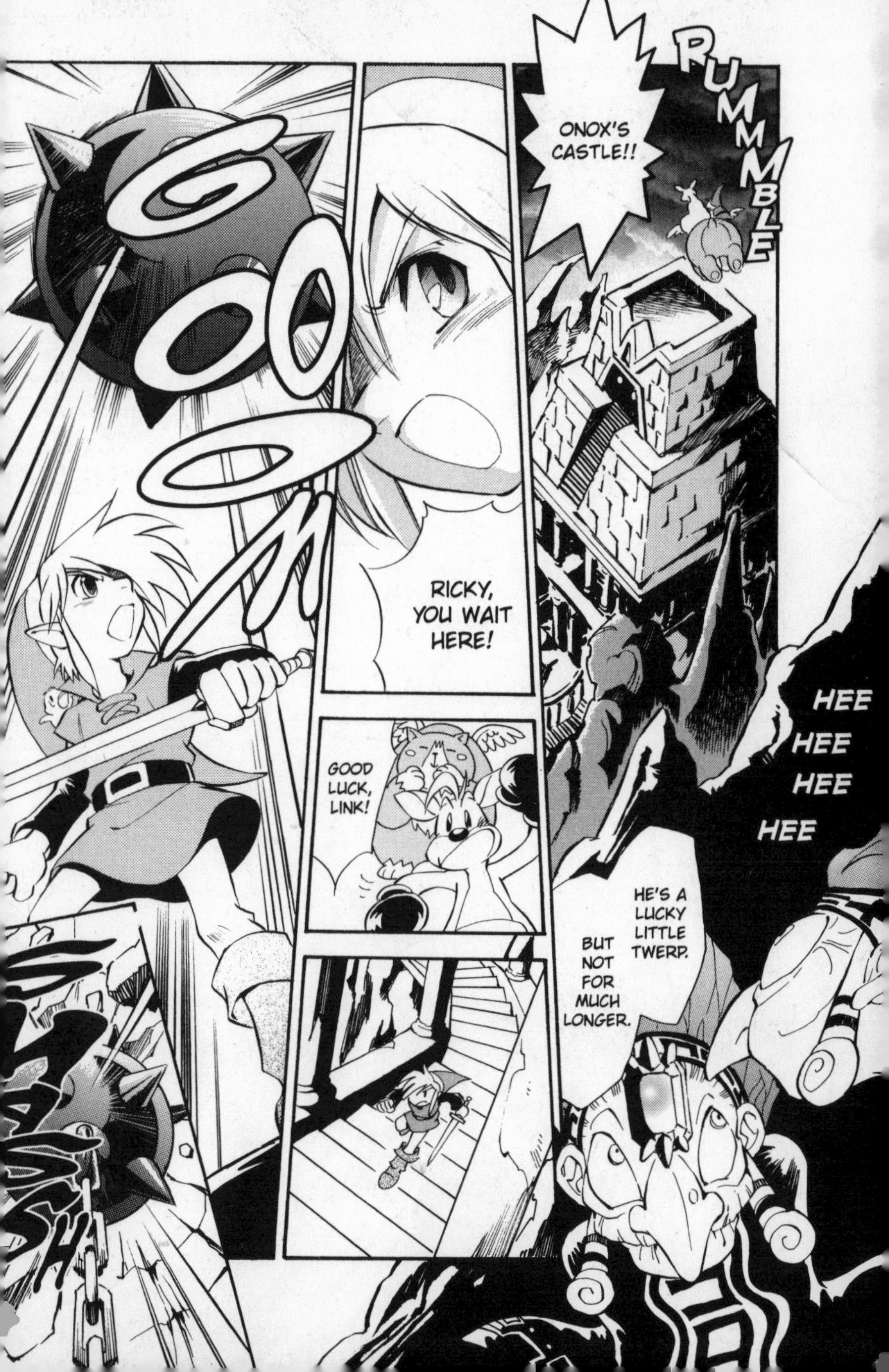
ONOX'S CASTLE!!
RUMMMBLE
HEE HEE HEE HEE
HE'S A LUCKY LITTLE TWERP.
BUT NOT FOR MUCH LONGER.
RICKY, YOU WAIT HERE!
GOOD LUCK, LINK!
GOOOM

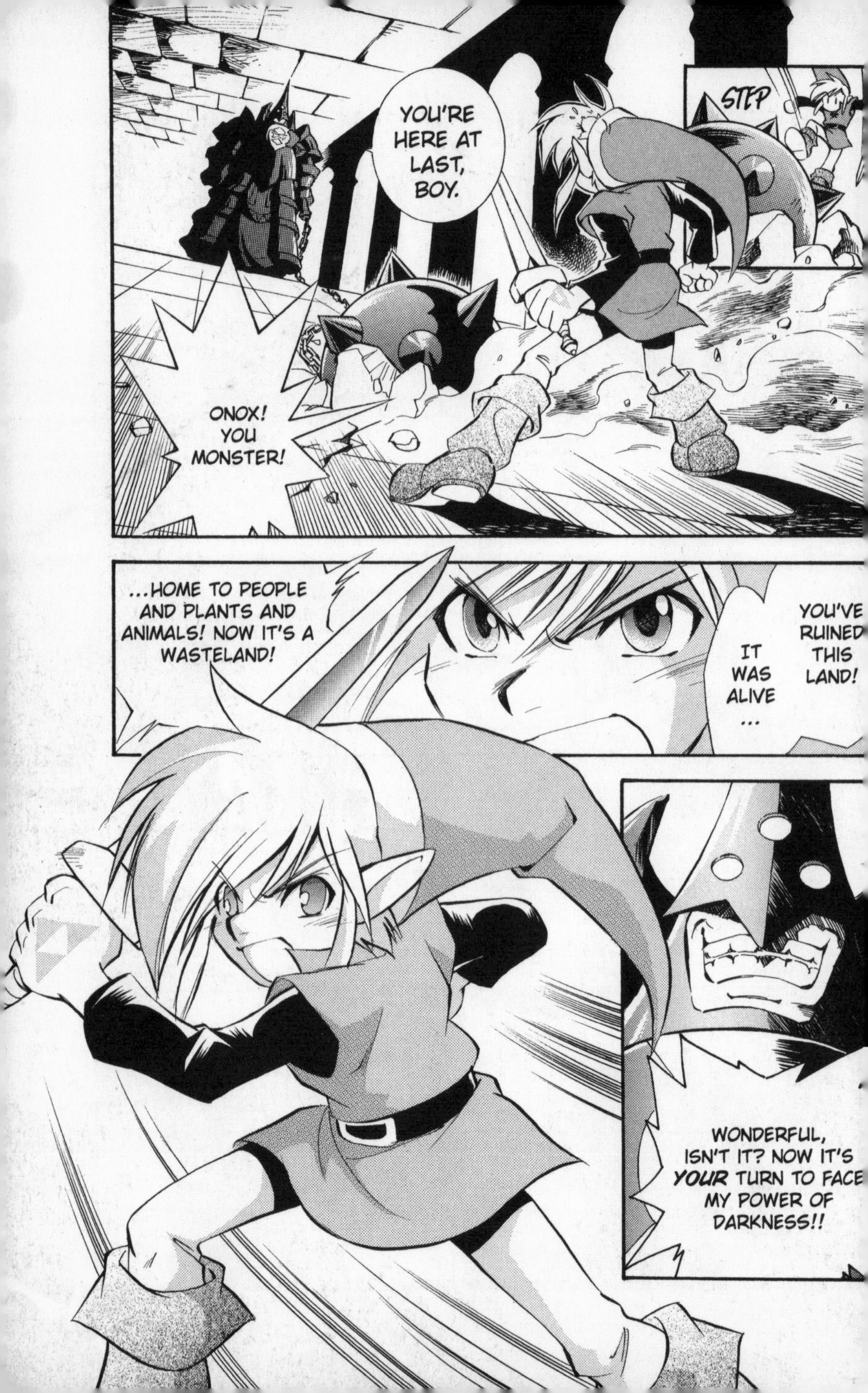
STEP
YOU'RE HERE AT LAST, BOY.
ONOX! YOU MONSTER!
YOU'VE RUINED THIS LAND!
IT WAS ALIVE...
...HOME TO PEOPLE AND PLANTS AND ANIMALS! NOW IT'S A WASTELAND!
WONDERFUL, ISN'T IT? NOW IT'S *YOUR* TURN TO FACE MY POWER OF DARKNESS!!

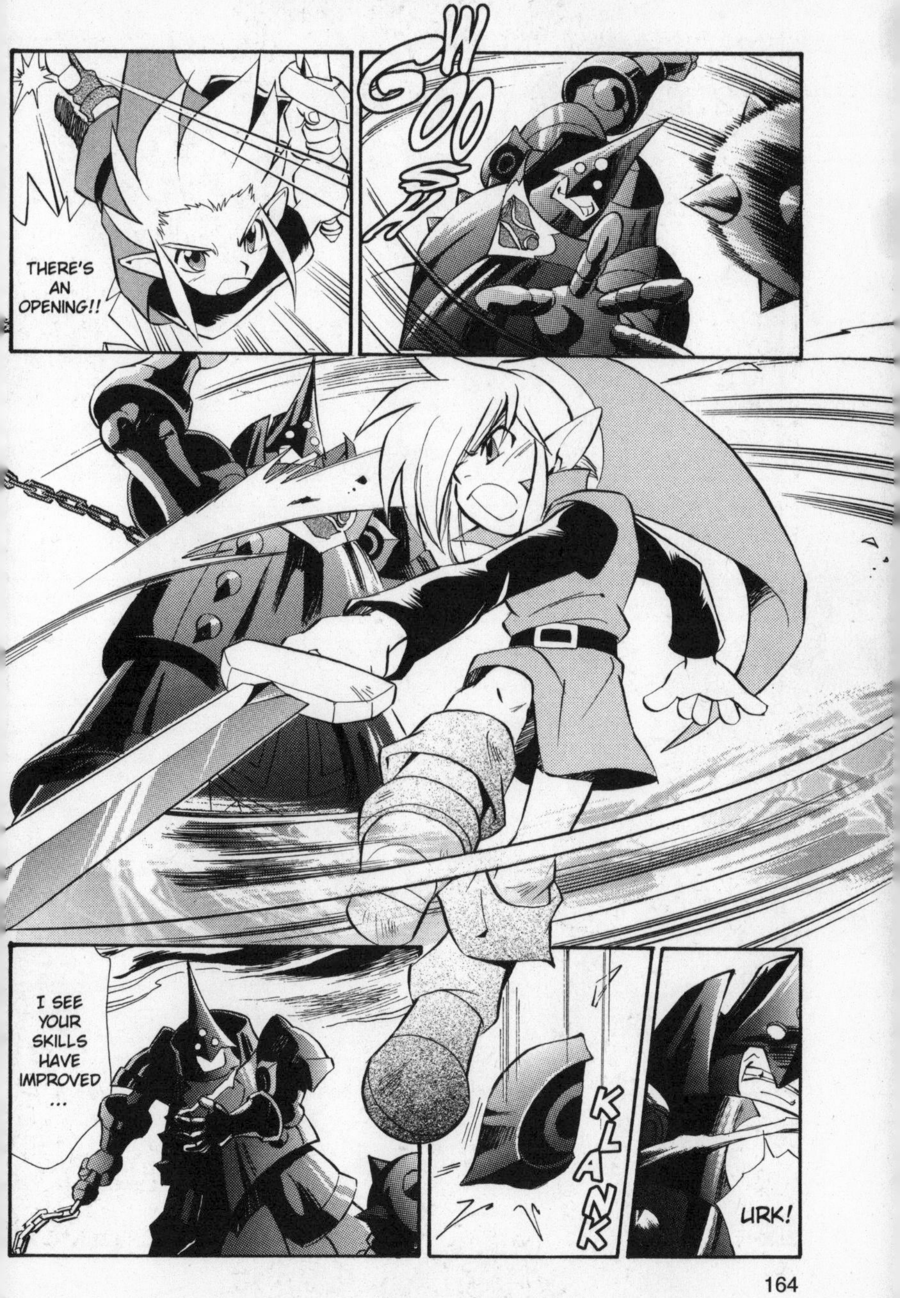
GWOOSH
THERE'S AN OPENING!!
URK!
KLANK
I SEE YOUR SKILLS HAVE IMPROVED...

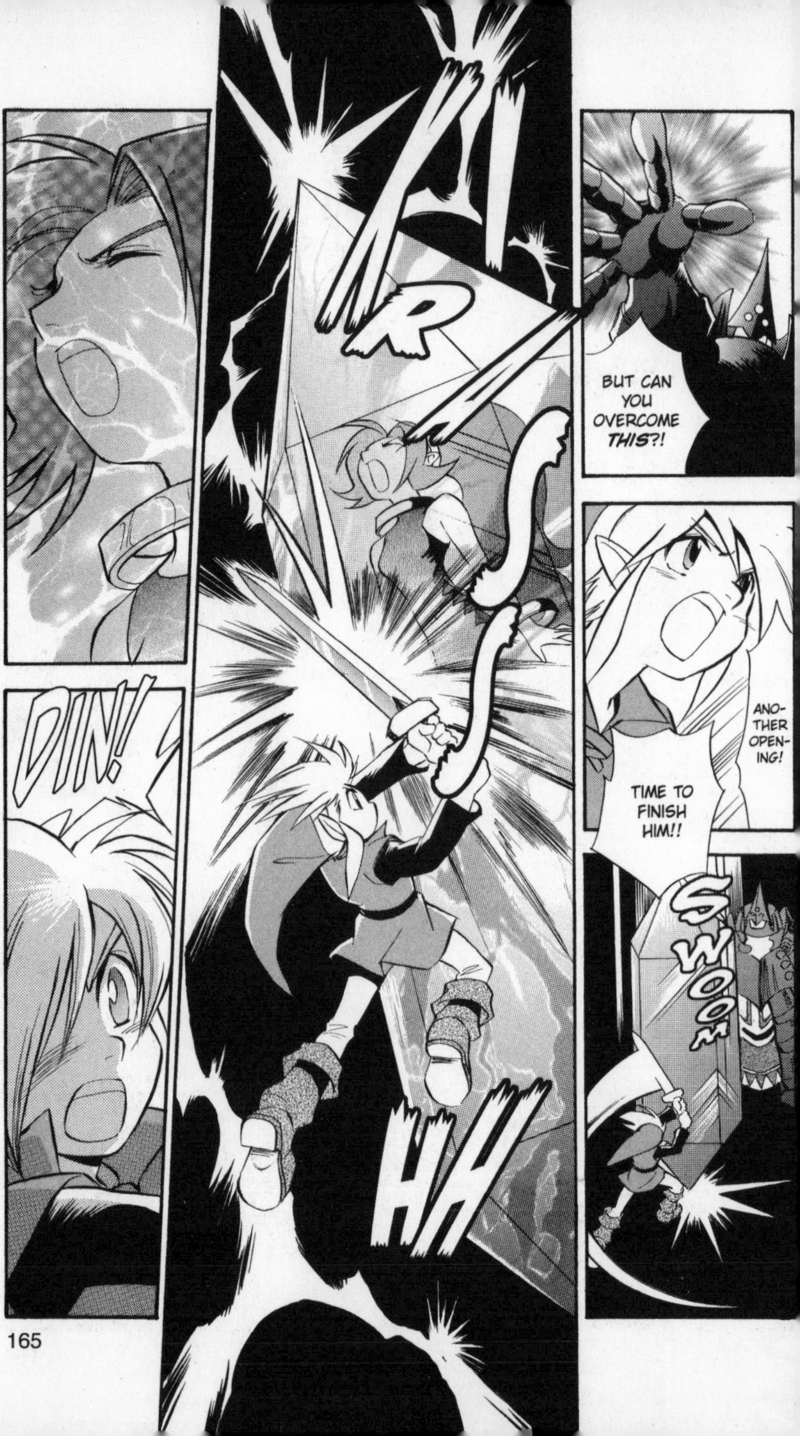
BUT CAN YOU OVERCOME THIS?!
ANOTHER OPENING!
TIME TO FINISH HIM!!
SWOOM
R
HH
DIN!!

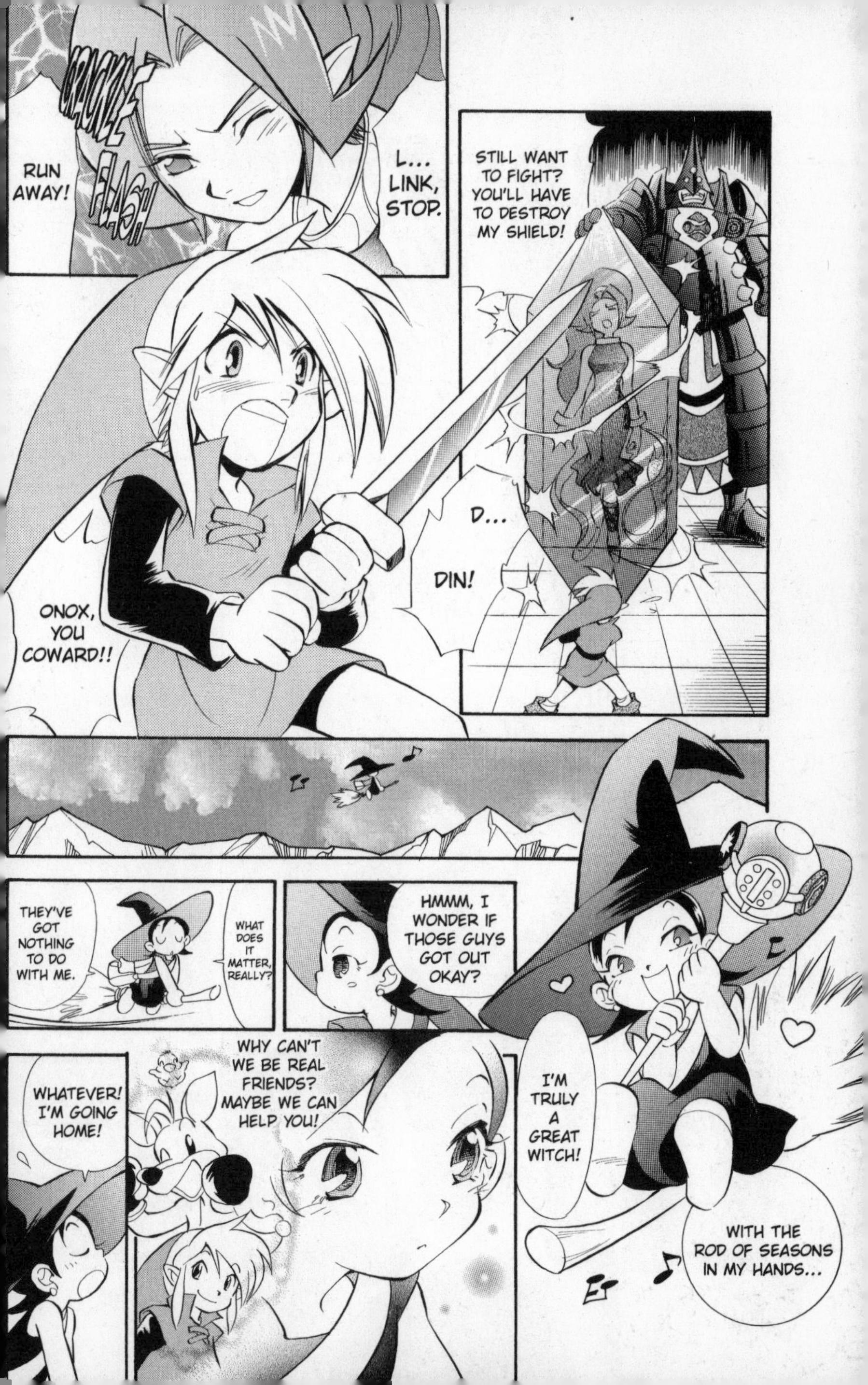
STILL WANT TO FIGHT? YOU'LL HAVE TO DESTROY MY SHIELD!
D...
DIN!
L... LINK, STOP.
CRACKLE FLASH
RUN AWAY!
ONOX, YOU COWARD!!
I'M TRULY A GREAT WITCH!
WITH THE ROD OF SEASONS IN MY HANDS...
HMMM, I WONDER IF THOSE GUYS GOT OUT OKAY?
WHAT DOES IT MATTER, REALLY?
THEY'VE GOT NOTHING TO DO WITH ME.
WHY CAN'T WE BE REAL FRIENDS? MAYBE WE CAN HELP YOU!
WHATEVER! I'M GOING HOME!

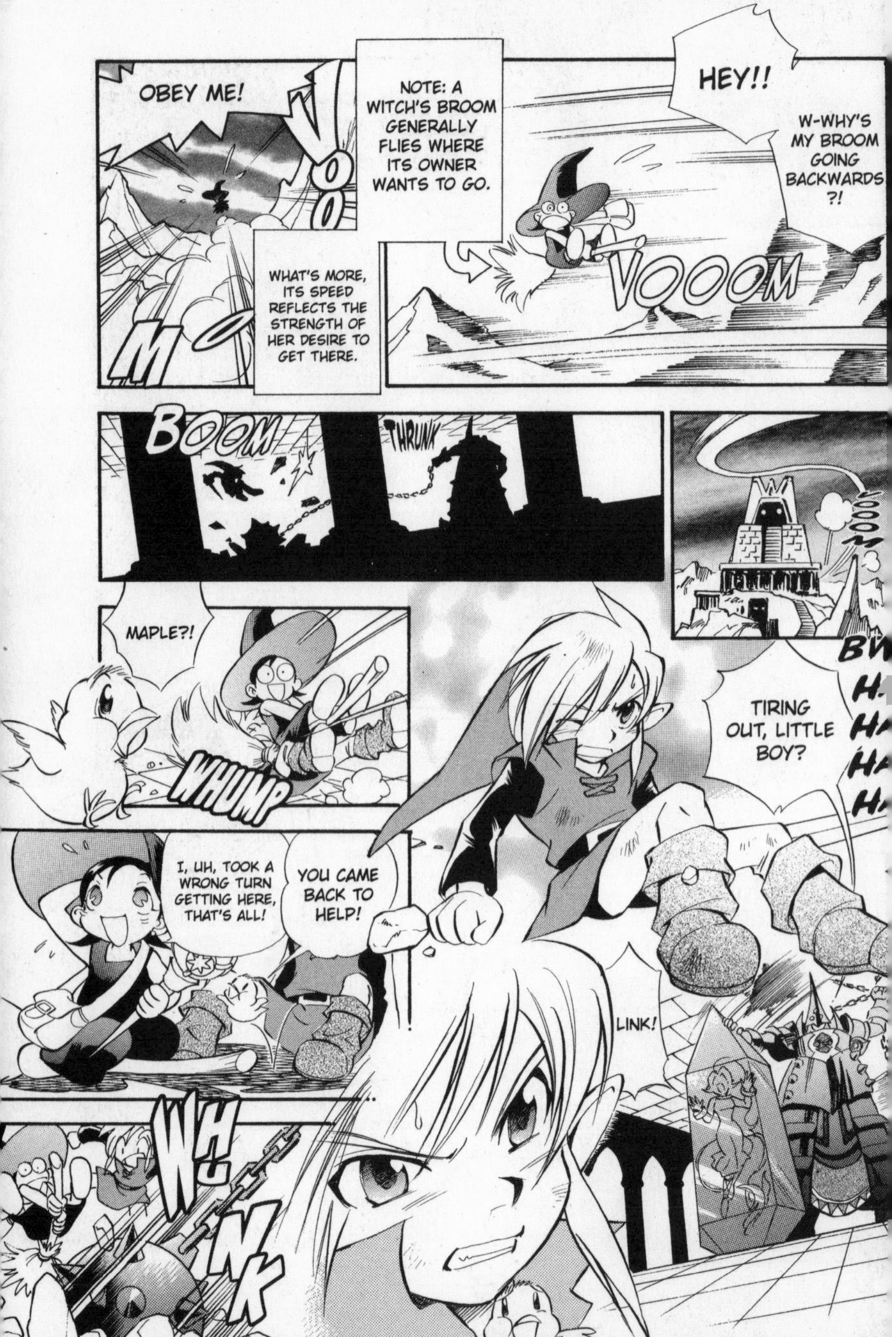
HEY!!
W-WHY'S MY BROOM GOING BACKWARDS ?!
VOOOM
NOTE: A WITCH'S BROOM GENERALLY FLIES WHERE ITS OWNER WANTS TO GO.
WHAT'S MORE, ITS SPEED REFLECTS THE STRENGTH OF HER DESIRE TO GET THERE.
OBEY ME!
VOOOM
VOOOM
BOOM
THRUNK
BWAHAHAHAHA
TIRING OUT, LITTLE BOY?
MAPLE?!
WHUMP
YOU CAME BACK TO HELP!
I, UH, TOOK A WRONG TURN GETTING HERE, THAT'S ALL!
LINK!
WHUNK

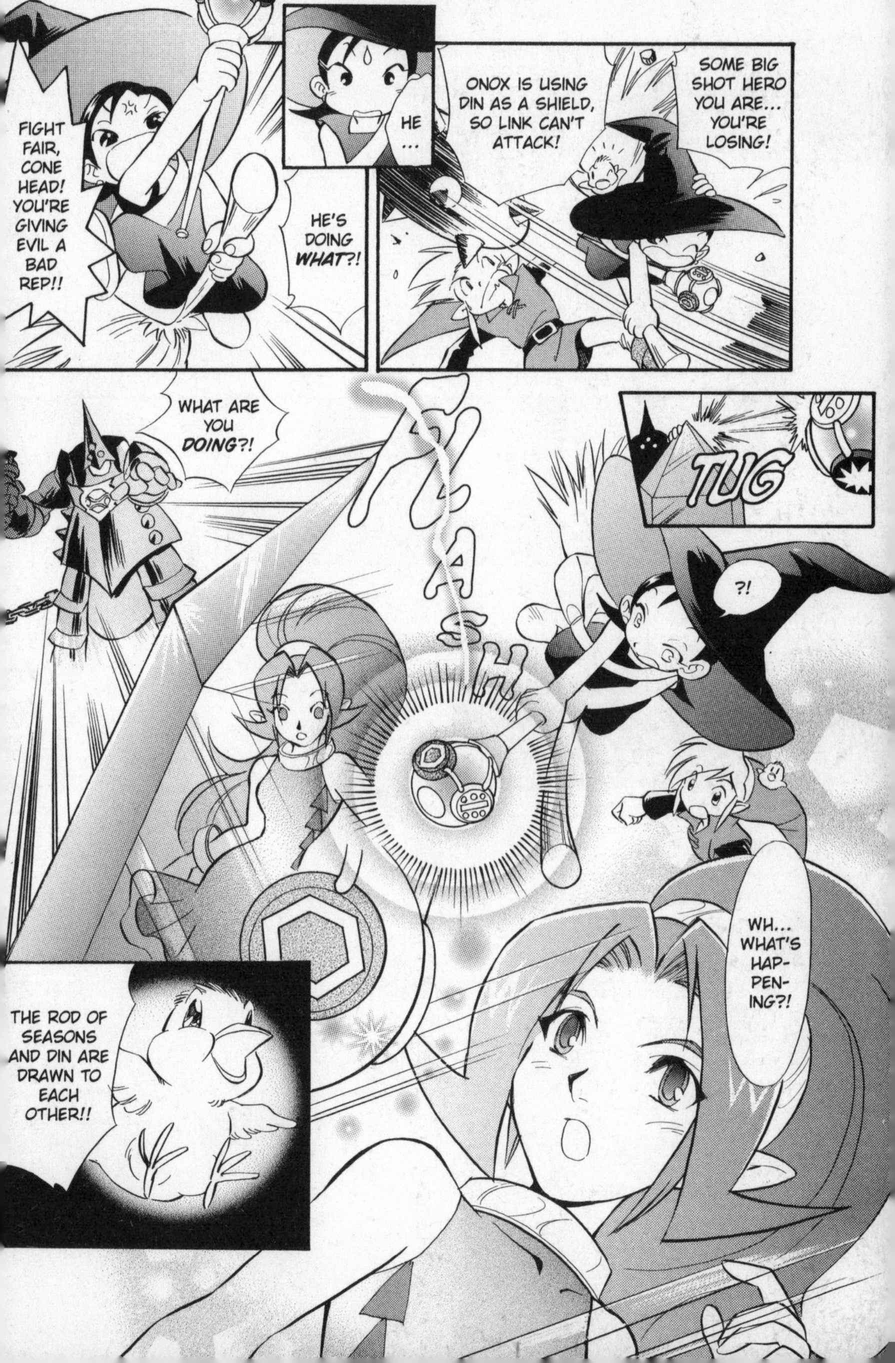
SOME BIG SHOT HERO YOU ARE... YOU'RE LOSING!
ONOX IS USING DIN AS A SHIELD, SO LINK CAN'T ATTACK!
HE ...
HE'S DOING **WHAT**?!
FIGHT FAIR, CONE HEAD! YOU'RE GIVING EVIL A BAD REP!!
TUG
?!
WHAT ARE YOU **DOING**?!
FLASH
WH... WHAT'S HAP-PEN-ING?!
THE ROD OF SEASONS AND DIN ARE DRAWN TO EACH OTHER!!

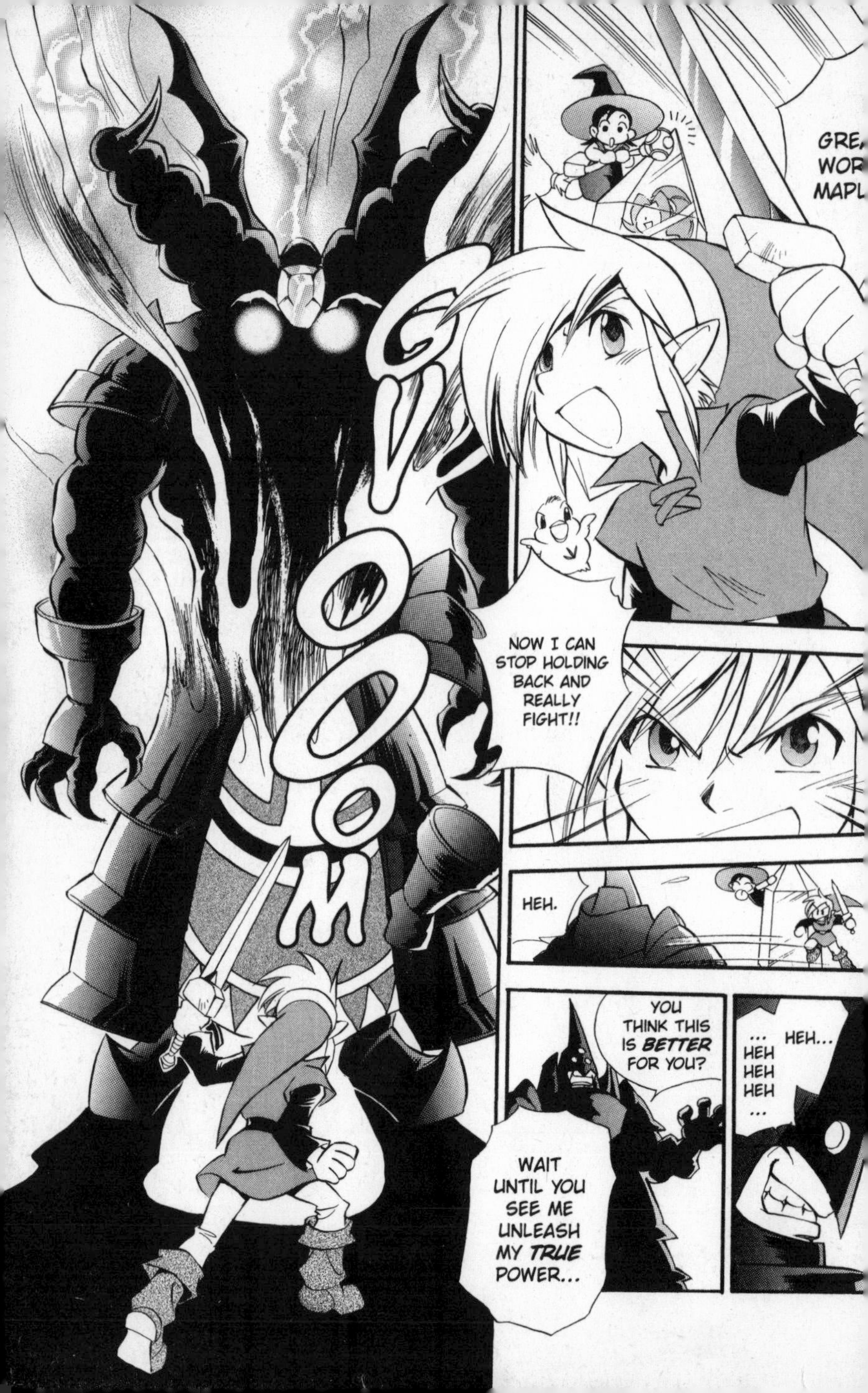
GRE,
WOR
MAPL
NOW I CAN STOP HOLDING BACK AND REALLY FIGHT!!
HEH.
HEH...
... HEH HEH HEH ...
YOU THINK THIS IS ***BETTER*** FOR YOU?
WAIT UNTIL YOU SEE ME UNLEASH MY ***TRUE*** POWER...
GOOOOM

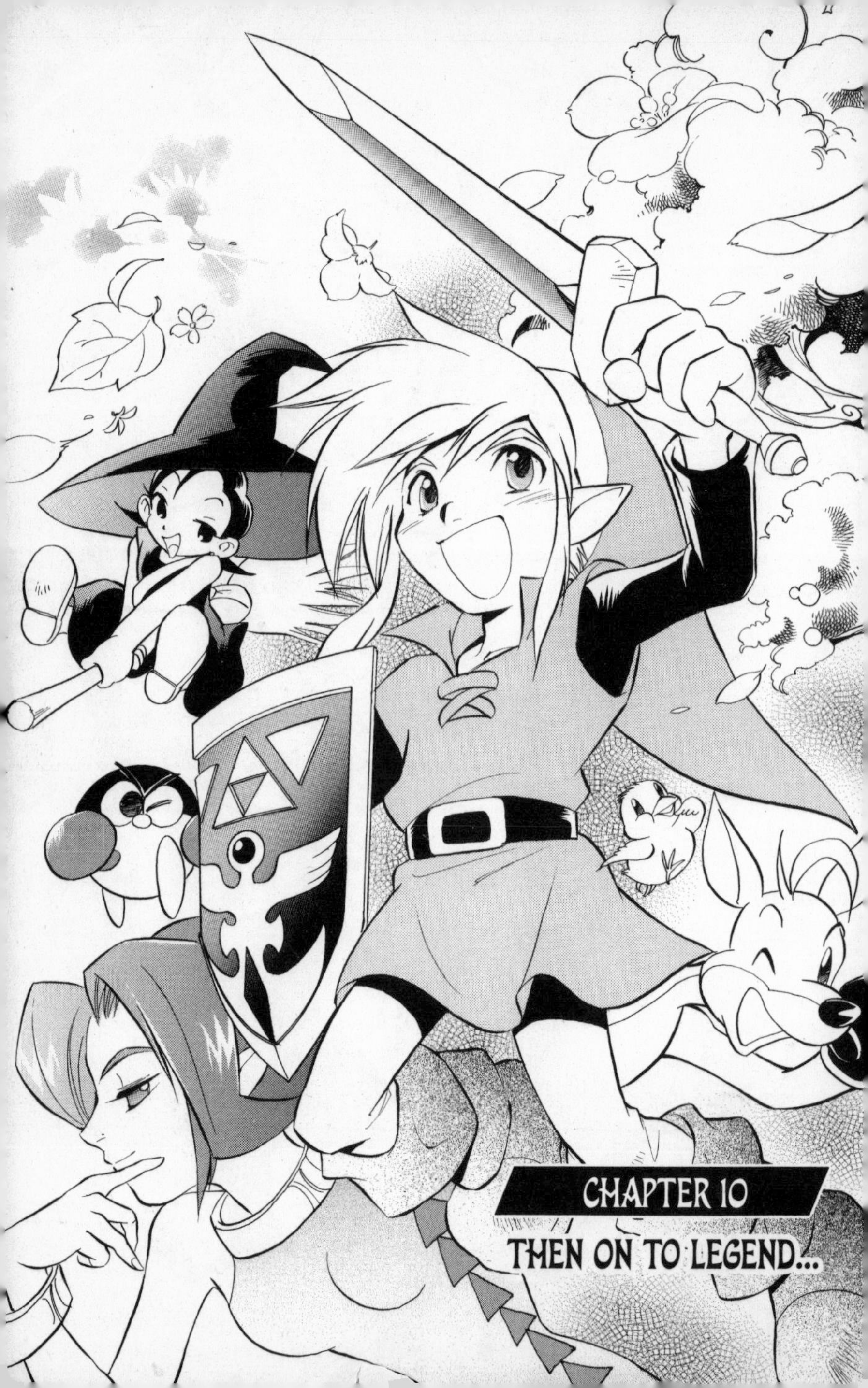
CHAPTER 10
THEN ON TO LEGEND...

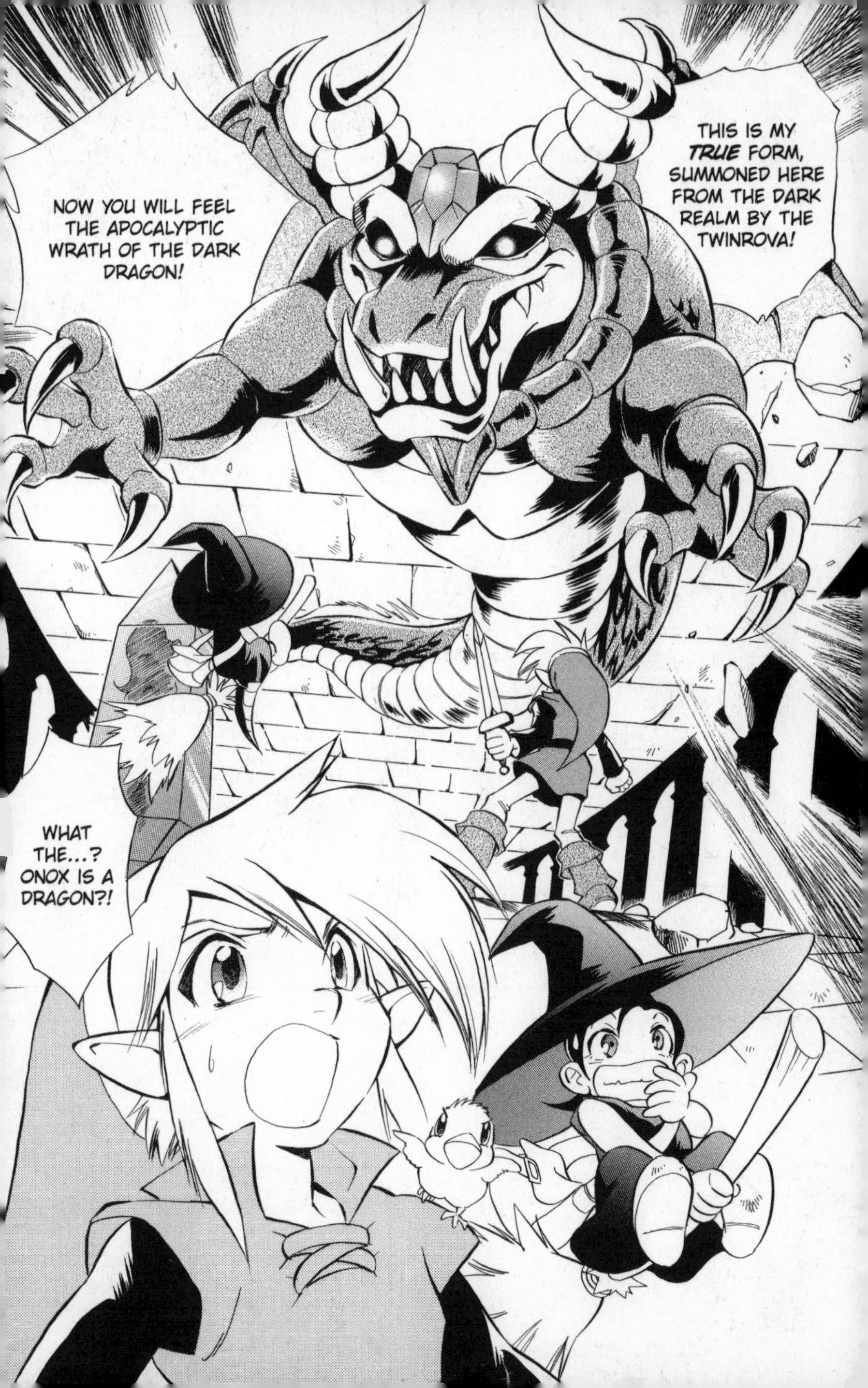
THIS IS MY *TRUE* FORM, SUMMONED HERE FROM THE DARK REALM BY THE TWINROVA!
NOW YOU WILL FEEL THE APOCALYPTIC WRATH OF THE DARK DRAGON!
WHAT THE...? ONOX IS A DRAGON?!

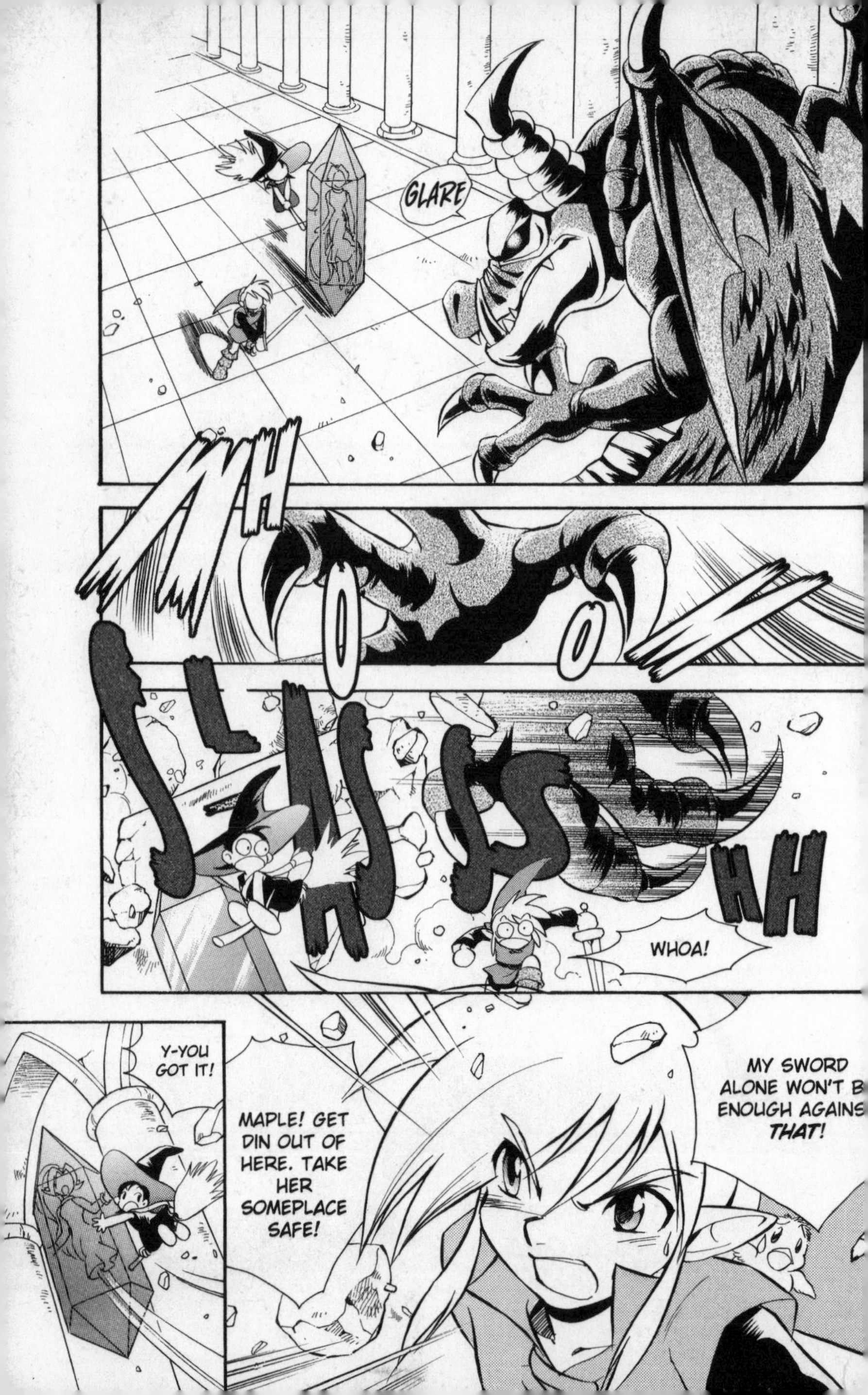
GLARE
WHOA!
MY SWORD ALONE WON'T B ENOUGH AGAINS THAT!
MAPLE! GET DIN OUT OF HERE. TAKE HER SOMEPLACE SAFE!
Y-YOU GOT IT!

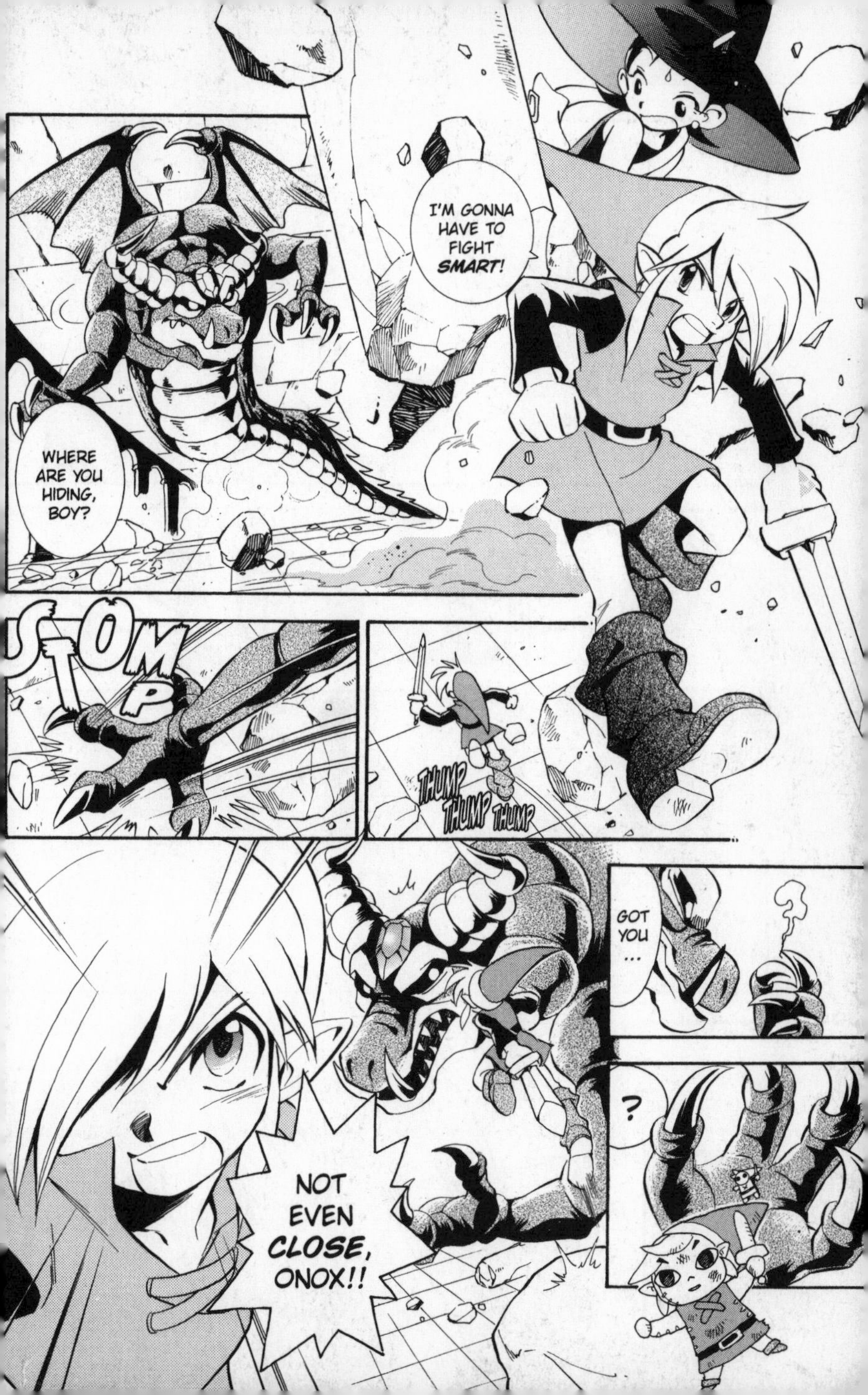
I'M GONNA HAVE TO FIGHT SMART!
WHERE ARE YOU HIDING, BOY?
THUMP THUMP THUMP
STOMP
GOT YOU ...
?
NOT EVEN CLOSE, ONOX!!

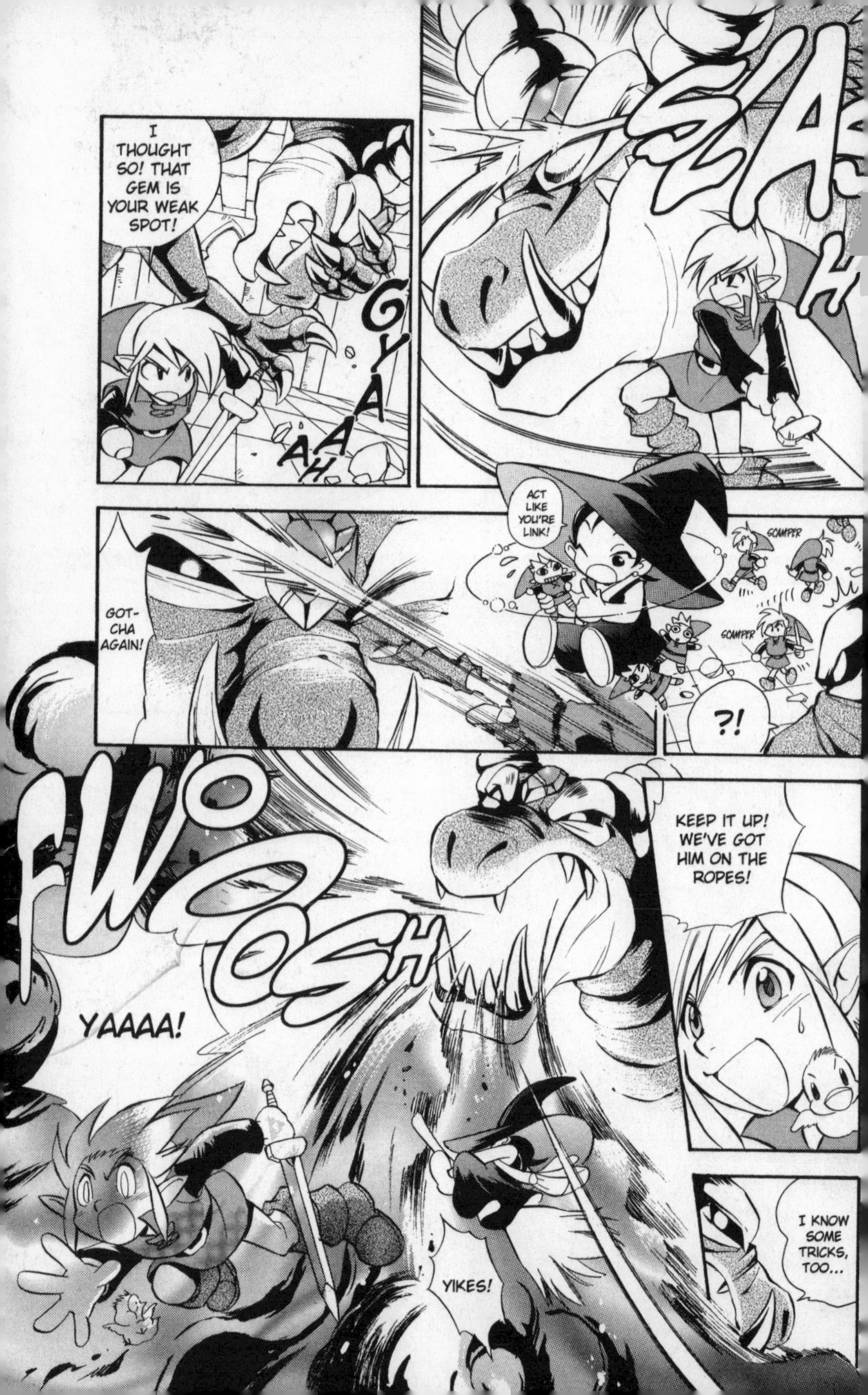
I THOUGHT SO! THAT GEM IS YOUR WEAK SPOT!
GYAAAAH
ACT LIKE YOU'RE LINK!
SCAMPER
SCAMPER
?!
GOT-CHA AGAIN!
KEEP IT UP! WE'VE GOT HIM ON THE ROPES!
I KNOW SOME TRICKS, TOO...
FWOOSH
YAAAA!
YIKES!

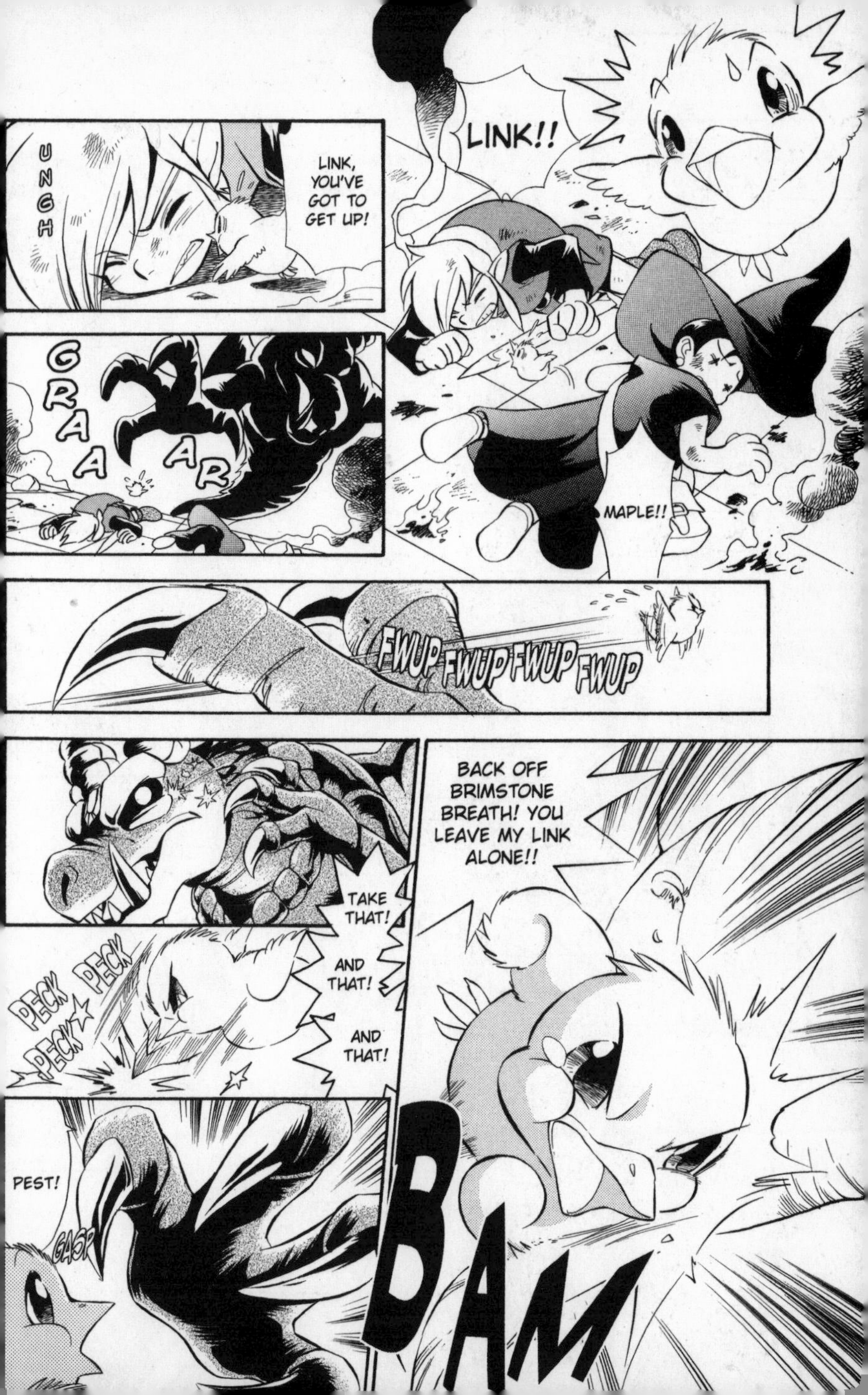
LINK!!
MAPLE!!
LINK, YOU'VE GOT TO GET UP!
UNGH
GRAAAAR
FWUP FWUP FWUP FWUP
BACK OFF BRIMSTONE BREATH! YOU LEAVE MY LINK ALONE!!
BAM
TAKE THAT!
AND THAT!
AND THAT!
PECK PECK PECK
PEST!
GASP

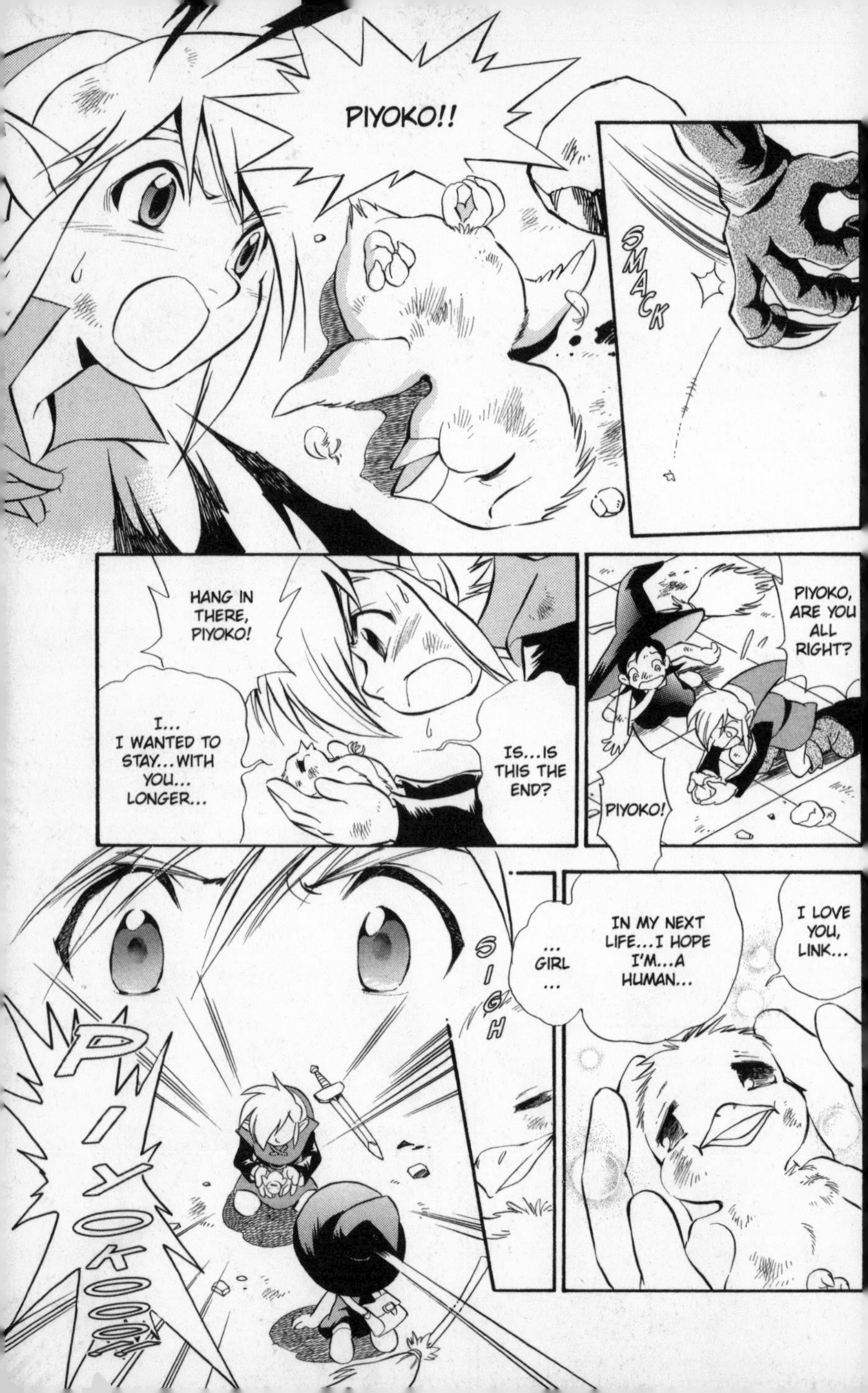
SMACK
PIYOKO!!
PIYOKO, ARE YOU ALL RIGHT?
PIYOKO!
HANG IN THERE, PIYOKO!
IS...IS THIS THE END?
I... I WANTED TO STAY...WITH YOU... LONGER...
I LOVE YOU, LINK...
IN MY NEXT LIFE...I HOPE I'M...A HUMAN...
...GIRL...
SIGH
PIYOKOOO!!

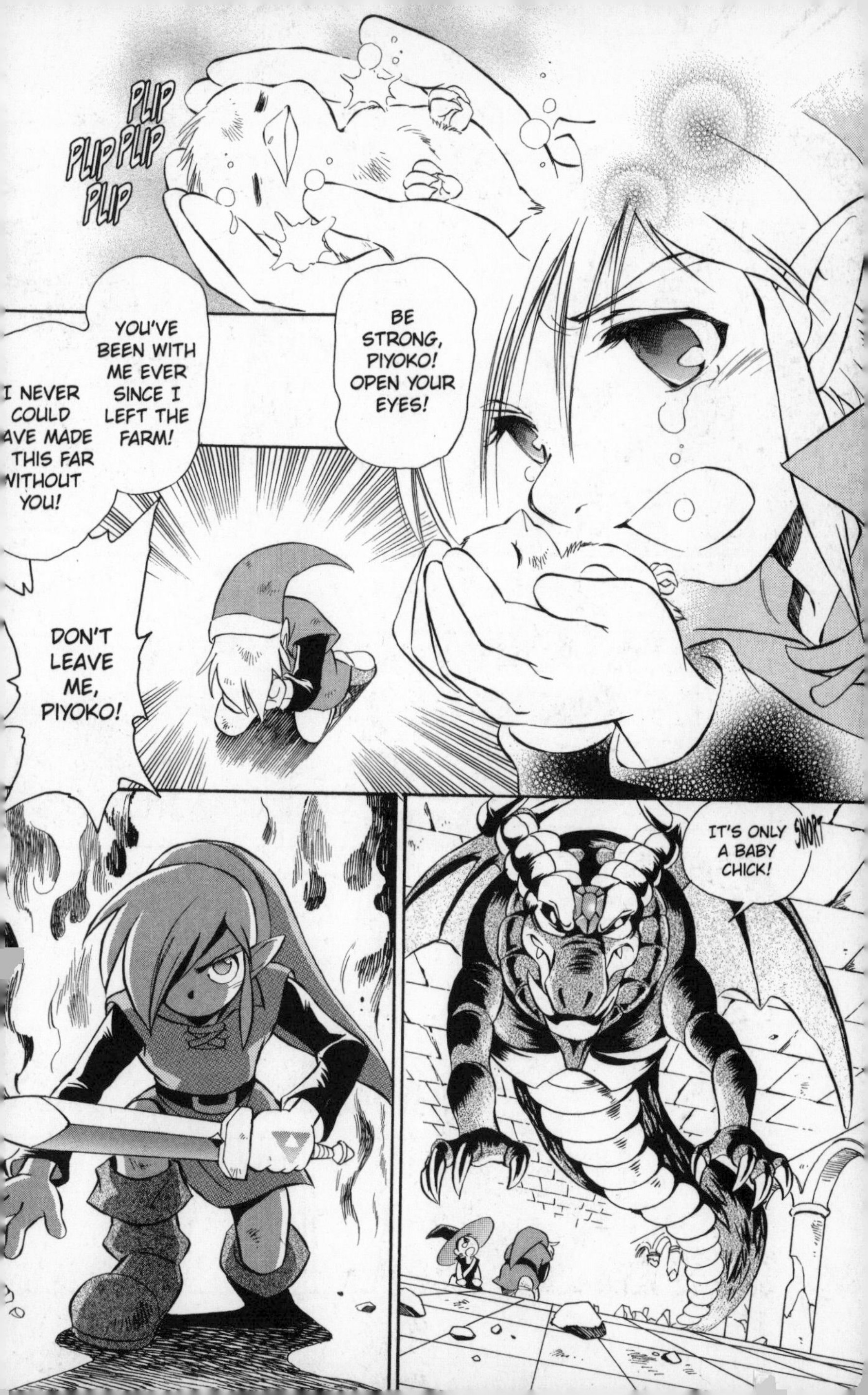
PLIP PLIP PLIP PLIP
BE STRONG, PIYOKO! OPEN YOUR EYES!
YOU'VE BEEN WITH ME EVER SINCE I LEFT THE FARM!
I NEVER COULD AVE MADE THIS FAR WITHOUT YOU!
DON'T LEAVE ME, PIYOKO!
IT'S ONLY A BABY CHICK!
SNORT

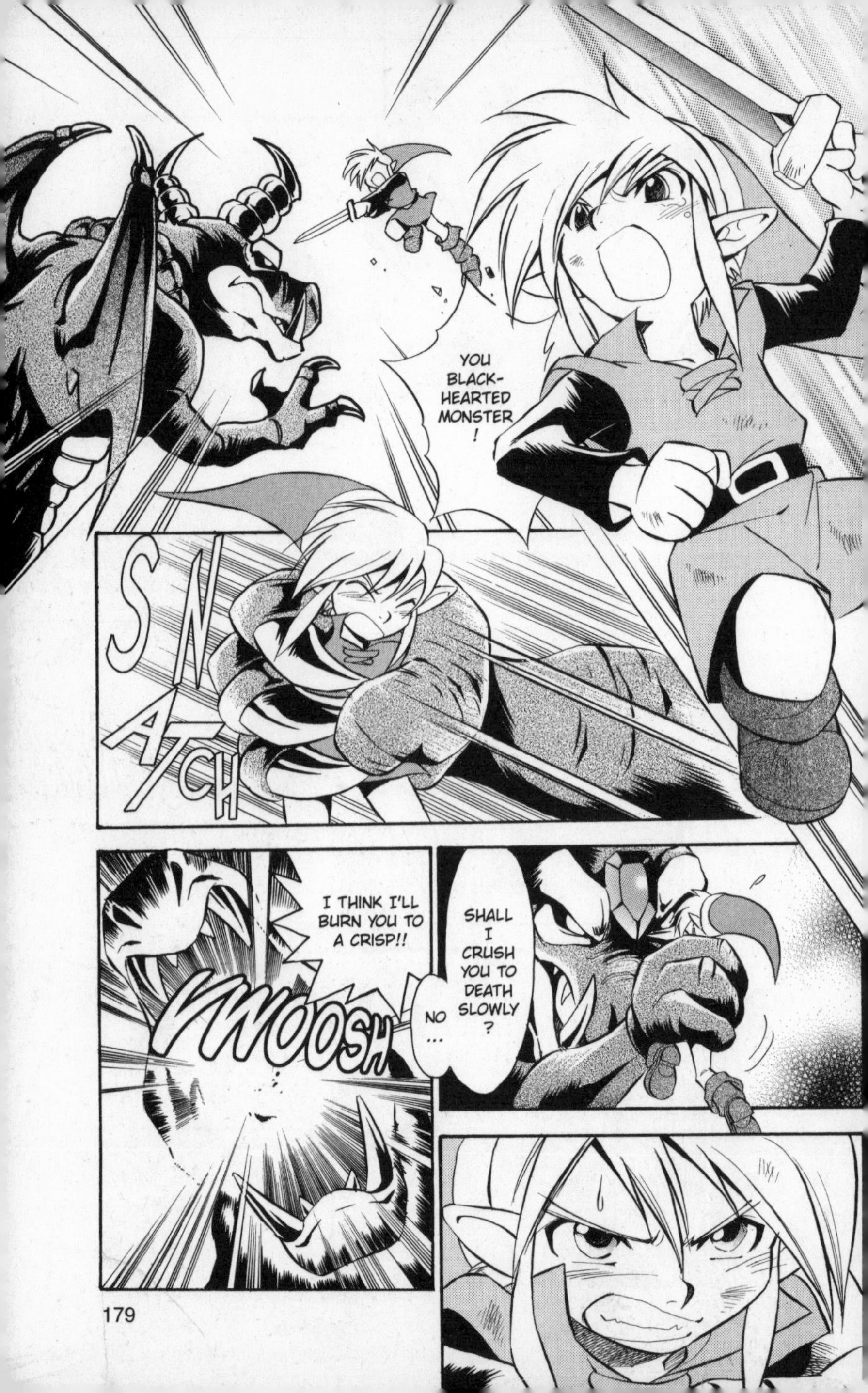
YOU BLACK-HEARTED MONSTER!
SNATCH
SHALL I CRUSH YOU TO DEATH SLOWLY?
NO...
I THINK I'LL BURN YOU TO A CRISP!!
WHOOSH

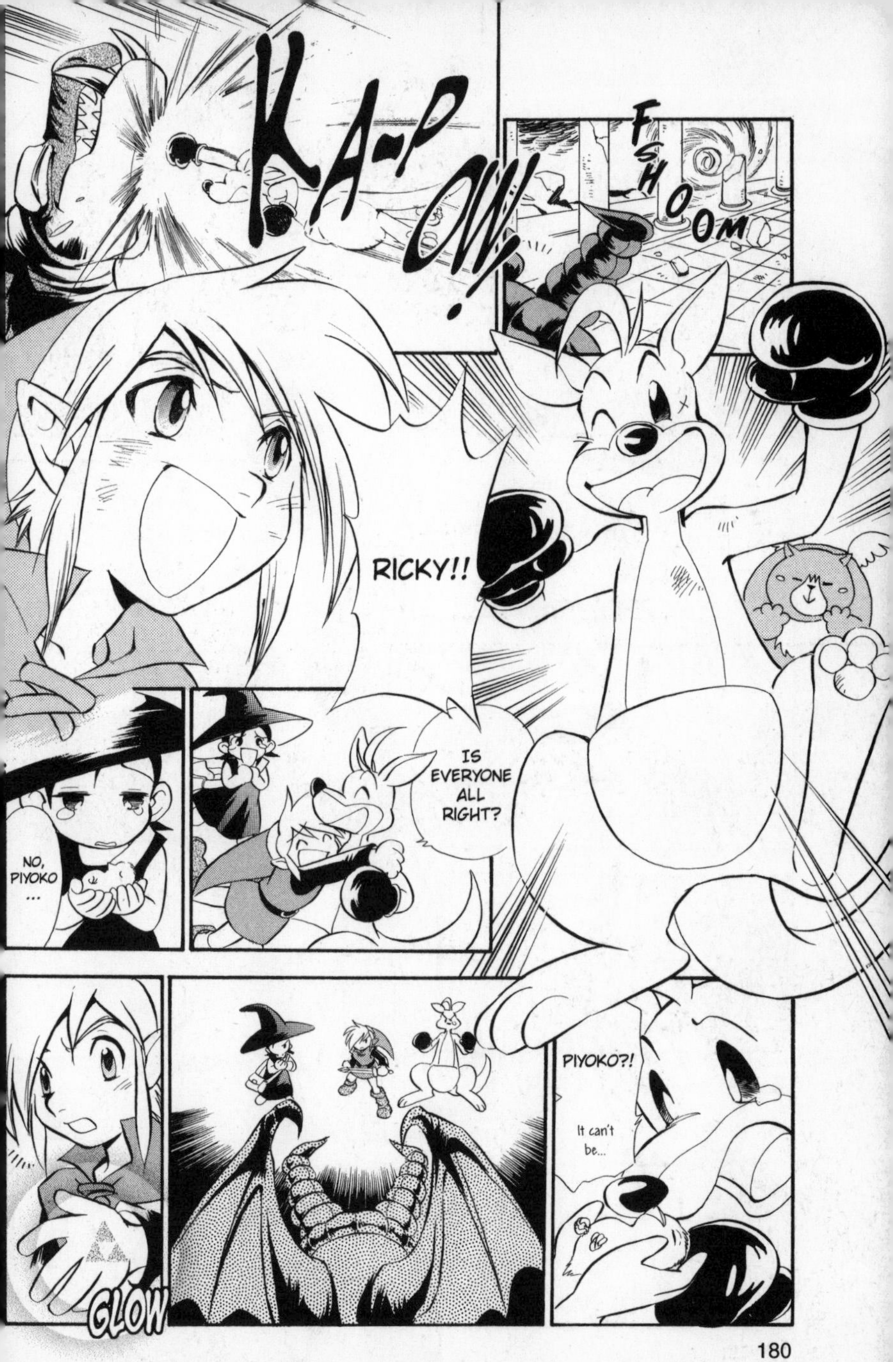
FSHOOOM
KA-POW!!
RICKY!!
IS EVERYONE ALL RIGHT?
NO, PIYOKO ...
PIYOKO?!
It can't be...
GLOW

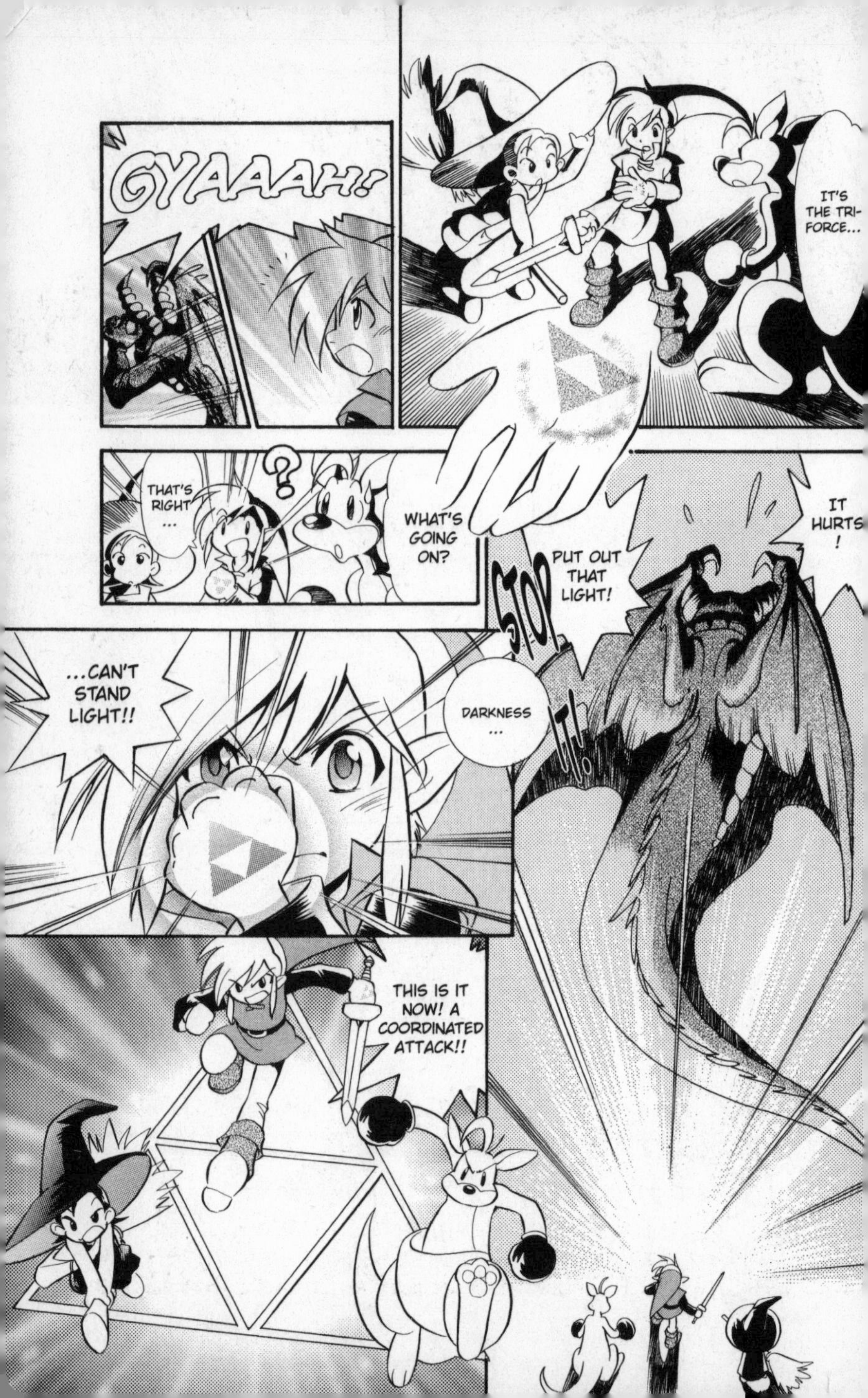
IT'S THE TRI-FORCE...
GYAAAAH!
IT HURTS!
PUT OUT THAT LIGHT!
STOP IT!
WHAT'S GOING ON?
THAT'S RIGHT...
DARKNESS...
...CAN'T STAND LIGHT!!
THIS IS IT NOW! A COORDINATED ATTACK!!

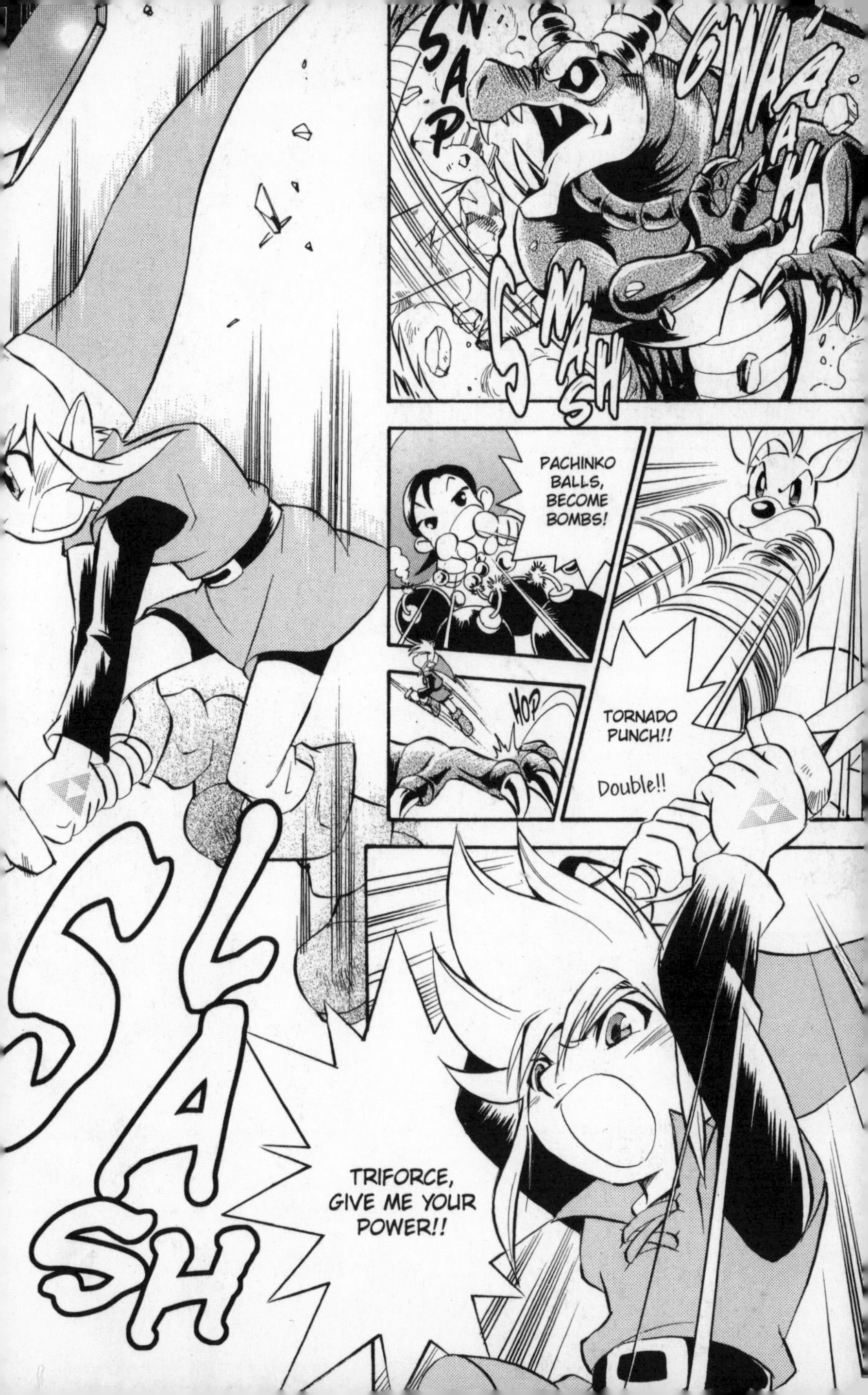
SNAP
GWA'A'AH
SMASH
TORNADO PUNCH!!
Double!!
PACHINKO BALLS, BECOME BOMBS!
HOP
TRIFORCE, GIVE ME YOUR POWER!!
SLASH

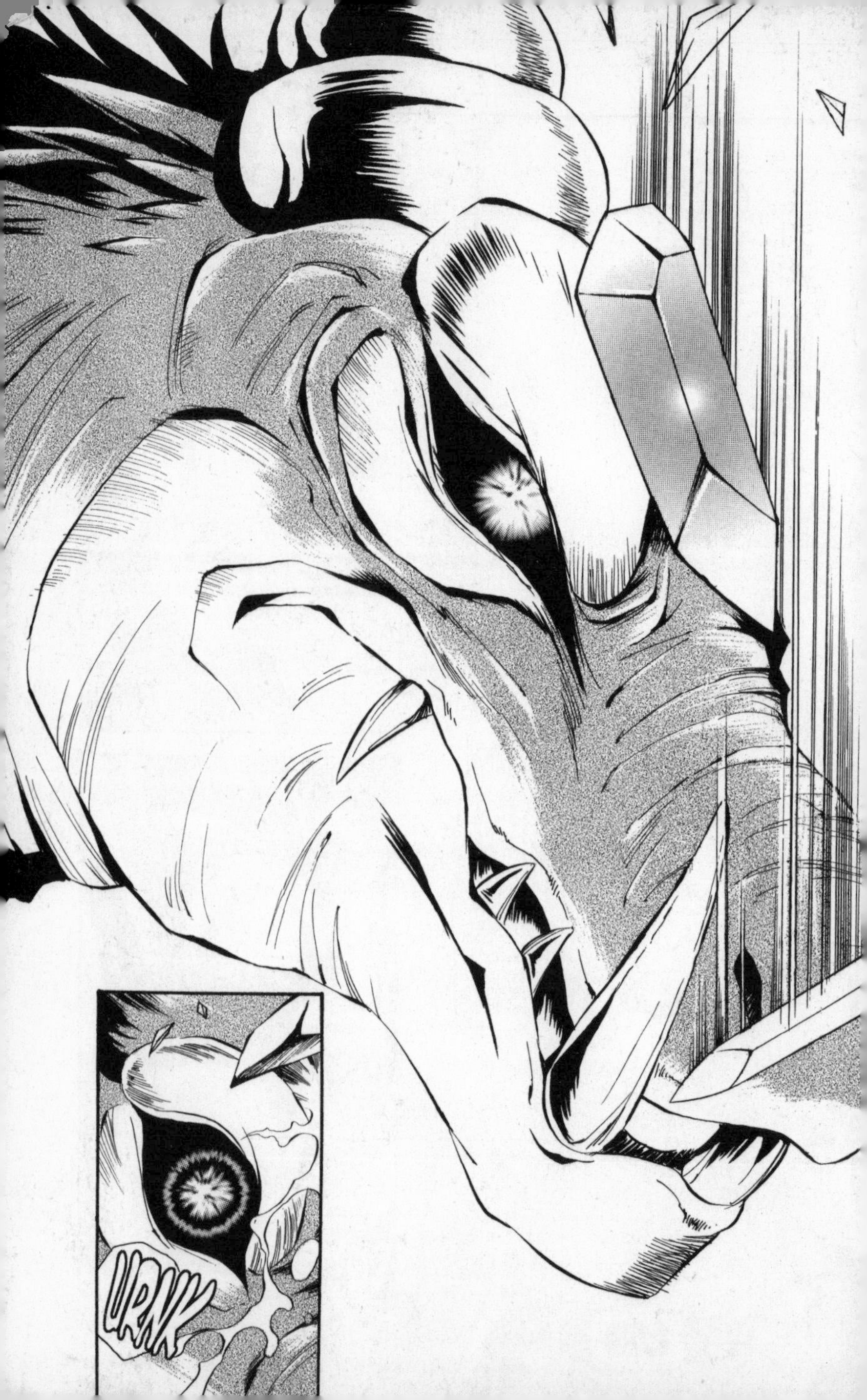
URNK

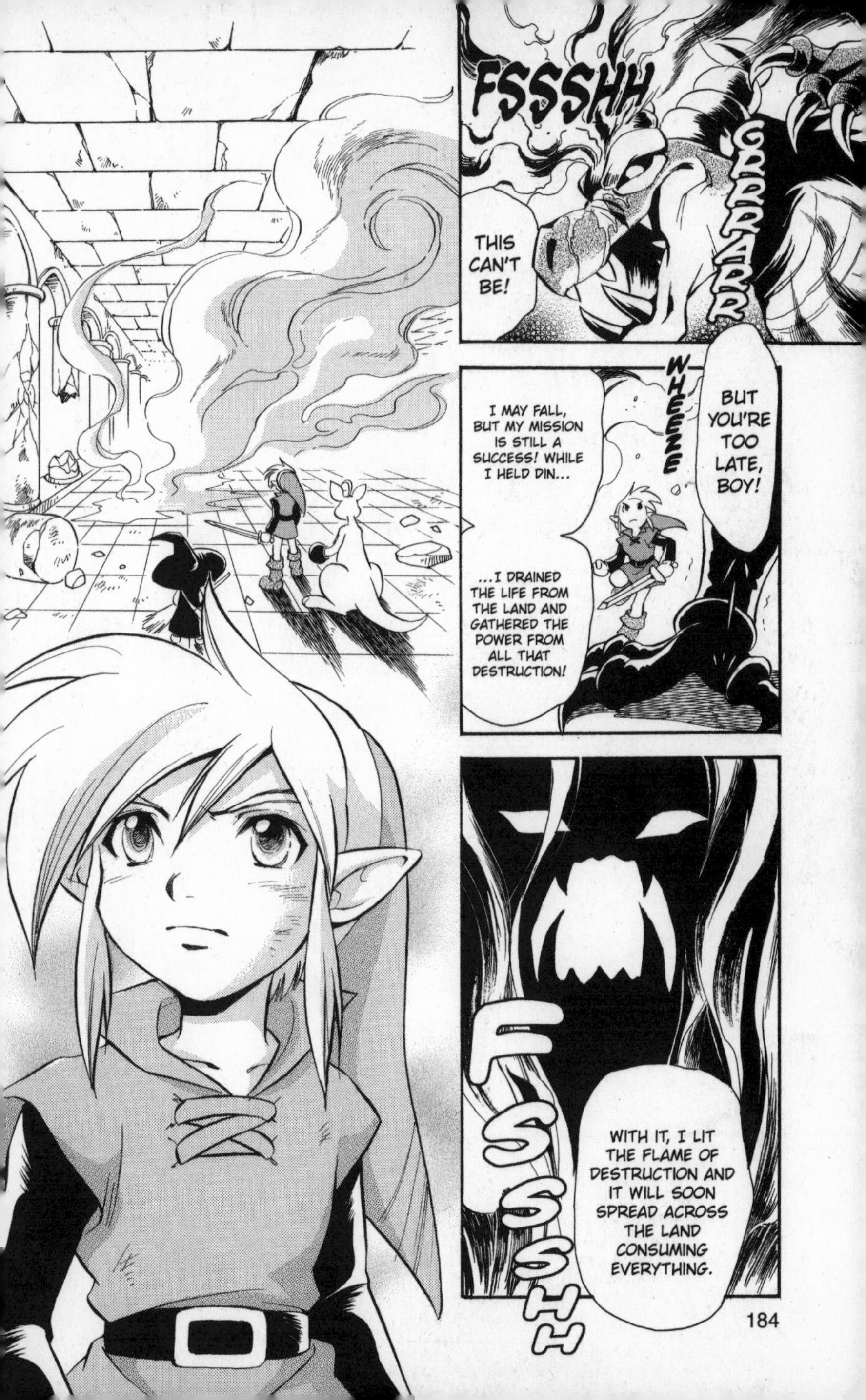
FSSSHH
GRRRARR
THIS CAN'T BE!
WHEEZE
BUT YOU'RE TOO LATE, BOY!
I MAY FALL, BUT MY MISSION IS STILL A SUCCESS! WHILE I HELD DIN...
...I DRAINED THE LIFE FROM THE LAND AND GATHERED THE POWER FROM ALL THAT DESTRUCTION!
FSSSHH
WITH IT, I LIT THE FLAME OF DESTRUCTION AND IT WILL SOON SPREAD ACROSS THE LAND CONSUMING EVERYTHING.

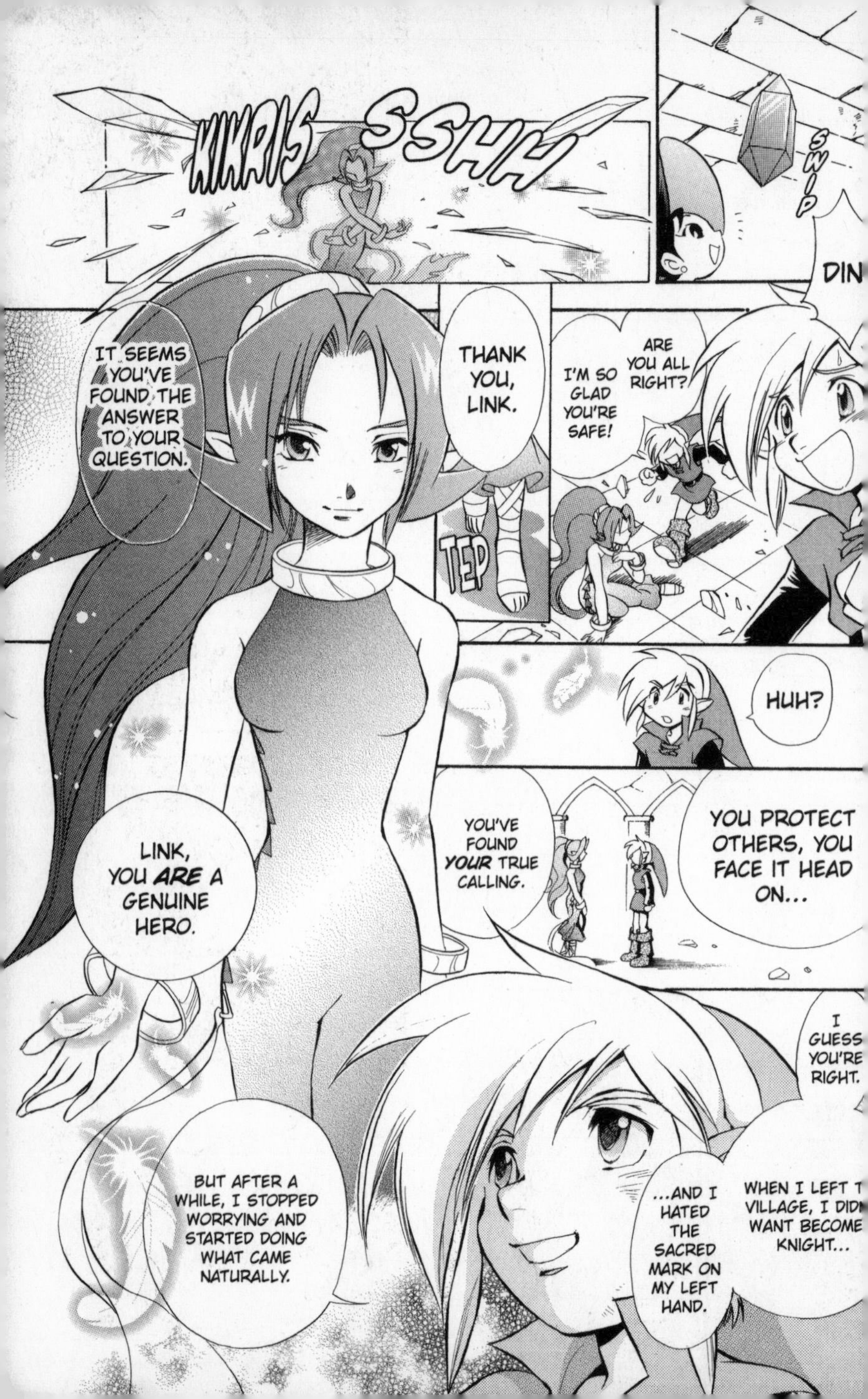
SWIP
KIKRIS
SSHH
DIN
ARE YOU ALL RIGHT?
I'M SO GLAD YOU'RE SAFE!
THANK YOU, LINK.
TEP
HUH?
YOU PROTECT OTHERS, YOU FACE IT HEAD ON...
YOU'VE FOUND *YOUR* TRUE CALLING.
I GUESS YOU'RE RIGHT.
WHEN I LEFT T VILLAGE, I DIDI WANT BECOME KNIGHT...
...AND I HATED THE SACRED MARK ON MY LEFT HAND.
BUT AFTER A WHILE, I STOPPED WORRYING AND STARTED DOING WHAT CAME NATURALLY.
IT SEEMS YOU'VE FOUND THE ANSWER TO YOUR QUESTION.
LINK, YOU *ARE* A GENUINE HERO.

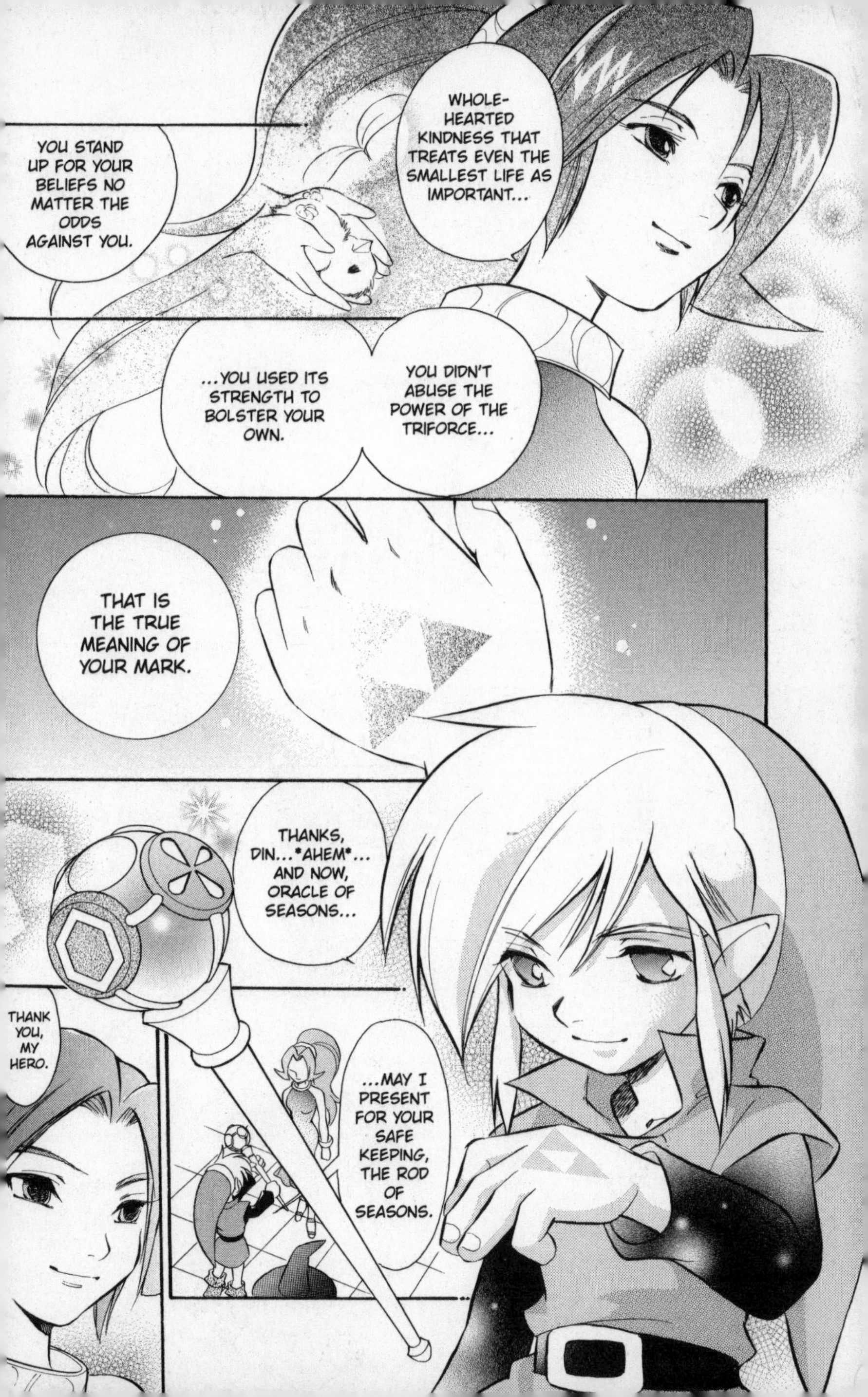
WHOLE-HEARTED KINDNESS THAT TREATS EVEN THE SMALLEST LIFE AS IMPORTANT...
YOU STAND UP FOR YOUR BELIEFS NO MATTER THE ODDS AGAINST YOU.
YOU DIDN'T ABUSE THE POWER OF THE TRIFORCE...
...YOU USED ITS STRENGTH TO BOLSTER YOUR OWN.
THAT IS THE TRUE MEANING OF YOUR MARK.
THANKS, DIN...*AHEM*... AND NOW, ORACLE OF SEASONS...
...MAY I PRESENT FOR YOUR SAFE KEEPING, THE ROD OF SEASONS.
THANK YOU, MY HERO.

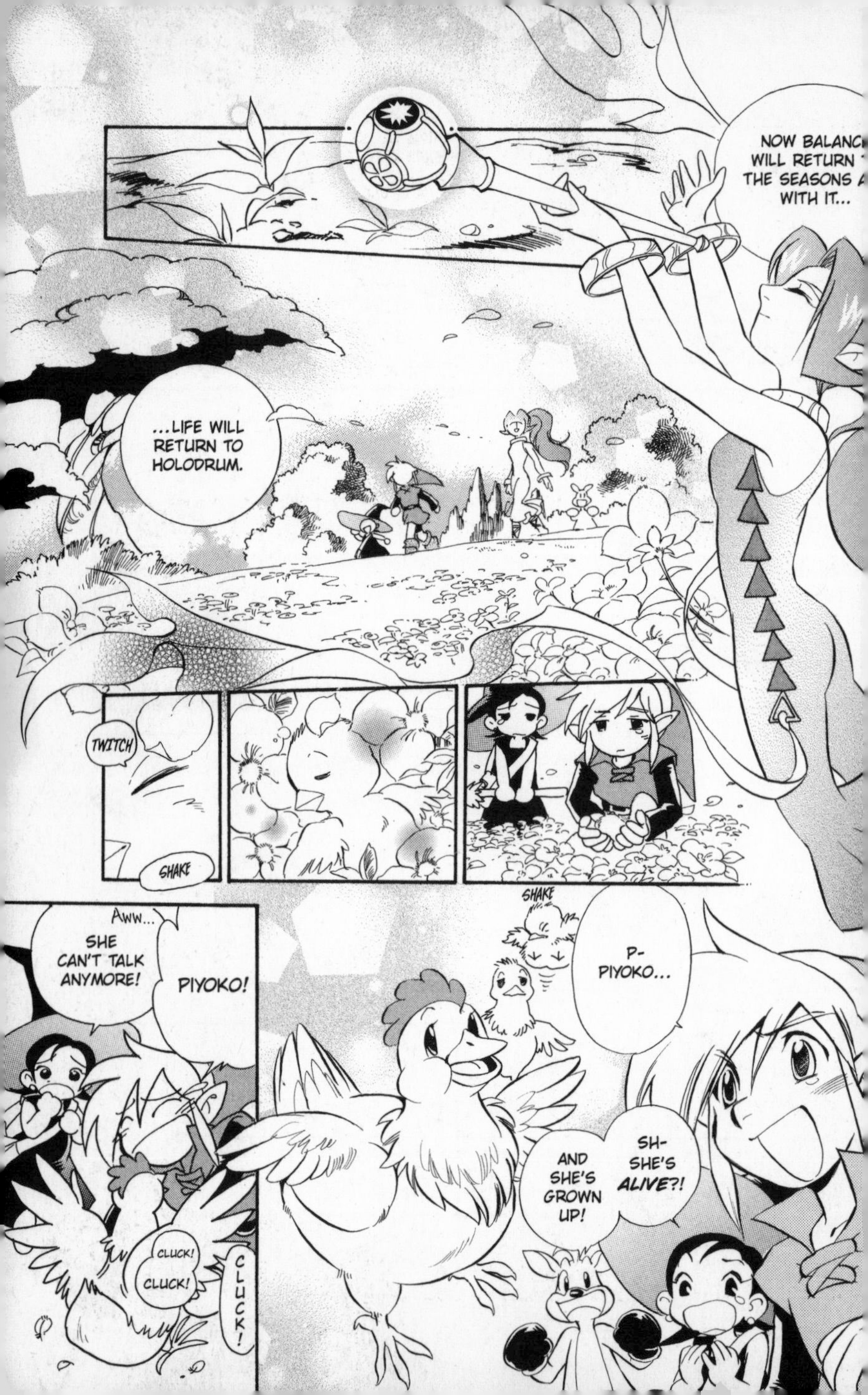
NOW BALANC
WILL RETURN T
THE SEASONS A
WITH IT...
...LIFE WILL RETURN TO HOLODRUM.
TWITCH
SHAKE
SHAKE
P- PIYOKO...
SH- SHE'S *ALIVE*?!
AND SHE'S GROWN UP!
PIYOKO!
AWW...
SHE CAN'T TALK ANYMORE!
CLUCK!
CLUCK!
CLUCK!

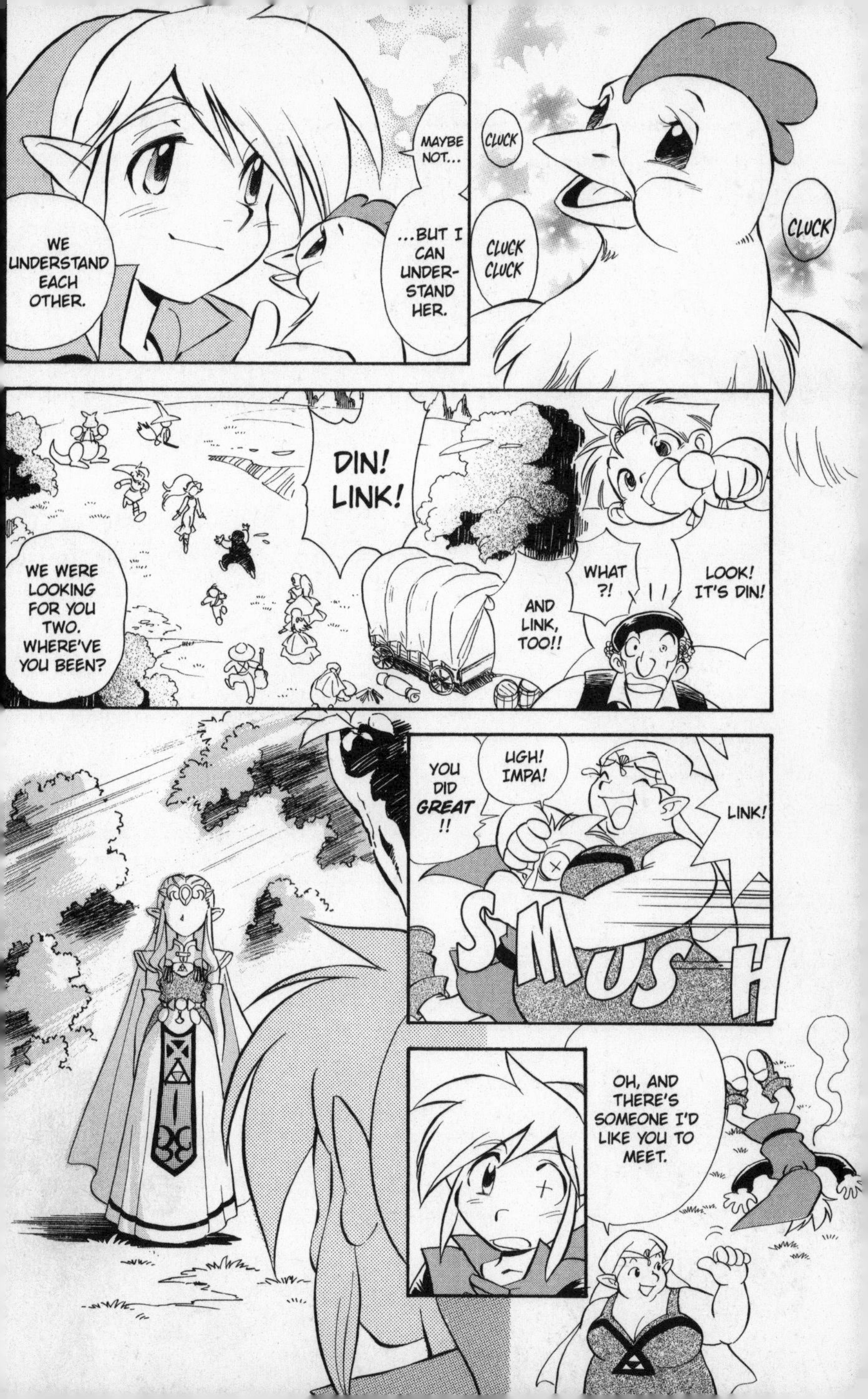
CLUCK
CLUCK
CLUCK CLUCK
MAYBE NOT...
...BUT I CAN UNDERSTAND HER.
WE UNDERSTAND EACH OTHER.
LOOK! IT'S DIN!
WHAT?!
AND LINK, TOO!!
DIN! LINK!
WE WERE LOOKING FOR YOU TWO. WHERE'VE YOU BEEN?
LINK!
UGH! IMPA!
YOU DID GREAT!!
SMUSH
OH, AND THERE'S SOMEONE I'D LIKE YOU TO MEET.

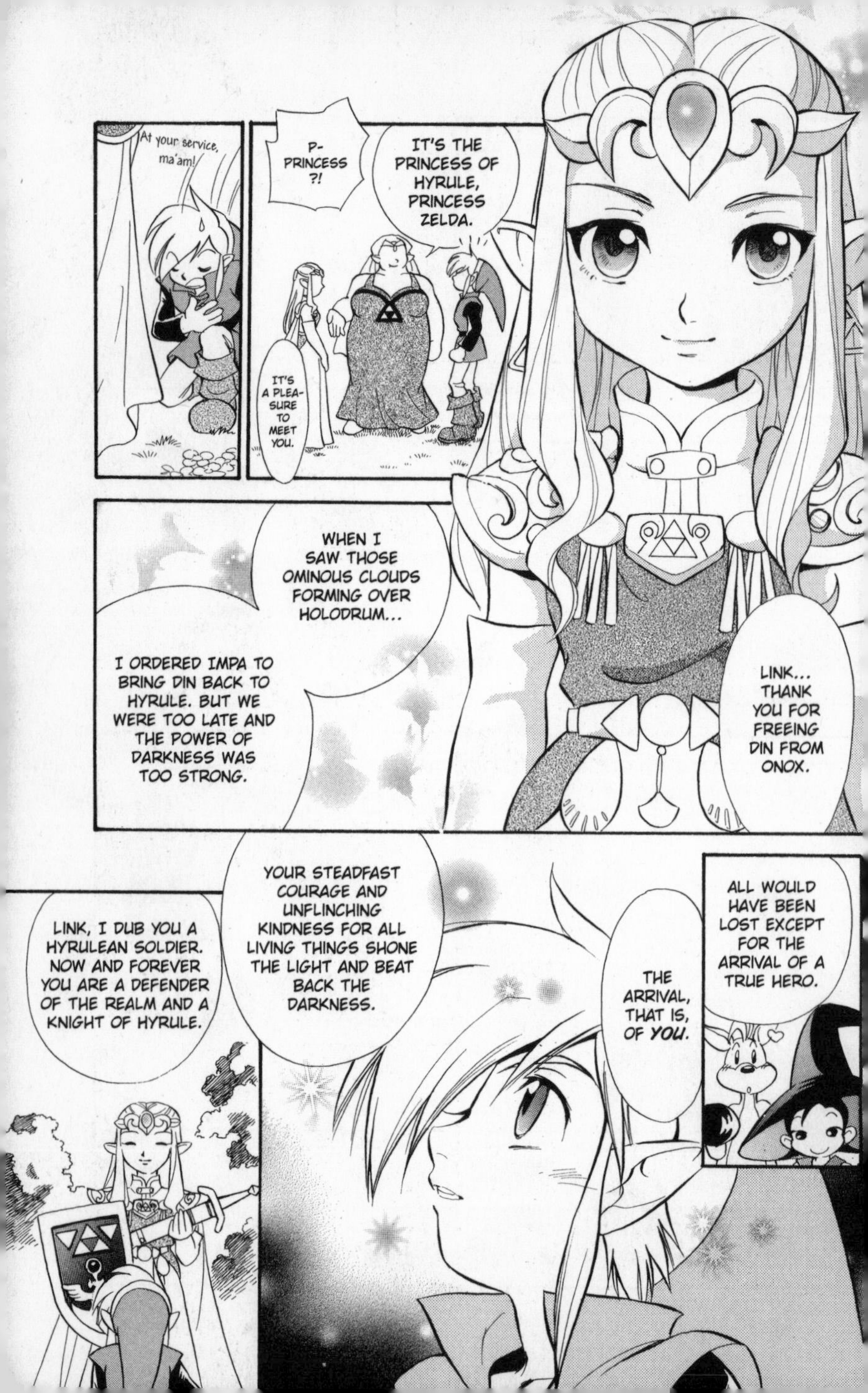
IT'S THE PRINCESS OF HYRULE, PRINCESS ZELDA.
P-PRINCESS?!
IT'S A PLEASURE TO MEET YOU.
At your service, ma'am!
LINK... THANK YOU FOR FREEING DIN FROM ONOX.
WHEN I SAW THOSE OMINOUS CLOUDS FORMING OVER HOLODRUM...
I ORDERED IMPA TO BRING DIN BACK TO HYRULE. BUT WE WERE TOO LATE AND THE POWER OF DARKNESS WAS TOO STRONG.
ALL WOULD HAVE BEEN LOST EXCEPT FOR THE ARRIVAL OF A TRUE HERO.
THE ARRIVAL, THAT IS, OF *YOU*.
YOUR STEADFAST COURAGE AND UNFLINCHING KINDNESS FOR ALL LIVING THINGS SHONE THE LIGHT AND BEAT BACK THE DARKNESS.
LINK, I DUB YOU A HYRULEAN SOLDIER. NOW AND FOREVER YOU ARE A DEFENDER OF THE REALM AND A KNIGHT OF HYRULE.

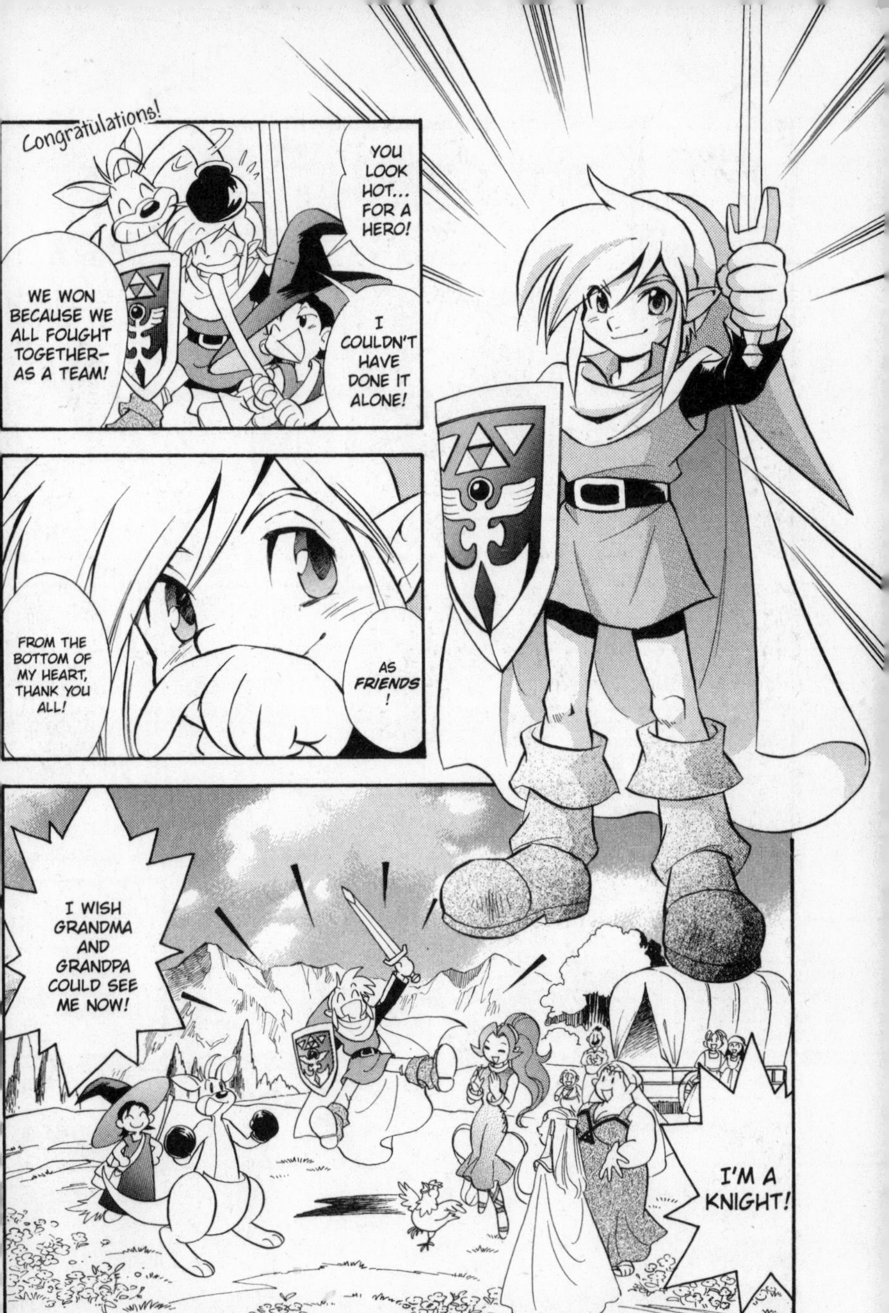
YOU LOOK HOT... FOR A HERO!
Congratulations!
I COULDN'T HAVE DONE IT ALONE!
WE WON BECAUSE WE ALL FOUGHT TOGETHER–AS A TEAM!
AS FRIENDS!
FROM THE BOTTOM OF MY HEART, THANK YOU ALL!
I'M A KNIGHT!
I WISH GRANDMA AND GRANDPA COULD SEE ME NOW!

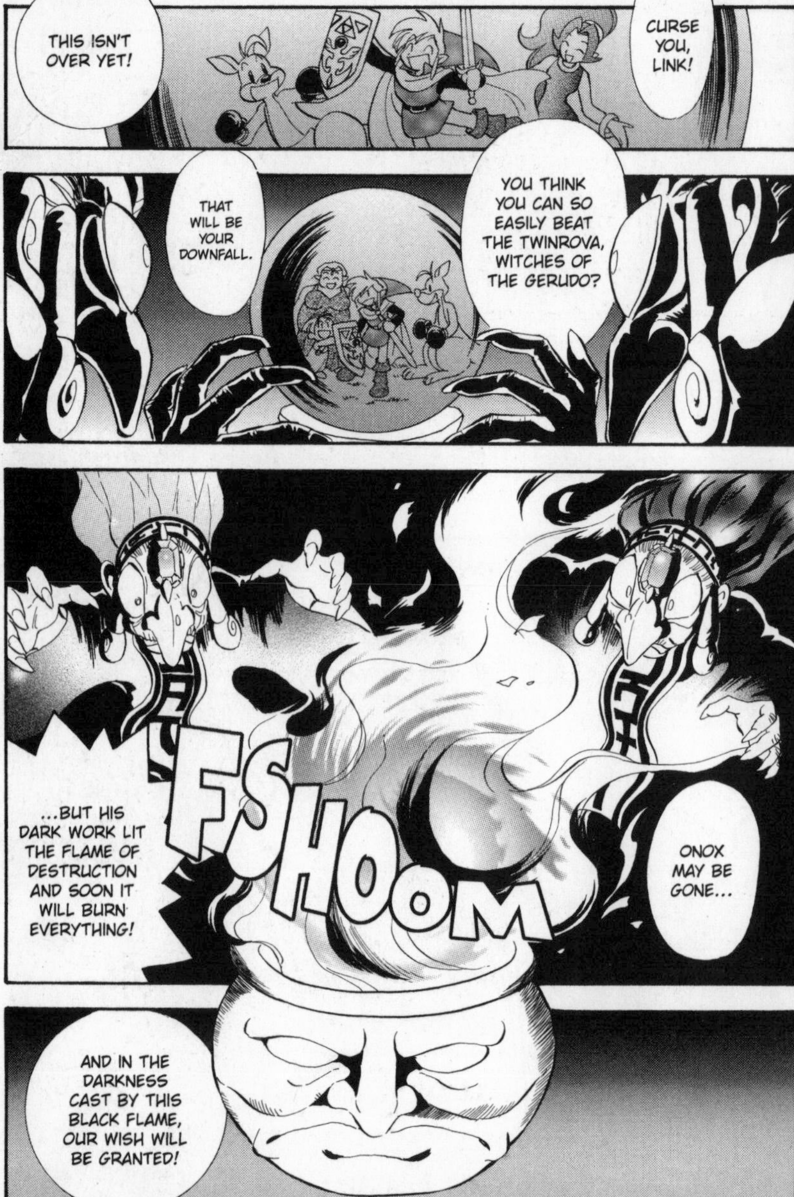
CURSE YOU, LINK!
THIS ISN'T OVER YET!
YOU THINK YOU CAN SO EASILY BEAT THE TWINROVA, WITCHES OF THE GERUDO?
THAT WILL BE YOUR DOWNFALL.
ONOX MAY BE GONE...
FSHOOM
...BUT HIS DARK WORK LIT THE FLAME OF DESTRUCTION AND SOON IT WILL BURN EVERYTHING!
AND IN THE DARKNESS CAST BY THIS BLACK FLAME, OUR WISH WILL BE GRANTED!

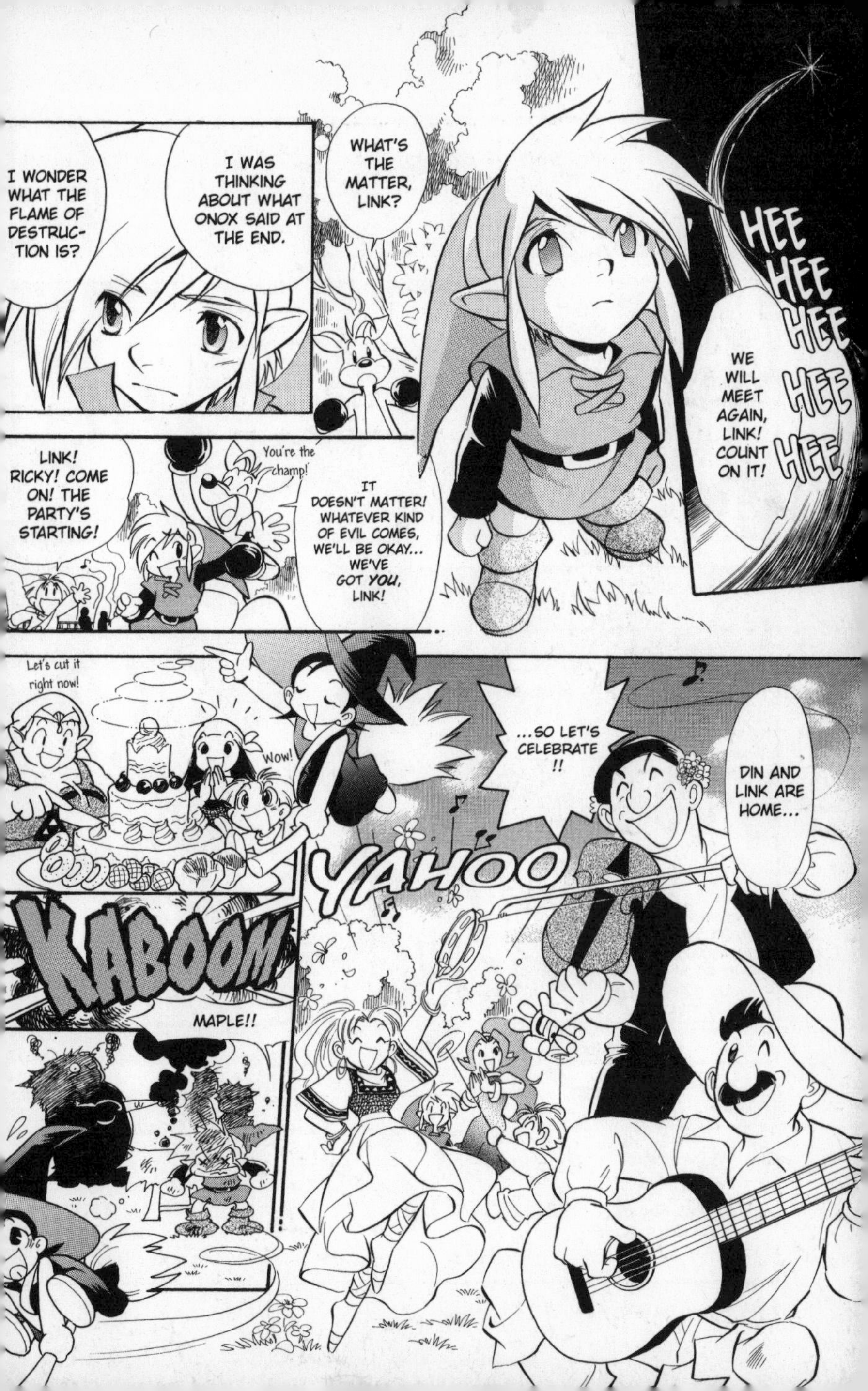
HEE HEE HEE HEE HEE
WE WILL MEET AGAIN, LINK! COUNT ON IT!
WHAT'S THE MATTER, LINK?
I WAS THINKING ABOUT WHAT ONOX SAID AT THE END.
I WONDER WHAT THE FLAME OF DESTRUCTION IS?
LINK! RICKY! COME ON! THE PARTY'S STARTING!
You're the champ!
IT DOESN'T MATTER! WHATEVER KIND OF EVIL COMES, WE'LL BE OKAY... WE'VE GOT **YOU**, LINK!
DIN AND LINK ARE HOME...
...SO LET'S CELEBRATE !!
YAHOO
Let's cut it right now!
WOW!
KABOOM
MAPLE!!

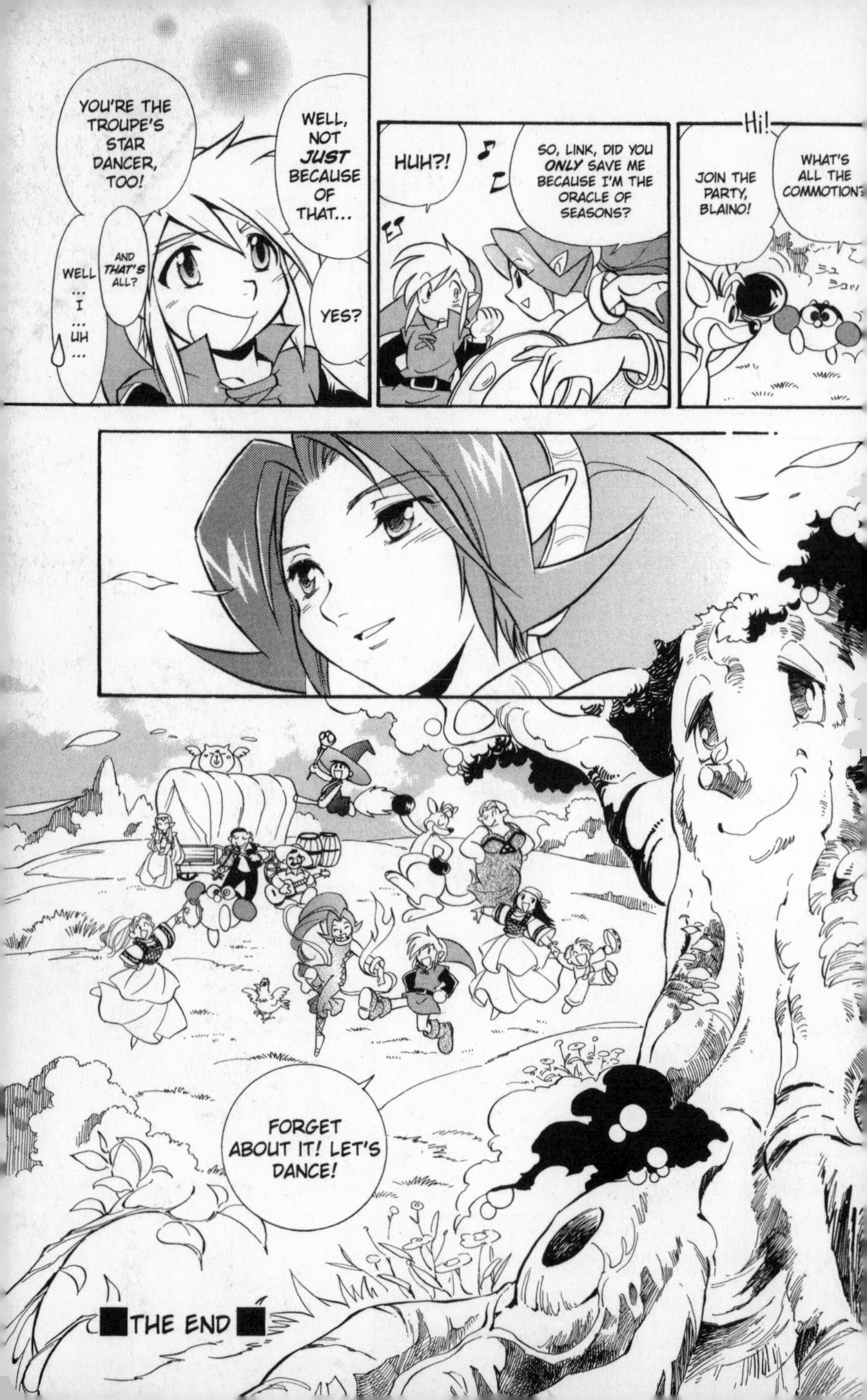
Hi!
WHAT'S ALL THE COMMOTION?
JOIN THE PARTY, BLAINO!
SO, LINK, DID YOU ONLY SAVE ME BECAUSE I'M THE ORACLE OF SEASONS?
HUH?!
WELL, NOT JUST BECAUSE OF THAT...
YES?
YOU'RE THE TROUPE'S STAR DANCER, TOO!
AND THAT'S ALL?
WELL ... I ... UH ...
FORGET ABOUT IT! LET'S DANCE!
THE END

Coming Next Volume

After defeating the evil General Onox in Holodrum, Link returns to Hyrule. Impa, Princess Zelda's attendant, asks Link to accompany her into the forest to find Nayru, the Oracle of Ages. But Veran, the evil Sorceress of Shadows, has plans to travel back to the past in order to kill one of Link's ancestors so that Link will never be born! Link once again battles across time to save Hyrule—and himself!

Available Now!